TRAINING MANUAL FOR

Food and Beverages Services

TRAINING MANUAL FOR
Food and Beverages Services

Mahendra Singh Negi
Assistant Professor
Faculty of Hospitality Management
Amrapali Group of Institutes
Haldwani, Uttarakhand

TECHSAR™
NEW DELHI

Published and Printed by
Techsar Pvt. Ltd.
4435-36/7, Ansari Road, Daryaganj
New Delhi-110002 (India)
E-mail: tech_info@techsarworld.com
Website: www.techsarworld.com

ISBN 978-93-85909-18-4

Reprint 2025

PREFACE

ood and beverages service is a dynamic industry covering a wide range of job roles. rom baristas to head waiters, mixologists and sommeliers, it is a career with many pportunities for development. A positive attitude and hard work can lead to great things. is now an integral part of modern hospitality and tourism industry. A well-trained od and beverages personnel combines his inherent creativity with an understanding of ie business world to manage the customer side of a restaurant, bar, café, or other food ervice establishment. This manual helps enhance your present career and prepare you or a new career in this diverse industry.

The content, scope and application of this training manual are reflective of the best global practices in the field of food and beverages service operations from an organizations and vis-a-vis-customer's perspective. This manual is integrated with innovative training methods along with photographs to facilitate professional and academic excellence as only a few books cover the operating procedures as applicable in the hotel and catering industry.

Training Manual for Food and Beverages Services covers the syllabuses of all major universities, technical boards, autonomous bodies and NCHMCT as applicable in all semesters/years. Photographs, images and tables related to service procedure and others have been included to ease the understanding on concerned topics. This manual also discusses new trends in the bar and drinks such as mixology and infusion. With the help of SOPs compiled from various five-star hotels it will help students to understand the right procedures of serving food, wine, spirits, cigarettes and cigars. Giving particular emphasis on food service sequence, restaurant hygiene, food and beverages knowledge, this manual can also be used by any restaurant or a hotel who wish to extend knowledge of their personnel working in food and beverages.

The manual will also benefit the students to prepare for their placement interviews and is also suitable for F&B professionals and aspiring bartenders as it will serve as a guide to them.

Divided into 43 chapters it elaborates the standard operation procedures required in F&B Service Department of any hotel from basics of food service sequence to service sequence of wines and cocktail making methods along with new trends. Practising these sops one can achieve excellence in the field of F&B services and would be able to learn and understand:

- The role of food and beverages services in hospitality industry
- Provide excellent customer service

- Maintain hygiene, and good attributes of a service personnel
- Prepare for food and beverages service
- Provide a food service to guests
- Provide a drink service to guests
- Understand risk and preventive measures at work
- Understanding of kitchen hazards and preventive measures
- Carry out general food and beverages and closing procedures in a restaurant
- Identify trends in the food and beverages industry
- Food and beverages services, selling techniques, promotions and marketing

I sincerely hope that its content and design will be found indispensible by the students of Hotel Management and a useful reference to the industry professionals.

Mahendra Singh Negi

ACKNOWLEDGEMENTS

From the moment I knew my book was going to be published, I had been anxious about the "thank you" page to express my gratitude to the people for their contribution and other help in creating this book. Without the interest and suggestions offered by a group of individuals *Training Manual on Food and Beverages Services* would have never seen the light of the day. First and foremost, I would like to thank God who gave me the power to believe in my passion and pursue my dreams. I could never have done this without the faith I have in you, the Almighty.

I wish to personally thank Prof. Shailendra Kumar Singh, C.O.O., Amrapali Institute of Hotel Management and Mr. Prashant Sharma, Dean, Amrapali Institute of Hotel Management for their encouragement, guidance and professionalism. My batchmate Ms. Archana Sharma (Duty Manager, the Grand Star, Gurnsey, United Kingdom) for helping me in designing and compiling the standard operating procedures and Mr. Dinesh Pandey for editing, technical support and smoothing out the rough edges in this manual.

I dedicate this book to my darling daughter Riddhima, whose beautiful smile acts as a catalyst to keep me going and inspires me to give my best in whatever I do. My lovely wife Tripti to whom I'm deeply indebted for being my pillar of support and for her unfailing belief in me. My dear students who are one of the major reasons for the conception of this book.

Finally, I would like to acknowledge with gratitude the love and support of my grandparents, especially my grandfather Mr. Govind Singh Tariyal and Mr. Khushal Singh Tariyal and also my friends. They all kept me going and this book would not have been possible without their support and love.

Mahendra Singh Negi

CONTENTS

1 INTRODUCTION TO FOOD AND BEVERAGES SERVICE INDUSTRY

Food service may be simply defined as the provision of food and beverages ready for consumption away from home. This definition however, fails to differentiate the food service industry from retailing industry – a distinction that is difficult to make in view of 'takeaway' and 'fast food' operations. A catering establishment may therefore be described as a place where:

- Food and beverages is consumed in the premises.
- The caterer determines the quality and quantity.
- The caterer is the processor as well as the seller of the product.

Chef's working kitchen

The concept of a place serving food and drink as a business or trade dates back to the very beginnings of organized societies. In ancient Greece every city had its bars and wine shops with their associated salons, and vendors of food and wine in marketplaces. The expansion of Roman cities and greater travel led to the development of a wide variety of eating and drinking places. In the Middle Ages, the main providers of lodging and food for travellers were the monasteries, guest houses and hotels operated by religious order. This led to the development of taverns and inns. In Britain, post coaches would stop here where the riders would rest their horses and find some refreshment. Following the introduction of coffee in the 17th century, coffee houses became fashionable meeting places

Trattoria

for gentlemen to debate and transact business. Lloyd's Coffee House, the first to be opened in London in 1688, became the centre for shipping insurance. By the end of the century there were close to 3000 coffee houses in London alone. Many inns followed suit by converting one of their public rooms into a coffee shop, as an informal restaurant open for long hours, serving light meals and refreshments for travellers and for local businessmen to discuss their business. Some of these coffee shops later became gentlemen's drinking and gambling clubs with the subsequent transformation of gentlemen's club. Similarly, France saw development of café in late 17th century when a Turkish ambassador introduced coffee to France. Café became popular with women and children as these served coffees and light meals located in shopping centres. These cafés diversified into patisseries or pastry shops and tearooms. Cook shops existed where processed meats were available for people who could not afford readymade fares—the modern-day delicatessen has its roots here. Boulanger in Paris first used the word 'restaurant' in 1765. Defying all food guilds he sold a restorative bouillon of sheep's feet in - white wine sauce in the market and called it 'restaurer' which literally means 'that which restores'. This controversy attracted an exclusive clientele to his shop. Following the French Revolution, many of the chefs from the houses of aristocracy became restaurateurs both in and out of France. This led to the widening of the range of food offered in these restaurants from set meals to à la carte dishes thus establishing the reputation of classical French (haute) cuisine. Monsieur Beauvilliers, as we know it today, opened the first restaurant, in the late 18th century. This had well turned out staff, a wine cellar, high cuisine and a beautiful salon. This term has today come to mean '*an establishment with a choice of different dishes and specialties of the house from which customers can choose*'. France also saw the birth of bistros, a word derived from Russian word 'bystro' which means 'quick'— a word supposedly shouted by the Russian soldiers to the café owners to hurry food service. Unlike café and restaurants, bistros are interpreted as relatively less sophisticated eating places with casual atmosphere, usually depicting the home setting of the owner. Around the same time Italy saw the development of *trattoria*, which were eating places offering local cuisine of quality and with style. Outside Italy *trattoria* has come to be identified with a trendy restaurant offering a wide range of traditional Italian dishes. Characteristically, the service is friendly and the atmosphere informal and lively. The railways provided the impetus to the growth of hotels, and subsequently food service industry. The profitable companies began to invest in large comfortable hotels and coaching inns generally located near main railway stations. This stimulated hotel buildings by other companies in city centres and at seaside resorts, and the result was a transformation from a relatively poor culinary standards of old coaching inns to the highest and more sophisticated standards of cuisine. The development of motorcar revitalized hospitality sector that had got saturated after an immediate boom during railway age. Where a tavern provided an eating place, it was usually called chophouse or a chop room from which was evolved the concept of grill room in hotels and modern steak houses. The increase in travel led to two major developments, i.e., development of transportation catering and development of ethnic or specialty restaurants, essentially with an aim of providing home food to travellers in foreign land. These restaurants also served to educate the locals about international cuisine and also provided alternatives to the local cuisine. The First World War interrupted the development of industry and severely limited food services in particular, due to the imposition of restrictions, regulations and towards the end of the war, rationing. The greatest impact was in the field of industrial catering, which hitherto had been virtually non-existent. The need to feed millions of service personnel and, eventually the whole population compelled the government to consider national dietary requirements. This led the government to convince employers to recognize the importance of adequate nutrition for workers. By the end of the war, the concept of industrial canteens supplying food to workers developed. Despite the depression years of 1930s, overall inter-war era was all right for food service business. Restaurant sales boosted by the Licensing Act of 1921, which allowed for drinks to be served after 11 p.m. As a result this era saw the development of public houses in England, leading to the proliferation of pubs and bars. At the same time, the Parisian brasserie, originally attached to the breweries of Lorraine and Alsace, came into the cities. The word has come to mean a restaurant with long wooden tables, foaming mugs of beer and an extensive range of simple food.

CLASSIFICATION OF FOOD AND BEVERAGES SERVICE OPERATIONS

There are many ways to classify food and beverages service operations. It could be classified on the basis of its menu, service style or market orientation. However, for our purpose we classify the F&B service operations into two as follows:

1. Profit oriented
    - Restricted market – Transport catering, Clubs, Private welfare.
    - General Market – Hotels/Restaurants/Bars/Pubs/Discotheque/Drive inn and many more.
2. Non-profit oriented or subsidised
    - Industrial catering/Institutional catering/Welfare catering/Schools Hospitals/Prisons

A restaurant

RESTAURANT TRENDS

The design and description of restaurants keep on changing with the change in demand and supply. Some of the common factors influencing food service industry are:

- Demographic structure
- Economy
- Buying power of the customer
- Competition
- Influences of immigration and tourism
- Dietary habits

Restaurants have been through a revolution in terms of design and concepts in the recent past. Some general trends include the following:

- Display of showmanship in preparation skills (Sushi bars, tepan tables), cooking (barbeques, grills) and serving (chef's table).
- Introduction of new foods with special emphasis on atmosphere and characterisation such as fruit counters, breakfast bars, starter carousels, etc.
- Openness in a restaurant or 'bringing the outside inside' by extension into patio, al fresco, presence of water bodies, etc.
- Live entertainment and music.
- Distinctive styling of coffee shops and all-day dining restaurants buzzing with lots of activities and interaction with the guests.
- Trend setting bistros and pubs with emphasis on ambience orientated towards younger generation.
- Characterisation of restaurants in converted buildings, restored monuments and unique settings.
- Development of retail malls and food courts incorporating a variety of specialty restaurants.

- Merchandising of food products.
- Franchised restaurants.
- Restaurants selling memorabilia.
- Simple food presentation but of high quality and giving a little bit of the unexpected.
- Minimalist decor.
- Children menus.
- Respect for the needs of guests on restricted diets - availability of organic foods, low calorie and low sodium meals.

Food and beverages operations is one of the major components of travel and hospitality industry. India is growing at an extremely fast pace in terms of hospitality industry. It is considered one of the highly profitable industries, contributing significant amount of foreign exchange to the economy. Hotels which are extremely important component of tourism industry where food service operation is available in the form of coffee shop, bar, night club, speciality restaurant, pastry and cake shop offering services and facilities of extremely high standards. The size of the hospitality sector of India is considered a sum of market share of two segments. The first segment is revenue obtained from travel businesses while the second is revenues acquired from hotel businesses. One of the most remarkable features of the Indian hospitality sector is that it has attracted significant amount of foreign inflows in the last few years. Several international hotel chains have established their presence in the country's hospitality industry. These hotel chains include: Accor, Starwood, Marriott, Hyatt, Le meridian, Premier Travel Inn (PTI), Cabana Hotels, Mandarin Oriental, Shangri la, Hampton Inns, Banana Tree, Best Western, Ramada and many more. Some reputed Indian companies leading in the hospitality sector include Asia Hotels, ITC, East India Hotels (EIH), Bharat Hotels, Hotel Leela and last but not the least, Indian Hotels Company (IHCL). Indian hospitality sector is the second largest employer in the country as it is capable of offering employment opportunities to a wide range of job seekers from professionals to unskilled workers in various departments of hotels like front office, food and beverages services, accommodation, food production and otherss.

ACTIVITIES

- Prepare a PowerPoint presentation on the growth and evolution of food service industry in India.
- List any ten international hotel chains operating in India along with the services and facilities provided by them.

2 FOOD AND BEVERAGES SERVICE PERSONNEL

A Food and Beverages (F&B) service personnel in a hotel/restaurant could be regarded as a person who takes the food and beverages orders from the guest and serves it to the guest and also takes care of the guest or we can say that an F&B personnel does anything to make the guest's dining experience memorable so that the guest visits the hotel or restaurant again to have the same dining experience.

STAFF ORGANISATION

In F&B department there are many personnel to carry out the administrative and operational functions. Staff organization is basically concerned with matters such as: identify, divide, distribute and group the tasks to be done. Delegate authority and responsibility for decision making to accomplish the tasks. To establish and determine working relationships among persons and groups for efficient implementation of hotel policies and to provide quality services to the guest. The organizational hierarchy of the F&B department is shown in below.

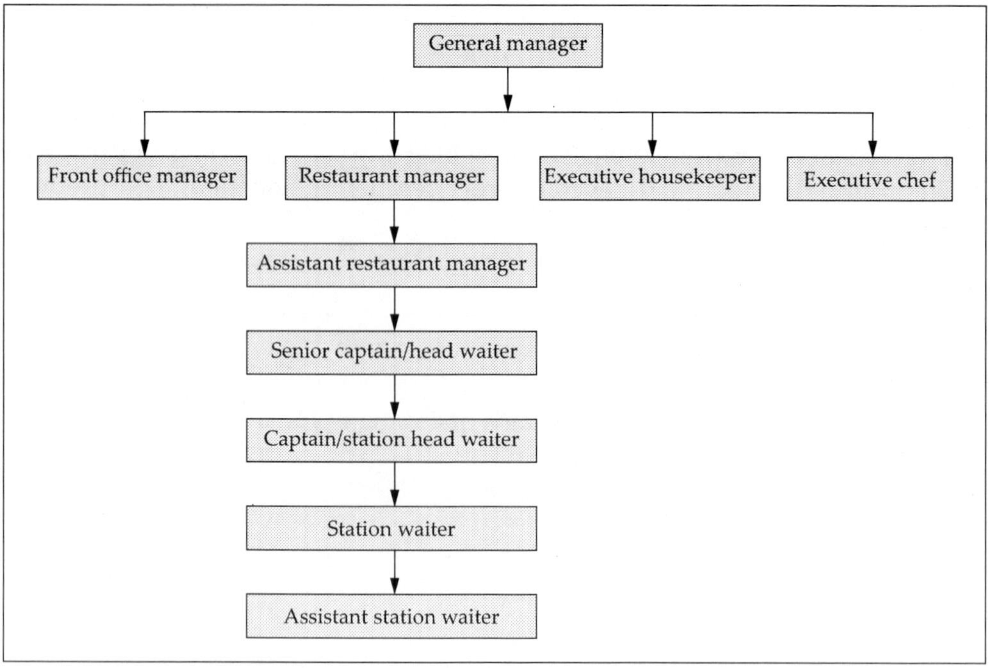

Organisational hierarchy of a small hotel

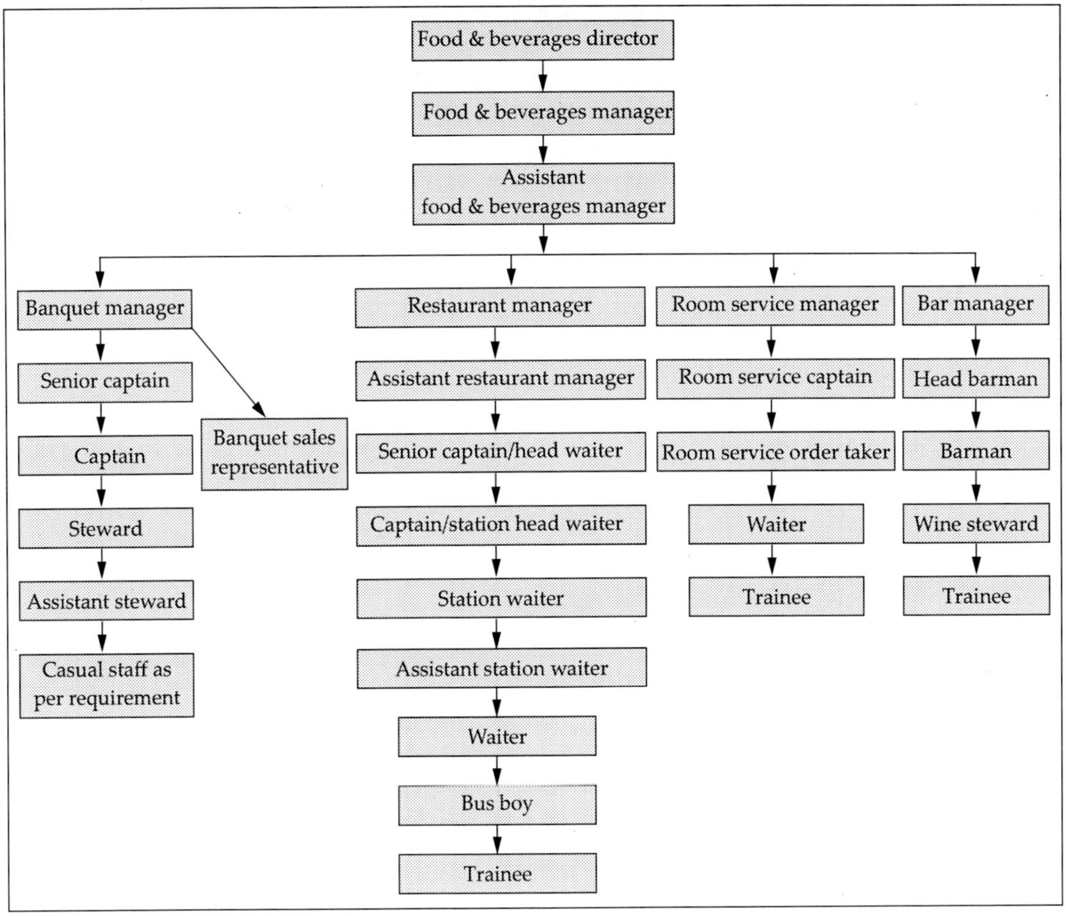

Organisational hierarchy of a large hotel

DUTIES AND RESPONSIBILITIES OF RESTAURANT STAFF

Every hotel has its own set of requirements from the F&B professionals working with them. Hotels want their F&B professionals to carry out certain duties and responsibilities.. They require a variety of staff positions in order to operate effectively and efficiently for smooth any operation of the F&B department. The F&B service department generally has the largest staff in hotel. These F&B personnel must have practical as well as theoretical knowledge of the operations. They are committed to provide quality service to the guest as any mistake done by them can lead to dissatisfaction in guests. They all work with a team spirit for the effective and smooth operation of the department. The important duties and responsibilities of the key staff of the F&B department are:

WAITER/STEWARD/FOOD AND BEVERAGES ASSOCIATE

Waiter, waiting staff, wait staff, are the persons who are assigned to serve food and beverages to the customer or supply the guest with food and drink as requested – promptly and pleasantly. In America a waiter is known as a steward and in French Commis-de-Rang. A female wait staff is known as waitress and stewardess. To accomplish this job a waiter must know various skills, attributes and have a positive attitude.

DUTIES OF A WAITER

- Reports to Senior Captain/Captain to receive necessary instructions for the shift and for any changes in the menu.
- Attends briefing taken by Senior Captain or Maitre d' hotel.
- Sets the assigned tables and ensures that the sideboard and back area is well-stocked with linen, silverware, glassware, chinaware and other required items.
- Greets guests and assists the host/hostess in seating the guest.
- Order taking and recording.
- Recommends dishes from the menu.
- Observes the guests in order to anticipate any additional request and to perceive when the meal has been completed.
- Clear the table after the meal is over and reset the table for the next guest.
- Maintaining good guest and staff relations.
- Performs other tasks as directed by the supervisor.
- Sometimes a waiter is also required to perform other duties such as singing birthday songs to customers.
- Ensures that guests enjoy their meal and leave the restaurant fully satisfied by the food and service provided to them.

French Terminology

(i) **Waiter:** *Commis de rang/Garcon*
(ii) **Restaurant Manager:** *Directeur de restaurant*
(iii) **Senior captain/Head waiter:** *Maitre d' hotel*
(iv) **Station head waiter/Captain:** *Maitre d' hotel de carre*
(v) **Station waiter:** *Chef de rang*
(vi) **Carver:** *Trancheur*
(vii) **Wine waiter:** *Chef de vin*
(viii) **Assistant wine waiter:** Commis de vin
(ix) **Floor waiter:** *Chef d' etage*
(x) **Lounge waiter:** *Chef de salle*
(xi) **Assistant lounge waiter:** *Garcon de salle*
(xii) **Trainee:** *Debarrasseur*

Waiter's Kit

Note pad:	To write down the orders	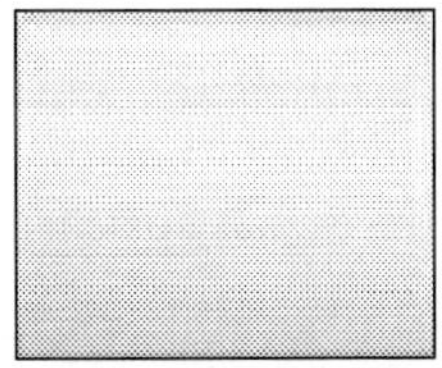
Nameplate:	So the guest can recognize him by his name	
Waiter's cloths:	Purpose of waiter's cloths is a follows: *Carrying hot plates* *Final polishing of plates* *Wiping small spills* *Brushing crumbs onto a service plate* *Wiping the undersides of the plates before placing them on the table.* *Size:* 27" × 18"	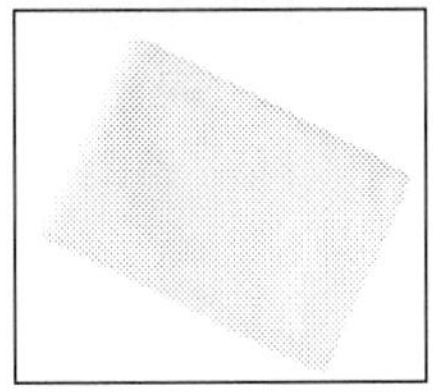
Ballpoint pen (Click type):	To write down the orders. Click-type pen is used because it reduces the time to open the cap of other types of pen	
Bottle opener:	To open the bottles	
Matchbox/Lighter:	To lit guest s cigarette.	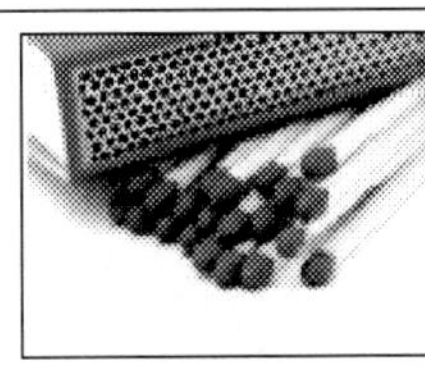
Waiter's Friend:	To open bottles, cork of the wines and to cut foil of the wine bottles Waiter s Friend patented in 1982 by German inventor Karl Wienke.	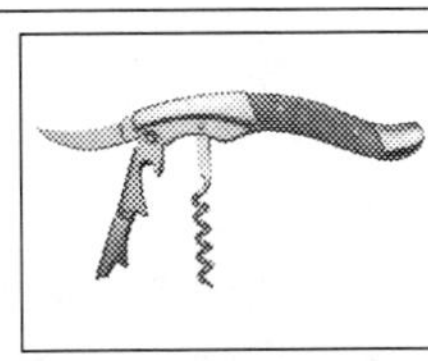

ATTRIBUTES OF A WAITER

Service industry, especially hotels require their staff to possess certain attributes that are prerequisites to perform well. Food & beverages professionals are expected to build upon the following attributes.

Professional and hygiene appearance: Waiter must be groomed and have a professional appearance as they reflect the image of the hotel. Grooming is important as waiter works in front of the guest and handles food and beverages. Service should be done in a clean way to protect guests against food contamination and other food-borne diseases. Unhygienic appearance makes the dining experience unpleasant as well as unhealthy.

Important points to be considered for maintaining personal hygiene by every F&B professional are:

- Bath every day before coming to the shift.
- Hair must be trimmed and free of dandruff.
- Hair must not come over the forehead.
- Hair must not be greasy or oily.
- Males should shave every day, before coming to shift.
- Moustache, if kept must be neatly trimmed.
- Strong perfume and deodorant should be avoided as some guests may have allergy related to this. Light talcum powder and perfume are preferred.
- Waitress should wear light make up.
- They should have a hair bun.
- Excessive jewellery should be avoided.
- Use mouthfreshener after smoking while coming to the shift.
- Wash hands with soap, before shift.
- Nails should be short, clean and well trimmed.
- Uniforms should be clean, laundered and ironed.
- Always carry a neat handkerchief.
- Shoes must be black and oxford.
- Ring should be avoided but a wedding ring can be allowed.
- Cuts and burns should not be open but covered.
- Body language is of great advantage while dealing with guests. Body language involves many body postures, gestures and movements, and each one having different meanings. Good posture when standing or seated indicates that we are in control and have confidence in yourself.

Some postures expected inside the restaurant are as follows:

- A firm handshake.
- Smile.
- Eye contact.
- No physical gestures while speaking to the guest.
- Standing erect.
- Slight leaning towards guest while hearing the guest.

Punctuality: Punctuality is very important for a waiter. If a waiter is not punctual in his job or shift he will miss the briefing and the whole day he will be in chaos. Late arrival in job shows disrespect and lack of interest towards job which gives a negative impact about an individual. Coming half an hour before in shift enables the waiter to acquire information regarding last day's sales, logbook, etc.

Communication Skills: Communication means to understand, perceive and express views among each other. In hotel industry it is mandatory for the front staff to be skilled in English as a language as knowledge of English language plays an important role in understanding the requirements of guests both domestic and foreign because English language is known as an universal and business language. The waiter must be fluent in English and must strive to improve his communication skills. Most of the communication in the department is done in English whether written or verbal therefore a waiter must know how to draft a letter, notice, memos, etc.

Team Work: Team work is an essential element of a waiter. All departments of F&B work together, coordinating with each other to achieve the goal. Delivering best to the guest is possible only when F&B professionals work with a team spirit within and among all other departments. This can be achieved through coordination and cooperation. Example: a prompt service of a meal is done when there is team spirit between the kitchen and F&B department.

Discipline & Honesty: In every shift specific jobs are assigned to each staff member. One must adhere to these jobs and complete them on time for efficient operation of the department. Honesty is also one of the attributes required by the waiter. It is expected that if a guest forgets some valuable in the restaurant it should be reported to the seniors immediately or to find the right owner of the valuable and returned.

Zeal to Learn and Yield: Zeal means *enthusiasm to learn* and yield means *produce*. F&B professionals should strive to know all standard operating procedures and practise them. A waiter should have a fire in the belly to learn and must practise the habits of constant learning. Learning alone will not be benefitted if not shared with the other staff. The waiter should attend the various training programmes conducted in the department and share the acquired knowledge with others.

Local Knowledge: A waiter should have knowledge about the working area as well as of city because sometimes guest may ask questions regarding this, for example, the guest can ask about the visiting places in the city. Who is the owner of the hotel? What are the various promotions going on in the hotel and many more? Failing to answer these questions gives negative impact to the guest.

Product Knowledge: Product for a F&B professional is menu. Waiter must have a detailed knowledge of menu, i.e., brief description of the food items in menu along with their preparation, accompaniments. Not only food but knowledge of beverage is also required by the waiter. A waiter can give recommendations to the guest only if he has thorough knowledge of the menu.

Eye for Detail: Waiter must be observant. He must observe each and every detail inside the restaurant. He must know what is the food order of guest sitting in table no. 5? Has cheque been produced to guests no 6? Why the food is late in the table no 9? and many more.

Flexibility: Nowadays new trends are being introduced in the restaurants, which also bring new technology and other skills. F&B professionals should be flexible in nature to adapt the changing environment.

Sense of Urgency: A waiter should know his importance to the organization and must be there when he is needed. Sometimes waiter is called by the manager even when his shift is over due to many reasons such as sudden reservations of table and lack of staff in the restaurant.

Salesmanship: A waiter is even called a salesman as he presents and sells the food prepared by the production/kitchen department. He is responsible for generating revenue for the restaurant. No matter how delicious the food is but if it not presented in the right manner the guest will not be satisfied because he expects quality service as well as value for money. A waiter must be a good presenter.

Suggestive selling: It is a simple, effective and commonsense technique of using power of suggestion to ensure:

- Dining experience for guests
- Profit maximization
- Repeat guests in the restaurant
- Suggest options and guide the guests. Ask what you can get them rather than what they want. Offer enough options from which it is easy to choose.

Use appetizing descriptions and phrases such as:

Tangy, juicy, succulent, appetizing, will enhance your taste buds. Ours chef's special is….. You must try our…….

This is the most preferred dish by the guest. The star of the menu is …..

Upselling: It is a concept wherein the guest is suggested to buy a similar kind of product, which is a level higher than his/her original choice. It's a process of upgrading sales. There are n number of opportunities for up selling like:

- Non-alcoholic beverages, especially soft drinks to ladies and children.
- Selling mineral water, spring water and aerated water instead of regular water.
- Offering to refill the glasses.
- Suggest accompaniments/side dishes that go well with the main course.

Order Taking: *Sir, What would you like to have?*

Selling: *Would you like to have crunchy goat cheese tart as a starter?*

Always go for selling rather than order taking to be a successful waiter.

Computer Skills & Tactfullnes: As we all know nowadays knowledge of computer is must for day-to-day operations in any organization, same is applicable for the waiters. A waiter must have the knowledge of operating computer and to work in MS Office. Apart from this a waiter must be tactful to handle the various situations inside the restaurant.

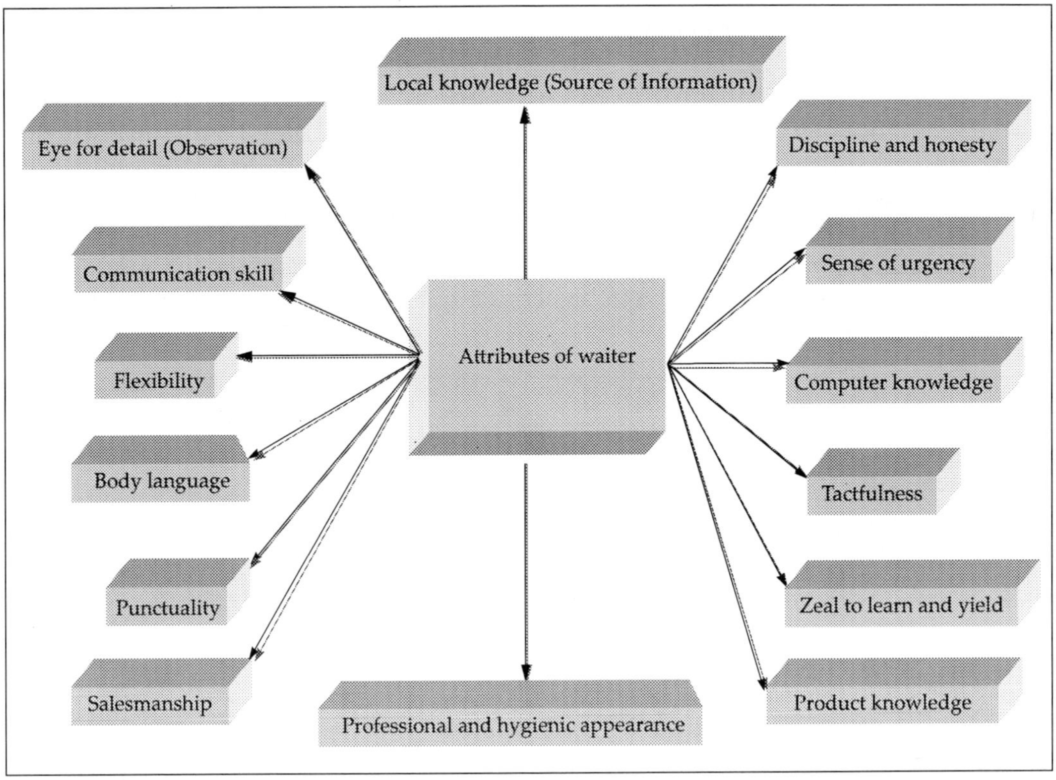

ACTIVITIES

- Visit a restaurant nearby your place and list down the various attributes followed by a waiter.

3 RESTAURANT ETIQUETTE

Guests observe more than grooming and appearance. They observe how staff members carry themselves. Therefore, hotel staff must know the etiquette and manners and should practise them. Courtesy enhances workflow and it is imperative for a good working environment. Etiquette and manners enhance the ability to get along with those around you, making others feel comfortable and important. It enables us to present ourselves to our best advantage but one must remember that the world is changing and the rules must change as a result. The hotel and restaurant business is a cocktail of showmanship, diplomacy and sociability. All food and beverages personnel are required to communicate effectively with manners and etiquette inside the hotel to provide a better service and hospitality to the guest.

PROPER HYGIENE AND GROOMING

Hygiene involves care for the health of others and oneself. F&B associates are involved in physical work about lifting trays, carrying plates and others so look after your health; guard against leg or feet weakness; maintain good sight; and clean teeth and mouth. A balanced diet, fresh air, and suitable recreation help all. Service must be done in a clean way to protect guests against food poisoning or passages of disease. Dirt and dirty practices make dinning unpleasant as well as unsafe. Points to remember for maintaining personal hygiene:

- A shower or bath should be taken daily.
- Always use either deodorant or talcum powder.
- Sufficient sleep (minimum 6 hours), and adequate healthy intake of food (more vegetable, less oil) and regular exercise keeps body healthy.
- Always trim nails and keep hands clean.

- Men should be clean-shaven with well-trimmed moustache.
- Wear clean uniforms.
- Always wear clean undergarments.
- Hair must at all times be clean and well groomed.
- Always brush your teeth after having breakfast, lunch, and dinner.

These hygiene standards must be followed by every F&B professional.

Bathe	Bathe every day before coming to the shift.
Hair	Shampoo hair regularly to avoid dandruff. Hair must be trimmed and clean all times. Hair must not touch the face. Hair must not be greasy or oily.
Face	Males should shave every day, before coming to shift. Moustaches must be neatly trimmed. Do not use strong aftershave lotions. Ladies should wear only light make up. Excessive jewellery should be avoided. Do not use heavy perfumes. Fresh light cologne is preferable to strong ones.
Teeth	Brush your teeth immediately before coming to the shift. Do not eat onion, garlic or smoke before your shift. If you smoke, use mouth freshener.
Hands	Always wash hands with soap before shift. Keep your nails short and clean. Hands must always be clean, free of any stains or any skin breaks.
Uniforms	Should be clean, laundered, ironed. Change whenever it is soiled. Change socks and undergarments every day. Always carry a neat handkerchief.
Feet	Must be washed regularly and toe nails kept trimmed.
Shoes	Wear comfortable closed toed shoes. Shoes must be well polished. Do not wear high healed or open toed shoes.
Cuts and burns	Cuts and burns must be covered with correct dressing. The dressing should always be in proper condition.
Illness	Inform if you suspect or know that you are not physically fit.

HINTS FOR ENTRANCES AND EXITS

Revolving Doors

- While moving through a revolving door, generally whoever comes first leads the way.
- In case of hotel staff, they should make way for guest, people with physical disabilities, old people, slow travellers and people with bulky packages.
- Maintain a steady pace and never stop or change once inside.

Stairs and Elevators

- The hotel staff should always let the guest pass unless leading the way.
- Do not rush or push people on staircase, even if in a hurry. Do not attempt to run on the escalator.
- Help people with disabilities, children, luggage and people with loose clothing to alight and get off elevators and escalators.
- The hotel staff should show the way using an open palm gesture whilst holding the door using the elevator door button.
- One must always hold the door and help people with disabilities or heavy packages.
- Make room for guest, do not crowd or push. If the lift is too crowded then the hotel staff should volunteer to exit.
- Never gossip or discuss other guest or hotel issues whilst in the elevator.
- Hotel staff should always use service elevators unless accompanying a guest.
- The hotel staff should not stare at the guest or themselves through the mirrors inside the guest elevator.

Doors

- The hotel staff should always observe guests approaching the door and open it as the guest walks through.
- The door should be opened in the direction in which the guest is going.
- Always open the door for the person behind.
- The hotel staff should greet the guests as he/she passes through the door.
- The hotel staff must thank anyone who keeps the door open.

ETIQUETTE WITH GUESTS

While Talking to Guest

- Always smile while welcoming a guest in the restaurant.
- Always give the guest full attention and do not say, "yes" until you completely understand what he is asking for. Always provide the guest with at least two alternatives while solving a problem.
- Never say "I don't know". Tell the guest you will find out for him and ensure him that he will be provided with correct information.
- Never argue with the guest, speak softly and clearly without any artificial accent.
- Never discuss negative views about the hotel or other staff with the guest.
- Maintain eye contact, even if you are busy writing or serving, look up once in while to maintain eye contact.
- Avoid using hotel jargons with guests.

While Standing

- While standing to take an order or standing at the restaurant door, stand at erect ease, and not in casual manner.
  - □ Weight balanced on both feet
  - □ Shoulders straight
  - □ Chest out
  - □ Stomach in
- Keep your hands on side or behind your back.
  - □ Do not keep your hands in the pockets or on the hips.
  - □ Do not cross your arms across the chest.
- Do not lean against the sideboard, panels or the hostess desk.
- Remember, you are in the view of the guest even when you are not directly interacting with the guest.
- Do not huddle together in bunches inside the restaurant.
- Avoid turning your back to the guest whenever possible.

Maintain correct body posture without using unwanted gestures or awkward facial expressions.

While Walking

- Walk at an even pace inside the restaurant, avoiding any sound of the footsteps.
- Never run inside the restaurant.
- While walking inside the public areas, if guests are approaching, get aside and give them first right of way. If near a door, open the door for the guests to pass through.

- If accompanying a guest, walk on his/her right-hand side and open the door for the guest.
- Walk erect and maintain the poise.
- Never push or shove colleagues, no matter what the hurry.
- Everyone should follow the generally accepted rules of traffic while walking through the restaurant. Walk to your left side.

COURTEOUS BEHAVIOUR

- Anticipate needs of the guest and fulfil them without being asked. For example:
  - Identify that the guest needs something without him having to call for someone.
  - Open the restaurant door and let the guest pass ahead.
  - Hand him a pen as he reaches for his own.
  - Light his cigarette, as he gets ready to light it.
  - Reach out for the heavy bag he is carrying.
- Do not get familiar with the guest, even when he treats you like a friend. Maintain professionalism.
- Be consistent in recognising guests.
- If a guest asks for directions, do not point. Escort the guest to the destination.
- Treating guests courteously and turning to a colleague and talking to him impolitely destroys the image.
- Treat non-resident guests with as much respect as resident guests as they are potential guests too. Do not forget the power of *"word of mouth publicity"* that the guests do for the restaurant.
- Give attention to single diners also.
- Always remember that service continues until the guest leaves the restaurant and not when the bill is settled.
- Take ownership of the guest's problem.
- Never cross the guest's middle line during service or clearance.

COURTESY AMONG COLLEAGUES

- While communicating with your colleagues, do not point your finger towards any guest. Use cover numbers to inform who has ordered for what.
- Do not use abusive language with your colleagues.
- Speak politely while ordering food, calling for pick-up, etc.
- Be aware of your conversation over the telephone. Guests may be watching or hearing you:
  - Never shout into the telephone.
  - Do not have long conversation over the phone, while a guest is waiting.

□ Do not entertain personal calls while at work.

- When a guest requires assistance, do so regardless of whether it is your job or not.

DOS AND DON'TS

- Attend the guests as soon as they enter the restaurant addressing their name as it gives recognition. Pronounce name correctly. Acknowledge the guests within 30 seconds.
- Welcome and wish them according to the time of the day. Example. *Good Afternoon Mr Robert, Welcome to the, (name of the restaurant).* Escort the guest to the table.
- Help guests to be seated. Assist guests to remove and wear heavy warm coats and bags.
- Provide extra cushions or special chairs for children.
- Do not overhear conversation.
- Avoid mannerisms such as touching the hair, scratching oneself, etc.
- Stand erect at all times a gentle bow at the time of service is permissible.
- Talk softly and politely
- Always wear smile on your face.
- Avoid arguments.
- Do not run inside the restaurant.
- Do not make clusters inside the restaurant.
- Avoid talking inside the restaurant.
- Carry pen in the trousers pockets and not behind ears or clipped in front of the jacket.
- Desist from chewing gum or beetle nut.
- Present the bill/check to the guest in the bill folder.
- Avoid soliciting for tips. Remove tips after guests have left.
- Lead the guest to the clean tables only.
- Keep your working area neat and clean as the guests are very observant.
- Remember you may be in the view of a guest even when you are not directly interacting with him/her.
- Avoid using inappropriate language inside the restaurant and in front of the guest.
- Do not show disregard for other's time.
- Always be in appropriate dressing or grooming.
- Don't misuse the telephone.
- Do not fail to greet the guest.
- Have proper listening skills.
- Don't show disregard to shared property and other's space.
- Don't embarrass others.

- While approaching the guest, use words like "May I assist you" or "May I help you Sir/Madam".
- Enter and leave the restaurant through the service entrance only.
- After service always use words like, "Thank You, It's been a pleasure serving you. Please visit soon."

TIPS ON TIMING AND HONOURING SCHEDULES

- Hotel staff should always specify time that they expect to be taken while fulfilling guest's requests or responding to a query.
- Guests are more important than staff or other work. They should always be given the first priority.
- Orders must be served within the standard time.
- In case an order is expected to take additional time, the service of food and beverages should be planned in such a way that the guest is kept waiting for the least duration.
- The staff should offer fast beverage replenishments in order to create a positive impression of alertness.

HANDLING FOOD

- Always wash your hands before touching food, and always after coming from toilet.
- If you are suffering from any skin, nose, throat or stomach problem or trouble at work, tell your senior and don't handle food.
- Use waterproof dressings on cuts and sores. And remember to keep those dressings clean.
- Be clean in yourself and in the clothes you wear.
- Don't smoke in a kitchen or dining room. And never cough or sneeze over food.
- Clean as you go in the kitchen, if anything get spilled, wipe it immediately. See that all utensils are clean.
- Cover food, keep it clean.
- Use tongs, spoons, etc., when handling food, rather than your fingers.
- Always keep the lid on a dustbin.
- In restaurants, remember that clean, fully equipped, well-lit, and airy conditions are required for maintenance of hygiene.

ETIQUETTE FOR USING RESTAURANT EQUIPMENT

- Learn how to use the equipment properly.
- If it is empty and requires refilling, do so to avoid inconvenience.
- In case you have borrowed the equipment, return it to the original user as soon as possible and in the same condition as received.

- Do not borrow equipment without prior permission.
- Use correct method and technique to use and carry the equipment.
- Do not rest foot sole against walls or furniture?
- Do not bang the door of the sideboards.
- Do not carry trays, peppermills, dirty linen and other such items under your arms when your hands are full.

BRIEFING

A restaurant starts a shift with a briefing. It is an important two-way communication process between the management and staff to ensure harmony in the thought process before a restaurant opens. Prior to the briefing, the servers are required to come prepared with the following as they will be checked by the manager.

- Be in the correct uniform and be properly groomed such as:
  - ☐ Fingernails are manicured and clean.
  - ☐ Shoes are well polished.
  - ☐ Hair is well combed.
  - ☐ Uniform is well ironed and clean.
- Equipped with KOT (kitchen order tickets) and scribbling pads.
- Waiter cloth.
- Clean handkerchiefs.
- Click type pen.
- Cigarette lighter/matchbox.
- Bottle opener.
- Be informed about non-available menu items listed on the board in the kitchen so as to alert guests immediately when they place orders.
- Daily specials (Carte du jour).
- Method of preparation of all menu items.
- Time taken for the preparation of each dish.
- Sauces used for each dish.
- Accompaniments and garnishes of each dish on the menu.
- Whether dish is vegetarian or non-vegetarian.
- Method of service.
- Appropriate wines with each dish.
- The course each dish belongs to.
- Price of dishes.
- Alternative suggestions for dishes.
- Whether to fetch various items from the different sections of the kitchen.
- Portion sizes.
- Popular menu items.

Briefing format **Date:**

Room count :____________________ Occupancy :____________%

House count :____________________

VIPs in house :____________________

Club members :____________________

Hotel :____________________(MTD)

:____________________(YTD)

Revenue

Last day sale :____________________

Food :____________________(MTD) ____________________(YTD)

Beverage :____________________(MTD) ____________________(YTD)

Not available item

Food :____________________

Beverage :____________________

Supervisor present on shift :____

F&B associate present on shift :____

Weekly off :____________________

On leave :____________________

Any special event/bulk booking :____

At the Briefing Following is Also Discussed

- New policies of the management.
- Table reservation status.
- VIPs expected in the restaurant.
- Service standards that need re-enforcing.
- Guest complaints and how they can be avoided.
    - □ Training tips.
    - □ Revenue performance of the restaurant to date.
    - □ Sales targets for the day.
    - □ Recognition for jobs well done.
    - □ Transfer, promotions, new staff and exits.
    - □ Introduction to new staff joining the team.
    - □ Encouragement and motivation.
    - □ Staff schedule and station allotments.
    - □ Cost control measures.
    - □ New menu items.
    - □ Management observations and suggestions.

ACTIVITIES

- Visit any nearby restaurant for a cup of tea along with your friends and observe the etiquettes and manners followed by the staff.

4 RESTAURANT EQUIPMENT

F&B service equipment is divided into chinaware, glassware and tableware which can be used for eating, for service or for preparation in front of the guest. Tableware is further divided into flatware, cutlery and hollowware. There is a huge variety of tableware used in restaurants. Not only does the basic cutlery come in a variety of styles, but the range of specialist equipment is also endless. In this chapter you will be able to understand various types of equipment used in restaurants and hospitality industry along with their uses.

CHINAWARE

- Chinaware is made of silica, soda ash and china clay and is glazed to give finish. It should be opaque and free from air bubbles.
- Chinaware is a breakable item so it should be handled carefully.
- Chinaware can be found in different colours and designs, which are always with glaze.
- Patterns on the top of the glaze wear and discolour quickly.
- Chinaware is more resistant to heat than glassware.
- Recent developments in chinaware include the ovenproof ware (dishes, casserole and cocotte dishes), which allow food to be brought straight from the oven to the table.
- Chinaware should be kept covered to prevent dust and germs settling on it.
- Chipped and cracked items harbour germs and should, therefore, be not used and disposed of carefully.
- Should be wiped/polished using a slightly damp cloth just before being set on table to give some shine.

Examples of Chinaware with Standard Sizes and Purpose		
Name	**Size**	**Image**
Side plate	6 inches	

Fish plate	8 inches	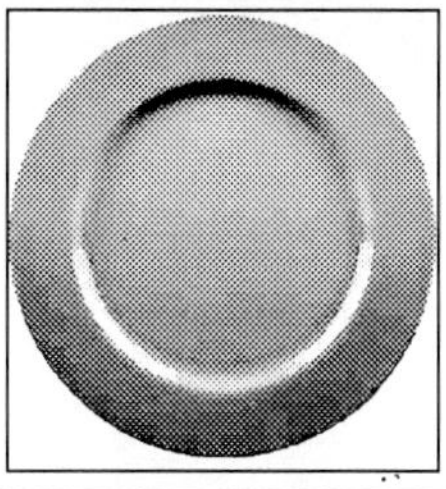
Soup plate	7 inches	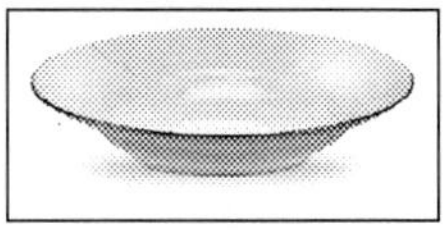
Dinner plate	10 inches	
Joint plate/Show plate	12 inches	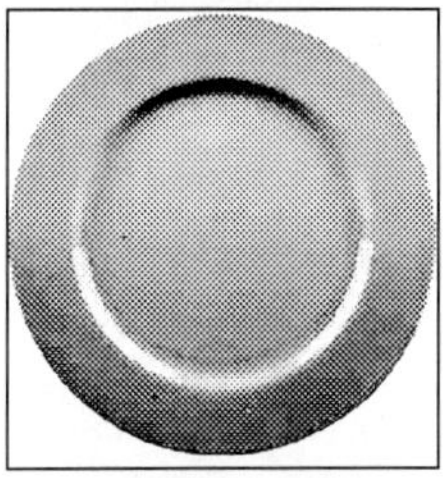
Cereal bowl	5 inches	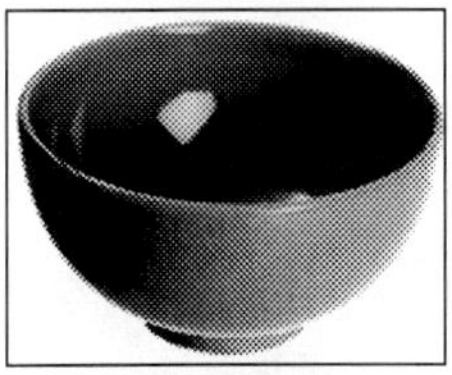
Demitasse cup (small cup for serving espresso)	97.5 ml	

Teacup with saucer	200 ml	
Cappuccino cup	240 ml	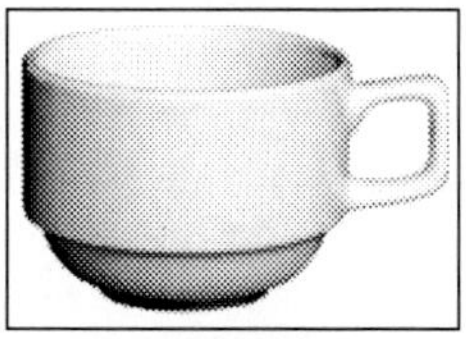
Saucer (placed as an under liner with cups)		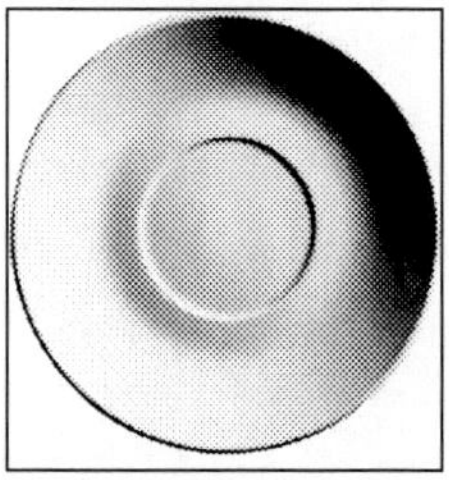
Soup bowl	240 ml	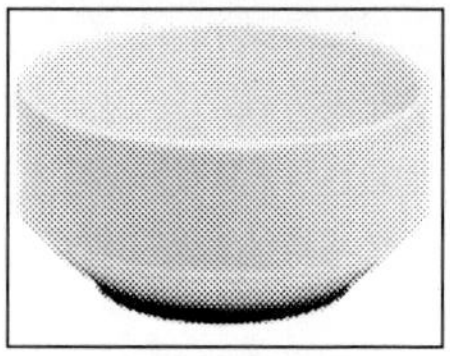
Consommé cup with saucer (have handle/ears)	240 ml	
Oval platter (can be used for serving salads)	One portion	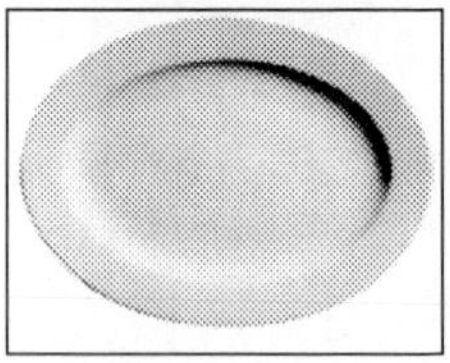
Tea/coffee pot	To serve tea and coffee. Stainless tea pot has multiple hole to strain tea. Comes in many sizes.	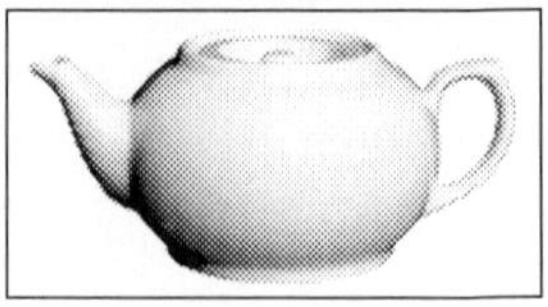

Creamer	To serve milk with tea	
Ashtray	To put cigarette and cigar ashes	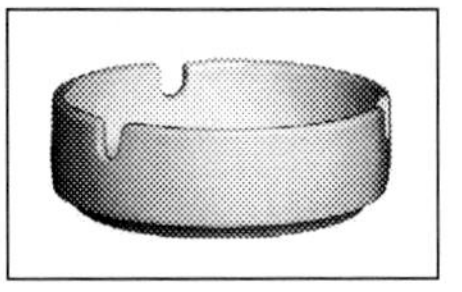
Bud vase	For small flower arrangement on table	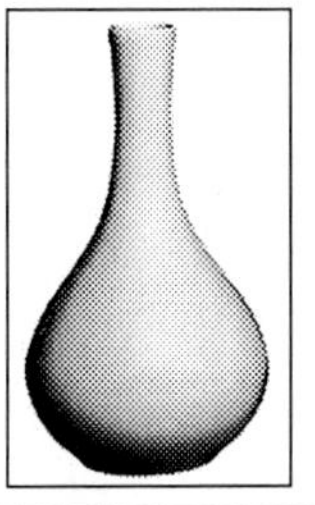
Cruet set	Salt and pepper cellars. Salt pepper has one or few holes whereas pepper has many (ashtray, budvase and cruet set-ABC all together are also known as table appointments)	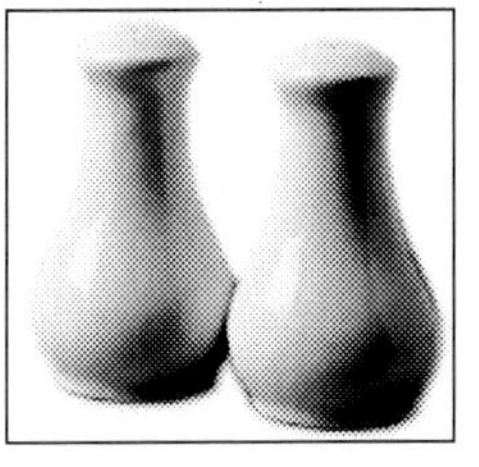
Egg cup	To serve boiled egg	

CUTLERY AND FLATWARE

Sizes of spoon

Teaspoon: 5 ml

Tablespoon: 15 ml

Dessert spoon: 10 ml

Soup spoon: 10 ml

Cutlery refers to all kinds of knives and cutting implements whereas flatware refers to all kinds of spoons and forks. In general, all knives, spoons and forks are called cutlery. One should always keep in mind that cutlery is for guest's use and its quality will reflect the image of the service outlet. Most food service operations now prefer the use of stainless steel cutlery rather than EPNS (electroplated nickel silver) as these are cheaper, easy to clean and resists scratch. Nowadays, the manufacturer understands the needs of various catering operators and produces a wide range of cutlery and flatware with varied designs and prices to cater to these needs. The commonly used cutlery and their uses are shown below.

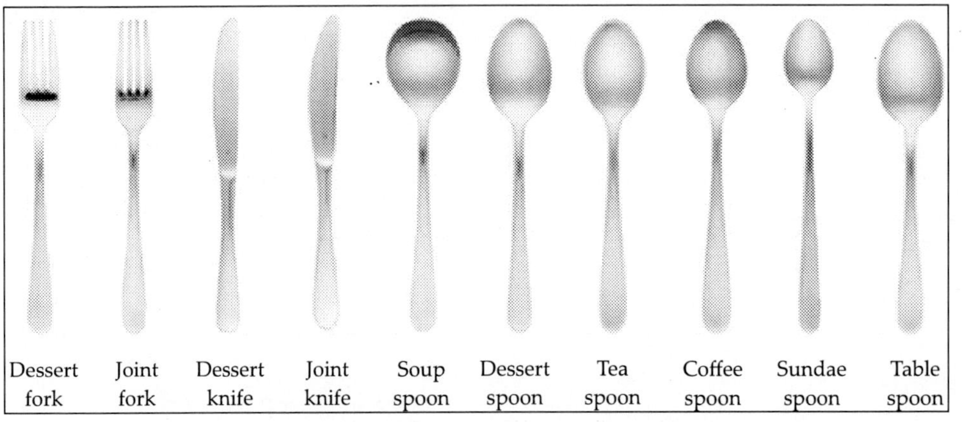

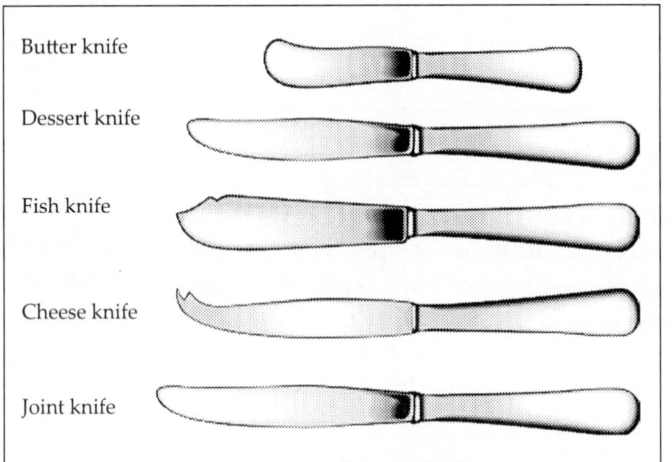

Types of knife

Types of spoon

Cutlery	Uses
Soup spoon	For thick soup.
Dessert spoon	For dessert.
Dessert fork	For dessert.
Joint fork and joint knife	For main course.
Service spoon and service fork	Also known as service gears. Used for transferring dishes from the platter to guest's plate.
Tea spoon	Tea/coffee/juice served with accompaniments, fruits cocktails, sweets served in coups or glass bowls.
Coffee spoon/Demitasse spoon	For coffee served in demitasse after lunch or dinner.
Side knife	Placed on the side plate for bread, toast, rolls, cheese.
Cheese knife	To serve cheese.
Fish knife	For all fish dishes.
Fish fork	For all fish dishes.
Steak knife	For steaks.
Fruit knife and fruit fork	For fruits.
Sundae spoon /Parfait	Ice cream or any shakes with ice cream served in tall glass.

HOLLOWWARE

This refers to all tableware other than cutlery which are hollow in shape. It includes the following:

- Stainless steel pots
- Water jugs
- Platters
- Finger bowls

- Wine chiller
- Bread basket
- Butter dish
- Sauce boat

SPECIAL EQUIPMENT

Though the list covers important special equipment, it does not cover the entire range. Some items listed will be found in all types of food service operations and the rest according to the menu offered.

Name	Purpose	Image
Trays	Rectangular in shape and used for carrying cutlery, glassware and hollowware. Mostly used to serve small orders and tea/coffee in guest room.	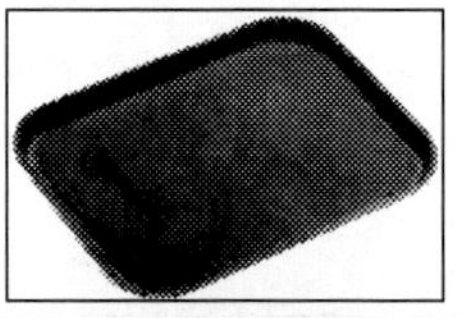
Salver/Beverage round	Round in shape and used for carrying cutlery, beverages, glassware hollowware, dishes, and so on. Size of salver should be 12 – 18 inches in diameter.	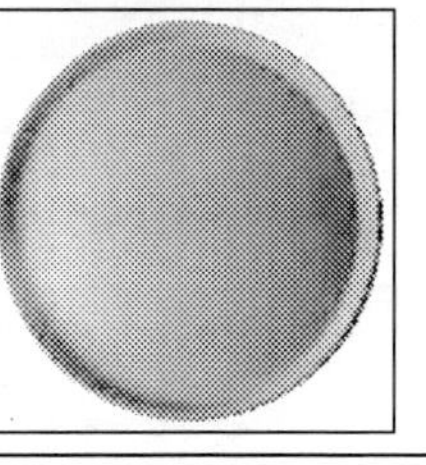
Tray jack	Used to keep the trays and salvers on it while clearing the long table in the restaurant and banquets. Tray jack has a folding stand which makes it easy to keep anywhere in the restaurant.	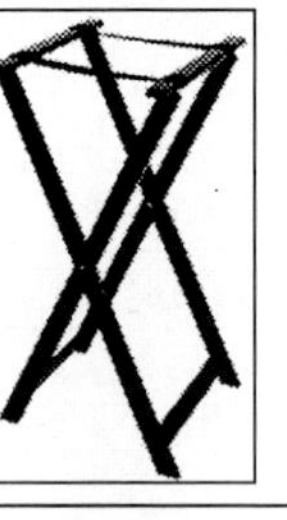
Water jug	For the service of water.	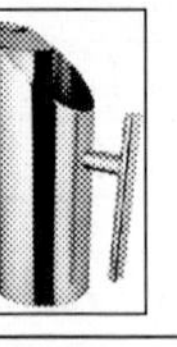
Entree dish	For portioning out dishes and taking to guest table. Many portion sizes are available such as one portion, two portion and more.	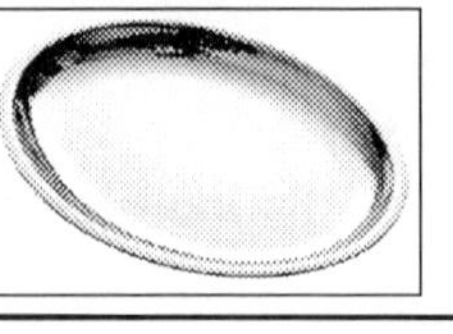

Oval platter	For carrying food to the guest table, many portion sizes are available.	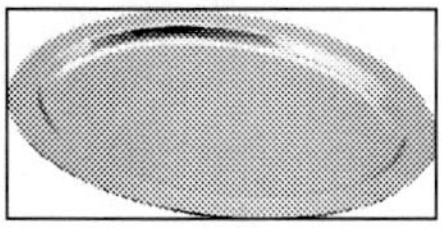
Bread basket	Mat finish stainless steel or can basket. Used for carrying bread rolls and Indian breads.	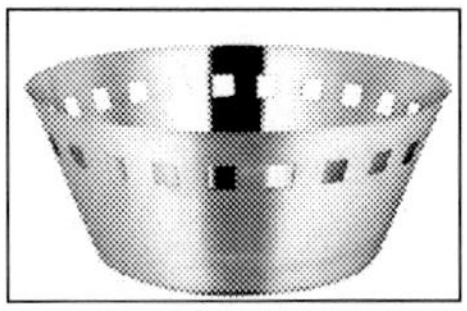
Butter dish	Used for serving butter.	
Menu stand	To hold table d' hote menu card. Can also be used to place buffet tags. Comes in many shapes and sizes.	
Soup tureen	To serve soup in buffet.	
Soup ladle	To serve soup from soup tureen.	
Chafing dish	To place food in buffet.	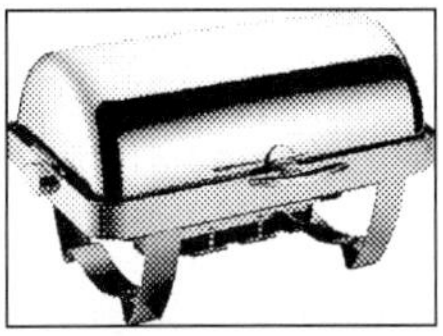

Serving ladle	To serve food from chafing dish in buffet.	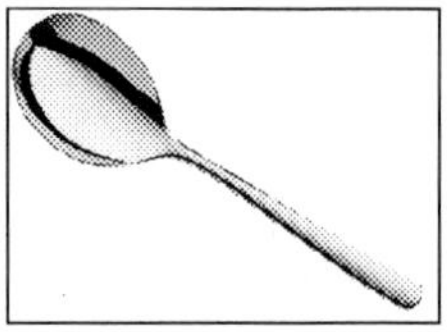
Sauce boat	To accompany sauces and serve.	
Ice bucket	To serve ice cubes.	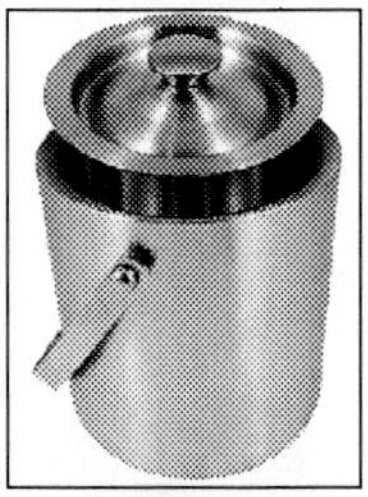
Wine chiller	To serve white wine, champagne and sparkling wine.	
Toast rack	To present toast. Has 8-10 slots for toast.	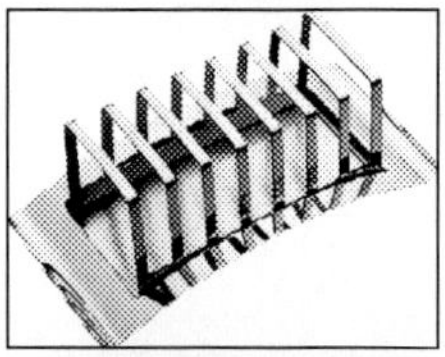
Preserve boat	To hold preserves such as jam, honey and marmalade.	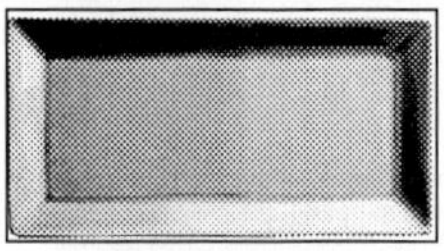
Sugar basin	To place sugar sachets.	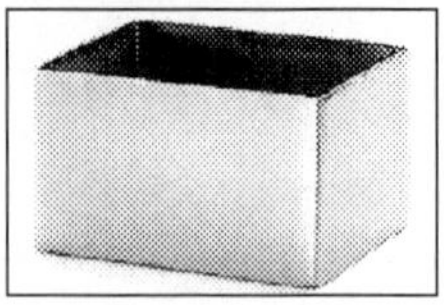

Tea strainer	To strain tea while serving tea.	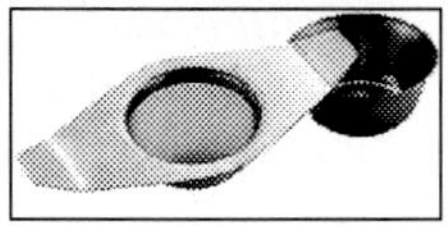
Sugar tong	To serve sugar cubes.	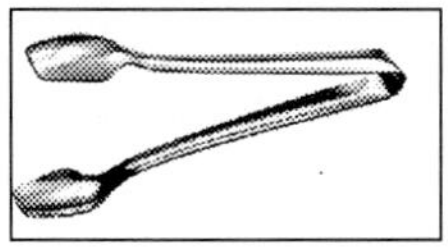
Multipurpose tong	To serve breads, salads, lettuces and pastry.	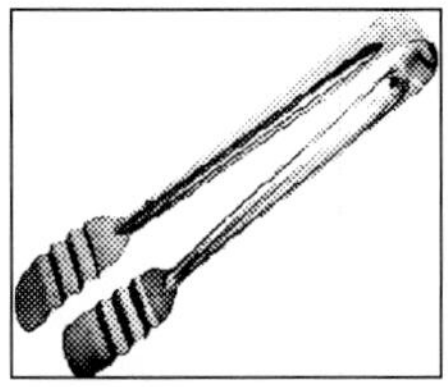
Ice tong	To serve ice cubes	
Snail dish	Round dish with 8-10 indentations to pick-up counter hold snail.	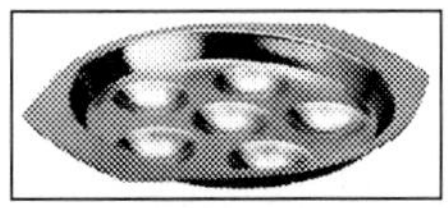
Snail tong and snail fork	A two-pronged fork, used to pick flesh pantry from shells	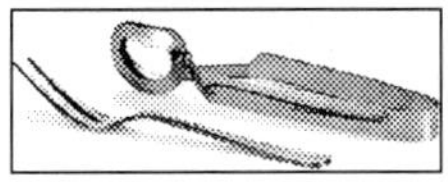

GLASSWARE

Any vessel made of glass and is intended to drink beverages from is known as glassware. Detail about glassware is discussed in chapter "Bar Glassware and Equipment".

TROLLEYS

Some of the various trolleys used in the food and beverages service outlets are:

- **Gueridon or Flambe Trolley:** A gueridon or flambe trolley is a small mobile trolley that can be placed alongside the guest's table. It consists of one or two burners, a gas cylinder and a work and storage space for plates and cooking equipment. Using this trolley, the food is flambéed at the guest's table. Only skilled and well trained waiters are allowed to handle this service as there is risk of spoiling food by overcooking it, and of the flame causing a fire in the premises.

- **Room Service Trolley:** This trolley is known for its versatility. It is used for the service to guests in their rooms. The waiter sets up the meal and covers on the trolley and wheels it into the guest's room. This trolley may also be used as a dining table in the privacy of the guest's room. Beneath the trolley top, provision is made for mounting a hot case to keep the food warm.

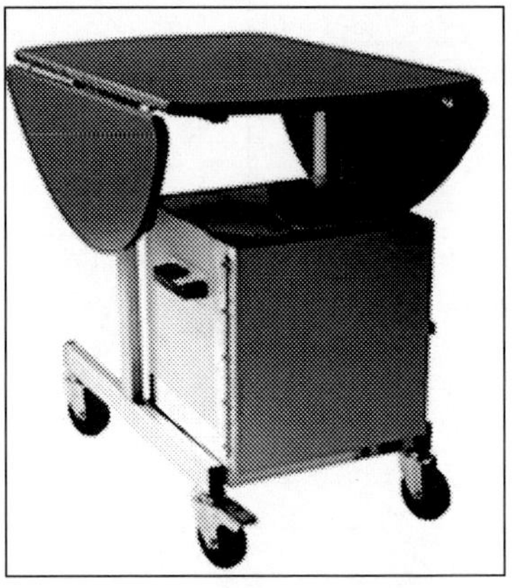

Room service trolley

- **Dessert Trolley:** This trolley serves as a visual aid to selling desserts. Guests are more likely to order a dessert if they can see what is available, particularly if it is well presented. Some dessert trolleys are refrigerated. Gateaux, pastries, jellies, tarts, pies, flans and soufflés can be served from a dessert trolley. This trolley has several shelves and the bottom shelf is reserved for plates, cutlery, linen and other service equipment. A glass or transparent trolley top makes it easy for guests to select a dessert of their choice.

Dessert trolley

- **Hors d'oeuvre Trolley:** A hors d'oeuvre is the first course of a menu usually consisting of a selection of small items of egg, fish, meat, fruit and vegetables in pungent dressings. This hors d'oeuvre trolley is used to carry a variety of appetizers. This trolley is probably the least popular in India, as a majority of guests are not too keen on hors d'oeuvre as a starter. They prefer soups instead. However, this trolley can be used to popularize special dishes that are introduced in the restaurant from time to time.

Hors d'oeuvre trolley

- **Cheese trolley:** It is used to serve variety of cheese to the guest.
- **Liqueur trolley:** This trolley contains variety of liqueurs to be served to the guests.

Liqueur's trolley

TABLES AND CHAIRS

The size and shape of tables depends entirely on the availability of space and the kind of service envisaged. Normally, three types of tables are used. These are round, rectangular and square. Commercial table tops come in a variety of materials: wood, metal, stone, tile and melamine. Many restaurant table tops are available with edged finishes to prevent scuffs and dents. In some expensive tables, another table top is placed with revolving facility, on top of which the food is placed where the guest can rotate revolving top and serve himself, if he chooses so. Normally, tables used in restaurants have a central pedestal to allow maximum leg space with a heavy base to provide stability.

Square Table

- 2.5 feet × 2.5 feet – For seating two people
- 3 feet × 3 feet – For seating four people.

Round Table

- 3 feet diameter: for seating four people
- 5 feet diameter: for seating eight people.

Rectangular Table

- 4.5 feet × 2.5 feet: for seating four people

Hostess Desk

- 42 inches height working surface
- Covered from the front
- Shelves to store items such as reservation register, paging board, telephone, menus, etc.

Chairs: Chairs are available in various shapes, colours and sizes to suit various occasions. Because of the wide ranges of style, chairs come in varied height and width. However, the dimension of chairs should be relative to table dimensions. The average height of a chair should be 36 inches. The seat should be 18 inches from the floor and 18 inches from the top of the table. This would enable guests to sit and eat comfortably, without their legs touching the underside of the table. Chairs may be with arms or armless. Chairs with arms are used for a luxurious and more comfortable dining experience. They may also have rubber shoes which prevent damage to the floor and the chair both.

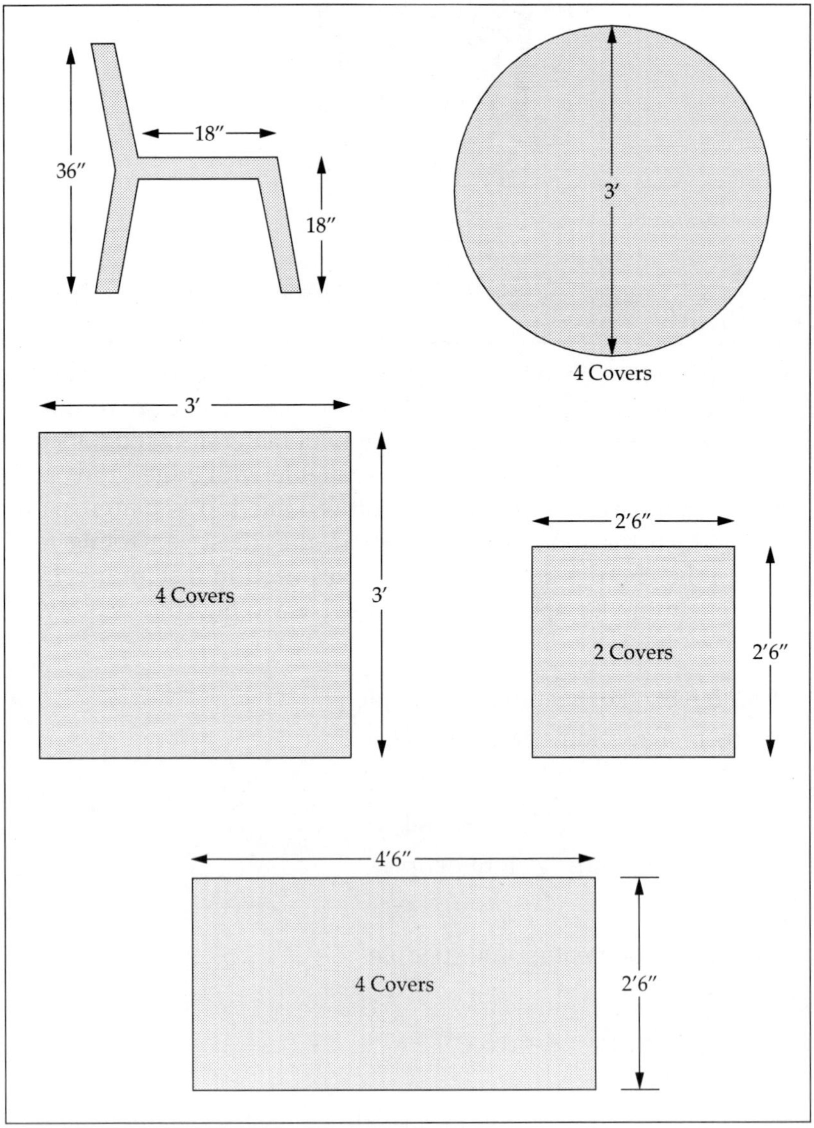

Chairs and Tables

LINEN

Linens are fabric goods, such as tablecloths, napkins and slip cloths. Linen is a material made from the fibre of the flax plant. Originally, many such as bedsheets and tablecloths, were made of linen. Today, the term "linen" has come to be applied to all related products even though most are made of cotton, various synthetic materials, or blends. The main items of linen in a restaurant are: tablecloths, slip cloths, buffet cloths, trolley and waiter's cloths and service cloths.

Damask is a form of weaving in which weft produces a self pattern. Damask is traditionally, but not necessarily, white. Double or single damask are terms used to describe difference in weave.

Table Cloths: Table linens made from cotton or linen are not only more absorbent but also last longer. The fibre does not pill or pile as easy as with synthetic table linens and they don't become shiny when exposed to an iron's heat. Egyptian cotton and Irish linen are considered the finest materials for table linen because of their long, durable fibres. White is the most popular colour for table linen because it's considered formal. Table linens in off white or ivory are also acceptable. A damask (woven) or embroidered pattern is a perfectly acceptable tablecloth. Tablecloths should be large enough to cover the top as well as a portion of the legs of a table without interfering with the guest' comfort while he is seated at the table. The size of the tablecloth varies according to the size of the table it is required to cover.

- 54 inches × 54 inches to fit a 2 feet 6 inches square table or round table of 3 feet diameter.
- 72 inches × 72 inches to fit a table of 3 square feet.
- 72 inches × 96 inches to fit a rectangular shaped table.
- 72 inches × 54 inches to fit rectangular shaped table.

Slip Cloths or Naperons: These are designed to be laid over the tablecloth to protect it from spillage and give it a longer life. Using a slip cloth reduces the number of tablecloths used and thus reduces the cost of inventory and laundry. Slip cloths may measure 1 square metre approximately. It also adds to the theme or décor of the restaurant.

Napkins or Serviettes: A napkin or serviette is a rectangular cloth or paper used at the table for wiping the mouth while eating. It is usually small and folded. Conventionally, the napkin is folded and placed to the left of the place setting, outside the outermost fork. In an ambitious restaurant setting, it may be folded into elaborate shapes and displayed on the empty plate. A napkin may also be held together in a bundle (with cutlery) by a napkin ring. Alternatively, paper napkins may be contained with a napkin holder. Napkins may be of the same colour as tablecloths, or in a colour that blends with the decor of the restaurant. Napkins should be spotlessly clean and well-ironed.

- Dinner napkin: 20 square inches
- Lunch napkin: 18 square inches
- Tea napkin: 12 square inches

- Cocktail napkin: 9 square inches
- Paper napkin: 14-17 square inches

Buffet Cloths: For a buffet table, the minimum size of the tablecloth required is 2 m × 4 m.

- 6 feet × 12 feet

Trolley Cloths and Sideboard Cloths: These are usually made from tablecloths well worn and not suitable for use on tables, mended by the housekeeping department and folded to fit a sideboard or trolley.

Moultons: Also known as baize cloth. It is made of brushed cotton/baize cloth. Used as an underliner to the tablecloth to give smoothness to the table surface. Moultons help in absorbing spillages, cushions noise, protects table tops from heat and silverware from abrasion. It has a 9″ fall and fixed with drawstrings/thumb tacks/Velcro tape.

Waiter's Cloths or Service Cloths: A service cloth is an important part of service equipment as well as being part of the food server's uniform. It must be kept clean and ironed and only used as a service cloth for certain activities such as:

- Carrying hot plates
- Final polishing of plates
- Wiping small spills
- Brushing crumbs onto a service plate
- Wiping the undersides of the plates before placing plates on the table. Service cloths are also used as protection against heat and to keep uniforms clean.
- Daily care and cleaning

After any service, the soiled linen is collected in the side stations and it is sorted as per size in bundles of ten before sending to the laundry for processing. It should also be segregated as heavy or light soiled linen to facilitate appropriate treatment.

Storage

- Fresh linen should be handled as less as possible for reasons of hygiene.
- It should be stacked in paper-lined shelves with correct sizes together and the folded end facing outside for ease of counting. Each shelf should be labelled with the names of the items that it holds.

SILVER CLEANING METHODS

During service, all soiled flatware and cutlery used is deposited in a plastic tray immersed in a tank containing soap solution to degrease it. After service, the tray is passed through the dishwasher for washing, rinsing and sterilizing. For best results, silver should be polished lightly by hand before it air-dries. A waiter's cloth is used for this purpose. 6-8 pieces are polished at a time. You should take care not to touch any cutlery or flatware while and after polishing it. In silver cleaning, hollowware is usually the responsibility of the kitchen stewarding and flatware is the responsibility of restaurant staff. Routine washing is done through dishwashing. Generally, in most of the hotels it is the kitchen stewarding who takes care of silver cleaning. Some of the silver cleaning methods are as follows:

Burnishing machine

- It is the most efficient way to clean silver on a daily basis.
- It has a revolving drum with a safety shield and lead ball bearings.
- The drum is lined with rubber to protect the silver.
- It is plugged to the water supply to maintain a constant flow of water. A proprietary soap solution is used with the machine.
- When the machine is plugged on, the drum starts revolving. The mixture of water and detergent acts as a lubricant between the ball bearings and the silver, removing any tarnish without scratching the silver.
- Depending on the size of the burnishing machine being used, it may be divided into compartments to hold specific size of silver.
- A rod may be inserted from one end to the other. This rod is removable and is used to hang the hollowware having handles like tea pot, coffee pot, sauce boat and others to hold them in a position while the drum is revolving.
- Burnishing machine is always kept filled with water so that ball bearings do not rust.
- On being removed from the burnishing machine, the silver should be rinsed in hot water and dried with clean cloth.
- This method of silver cleaning keeps the silver in good condition with minimum efforts and gives a lasting polish.

Polivit/Soda aluminium

- A perforated aluminium sheet and some soda are used in an enamel bowl, which contains the silver to be cleaned.
- Hot water is then poured in the bowl.
- The reaction among perforated aluminium sheet, water and soda lifts the tarnish from the silver.
- The silver is then rinsed in hot water and dried with a clean cloth.

Plate powder

- It is a very effective method but time consuming.
- Proprietary silver cleaning powder (in paste form, made with methylated spirit) or a pink powder which needs mixing with a little methylated spirit to obtain smooth paste.
- This paste is rubbed on the article and methylated spirit evaporates as a result removing tarnish from the silver.
- Water can also be used instead of methylated spirit but it is more time consuming.

- This method is very effective for all types of tarnish and is recommended for silver articles with a lot of intricate designs on them.

Silver dip

- This is a pink coloured liquid that must be used in a plastic bowl.
- The silver to be cleaned is placed into a wire basket and dipped into the plastic bowl containing the silver dip.
- All silver articles cleaned should be covered by the liquid.
- The silver should be left in the bowl for a short while and then lifted out and drained.
- After draining it is placed in warm water, rinsed and then polished with a clean, dry cloth.
- This method is very quick and produces good results, but is harder on the silver than other methods because of the chemical reaction between liquid and silver.

Buffing: To shine the silverware and stainless steel buffing is done. In this process stainless steel or silverware is scrubbed in a machine, it is a very effective process to shine the silverware and stainless steel but very hard on it as buffing removes the outer covering which results in shining of tableware and reducing the content of silverware and stainless steel.

After each one of the above processes, the silver is rinsed in hot water before giving a final polish. Silverware is cleaned daily and on the weekly basis like all cutlery on Monday, hollowware on Wednesday.

Storage

- Silverware should be stored in trays on shelves with all flats of one size together. Each shelf should be labelled with the names of the items that it holds.
- Heavier items should always be stored at the bottom of the shelf and lighter ones on top.
- All cutlery and flatware and small items such as cruet sets, etc., should be stored in drawers lined with baize cloth.

ACTIVITIES

- Find and make a list the various restaurant equipment suppliers in your city. Also find out the brand names of various crockery and cutlery available with them.

5 MISE EN PLACE

Mise en place means *putting in place* or *things prior to operation.* All the activities are done before the start of the shift for the smooth running of the operations. It is an international term used for preparing a restaurant for flawless service subsequently. It helps the team members to be prepared with all the necessary items to be ready/required for the shift. The server has to ensure that his station is adequately equipped with the serviceware and other necessary items for service. Activities to be done under mis en place are:

- Changing linen: Exchange all soiled linen against fresh linen from the housekeeping department.
- Placing and setting of tables.
- Laying covers on table.
- Arranging sideboards as per its checklist.
- Arranging back areas: Setting up the pickup counter with serving dishes and their covers, pick-up trays, bread baskets, butter dishes.
- Menu cards to be made presentable.
- Prepare all necessary items to be used in food service such as:
  - □ Cutlery and glassware.
  - □ Service gear.
  - □ Crumbing down equipment.
  - □ Service plates.
  - □ Tea/coffee service equipment.
  - □ Service trays.
  - □ Ashtrays.
  - □ Wine lists.
  - □ Condiment bowl.
  - □ Additional items to meet the specialist requirements of the organization.
  - □ Stacking sideboard.

WIPING GLASSWARE

Glassware is a breakable item therefore utmost care to be taken while wiping to avoid breakage and without hurting your hand.

Equipment Required

- Glassware
- Water pan containing lukewarm water
- Wiping cloth/sheet
- Glass rack.

Knowledge Required

- To know the right procedure of cleaning glasses
- Types of glasses
- Handling glasses

Procedure

1. The glassware is placed in the glass racks above the stewarding counter.
2. The kitchen stewarding person deputed for rinsing glasses brings the rack to the rinse basin.
3. Wipe the glasses with the wiping cloth.
4. Hold the base of the glass in hand using one corner of the wiping cloth.
5. If the glass is not chipped or cracked, insert the remaining cloth in the glass using the right hand. Insert the index, second and ring fingers in the glass and use the thumb as support on the outer side. Wipe the glass with the right hand in swift clockwise motion.
6. Hold the glass against the light and check for marks.
7. Stack the clean glasses directly into the shelves in the beverage stacking rack at the wash up area or stack into a salver to take inside the restaurant.
8. If the glass is chipped or cracked, it should be placed in the "discard bin". At the end of every shift the associate reports the breakages for shift to the concerned supervisor.
9. The supervisor takes stock of the breakage and notes it on the "breakage report".
10. The supervisor totals the breakages at the end of every month and places value to these breakages. This month end report is submitted to the F&B Manager.

Standards

- The steward should always dispose of any extra beverage in the glass.
- The glasses should always be placed inverted in the glass rack.
- The glasses should be carried on the glass rack and not individually by hand.
- Care should be taken to not dirty the floors with droplets from the glass rack.
- Hand should never be in direct contact with the glass.
- Only one cloth should be used to wipe the glass.
- The discarded tablecloths are used as wiping cloths with colour codes.

- The wiping cloth should not be damp.
- The wiping cloth should not smell.
- The wiping cloth should be changed regularly.
- Check the glass for cracks or chip.
- The glass should be free from water marks or any other stain.
- The glasses should be stacked according to the glass type in neat rows.

Step 1	Put the glasses in the pan containing lukewarm water. Vinegar may be added if the glasses are very dirty.	
Step 2	Hold the base of the glass in the left hand using one corner of the wiping cloth.	
Step 3	Insert the wiping cloth inside the glass and start wiping by rotating the cloth clockwise and anticlockwise simultaneously.	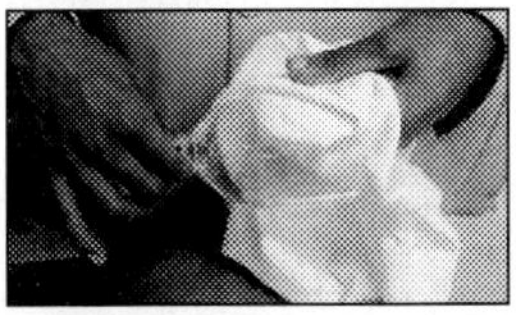
Step 4	Hold the glass against the light and check for any stains.	

Step 5	Stack the wiped/clean glasses in the glass rack and later on stack them in the designated places.	

TABLE SETUP

Equipment Required

- Appropriate cutlery and flatware
- Table appointments
- Appropriate glassware
- Salver

Knowledge Required

- Types of cover setup
- Size of a cover
- Carrying salver
- Handling glasses
- Hygiene and sanitation
- Restaurant etiquette
- Eye for detail

Procedure

- When the breakfast session ends, the steward clears the following items from the table.
  - □ Teacups
  - □ Preserves
- Wipe the table with an appropriate table duster.
- Ensure that the tables are not wobbling and are arranged symmetrically. If the table is wobbling, please get it rectified.
- The steward places the tablemats in front of each cover on the table.
- The steward places the spoon, knife and fork on place mat.
- Place the side plate on the left-hand side along with the napkin on top of the plate.
- Collect the water glasses and place them on the table.

Standard

- The steward must use a salver to clear all items.
- The teacup, saucer and teaspoon should be cleared and taken to the side station.
- Ensure that the waiter's cloth is clean.
- Table should not have water marks or protrusions.
- Inner side of the table should be free of any dirt, or any remnant of grease.
- The base tip of the table mat should one inch away from the edge of the table.
- The upper tip of all the place mats should be in a straight line when placed opposite to each other.
- The cutlery should be stain free and sparkling clean.
- The quarter plate should be clean and free from any stains and chips.
- Napkin should be well folded, crisp, and cleaned.
- Water glass to be placed on a coaster if table does not have place mats or tablecloth.
- Logo on the coaster to be facing the guest.

Step 1	Wipe the table with the help of neat and clean duster/ waiter 's cloth.	
Step 2	Check the table alignment and ensure that tables are not wobbling. If so, get them rectified.	
Step 3	Ensure that chairs are not wobbling. If so, get it rectified.	

Step 4	Place cruet set and other table appointment on the table.	
Step 5	Place side plate on the left side on the table.	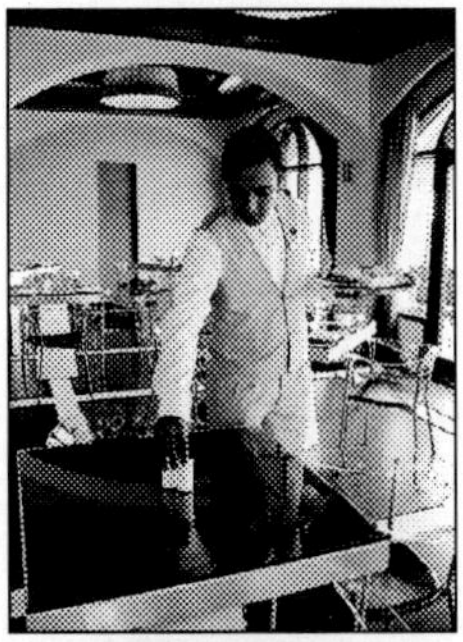
Step 6	Place water glass on the right side on the table.	

BREAKFAST SETUP

Equipment Required

- Appropriate cutlery and flatware.
- Table appointments
- Appropriate glassware
- Salver

Knowledge Required

- Types of breakfast
- Breakfast accompaniments
- Size of a cover
- Carrying salver

- Handling glasses
- Hygiene and sanitation
- Restaurant etiquette
- Eye for detail

Procedure

- Wipe the table with an appropriate table duster.
- Ensure that the tables are not wobbling and are arranged symmetrically. If the table is wobbling, get it rectified.
- Place cruet sets on the table.
- Place the sugar basin next to the cruet set.
- The steward places the place mats in front of each cover on the table.
- The steward places the spoon, knife and fork on place mat.
- Place the side plate on the left-hand side along with the napkin on top of the plate.
- Collect the water glasses and place them on the table.
- The steward places the teacup and teaspoon on the table.

Standard

- Ensure that the cloth is clean.
- Table should not have water marks or protrusions.
- Inner side of the table should be free of any dirt, or any remnant of grease.
- To be placed on the side closest to the restaurant entrance.
- The base tip of the table mat should be one inch away from the edge of the table.
- The upper tip of all the place mats should be in a straight line when placed opposite to each other.
- The cutlery should be stain free and sparkling clean.
- The quarter plate should be clean and free from any stains or chips.
- Napkin should be well folded and crisp, cleaned.
- To be placed on a coaster if the table does not have place mats.
- Logo on the coaster to be facing the guest.
- To be placed in line with the knife.
- The teacup, teaspoon and saucer should be clean, free from stains and chips.
- The teacup and teaspoon should be placed on the right-hand side of the cover.
- The teaspoon should be on the top half of the saucer, parallel to the handle of the cup and the edge of the table.
- No ashtrays to be placed in the all-day dining restaurant.
- The F&B associate should ensure that the butter is firm and melted.
- The steward should ensure that the butter is firm and not melted.

For Breakfast setup - Steps 1 - 4 is same as for table setup		
Step 5	Place sugar caddy on the table.	
Step 6	Place preserves tray on the centre of table • Jam • Honey • Marmalade	
Step 7	Place the butter dish	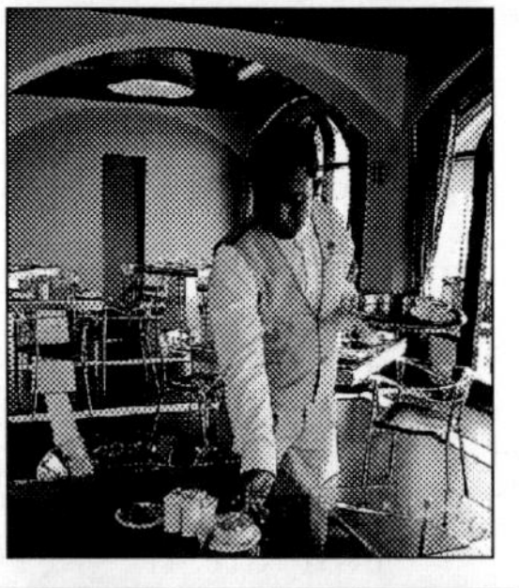
Step 8	Place spoon, knife and fork on the left-hand side.	

Step 9	Place water glass on the right-hand side.	
Step 10	Place teacup with saucer and teaspoon on the right-hand side. Handle of the teaspoon should be at 5'o clock whereas the teaspoon should be at 4'o clock.	

WIPING CUTLERY AND FLATWARE

Equipment Required

- Cutlery and flatware
- Water pan containing lukewarm water
- Salver
- Wiping cloth

Knowledge Required

- Types of cutlery and flatware
- Carrying salver
- Hygiene and sanitation

Procedure

- The cutlery is placed in the cutlery racks above the stewarding counter.
- The associate deputed for rinsing cutlery brings the rack to the rinse basin.
- Wipe the cutlery with the wiping cloth.
- Hold the base of the cutlery in the hand using one corner of the wiping cloth.
- Wipe the cutlery using swift front and back motion.
- Check completion by visual observation for stains or marks and dryness.

- Damaged cutlery to be placed in the "discard bin" along with the other breakages. At the end of every shift the associate reports the breakages for shift to the concerned supervisor.
- The F&B supervisor and KST in charge to decide on discarding of the cutlery.
- The supervisor takes stock of the breakage and notes it on the "breakage report".
- The supervisor totals the breakages/damages at the end of every month and places value to these breakages. This month end report is submitted to the F&B Manager.

Standard

- The steward should always dispose of any extra food particle left in the cutlery. The cutlery should always be placed in soap solution tub kept for cutlery.
- The cutlery should be carried on the cutlery rack and not individually by hand.
- Care should be taken not to dirty the floors with droplets from the rack.
- The hand should never be in direct contact with the cutlery.
- Only one cloth should be used to wipe the cutlery.
- The discarded tablecloths are to be used as wiping cloth.
- The wiping cloth should not be damp.
- The wiping cloth should not smell.
- The wiping cloth should be changed regularly.
- The cutlery should not be bent, damaged or dirty.
- The cutlery should be stacked according to the type in neat rows.

Step 1	Wipe the cutlery/flatware with the help of a wiping cloth.	
Step 2	Hold the base of the cutlery with left hand using one corner of the wiping cloth.	

Step 3	Wipe the cutlery using swift front and back motion.	
Step 4	Place the cutlery on the clean salver and later in the designated areas.	

WIPING CROCKERY

Equipment Required

- Crockery
- Water pan containing lukewarm water
- Wiping cloth

Knowledge Required

- Types of crockery
- Hygiene and sanitation

Procedure

- The washed crockery to be taken to the table meant for wiping.
- Wipe the crockery with the wiping cloth.
- Check the plates for cracks or chips.
- If the plate is in good condition, hold one side of the crockery using one corner of the wiping cloth.
- Hold the remaining cloth in the other hand and wipe using a circular motion first the top part of the crockery and then the bottom side.
- Check completion by ensuring no visual stains or marks are seen.
- The crockery is stacked in the designated racks.
- If the crockery is chipped or cracked, it should be placed in the "discard bin". At the end of every shift the associate reports the breakages for shift to the concerned supervisor.

- The supervisor takes stock of the breakage and notes it on the "breakage report".
- The supervisor totals the breakages at the end of every month and places value to these breakages. This month end report is submitted to the F&B Manager.

Standard

- Hand should never be in direct contact with the crockery.
- Only one cloth should be used to wipe the crockery.
- The discarded tablecloths are to be used as wiping cloth.
- The wiping cloth should not be damp.
- The wiping cloth should not smell.
- The wiping cloth should be changed regularly.
- The crockery must be dry, stain free and lint free.

Step 1	Hold the plate with one end of wiping cloth.	
Step 2	Wipe using a circular motion. First the top part and then the bottom part.	
Step 3	Stack the plates/crockery in a designated place.	

FILLING CRUET SET

Equipment Required

- Cruet set
- Plate
- Salver
- Waiter's cloth/ duster

Knowledge Required

- Type of salt and pepper to be used
- Hygiene and sanitation

Procedure

- On a daily basis the cruet set to be checked by the associate while doing the breakfast table setup.
- On a daily basis the cruet sets to be taken to the back area on a salver for washing and refilling.
- Remove the cap of the cruet set and empty the contents on a plate.
- Wash the cruet set.
- Once the cruet set has been washed, dry it by keeping it over a hot salamander/ oven.
- When the cruet set is completely dry, fill it with fresh salt and pepper.
- Check if the contents are free flowing.

Standard

- Cruet containing single hole contains salt and cruet with multiple holes contains pepper.
- The cruet set contents to be free flowing.
- The holes should be cleaned with a clean toothpick regularly.
- The cruet set to be free from stains.
- The cruet set should not be more than half filled and not less than one-fourth filled.
- The cruet set is always carried on the salver and not in the hands.
- Caps to be stored in a safe manner in a bowl.
- The steward should ensure that there is no spillage of salt / pepper from the cruet set.

Step 1	Collect the cruet set and remove the lid of the cruet set.	
Step 2	Empty the cruet set.	
Step 3	When the cruet set is empty and dry fill it with fresh salt and pepper	
Step 4	After filling the cruet set close the lid tightly.	
Step 5	Wipe the cruet set after filling	

PREPARING BREAD BASKET

Equipment Required

- Bread basket
- Napkin
- Wiping cloth

Knowledge Required

- Types of bread
- Hygiene and sanitation

Procedure

- The stainless steel bread baskets to be washed every night with hot water.
- Wipe with a dry wiping cloth.
- Stack the baskets at the designated place along with a neat and clean folded napkin.

Standard

- Stained or dirty napkins should be replaced with the clean and new.
- Basket to be stain free and not damaged.

Step 1	Remove any debris or leftover bread crumbs.	
Step 2	Wipe the bread basket with a dry wiping cloth.	
Step 3	Fold a napkin half way and place it on the bread basket ready for service.	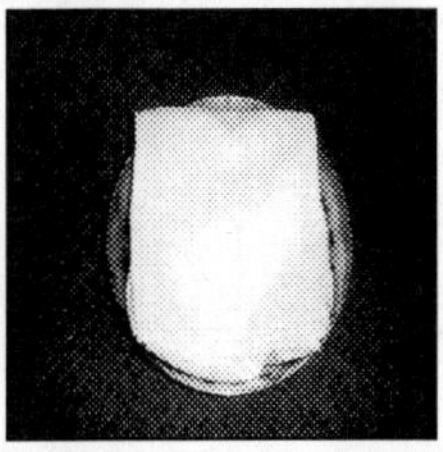

FILLING SUGAR CADDY

Equipment Required

- Sugar basin
- Wiping cloth

Knowledge Required

- Types of sugar
- Hygiene and sanitation

Procedure

- Collect the sugar basin from all the tables using a salver.
- Take these sugar basins to the back area and empty them and place the sachets into a separate basket.
- Check and discard basins that are cracked or chipped.
- Wipe the sugar basin with a damp cloth.
- Arrange the sugar basins in rows on the salver and then arrange the sugar sachets in this basin.

Standards

- Sugar basin is generally filled after the dinner session.
- The sugar basin should be free from any sugar deposits, food stains and chips.
- A standard sugar basin consists of:
  - □ 6 castor sugar
  - □ 2 demerara sugar
  - □ 4 sugar free (this composition can differ from establishment to establishment).
- The names on the sachet to be facing upright.
- The sugar basins should be arranged in a single layer to avoid them from sliding off the slaver.
- The sugar basins to be carried back to the table using a salver.

Step 1	Wipe the sugar basin with a damp cloth/ wiping sheet	
Step 2	Place and arrange sugar sachets in sugar basin	

STACKING SIDEBOARD

Equipment Required

- Sideboard
- Salver
- Necessary cutlery and flatware to be stacked
- Wiping cloth
- Vacuum cleaner

Knowledge Required

- Equipment required to be stacked
- Hygiene and sanitation
- Eye for detail

Procedure

- Empty the inside of the sideboard and place all the items on top of the side-board.
- Clean the inside of the side-board.
- Restack the lower half of the sideboard.
- Remove the drawer mats (felt), dust, and vacuum and place it back.
- Place the cutlery back into the drawers.
- Clean the top and the side of the side station with a dry wiping cloth.
- The steward cleans the trays and salvers with a damp wiping cloth in the back area.
- In case any of the trays or salvers are damaged or cracked, they should be discarded immediately in the "discard bin" placed near the stewarding area and breakage report to be made for the same.

> The side station is also called the **"dummy waiter"**. It is used by the service staff for keeping all the service equipment at one place. For the convenience of the service staff, the side station should be strategically located in a restaurant. It should be kept clean and presentable as it can be seen by the guest. The style and design of the sideboard varies from establishment to establishment. It depends upon:
>
> 1. The style of service and menu offered.
> 2. The number of waiters working from one sideboard.
> 3. The number of tables to be served from one sideboard.
> 4. The amount of equipment it is expected to hold.
> 5. The top should be of heat-resistant material which can be easily washed.
> 6. After service, the sideboard is either completely emptied or restocked for the next service.

- The F&B associate wipes the laminated menu cards.
- Wipe the neck of the bottles with a clean duster.
- The water jugs to be filled with water.
- Nothing should be placed in the upper deck of the sideboard.
- Sideboard should always be neat and clean as it is in the view of the guest.

Standards

- Place a baize cloth or napkins in the drawers of sideboard to prevent noise of cutlery.
- Place one type of cutlery in one drawer and another type of cutlery in another drawer.
- Same criteria to be followed for the other sideboards situated in the restaurant for easy access to the food and beverages associate.
- On opening of the drawers and cupboards of the side station no noise should be made.
- The hinges to be intact.
- All maintenance job orders to be routed to engineering.
- The station setup during breakfast should have the following:
  - □ Napkins
  - □ Table mats
  - □ Wiping cloths
  - □ Paper napkins
- Crockery and glassware
  - □ Saucers
  - □ Side plates
- Accompaniments
  - □ HP sauce
  - □ Tabasco
  - □ Mustard
  - □ Pepper mill
  - □ Water glasses
  - □ Finger bowl with underliner
  - □ Lemon slices in a covered saucer
  - □ Rosewater bottle
- Inner part of the drawer should be free from any debris.
- Following cutlery and flatware to be stacked neatly.

Stacked sideboard

- □ AP spoon
- □ Soup spoon
- □ Tea spoon
- □ AP fork
- □ AP knife
- □ Steak knife

- Trays and salvers to be clean and free from food deposits.
- Each sideboard to have at least two shelves.
- High levels of hygiene is maintained in the restaurants. Sideboard should be neat and clean. Dirties to be cleared immediately and not allowed to pile on the sideboard.
- All bottled accompaniments to be checked for expiry dates.
- The menus should be wiped thoroughly with disinfectant solution to remove all food and oil stains.
- The menu should not be dog-eared or torn. All torn menus should be discarded immediately (if beyond repair).
- One jug to be filled with room temperature water and one jug with ice cold water. The jugs should be covered with a fresh napkin.
- The outside of the flask to be wiped dry.

SETTING COFFEE MACHINE

Equipment Required

- Operation of the coffee machine
- Maintenance schedule of the machine
- Working parts of the machine

Knowledge Required

- Hygiene and sanitation
- Safety
- Eye for detail

Procedure

- The steward ensures cleanliness of the coffee machine area.
- The steward checks the drip tray for accumulation of milk and water.
- Clean the dip dray.
- The steward checks the level of coffee beans and fills the container if necessary.
- The steward checks the level of milk in the container and fills if necessary.

Standards

- The coffee machine and its surrounding should be free from dirt, dust and liquid waste.
- The drip tray and the basin should be checked regularly for milk and water accumulation.
- In case the water outlet is blocked, clean the same and inform the maintenance representative of coffee machine suppliers.
- Refill the coffee beans when level is half.
- Refill the milk when level is one-fourth.
- Always use milk cover to avoid milk burn.

Cleaning of coffee machine

EXCHANGING LINEN

Equipment Required

- Linen hamper
- Linen exchange register

Knowledge Required

- Par stock of linen
- Types of linen
- Eye for detail

Procedure

- The F&B associate counts the soiled linen in the dirty linen hamper.
- The F&B associate checks all the linen for damages before bundling them.
- Make the bundle of ten linen/napkins.

- The F&B associate counts the linen, enters the count of each type of linen in the linen exchange register and hands it over to the housekeeping department by 07.30 hours & 1600 hours (time may differ from establishment to establishment).
- On deposit of the soiled set of linen an equal quantity of fresh linen is issued.
- The associate random checks the condition of fresh linen issued before accepting it.

Linen hamper

Standards

- The linen is counted and handed over to housekeeping department at the specific time allotted by housekeeping department.
- The F&B associate keeps the soiled napkins in bundles of ten each by bounding nine soiled napkins together with the tenth soiled napkin.
- All linen other than napkins are segregated as per type.
- Check whether the linen is torn, frayed, worn, damaged heavily stained or with the stitching at the borders has come out.
- All the sets of soiled linen are bundled inside a large wiping cloth before carrying it to the housekeeping department.
- All linen which is torn, frayed, worn, damaged heavily stained or with the stitching at the borders come out is separately handed over to the housekeeping department for damage rectification/discarding.
- The F&B associate writes the quantity of fresh linen is issued in the register.

- If the quantity of fresh linen issued is less than the quantity of dirty linen deposited it is highlighted in the linen exchange register and the same is collected the same day/when available.
- Linen should be clean, well pressed, colour-resistant and not torn, frayed, worn, damaged or stained. If not, it is returned to the housekeeping department before bringing it to restaurant

HOTEL ABC

Food and Beverages Department

1. The soiled linen is to be taken to the housekeeper and exchanged against fresh linen. The person in-charge of exchanging the linen has to verify that he received exactly the same amount of linen as recovered on the exchange slip.
2. The captain must supervise to avoid any misuse of linen for cleaning or polishing purpose.
3. Once a month an inventory has to be taken in the restaurant to verify the par stock.

LINEN EXCHANGE FORMAT

Name of the Restaurant..

Time........................

Date........................

Description	Balance Forward	Soiled Linen Received	Fresh Linen Issued	Balance

Linen Issued By..............................

Linen Received By..............................

CLEANING PRESERVE CONTAINERS

Equipment Required

- Preserve containers
- Cloth

Knowledge Required

- The preserves used in IRD setup area
- Need for aesthetic appearance

Procedure

- At the end of the breakfast session collect the unused preserve sachets in a tray.
- Segregate the sachets according to the type of preserve.
- Ensure that the sachet is not greasy, sticky or spotted.
- If the sachet is clean and the seal is secure keep it in its respective storage unit.
- If the sachet is not clean, wipe it clean with a damp cloth ensuring that the seal is intact.
- Dispose of all used and damaged preserver sachets.
- Place one number of each preserve sachet on each pre-set breakfast trays.
- Extra sachets to be placed in their respective storage units in IRD preset area.
- Confirm completion of task by conscious visual observation.

Standards

- Used preserve sachets should not be used
- Preserve sachets should be sealed
- Check the preserve sachets for expiry date

CLEANING PROPRIETARY SAUCE BOTTLE

Equipment Required

- Proprietary sauce bottle
- Cloth

Knowledge Required

- Proprietary sauces kept in the IRD pantry.
- Brands of proprietary sauces served in the IRD pantry.
- Knowledge of the methods of cleaning.

Procedure

- Check the proprietary sauce bottles for damages/expiry date.
- Ensure that the bottle is within expiry date and the label is intact.
- Check whether the bottle is worn, damaged, cracked or chipped.
- If the bottle has expired, worn, damaged, cracked or chipped discard into the "waste bottle bin" kept in stewarding area after disposing of any sauce left in the bottle into the "food waste bin" kept in stewarding area.
- Keep proprietary sauces refrigerated below 5°C once it is opened.
- Fill the bottles that are relatively full with sauce from relatively empty bottles discard the empty bottles.

  Some proprietary sauces used:
  - □ Tabasco
  - □ Capsico
  - □ HP
  - □ Worcestershire
  - □ Mustard
  - □ Chilli sauce
  - Tomato sauce
- Remove the cap and clean the neck and mouth of the bottle.
- Wipe the neck and mouth of the bottle with a paper napkin and not with a wiping cloth.
- All proprietary sauces are served in manufacturer's bottle/sachet.
- The steward should ensure that there is minimal spillage when the sauce is being transferred.
- Remove the cap of the bottle, wash it in running tap water and wipe it dry using a wiping cloth.
- Wipe the body of the bottle with a damp wiping cloth.
- Ensure that the cap is free from deposits.
- Replace the cap tightly on the bottle and shake it well and then wipe the body of the bottle with a damp wiping cloth.
- Ensure that the label is clean and intact.
- Store the sauce bottles inside the refrigerator.
- Sauce bottles are to be kept in the designated racks in the refrigerator.
- Confirm completion of task by visual observation to ensure that the neck, mouth and body of the bottle is free from any deposits and the bottle is in an impeccable condition.

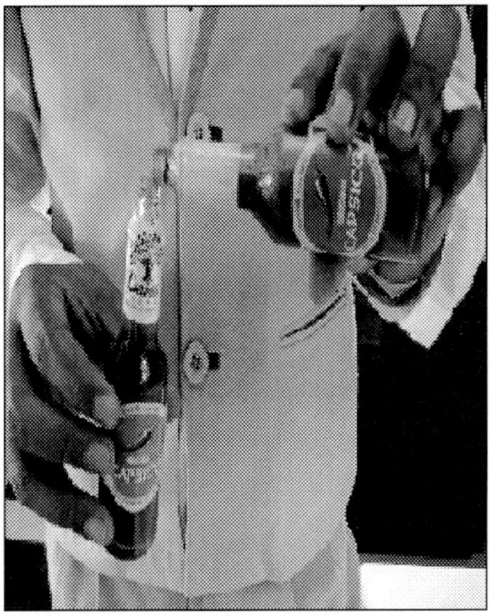

Fill the bottle relatively full
with sauce from empty bottle

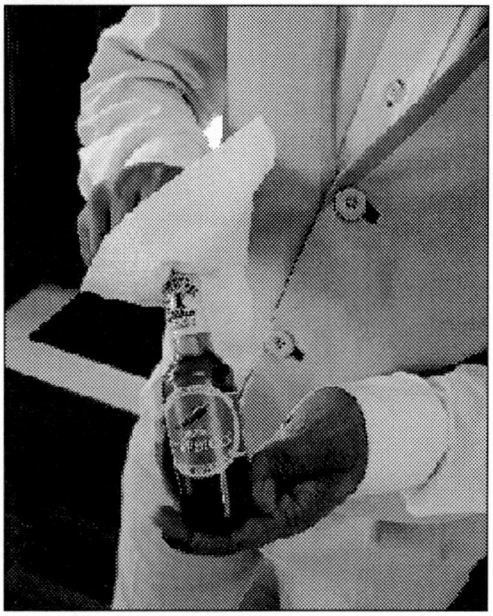

Remove the cap and clean
the neck of the bottle

Clean the cap in running wear

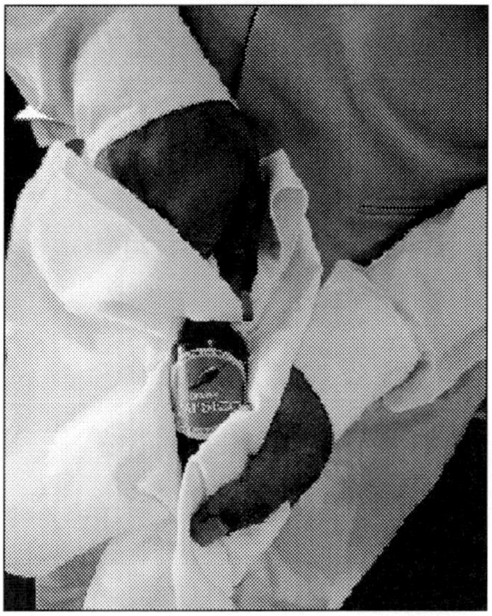

Wipe the bottle with damp wiping cloth

6 RESTAURANT PREPARATION

It is essential to make the restaurant ready for the smooth operation of food and beverages service. Careful and thorough preparation of the restaurant and other dining areas is of utmost importance to give the guest a memorable dining experience. It is the duty and responsibility of food and beverages associates to prepare and maintain the restaurant as per the standards set by the management. In this unit you will understand about the following:

- Handling reservation.
- Layout of restaurant.
- Table alignment.
- Laying a tablecloth.
- Mis en place and Mis en scene.
- Laying àla carte and table d'hote cover.

HANDLING RESERVATION

The booking sheet or reservation diary

- It could be manual or electronic.
- It gives the maximum number of covers to be booked.
- Written confirmation of bookings may be required or credit card numbers taken.
- The customer's preferences about the size, shape and location of a table may be included.
- Bookings may be taken by post, email, internet, telephone and in person.
- It is important to give a good impression while taking bookings.

Restaurant reservation system involves usage of a well trained personnel as it is the first contact with a potential guest and a booking sheet which records the essential information about the booking. Prior taking reservation you must be aware of the following:

- What cuisine do you offer?
- What style of menu do you offer?
- Do you accept credit cards?
- Is there any cover charge?
- What is the service tax and beverage tax applicable?
- What are the opening and closing times?

Booking Sheet						
Restaurant……………. Day………. Date……. Maximum Covers…………						
Table No.	Name of the Guest	Room No./ Telephone No.	Covers	Arrival Time	Special	Remarks

Reservation Diary							
Occupancy_______________						Date______________	
House Count______________						Day_______________	
Manager on Duty_________						Meal Period______	
Hostess on Duty__________							
S. No.	Name	Pax	Time	Table	Contact No.	Remarks	Taken By

Mostly, reservations are taken over telephone. While taking booking by telephone make sure of the following:

- Pen and reservation diary/booking sheet is close to hand.
- Always answer the phone promptly within three rings. Greet the guest in a polite manner. The standard phrase may be "*Good morning Sir/ Madam, How may I assist you?*"
- Answer any question clearly and politely.
- If the table is available as per the guest's request continue taking the reservation or else apologize and ask if you can taken booking for any other occasion.
- Note down the essential information required as follows:
    - □ The guest's name and telephone number.
    - □ The host's name.
    - □ The day and date booking is required.
    - □ The number of covers.
    - □ The time the booking is required.
    - □ Any special requests.

When this information is received from the guest, it is advisable to repeat all the details back to the guest for confirmation. If it is a policy of the establishment to take a minimum cover charge for a table, it is essential to inform the guest of the same. If the cancellation is being received, confirm the cancellation with the guest by repeating his/her request and then ask if you can take booking for any other occasion in place of cancellation. At the end thanking the guest is essential. When taking bookings by email the information that is required is the same as that mentioned above. Confirmation is normally sent back to the guest by the same method as the booking was received such as by email or post.

LAYOUT OF RESTAURANT

Restaurant can be S-shaped, L-shaped, rectangular, square and any other shape depending on space availability, types of menu to be served, location and others. Below shown is the basic rectangular shape layout of restaurant.

TABLE ALIGNMENT

The table alignment for a restaurant depends on the number of covers and the style of service to be offered. When these have been established table alignment is prepared as a guide for the setup of restaurant and to assist in the seating of the guest. Table numbers are also allocated to each table for its identification.

Table should be positioned in such a manner so that it allows sufficient space for the movement for guests and staff. Tables should also not be placed near doorways, kitchen, washroom, behind pillars or in any area where guest may feel uncomfortable.

Layout of restaurant

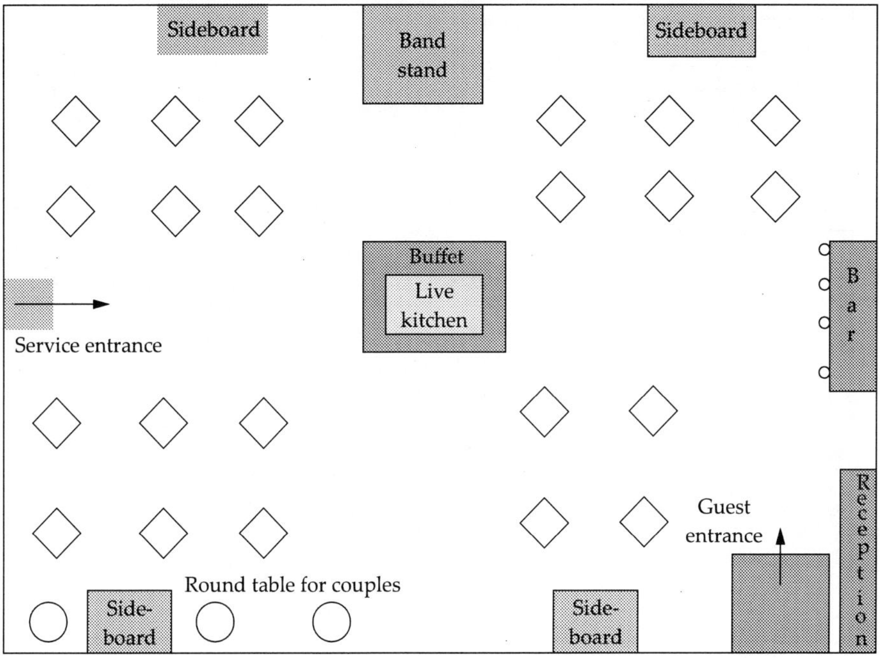

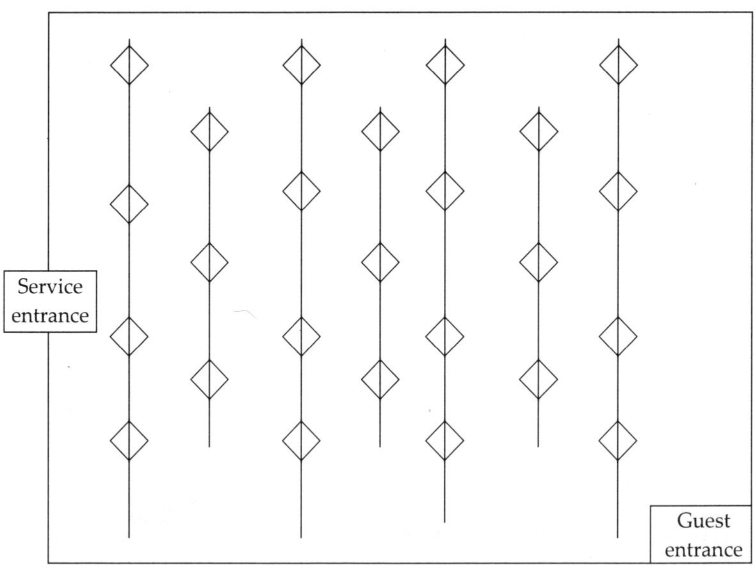

Table alignment for a rectangular restaurant

A well alligned restaurant

LAYING A TABLECLOTH

Tablecloth is one of the most important linens used in the restaurant. It is made up of cotton, linen or damask among them damask is best. Nowadays most of the restaurants use place mats rather than tablecloth to curtail the laundry costs. However, tablecloths are still in vogue in fine dining restaurant and specialty restaurant as it helps in creating a favourable ambience and decor. Apart from this tablecloth protects the guest from the edges of the tables and helps in hiding any stains or marks on the table. It also reduces the sound created by the cutlery while placing them on the table for the food service. Before laying a table cloth mouton or baize cloth is placed on the table so that table cloth does not fall.

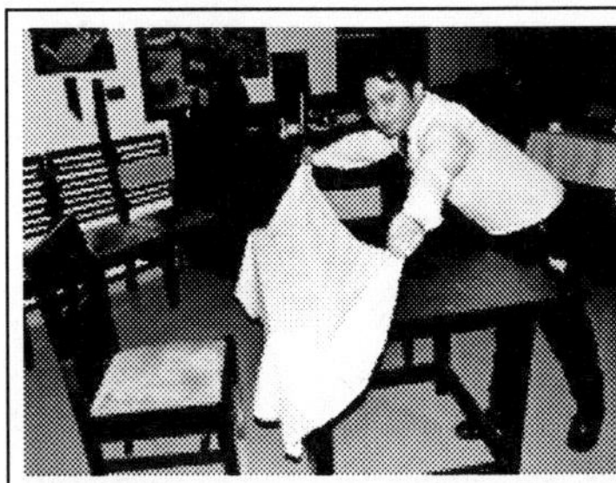

Step 1

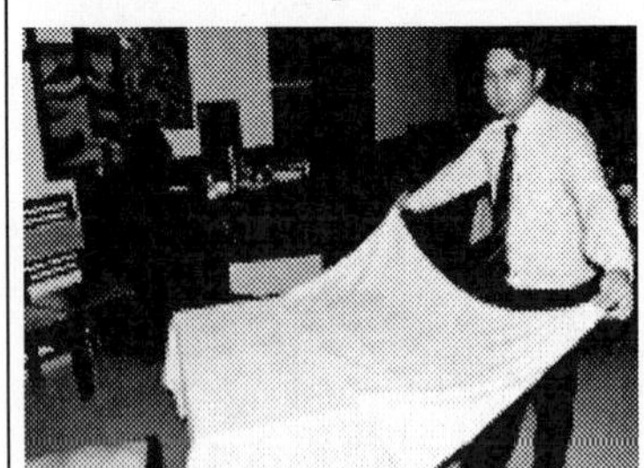

Step 2

Laying tablecloth

While handling tablecloth ensure the following points:

- Tablecloth is neat, well ironed and free from any stains.
- Tablecloth is folded and creased properly while receiving it from laundry.

Procedure for laying tablecloth is as follows:

- Make sure that the table should not wobble.
- Stand in the centre between the two legs of the table holding the tablecloth.
- Place the clean tablecloth on the table with the two woven edges towards you and the two folds facing away from you.
- The edges of the folded cloth should hang evenly over the width of the table. The folds of the tablecloth should be facing you.
- Lean across the table and release the bottom layer of the cloth to hang over the far edge of the table.
- Hems should face inwards.
- Release the hold on the centre fold and draw the top fold towards you.
- Having centred the cloth both vertically and horizontally the tablecloth should now be positioned with an equal drop all round with the folds of the cloth covering the legs.
- The corners of the tablecloth should cover the legs of the table.
- The overlap should be even all round the table: 30-40 cm.
- If you are laying tablecloths for larger parties, overlap the two tablecloths with the overlap facing away from the entrance.

ADVANTAGES OF BAIZE CLOTH

- Protects the table surface.
- It allows the table cloth to hang freely and firmly in the table surface.
- Reduces the noise of cutlery, crockery and glassware while placing them on the table.
- It protects the wrists and elbows of the customer from the sharp edges of the table.
- It protects the tablecloth from getting torn by sharp edges of the corner.

Slip cloth or napperon is also laid in some restaurants over tablecloth. It comprises a decorative part of the table, it is always laid in length or diagonally on the table over tablecloth.

MIS EN SCENE

To make the working environment of the restaurant pleasant, safe, hygienic and comfortable for the guest, activities to be done under mis en scene are:

- Open all the doors and windows to let in the fresh air. Carpet and tiles to be free from and clean of any stains and debris.
- Brush or vacuum clean the carpet, i.e., if housekeeping has not done so earlier.
- Light fixtures to be fully illuminated. Switch on all lights to check for fused bulbs.
- Air condition is working properly.
- All walls to be clean and free from any chips or marks.

- All mirrors/glass should be polished and free from any smudges.
- All windows should be clean and free from any streaks.
- Side stations should be stacked properly and must be neat and clean.
- Tables and chairs should be steady. Tables and chair legs should be free from any scuffs and scratches.
- Chair/couch upholstery should be clean, matching and in good condition.
- Appropriate music should be played.
- Hotel pad, pen and matchbox should be available on request.
- Check and clean all the furniture.
- Remove all unserviceable items to the maintenance department for repairing.
- Sort the menu cards and remove those that are dirty or torn.
- Ensure that all the promotional and sales material is presentable.
- Clean all display counters and arrange the display items.
- All plants and floral decorations to be fresh, remove all withered and wilted flowers from the bud vase and replace them with the fresh ones.
- Additional items to meet the requirements of the organization.

Set restaurant table

MIS EN PLACE (PUT IN PLACE)

Things prior to operation which help in smooth operation of the restaurant operation. Activities to be done under mis en place:

- Placing and setting of tables and chairs.
- Changing linen: Exchange all soiled linen against fresh linen from the housekeeping department.
- Laying covers on table.

- Arranging sideboards as per its checklist.
- Arranging back areas: Setting up the pick-up counter with serving dishes and their covers, pick-up trays, bread baskets, butter dishes.
- Menu cards to be made presentable.
- Stacking sideboard.
- Prepare all necessary items to be used in food service such as:
  - □ Cutlery and glassware
  - □ Service gear
  - □ Crumbing down equipment
  - □ Service plates
  - □ Tea/coffee service equipment
  - □ Service trays
  - □ Ashtrays
  - □ Wine lists
  - □ Condiment bowl
  - □ Additional items to meet the specialist requirements of the organization.

Activities of mis en place are well explained in the next chapter.

7 THE MENU

INTRODUCTION

Menu is the statement of food and beverages items available or provided by food establishments primarily based on consumer demand and designed to achieve organizational objectives. Menu is a list of food items which a restaurant offers to its guests. Menu is also known as the "bill of fare'. It is said that in year 1541 Duke Henry of Brunswick was seen referring to a long slip of paper. On being asked what he was looking at he said it was a form of program of dishes and by referring to it he could see what was coming and reserve his appetite accordingly. It is believed that perhaps it was this event that led to development of menu cards. In 19th century the Palais Royale in Paris introduced modern menus. Earlier 'bill of fare' of ceremonial meals used to be displayed on the walls to enable the kitchen staff to follow the order in which the meal had to be served. Nowadays menu has become short and smaller allowing number of copies per table. Compiling menus in is both science and art. It varies from one page to two or three. Menu can be referred as a visiting card of the catering establishment. A menu has the following functions:

- **Act as a bridge:** Menu acts as a bridge between the establishment and the guest.
- **Information:** It provides the information to the guest regarding food available, cooking method, portion size, price range. Menu gives a brief description of the food item.
- **Order:** It presents the dishes in a logical order, usually listing the menu items under course headings thereby making comprehension of the menu easy.
- **Choice:** It determines the freedom of choice that a guest may have.
- **Reflects Image:** Menu reflects the image of the restaurant.
- **Lessens Human Error:** As menu gives a brief description of the food item therefore it is easy for the guest to understand. Due to language problem waiter may not announce the dishes properly and menu lessens this error.
- **Tool to Communicate:** Menu is the tool by which we can communicate with our guests. As the food dishes are listed in the menu it makes the waiter's job easier.
- **Menu as a Sales Tool:** Menu acts as a silent sales person. To the customer menu is an introduction to the restaurant. It helps in promoting sales by appropriately describing the dishes and a their price.

Menu in the form of a card is known as menu card. Menu card should be neat and clean and must be presentable. Menu card is in different forms from a page to a book shape menu card. Some restaurants have a menu card inserted in the silk cloth or in leather folder to give an elegant look to the menu.

TYPES OF MENU

There are two basic types of menu:

- Ala carte
- Table d'hote

À la carte: An à la carte menu is a multiple choice menu. It is a list of all dishes on offer, which are available in the restaurant. À la carte means 'from the card'. Brief description of the food items is given along with price of dishes. Guest selects from the menu what he has to consume. The charge of meal will be the total of the prices of individual dishes served to the guest with each dish priced separately. If a guest wishes to place an order, an à la carte is offered, from which one can choose the items one wants to eat. In an *à la carte* menu all items are cooked to order. Depending on the dish chosen by the guest, the cooking time will vary. It is necessary to inform the guests about the time the preparation might take. An extensive à la carte menu is impressive but involves a huge amount of mise en place. This type of menu is provided by the specialty restaurants, multi-cuisine

Advantages of à la carte menu

- Choice is provided to the guest.
- Guests choose their own meals.
- Gives opportunity to combine various kinds of dishes according to his choice or palate.
- Guest pays for the meal which he has ordered.
- Food is portioned by the kitchen which helps in portion control.
- Easy to add or remove food items from the menu according to demand and seasonal availability of raw materials.

Disadvantages of à la carte menu

- All guests are not able to combine the menu according to their choice hence they fail to choose appropriate combination of dishes.
- Wastage can be more as the availability of ingredients need to be maintained more.
- Sometimes waiting for the food order is too long.

restaurant, café, bars, coffee shops, fast food outlets and takeaway counters.This type of menu may be defined by the following points:

- It gives a brief description and full list of all the dishes that may be prepared and offered by the establishment.
- Each dish is priced separately and guest will pay for those food items which he has ordered.
- A certain waiting time has to be allowed for many of the dishes.
- Food is cooked to order.
- For an à la carte menu the cutlery and flatware for each course is laid just before each course is served.

À la carte menu can be made more effective by inserting **carte du jour** and **plat du jour** menus in it. Carte du jour means **menu for the day.** Sometimes chef prepares a menu apart from à la carte menu for the day it is called as "carte du jour" whereas "plat du jour" means "specialty of the day" or "dish of the day".

APPROXIMATE WAITING TIME OF FOOD ITEMS

- Hors d'oeuvre : 10 minutes
- Soup 1 : 5 minutes
- Omelette : 10 minutes
- Chautebriand : 15 minutes
- Lamb cutlets : 10 minutes
- Souffle : 30 minutes
- Tea/coffee : 5 minutes
- Fried fish : 10 minutes
- Grilled fish : 10 minutes
- Barbequed chicken wings : 20 minutes
- Caesar salad : 10 minutes
- Club sandwitch : 15 minutes
- Kathi rolls : 20 minutes
- Grilled lamb chops : 20 minutes
- Seak with black pepper or mushroom sauce : 20 minutes
- Pasta : 20 minutes
- Main course generally takes 20 minutes to get served.

Table d'hôte or TDH menu: Table d'hôte means **table of the host**. It is a fixed course menu and the guest has to pay for the full course, no matter of the food items he consumes from the course. It is a meal usually divided into various courses with little or no choice, and is available at a fixed price. Dishes of the table d'hôte will be ready. You can understand the table d'hôte menu by the following points.

Factors Affecting the Meal Experience	
Food & beverage	Range on offer, type and variety, quality, availability of special items.
Levels of service	Method of service, speed of service, reliability, booking facility and others.
Level of cleanliness	Cleanliness and hygiene of equipment, premise and staff.
Value for money	Price perceptions in the guest's mind.
Atmosphere	Contributed to by aspects such as décor, lighting, heating, furnishing, acoustics, etc.

- Table d'hôte means 'from the table of the host'.
- A fixed course menu or daily menu.
- Offers a small number of courses with limited choice within each course.
- A fixed selling price for the entire meal irrespective of whether the guest consumes the complete meal or not.
- Cutlery for the entire meal is laid according to the course on the table.
- Used to promote quick service.
- Suggested ideally to large groups/tour, banquets, wedding ceremonies and cafeteria. Example: Plate system in wedding reception, thali system in dhabas.

Advantages of table d'hôte

- Easy to choose as choices are limited.
- Prices are set and hence guest can choose accordingly.
- Easier to cook and control.
- Food is prepared in advance.
- Less wastage of food.

Disadvantages of table d'hôte

- Limited choice with 1 each course which may not satisfy all guest.
- Guest has to pay the price for the whole menu whether he has consumed it or not.

Other Types of Menus

- Cyclic menu
- Promotional menus
- Children's/kid's menus
- Ethnic menus
- Café menus
- Buffet menus
- Banquet menus
- Beverage menus

Cyclic Menus

Cycle or rotating menus are generally used in cafeterias, hospitals, institutional catering and industrial catering. Cyclic menus get repeated therefore the menu structure and the choices of dishes must be carefully selected. This is designed for a specific period. The average cycle with most institutional operations is 7 days or 28 days, then the whole cycle or menu is repeated. In cyclic menus the nutrients and the recommended dietary allowances are taken into consideration. This menu has limited courses or a limited choice within in each course.

Promotional Menu

Promotional menus are introduced during some special events or occasions such as Diwali, New year, Christmas and many more. In hotels food promotions are held regularly. To promote this hotel prepares menu according to the theme or event. This is also known as food festivals. During these festivals there is a temporary change in the décor, ambience and sometimes uniform of the F&B staff of the restuarnt to offer change and variety to the guests and to create interest among the F&B staff.

Children's/Kid's Menus

In same establishments you can find the children/kid's menu which is attractive to kids. The children's menu contains those food items which are liked by children and can be prepared quickly. Children have a short attention time so their need can be met with place mats, menus and takeaways.

Beverage Menu

Beverage menu includes list of all kinds of alcoholic and non-alcoholic beverages offered by the restaurant. It includes wines, spirits, liqueurs, beers, cocktail, mocktails and other drinks. To provide non-alcoholic beverages restaurant must possess the required licence from the authorities concerned and it is served as per the rules set by them.

Dessert Menu

This menu is offered after the main course. It consists of all kinds of desserts offered by the restaurant.

Function Menu

This menu is planned during some events in the banquets like wedding reception, conference, seminars and others. It mainly consists of two to three courses or fixed course menu and is decided by the host along with the discussion with the banquet manager and chef. Host pays in advance giving details about the number of people and service time.

Planning of a Menu

Planning menu is an important task. It requires careful planning and imagination. It is an important attribute for success in menu planning and optimum utilisation of all resources is essential. While planning a menu F&B manager, executive chef, purchase manager, accounts officer all sit together and discuss the budget, availability of kitchen staff, restaurant staff and raw materials. Regular menus of the day are normally planned by the chef in accordance with the management's catering policy but menu for a restaurant pre-ordered party/banquet will usually be compiled by the restaurant manager/banquet manager in consultation with the chef. The following are some important points to be considered when compiling or planning a menu.

1. Type of restaurant and menu
2. Skilled staff
3. Demographic
4. Capability of equipment
5. Competition
6. Budget
7. Seasonal availability
8. Local ingredients
9. Taste and preferences
10. Balance diet
11. Availability of raw material
12. Menu specifications
13. Menu composition
14. Menu balance
15. Product mix
16. Restaurant menu pricing
17. Language

BALANCING A MENU

While selecting dishes from the range possible in the foregoing courses and in deciding the number of courses, it must be remembered that menu should be balanced. It should harmonise each other.

- A menu should not contain two dishes which are composed of the same ingredients: The various ingredients forming one course should not be repeated in another course, e.g., if an egg dish is on the main course then eggs should not form any appreciable part of the hors d'oeuvre. This applies to all other dishes also, e.g., if the soup is Crème Dubarry, which contains cauliflower as its base, then cauliflower should not be served later as a vegetable. If pie or pastry is served, e.g., vol-au-vent then there should not be any starch food, e.g., apple pie, served as sweet. Each dish should be different in method of cooking and have different character.

- Two white meats or two dark meats should never follow each other, e.g., pork should not be followed by veal or beef by mutton. Colour of two food items in each course should not be same, e.g., if chilled melon is there as an appetizer then cream of tomato soup should not be included in the menu as the colour of both dishes is nearly same.
- A light entrée should be followed by a heavier dish.
- If the menu is long, dishes chosen should not be heavy, e.g., if a big banquet is being served, earlier dishes in particular, should be without much bulk. Note, the possibility in the middle of an elaborate banquet (say before the roast is served) of serving a sorbet or water ice to stimulate appetite and to counteract the effect of the dishes that have already been eaten.
- If the menu is short, dishes may be included which have consistency or bulk to ensure that diners will have sufficient meal.

FRENCH CLASSICAL MENU

Traditionally, the French classical menu has seventeen courses but due to the concept of shorter menus the classical order of the French classical menu has been reduced to thirteen and eleven courses which can be further reduced to seven, five or three course. Courses in modern-day menus are based on the French classical menu. Sequence of seventeen-course French classical menu is as follow:

1. Hors d'oeuvres (Appetiser/Starter)

- Hors d'oeuvre is of a tangy nature in order to stimulate the appetite.
- It can be hot or cold.
- It is composed of tangy and salty dishes.
- Generally, hors d'oeuvre contains different types of salads like Russian salad, Caesar salad and other compound salads.
- Small portion sizes are served in it.
- The term hors d'oeuvre also covers any item served or listed on the menu before the soup.

Classical example of Hors d'oeuvre

- Caviar served with blinis, butter, lemon wedges, sieved egg whites and yolks, chopped shallots and parsley.
- Melon Frappe (chilled melon) served with castor sugar and ground ginger.
- Les huitres (oysters) with cayenne pepper, Tabasco and chilli vinegar, lemon wedges and brown bread and butter.
- Saumon fume (smoked salmon) with lemon wedges, onion rings, capers, lettuce garnish, brown bread and butter.

- Escargots (snails) with melted butter and bread cubes.
- Shellfish cocktail—prawns or shrimps on a bed of shredded lettuce and coated with tomato-flavoured mayonnaise.
- Nicoise salad: It includes boiled potatoes, whole French beans, tomatoes, hard boiled eggs, kalamata olives, anchovy fillet and flakes of tuna fish.

International Soups

- ***Minestrone:*** Italian soup with pasta, grated parmesan cheese and grilled flute
- ***Petite Marmite:*** From France. It is beef and chicken flavoured, garnished with turned root vegetable and dice of beef and chicken.
- ***Soup a l'oignon:*** French onion soup served with grilled flute, parmesan cheese and a slice of French bread
- ***Potage Germiny:*** From France. It is a consommé thickened before service with egg yolk and cream along with cheese straws.
- ***Mulligatawny:*** Indian soup, originated in Sri Lanka.
- ***Cock-a-leekie:*** Soup from Scotland. It is a veal and chicken consommé garnished with shredded leeks and chicken.
- ***Tom Yum:*** Spicy Thai soup
- ***Batwinia:*** It is a **cold soup** from Russia made from puree of spinach, sorrel, beetroot and white wine.
- ***Bortsch:*** Duck flavour consommé from Poland.
- ***Bouillabaisse:*** French soup in the form of fish stew. Slices of French bread, dipped in oil and grilled are offered with it.
- ***Gazpacho:*** Cold soup from Spain.
- ***Chowder:*** Soup from America.
- ***Consommé madrinale:*** Cold consommé soup.
- ***Vichysoisse:*** Cold soup.
- ***Misoshiru:*** A Japanese soup.

2. Potages (Soups)

In the potage course you serve soups, both hot and cold soups can be served in potage. The function of soup on the menu is to stimulate the customer's appetite rather than act as a complete meal. For this reason many soups are of a light and delicate nature. Hot soups are a welcome feature on winter menus; conversely cold soups are ideal in the summers. Soups may be classified in the following manner Thickened and unthickened.

Thickened Varieties

1. **Purée soups:** A type of soup thickened either by the main ingredient or a starch-based additive.

2. **Cream soups:** Passed soups that have béchamel sauce as their main thickening agent.
3. **Veloute soups:** Passed soups that have veloute sauce or blond roux as their main thickening agent.
4. **Brown soups:** Passed soups produced from flavoured brown stock thickened by a brown roux.
5. **Bisques:** Passed shellfish soups that are traditionally thickened with starch in the form of rice, but may be thickened by the roux method.

Soup in a consomme bowl

Unthickened Varieties

1. **Broths:** Unstrained soups prepared from a stock base flavoured and garnished by vegetables, meats, fish and cereals.
2. **Consommés:** Consommé is clarified stock of meat, fish or poultry, which is flavoured with herbs and seasoned. Depending on the garnish, the consommé is named, e.g., **consommé, julienne, consommé brunoise, etc**.
3. **Bouillon:** It is a plain unclarified broth obtained from boiling meat or vegetables.

Unclassified Varieties

Specialty soups that cannot be listed with the above types because of their unique mode of preparation are called specialty soups.

Soups and the Menu: It is recommended that the more substantial types of soup be served at luncheon and those of a more delicate nature for dinner.

Luncheon: Purees, creams, broths and brown soups.

Dinner: Consommés, creams, veloute's and bisques.Two soups can be provided on the menu, one being a clear soup (consommé) and the other a thick soup (crème velute' or puree).

The clear soup is always placed first on the menu.

Classical Example of Potage

Consomme Julienne: garnished with strips of root vegetables.

Consomme Celestine: garnished with strips of savoury pancakes.

Petite marmite: Beef and chicken flavoured consomme.

Soup a l'oignon: Clear onion soup.

Bortsch: Duck flavoured comsomme.

3. Oeufs (Egg Dishes)

There are great number of egg dishes beyond the usual omlettes but these are not popular. Boiled eggs are not offered in this course.

Examples of Egg Dishes

- Omelette espagnole: Flat omelette with onions, peppers and tomato.
- Omelette fines herbs: Savoury omelette.
- Oeufs en cocotte a la crème: Egg cooked in its own dish in a Bain Marie and garnished with cream.
- Oeuf poche Florentine: Poached egg on a bed of spinach, coated with a cheese sauce and gratinated.
- Oeuf brouille au lard: Scrambled egg with bacon.
- Oeuf sur le plat bercy: Egg cooked in its own dish on the top of the stove then finished in the oven, garnished with a chipolata sausage and a thread of tomato sauce.

4. Farineux (Pasta and Rice Dishes)

This course comprises pasta dishes. Pasta is made up of three most common types of flour semolina flour, unbleached white flour, and whole wheat flour. Semolina flour, ground from hard durum wheat, is typically used in dried pasta. It has a large amount of gluten which makes the dough quite elastic, lending itself to shaping. Unbleached white flour is made from red winter wheat and produces lighter dough that is easy to work with. Whole wheat flour is becoming more popular as consumers look for healthier pasta options, and is made from whole wheat grain.

Types of Pasta	Description
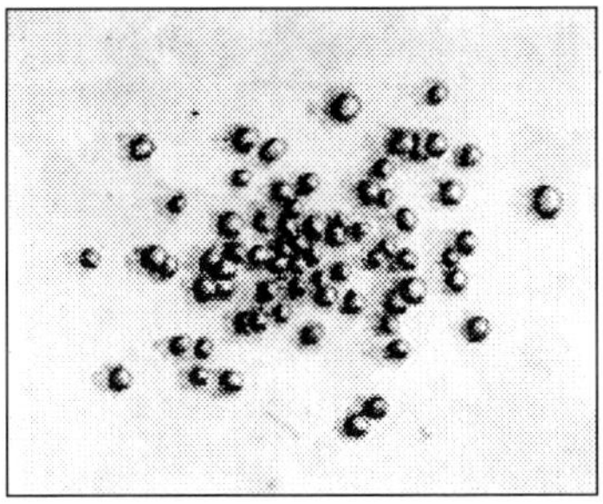	**Acini di Pepe** ("Peppercorn"): Acini di Pepe is perfect to use in soup recipes. These shapes are ideal to include in broths.
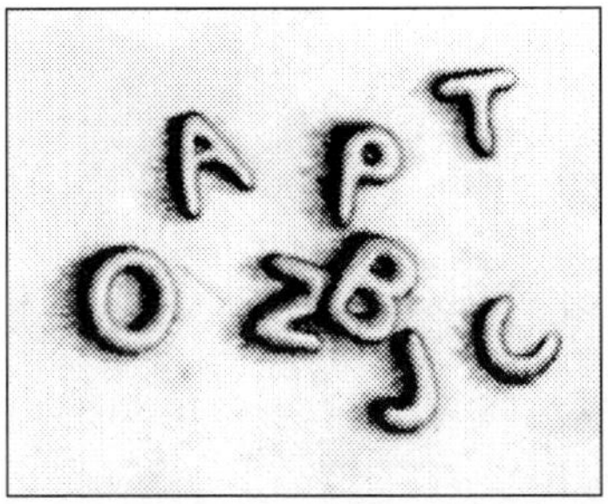	**Alphabet Pasta:** This favourite kids' shape is usually used in soups for a fun meal anytime.

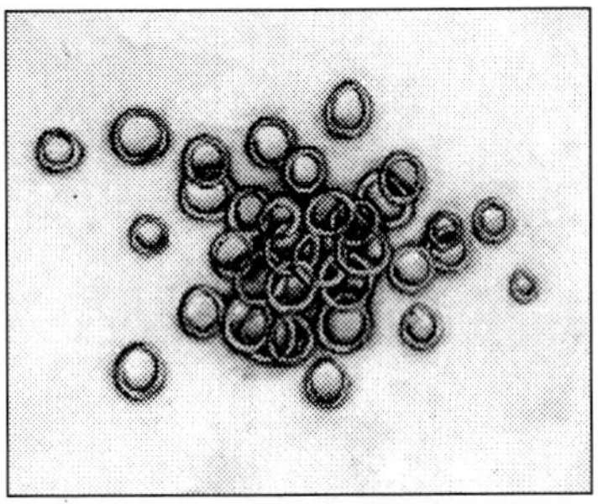

Anellini: Tiny rings of pasta. Anellini is a smaller version of Anelli pasta. It is used in various soups and is also a compliment to a number of salads.

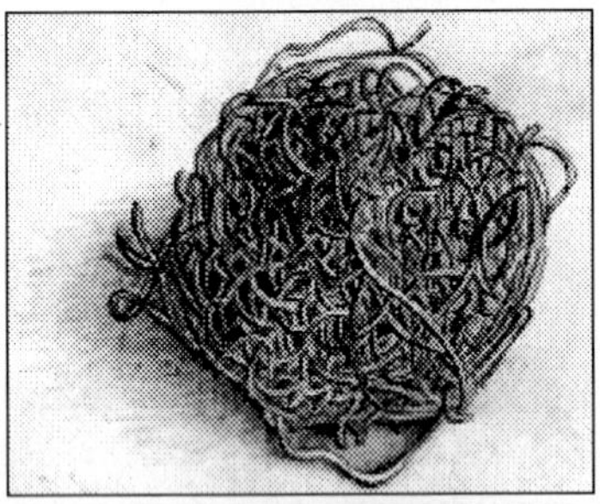

Angel Hair, Capellini ("fine hairs")**:** These thin, delicate pasta strands are best if used with thinner, delicate sauces. Other uses: break in half and put in soup; use in salads or stir-fry meals.

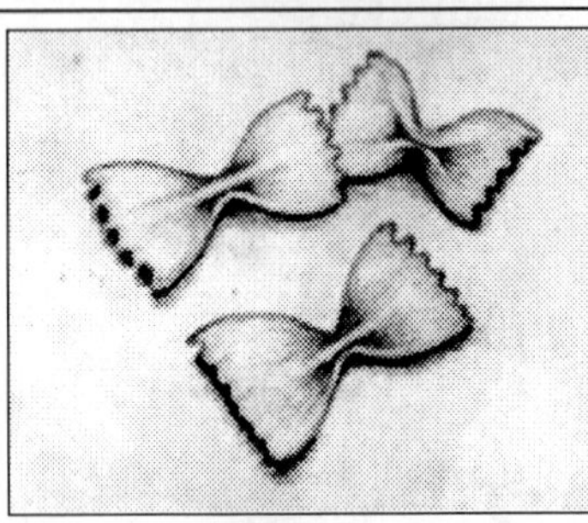

Bow Ties, Farfalle ("butterflies"): Bow Ties brighten any meal with their interesting shape. Thick enough for a variety of sauces, or a perfect addition to a number of salad or soup recipes.

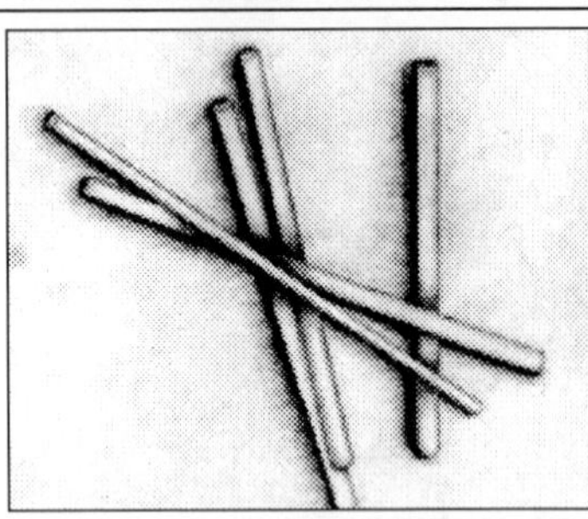

Buctani: Thick spaghetti shaped pasta that is hollow in the centre, similar to a thin straw. Bucatini is the perfect choice for nearly any sauce, or it can be used to make casseroles or stir-fry dishes.

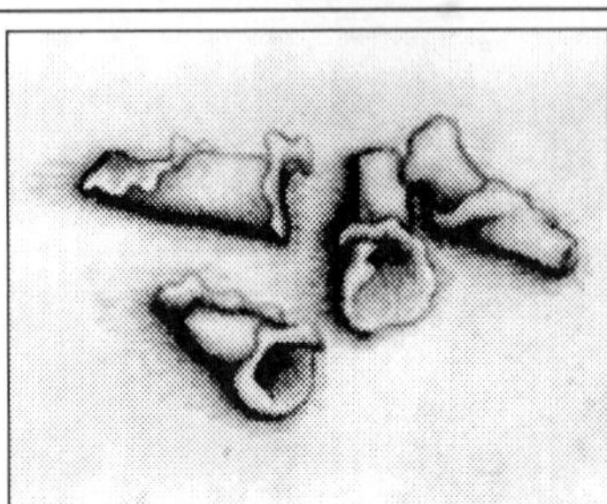

Campanelle ("Bells"): Campanelle pasta resembles a small cone with a ruffled edge. Pair Campanelle pasta with meat, cream, vegetable or oil based sauces. Also, these shapes are great when used in pasta salads.

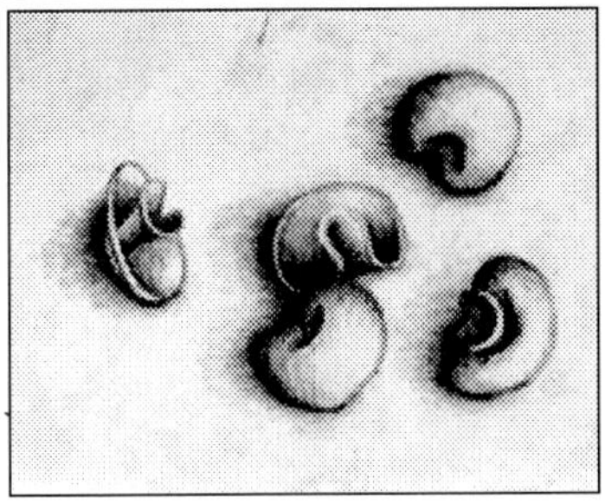	**Cappelletti:** Cappelletti pasta is folded and then twisted to form the shape of a small hat. This pasta is sometimes referred to as an alpine hat.
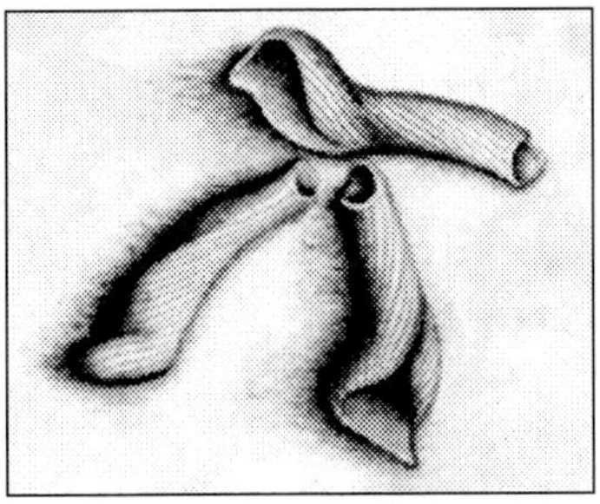	**Casarecce:** Casarecce pasta is shaped like a very narrow, twisted and rolled tube. This pasta is best used when serving a meat sauce and can be used in a variety of casserole dishes.
	**Ditalini** ("little thimbles"): This versatile shape can be used as the base of any dish. Bake it, stir it into soups, or create great salads and stir-fry dishes.
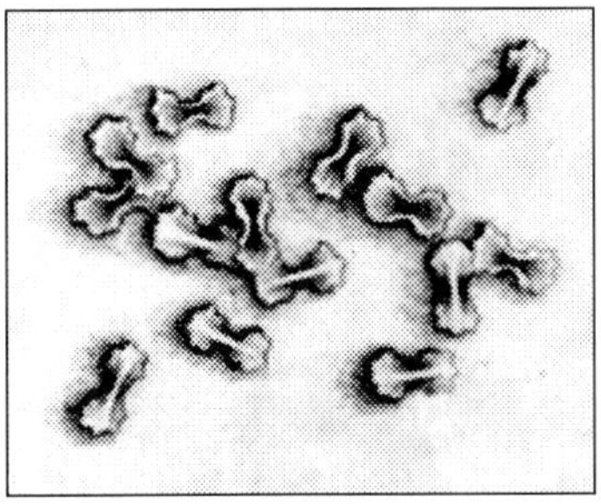	**Farfalline:** Farfalline is a small version of the bow tie or butterfly shaped pasta. This versatile shape can be used as the base of any dish. Bake it, stir it into soups, or create great salads and stir-fry dishes.
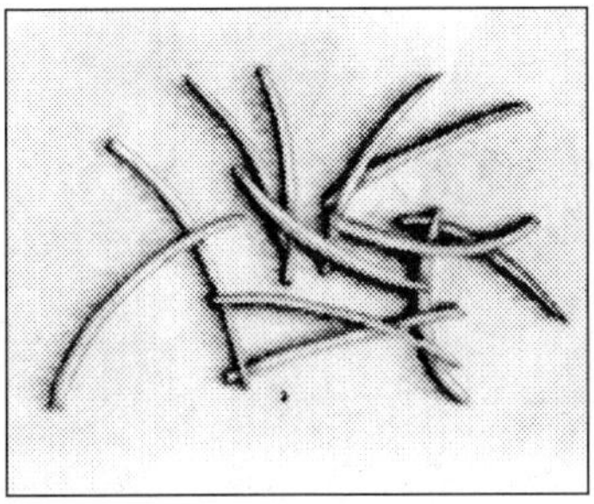	**Fideo:** Short thin strands of pasta that are slightly curved. Fideo pasta is commonly used in various soup recipes.

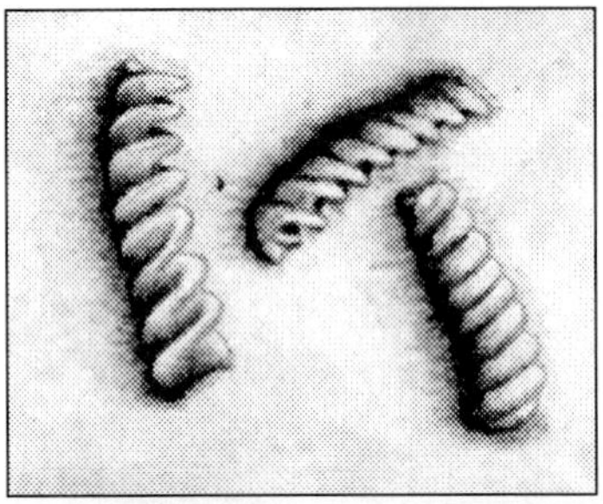

Fusilli ("twisted spaghetti"): This long, spiralled shape can be topped with any sauce, broken in half and added to soups, or turned into a beautiful salad. Fusilli also bakes well in casseroles.

Fettuchine: Fettuccine is classically paired with Alfredo Sauce, a rich cream sauce with Parmesan cheese.

Jumbo Shells: Best when stuffed with your favourite mixtures of cheese, meat and vegetables. Stuff with meat flavoured with taco seasoning, top with salsa and bake for a delicious Mexican dish, or create your own stuffed treat.

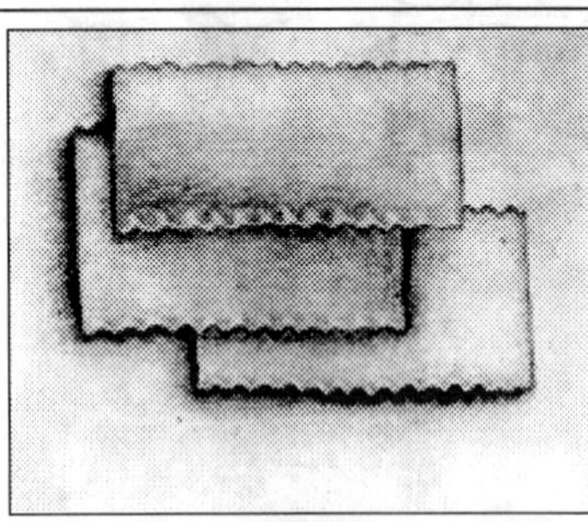

Lasagna (From "lasanum," Latin for pot): Create original Lasagna casseroles by using chopped vegetables, cheeses and any kind of sauce. You can also assemble your casserole and freeze it for later meal. The dish, lasagne is layers of pasta, meat sauce and béchamel sauce.

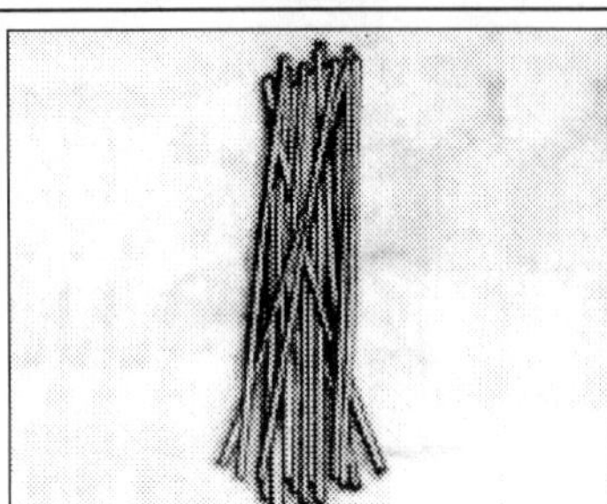

Linguine ("little tongues"): A great shape to compliment a variety of sauces. Also a good choice for salads and stir-fry dishes. It is frequently paired with white or red clam sauce. It matches well with pesto.

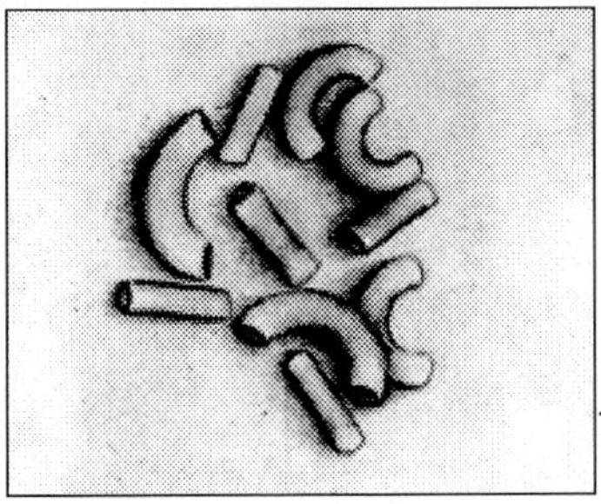

Macaroni: A highly versatile shape that can be topped with any sauce, baked, or put in soups, salads and stir-fry dishes.

Medium Shells, Conchiglie ("shells"): Shells make a great addition to soups or as the base of a wonderful salad. Try remaking your favourite Macaroni and cheese using shells, for a fun twist on a time-honoured tradition.

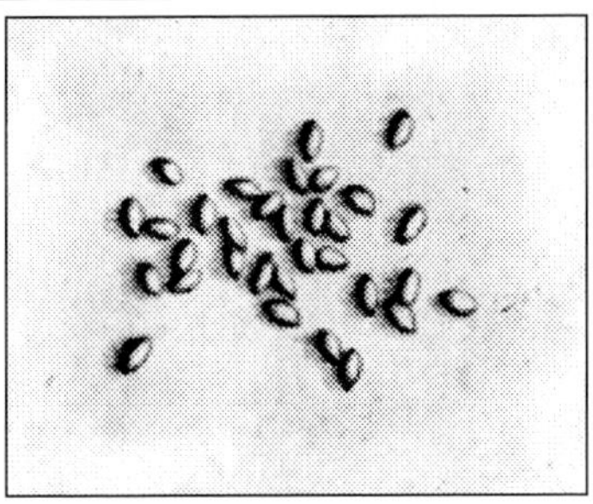

Orzo ("barley"): This small, grain shaped pasta can be topped with any sauce, added to soups, or baked as a casserole. Perfect as a side dish as well as a main course.

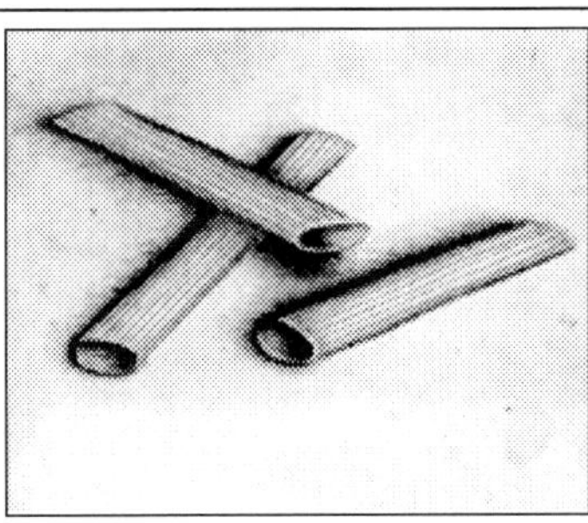

Penne, Mostaccioli ("quills" and "small moustaches"): This tubular pasta compliments a variety of sauces, is frequently used in salads, baked in casseroles, or made into stir fry dishes.

Penne ("quills" or "feathers"): Penne compliment virtually every sauce and are exceptional when paired with a chunky sauce. Penne pairs nicely with chunky meat, chunky vegetable, cream, or oil based sauces. Also, these shapes are great for baking dishes.

	**Ravioli:** Ravioli are square round pillows of pasta that have a filling consisting of ingredients such as cheese, meats, vegetables and seasonings. Ravioli can be served with a red sauce or it can be served with butter, oil or cream.
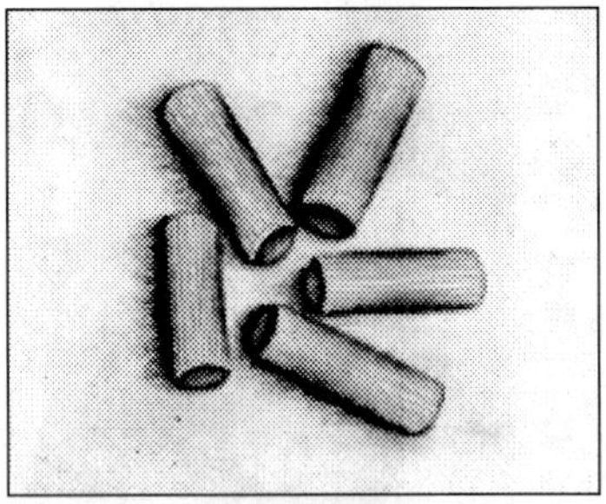	**Rigatoni** ("large grooved"): Rigatoni's ridges and holes are perfect with any sauce, from cream or cheese to the chunkiest meat sauces.
	**Rotelle** ("little wheels"): The cartwheel is not a classic Italian shape, but due to the variety of colour and entertaining shapes they are crowd favourite. Because the spokes of the wheels are good for capturing flavours, these shapes are easy to pair. Rotelle pasta pairs nicely with meat, cream, seafood and vegetables.
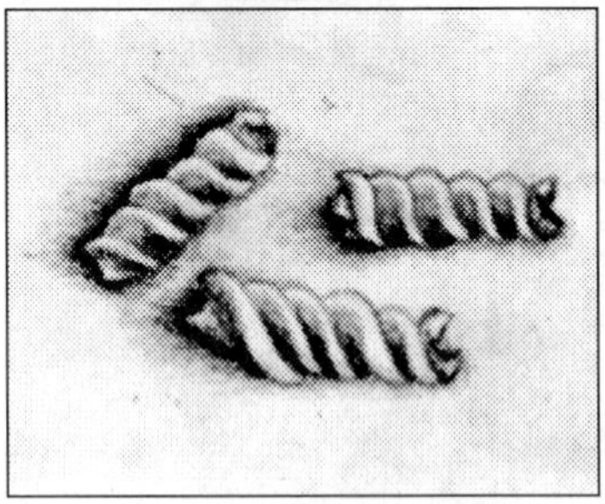	**Rotini** ("spirals" or "twists"): Rotini's twisted shape holds bits of meat, vegetables and cheese, so it works well with any sauce, or you can use it to create fun salads, baked casseroles, or stir-fry meals.
	**Small Shells:** Shells make a great addition to soups or as the base of a wonderful salad. Try remaking your favourite Macaroni and cheese using shells, for a fun twist on a time-honoured tradition.

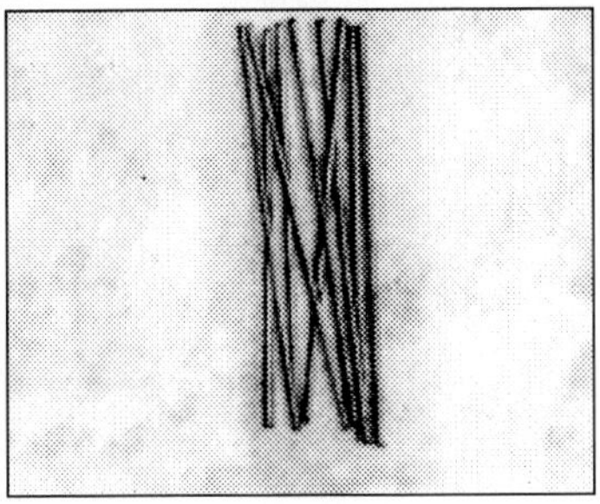

Spaghetti: ("a length of cord") America's favourite shape, Spaghetti is the perfect choice for nearly any sauce, or it can be used to make casseroles or stir-fry dishes. Go beyond tomato sauce and see what your favourite becomes.

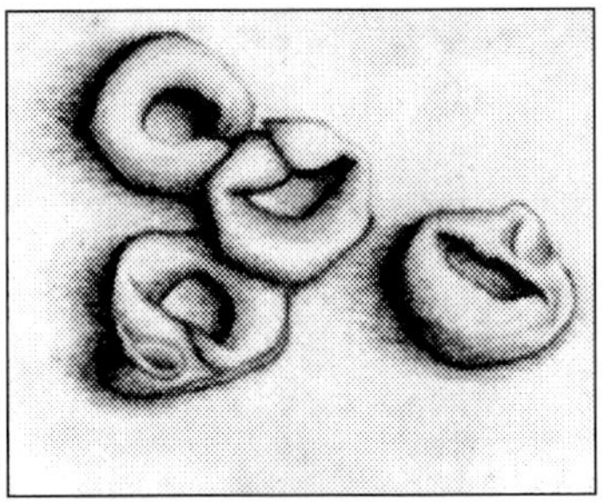

Tortellini: Tortellini is a ring-shaped pasta typically stuffed with meat, cheese or vegetables. Tortellini is commonly served in a broth or cream sauce.

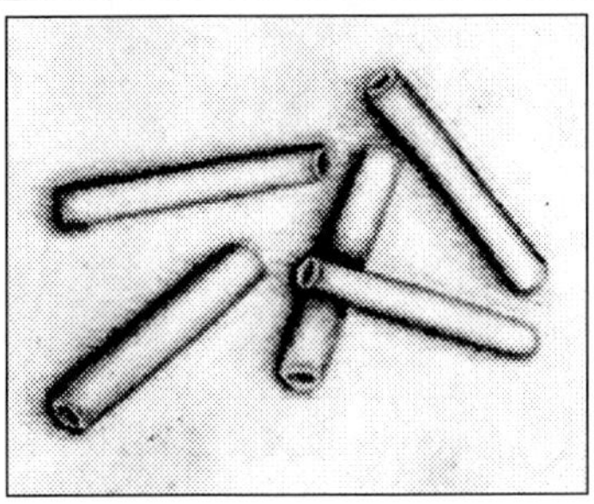

Tubini: A medium-sized, tubular pasta shape, Tubini is perfect for chunky sauces and meat dishes. It also makes wonderful salads, baked dishes and stir-fry meals.

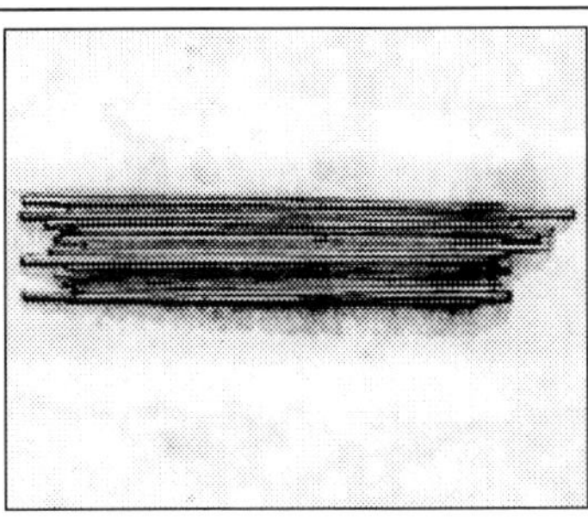

Vermicelli: ("little worms") Slightly thinner than Spaghetti, Vermicelli is good topped with any sauce, or as a salad or stir-fry ingredient.

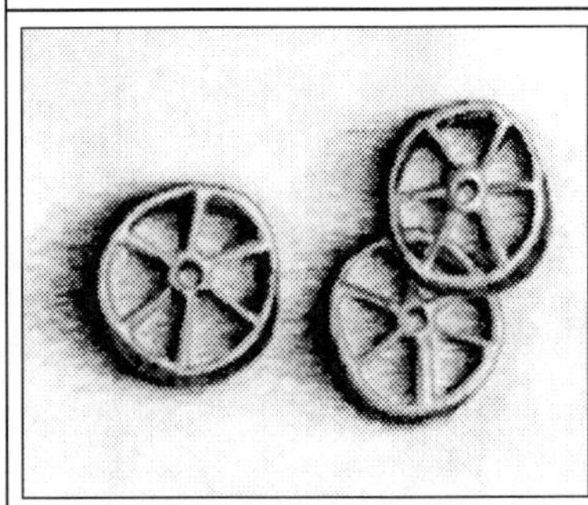

Wagon Wheels ("wheels"): Wagon Wheels make interesting salads, casseroles and stir-fry dishes. Add to soups, or simply top with sauce and enjoy.

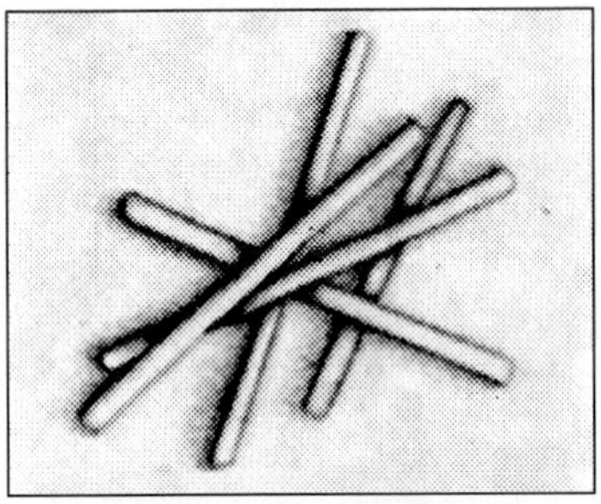

Ziti: A medium-sized, tubular pasta shape, Ziti is perfect for chunky sauces and meat dishes. It also makes wonderful salads, baked dishes and stir-fry meals.

Accompaniments

The various accompaniments to pasta are:

- Parmesan cheese
- Crushed chilly flakes
- Oregano
- Bruchettas
- Garlic breads
- Bread rolls

Pasta when served as an appetizer in a salad can be served up to 50 gm (pasta only).

When pasta is served as a main course it can be served at about 180 gm per portion along with the choice of sauce.

Pasta Sauces

- Arabiatta
- Marinara
- Bolognese
- Alfredo
- Puttanesca
- Pesto
- Carbonara
- Tomato basil (Nepolitana)
- Amatriciana
- Aglio olio pepperoncino
- Alcohol-based.

Example of Pasta Dishes

- Spaghetti napolitaine—spaghetti in a tomato and garlic flavoured sauce.
- Spaghetti Bolognese—spaghetti blended with minced lean beef in a rich brown sauce.

- Ravioli— noodle-type pasta filled with a variety of stuffings, such as chicken, beef and spinach.
- Cannelloni— rolls of ravioli paste filled with stuffings as for ravioli. Include all pastas such as spaghetti, macaroni, ravioli (stuffed pasta), penne, fettuccini, bow, orzo and other.
- Lasagne napolitaine.
- Macaroni au gratin.

5. Poisson (Fish)

Poached/steamed/baked fish is served in this course.

- Known as fish course.
- Fish is soft fibred and tender meat, which is easily digested and helps to prepare the appetite for heavier course to come.
- Fish course is presented simple without complicated garnishes.

  Served with appropriate sauce and boiled vegetables. Usually, baked, poached, steamed, grilled and fried fish.

  Meuniere: fish shallow fried in butter.

  Veronique: in white wine sauce, garnished with white grapes.

  Bonne femme: in white wine sauce with mushrooms.

> - **Hot fish with sauce:** No accompaniment
> - **Hot, without sauce:** With Hollandaise
> - **Fried (breadcrumbed) (a 'Anglaise):** With tartare sauce, or other mayonnaise based sauce.
> - **Fried or Grilled (not bread rumbed):** With hollandaise, or tartare.
> - **Deep fried dipped in better (a l'Orley):** Tomato sauce is offered with lemon.

Classical examples of fish dishes are:

- Sole meuniere: sole fish shallow fried in butter.
- Sole Colbert: sole fish coated with flour, egg and bread crumbs and deep fried.
- Sole bonne femme: fillet of sole in a white wine sauce with mushrooms.
- Fried fish with tartare sauce.
- Lobster Newberg: with thickened sauce of fish stock and cream, flavoured with brandy and marsala, finished with butter.

6. Entrée: First Meat Course

Usually, complete in itself does not have much accompaniments, if at all.

- The entrees are generally small, well garnished dishes which come from the kitchen ready for service.
- Small cuts of meat are served.

- They are always accompanied by a rich sauce or gravy.
- Entree is either a hot dish in a sauce or cold dish.
- Potatoes and vegetables are not served with the entree if it is followed by a releve. If releve is not being served then potatoes and vegetables can be served.

Classical example

- Poulet saute chasseur – chicken in rich brown sauce flavoured with tomato and mushroom.
- Minced chicken with savoury rice.
- Chicken liver with savoury rice.
- Steak Diane – minute steak shallow fried and flavoured with onion and mushroom finished with red wine sauce or cream.
- Chateaubriand – double fillet steak grilled.

7. Sorbet

Because of the length of the French classical menu, this course is considered to be the 'rest' between courses. You can say sorbet is a course intended to give a pause in the middle of the meal. Sorbet, therefore, must be able to counteract the richness of the dishes already served and stimulates the appetite for the courses to come. Sorbet is a type of water ice that is softer and more granular than ice cream, as it does not contain any egg or fat. The basic ingredient of a sorbet is a fruit juice or puree, wine, liqueur, etc. It should be piped into a champagne glass and served on a underplate with a teaspoon. Russian cigarettes and flavoured water may be offered.

Examples

- Sorbet au Citron
- Sorbet a l'orange
- Sorbet au Cassis
- Sorbet au Champagne

8. Releve (Grand Meat Dish)

Releve are normally larger than entrees and take the form of butchers' joints, which have to be carved. These joints are braised, poeled or roasted. A sauce or roast gravy and potatoes and green vegetables are always served with this course.

Examples of releve are:

- Gigot d'aigneau: roast leg of lamb with mint sauce.
- Contre fillet de Boeuf roti al'Anglaise: Boned and roasted sirloin of beef.
- Carre d'agneau roti: Roast best end of lamb.
- Cuissot de porc roti, puree de pommes: Roast leg of pork with applesauce.
- For vegetarian dishes such as au gratin, cutlets, vegetable kievs, etc., are served.

9. Roti (Roast)

Roti or roast items consists of roast game or poultry, i.e., chicken, turkey, duck, pheasant, quail

- Served with accompanying sauces or gravy.
- A dress salad is usually served along.
- Roast always consists of roast game or poultry: chicken, turkey, duck, pheasant, quail.
- Each dish is accompanied with its own particular sauce or gravy, with a green salad served separately on a crescent shaped dish, which is placed at the top left hand corner of acover.

Example

- Oie roti, puree de pommes: Roast goose with apple sauce.
- Faison roti: Roast pheasant served with bread crumbs.
- Poulet roti: Roast gravy and parsley and thyme.
- Venaison: Roast venison
- Agneau roti: Roast lamb with mint sauce or redcurrant jelly.
- Caneton roti: Roast duck.
- Cote de boeuf roti: Roast side of beef.

10. Legumes (Vegetables)

At this stage of meal the balance of the course is gradually returning from heavy to light.

Vegetables such as asparagus, artichokes, and corn on the cob, with hollandaise sauce or beurre fondue (melted butter) offered separately.

Example

- Pommes lyonnaise: saute potatoes blended with shallow fried shredded onions.
- Petits pois a la francaise: peas, button onions, diced bacon and shredded lettuce in a thickened sauce.
- Champignons grille: grilled mushrooms.
- Choufleur polonaise: cauliflower garnished with a mixture of fried bread crumbs, sieved egg white and yolk and parsley.
- Champignons grilles: grilled mushrooms.
- Choufleur mornay: cauliflower with a cheese sauce.
- Haricots verts au beurre: French beans tossed in butter.

Types of Dressing

- English Dressing
- French Dressing
- Vinaigerette Dressing
- American Dressing

11. Salade (Salad)

Example:

- Salade francaise: lettuce, tomato, egg and vinaigrette dressing.
- Salade vert: lettuce, watercress, cucumber and green pepper.

12. Buffet Froid (Cold Buffet): Cold Meat and Fish

This course consists of cold meat items. Froid means cold so all the items which come under this course are cold cuts which includes a variety of cold meats, fish, cheese and egg items together with a variety of salads and dressing.

- Jambon froid: cold ham.
- Galantine de volatile: cold chicken coated with a chicken flavoured sauce and decorated, then coated in aspic.

13. Fromage (Cheese)

All types of cheese may be offered together with the appropriate accompaniments. The ideal cheese board should combine hard, semi-hard, soft or cream, blue and fresh cheese along with various accompaniments of cheese such as salt, pepper and mustard, celery stick, olives, dry fruits, castor sugar for cream biscuits and cheese crackers. Cheese is explained in next chapter.

Examples

Name of Cheese	Type	Origin
• Cheddar	Hard	England
• Red Cheshire	Hard	Holland
• Brie	Soft	France
• Caerphilly	Semi-hard	Wales
• Gorgonzola	Blue	Italy
• Demi-sel	Soft	France
• Gruyere	Hard	Switzerland
• Gouda	Hard	Holland
• Ricotta	Fresh	Italy

14. Entremets (Sweet)

Consists of hot and cold items—hot dish such as soufflé, rum omelettes. Cold desserts are newer, modern versions of this course.

Examples of such dishes are:

- Crepes Suzette: pancakes in a rich fresh orange juice and flamed with brandy.
- Crepes Georgette: pancakes with pineapple sauce.
- Baba au rhum: yeast leavened light sponge soaked in rum.
- Jam omelets.
- Rum omelets.
- Peche Melba: poached peach copated with raspberry jam sauce topped with vanilla ice cream.
- Pineapples flamed with Kirtsch.
- Pancakes.

15. Savoureux (Savoury)

Savouries may take form of savoury items. It consists of a tid bit on a hot canapé of toast or fried bread.

Nowadays usually served as appetizers.

Examples of savories are:

- Scotch woodcock: Scrambled egg on toast and decorated with capers and anchovies.
- Welsh rarebit: Cheese sauce flavoured with ale on toast and gratinated.
- Scotch woodcock: Scrambled egg on toast decorated with capers and anchovies.
- Canape Diane: Chicken liver rolled in bacon and grilled, placed on warm toast.
- Croute Derby: Ham puree garnished with pickled walnut.
- Canapé Charlemagne: Shrimps in a curry sauce.
- Tartlettes: Round pastry cases with various fillings such as mushrooms, cheese soufflé mixtures with various garnishes or prawns or other fish in various sauces.
- Soufflés.
- Champignons sur croute: Mushrooms on toast.

16. Dessert (Dessert)

This course consists of fresh fruits and nuts. Sometimes placed on the table as decoration.

Nowadays served as an alternative to the entremets course. The dessert is usually dressed up in a fruit basket by the kitchen and is used as a central piece on a cold buffet until required.

- All forms of fresh fruit and nuts may be served accompanied with caster sugar and salt.
- Stewed fruits, fresh or nuts.

17. Beverages

All types of coffees and teas are served in this course. Apart from this Tisanes, Bovril, Horlicks and other milks can also be offered.

Example:

- Earl grey tea
- Darjeeling tea
- Green tea
- Cammomile tea
- Assam tea
- Russian tea
- Cappuchino
- Specialty coffee
- Espresso

- Café Latte
- Cafe Mocha

To make the menu course simple and easy to understand always remember that:

- Starters start from courses 1-4.
- Main courses from courses 5-12 (except 7th course which is generally a pause during meal).
- After from courses 13-16.
- Beverages are course no 17.

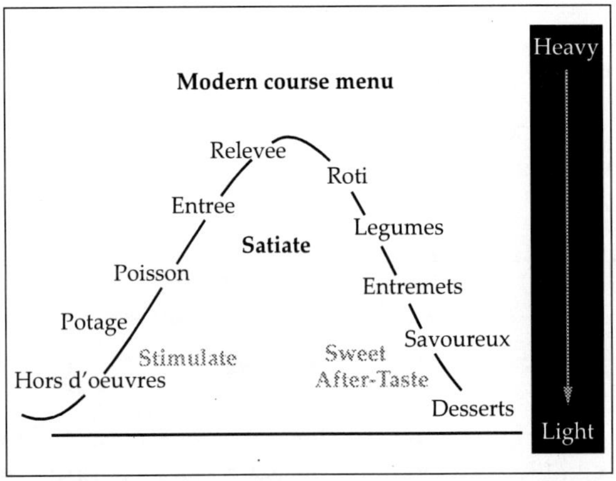

The following Table lists 13-course French classical menu

S. No.	French	English	Examples
1.	Hors d'oeurves	Appetisers	Oysters, smoked salmon, Caviar, Melon frappe
2.	Potage	Soup	Crème de tomato, Consommé julienne
3.	Oeuf	Egg dishes (except hard boil egg)	Oeuf sur la plat
4.	Farineux	Rice and pasta dishes	Sphagetti Bolognese Macaroni au gratin
5.	Poisson	Fish	Poisson al'Anglaise, Poisson Bonne Femme
6.	Entree	First meat dish	Noisette d'Agneau Roti
7.	Sorbet	Flavoured ice	Lemon & mint sorbet Champagne sorbet (Cigarettes/cigar may be Offered at this stage)
8.	Releve	Main meat dish	Pepper steak, Chateaubriand

9.	Roti	Roast of game Birds or joints	Roast turkey
10.	Legumes	Vegetables	Tomato farcis Hericots vertes au beurre
11.	Entremets	Sweet dish	Baba au rhum Crepe suzette, Choux Chantilly
12.	Savoureux	Savoury	Tartlettes Souffles Croute Diane(chicken livers wrapped in streaky bacon)
13.	Dessert	Dessert	Fruit and nuts

Note: Oeuf and Farineux courses will be removed while compiling 11-course French classical menu.

Order of Courses for a Dinner Menu

A full-course dinner is seldom served today, but the sequence of courses should be respected even if some are omitted. The general standard at present is for a four- or five-course meal to be served for dinner. Theoretically, however, all the courses of a full dinner menu must be studied and learnt by heart so that perfect compilation of menus can be achieved.

Three-course Dinner Menu

1. Hors d'oeuvre or soup.
2. Main course with vegetables and potatoes or salad.
3. Sweet or savory.

Four-course Dinner Menu

1. Hors d'oeuvre or soup.
2. Fish course.
3. Main course with vegetables and potatoes or salad.
4. Sweet or savory.

Five-course Dinner Menu

1. Hors d'oeuvre or soup.
2. Fish course.
3. Main course with vegetables and potatoes or salad.
4. Sweet.
5. Savory.

Six-course Dinner Menu

1. Hors d'oeuvre or soup (potage).
2. Fish (poisson).
3. Entrée.
4. Main (releve or remove) with (pommes et legumes ou salade).
5. Sweet (entremets).
6. Savory (savoureux ou bonne bouche).

Seven-course Dinner Menu

1. Hors d'oeuvres or soup
2. Potage
3. Poisson
4. Entrée
5. Releve/Remove-Pommes et Legumes
6. Roast (roti) - Salade
7. Entremets or Bonne/Bonne Bouche

Lunch Menu

Crème de tomates

(Cream of tomato soup with ricotta basil crostini)

--------------x----------------

Fish a'la orly

(Deep fried fish with lemon wedges, French fries and tartar sauce)

--------------x----------------

Gigot d agneau roti

(Roast leg of lamb with mint sauce)

---------------x----------------

Welsh rarebit

(Cheese sauce flavoured with ale on toast and gratinated)

---------------x----------------

Freshly brewed café/tea

Eight-course Dinner Menu

1. Hors d'oeuvres
2. Postage
3. Poisson
4. Entrée
5. Releve/Remove - Pommes et Legumes
6. Roti–Salade
7. Entremets
8. Savories/Bonne Bouche

Finally, he will often be required to comprehend and then explain to guests the French expressions of a menu. He should, therefore, become familiar with the words for food and methods of cookery.

STANDARD PORTION SIZE TO BE SERVED

Hors D'oeuvres

S. No.	Particulars	Grams Served Per Portion
1.	Vegetables/salads	90 gm
2.	Green leaves	125 gm
3.	Mushrooms	115 gm

4.	Truffles	25-30 gm
5.	Fruits and fruit cocktails	90 gm
6.	Eggs	1 No.
7.	Fish and fish products (a) Caviar (b) Oyster (c) Scallops (d) Snails	60 gm 30 gm 6 no. 5-6 no. 6 no.
8.	Charcuterie products (a) Cured and dried (b) Cured and cooked	 60 gm 125 gm
9.	Cold meats (galantine)	120 gm
10.	Offals/pate	60 gm
11.	Aspic	45 gm

Soups

S. No.	Particulars	Grams Served Per Portion
1.	Broth based	250 ml
2.	Consomme	175 ml
3.	Bisques	175 ml
4.	Veloute/cream and puree soups	175 ml
5.	Cold soups	175 ml
6.	Main course	500 ml

Eggs

S. No.	Particulars	Nos.
1.	For all breakfast items.	2
2.	For omelettes.	3
3.	Egg course (with sauce and accompanying vegetables).	2

Pasta

S. No.	Particulars	Grams Served Per Portion
1.	Dried pasta for main course (Raw)	120 gm
2.	Fresh pasta for maincourse (Raw)	160 gm
3.	Pasta for hors d'oeuvres	60 gm
4.	Pasta for soups	30 gm

Fish

S. No.	Particulars	Grams Served Per Portion
1.	Fish course (without bones and head)	120 gm
2.	Main course (without bones and head)	180 gm
3.	Fish (with head and bones)	375-500 gm
4.	Fish (without head but with bones)	250-350 gm
5.	Crustaceans (in shell)	500-750 gm
6.	Squid	180 gm
7.	Shrimps/Prawns/Scampi (in shell without head).	180 gm

Main Course

Meats – Beef, Veal, Lamb, Poultry

S. No.	Particulars	Grams Served Per Portion
1.	Tenderloin	200 gm
2.	Shoulder (without bone)	250 gm
3.	Chops/ribs (with bone)	375 gm
4.	Sirloin (without bone)	250 gm
5.	Leg (boneless)	250 gm
6.	Flank	250gm
7.	Brisket	250 gm
8.	Hamburger patties	175 gm
9.	Offals	175 gm
10.	Poultry boneless	200 gm
11.	Poultry with bone	375 gm

Pork Products

S. No.	Particulars	Grams Served Per Portion
1.	Spare ribs	375 gm
2.	Chops	375 gm
3.	Bacon (with fat)	125 gm
4.	Bacon (without fat)	175 gm
5.	Fresh sausage	175-250 gm
6.	Dry sausage	90-125 gm

Cheese Course

S. No.	Particulars	Grams Served Per Portion
1.	Soft cheese	125 gm
2.	Semi-hard cheese	125 gm
3.	Hard cheese	125 gm
4.	Blue vein cheese	90 gm

Sorbet

S. No.	Particulars	Quantity
1.	Sorbet	120-150 ml

Vegetables

S. No.	Particulars	Weight
1.	As main course	150 gm

Rice

S. No.	Particulars	Weight
1.	Long grain rice (180 gm raw rice makes 850 gm of cooked rice).	200 gm
2.	Short grain rice (180 gm of raw rice makes 750 gm of cooked rice).	180 gm

Curries

S. No.	Particulars	Weight
1.	Non-veg (with bone and gravy)	375 gm
2.	Non-veg (boneless and gravy)	275 gm
3.	Meat boneless, dry	200 gm

Lentils

S. No.	Particulars	Weight
1.	As dals	200 ml
2.	As salads	150 gm
3.	As sprouts	150 gm

Pulses

S. No.	Particulars	Weight
1.	As curries	200 gm
2.	As salads, etc.	180 gm

Desserts

S. No.	Particulars	Weight
1.	Cheeseckes	150 gm
2.	Fresh fruits	150 gm
3.	Pastries	150 gm
4.	Chocolate desserts	120 gm
5.	Souffle and mousses	220 gm
6.	Moulded gelatin desserts	220 ml
7.	Meringue desserts	80 gm
8.	Ice creams	150 ml

Savoury Products

S. No.	Particulars	Weight
1.	Pies/Quiche	150 gm

Accompaniments

S. No.	Particulars	Weight
1.	Potato preparation	100-120 gm
2.	Vegetables	60 gm
3.	Accompanying sauce	60 ml
4.	Raita	120 ml
5.	Curd	150 ml
6.	Chutney	75 ml
7.	Poppadoms	2 nos.
8.	Pickles	30 gm
9.	Preserves (3 varieties)	15 gm each
10.	Butter	20 gm
11.	Nan	160 gm
12.	Roti	90 gm
13.	Hash brown potato	60 gm
14.	Ham/bacon/sausage as side order of breakfast	45 gm each
15.	Rice in preplated food	90 gm

MENU TERMINOLOGY

Term		**Definition**
Aiguillettes	:	Long, thin, vertically cut strips of meat from he breast of ducks and other poultry.
A la broche	:	Cooked on a spit.

A l'anglaise	:	English style.
Aspic	:	Savoury jelly.
Au four	:	Baked in the oven.
Bain - marie	:	Hot water bath or well.
Barquette	:	A boat-shaped tartlet case, filled in a variety of ways.
Bechamel	:	Basic white sause.
Beurre manie	:	Butter and flour kneaded together and used to thicken soups and sauces.
Bisque	:	A fish soup, made with shellfish.
Bordelaise	:	Rich brown sauce flavoured with red wine.
Bouchee	:	Small puff paste patty; tiny savoury or hors D'oeuvre tit-bit; Bouchees may be filled in a variety of ways. Bouchees a la reine
Bouillon, court	:	Liquor for cooking fish
Braiser	:	To brown meat, game and poultry throughly and then finish cooking in a covered vesel with a little liquid or sauce. Vegetables are usually braised without browning in broth containing very little fat.
Breadcrumb	:	To cover a piece of meat, fish, poultry, etc., with bread crumbs after first dipping it in beaten egg or liquid butter. See bread crumbs.
Brunoise	:	A name used to describe vegetables, ham, or chicken cut in tiny dice. It is also a garnish for a clear soup.
Caviar	:	Role of female sturgeon.
Celestine	:	Strips of savoury pancake.
Champignons	:	Mushrooms
Chateaubriand	:	Double fillet steak
Concasse	:	Rough chopped (tomato)
Confiture	:	Jam
Citron	:	Lemon
Canapés	:	Small pieces of bread, plain, grilled, or fried, garnished and served mainly as hors'd'oevre.
Caramel	:	Burnt sugar, commonly known as 'Black Jack'.
Casserole	:	A fire-proof earthenware saucepan, casserole.
Cocotte	:	Small round fire-proof dishes for cooking an egg, a ragout, etc., also used to describe a larger oval casserole for cooking chicken, etc.

Court bouillon	:	Fish stock with white wine or vinegar and mirepoix.
Croutons	:	Fried bread, used as garnish. For soups they are cut in small cubes, for other dishes in a variety of fancy shapes.
Demi - glace	:	A basic sause of fairly thin consistency, frequently used to improve other sauces, soups and stews.
Escallops	:	Thin slices of flattened veal or beef.
Entrée	:	A meat dish served with a sauce. Formerly regarded as an intermediate dish, it is nowadays frequently served as the main course.
Entremets	:	Sweet, dessert.
Frappe	:	Chilled
Flambé	:	Flamed with spirit or liqueur.
Foie gras	:	Liver of a fattened goose.
Fromage		Cheese
Fricassee	:	A white stew in which the poultry or meat is cooked in the sauce.
Fumet	:	Essence of fish or herbs, game or poultry.
Gateau	:	Sponge cake
Glace	:	Ice cream
Galantine	:	A fine cold dish of poultry or meat, boned, stuffed, braised in concentrated stock and coated and garnished with aspic.
Garnish	:	An ingredient which decorates, accompanies or completes a dish. Many dishes are identified by the name of their garnish.
Hors d'oeuvre	:	Preliminary dishes intended to act as appetizers. Hors d'oeuvre may be hot or cold and are served before the soup.
Embrocher	:	To place on a pot for spit roasting or on skewers for grilling or frying.
Jus lie	:	Thickened gravy
Julienne	:	Term used to describe vegetables cut in very fine strips. Used as a garnish in soups.
Macedoine	:	Mixture of diced vegetables
Mise en place	:	Preparation beforehand
Marinade	:	To soak meat, game, etc., for a short while to improve flavour and make more tender.
Marmite	:	An earthenware pot in which soups and stews are cooked and served at table. The name is also given to some dishes cooked in such a pot.
Mirepoix	:	A garnish of diced, browned onions, bacon and carrots with various herbs used to flavour soups, sauces, stews, etc.

Mousse	:	A light of fluffy mixture, which may be sweet or savoury, hot or cold.
Poulet	:	Chicken
Poach (pocher)	:	Simmer dishes in a mould in a Bain-Marie until done. To cook food in water that is kept just on boiling point without actually letting it boil.
Profit roles	:	Small balls of choux paste. Garnish for soup. Sweet of same name.
Quenelles	:	A kind of dumpling, made from various kinds of forcemeat and poached, made in different shapes, balls, ovals, etc.
Roux	:	Flour stirred into melted butter, used for thickening soups and sauces. It may be white, blonde or brown.
Shred (emincer)	:	To cut meat or vegetables into thin slices or strips.
Supremes	:	The best parts, e.g., supreme de volaille – chicken breasts and wings.
Tabasco	:	A pungent Indian pepper sauce, also used extensively in countries with a hot climate.
Tartare	:	Cold sauce, base of mayonnaise.
Troncon	:	Portion of flat fish cut across the body (turbot)
Veloute	:	Velvety, smooth. A rich white sauce made from chicken stock, cream, etc. Also a name given to certain cream soups.
Vol au vent	:	A round or oval case made of puff pastry.

ACTIVITIES

- Plan a five-, four- and three-course lunch menu for a continental restaurant.
- Collect five menus from your nearby restaurants and compare them in terms of their designing, layout, typology, printing and other aspects.

8 TYPES OF SERVICE

There are many ways in which food and beverages are served to the guests in the food and beverages service industry. This may range from full silver service in a fine dining restaurant, where the dishes are served at the table by waiters with service spoon and fork, to a self-service cafeteria where guest collect their own food from the counter. Food service helps in meeting customer requirements, to increase the food sales and to make the dining experience pleasant. Food and beverages service styles can be broadly classified into five groups:

1. Table service
2. Assisted service
3. Self service
4. Single-point service
5. In situ/specialized service.

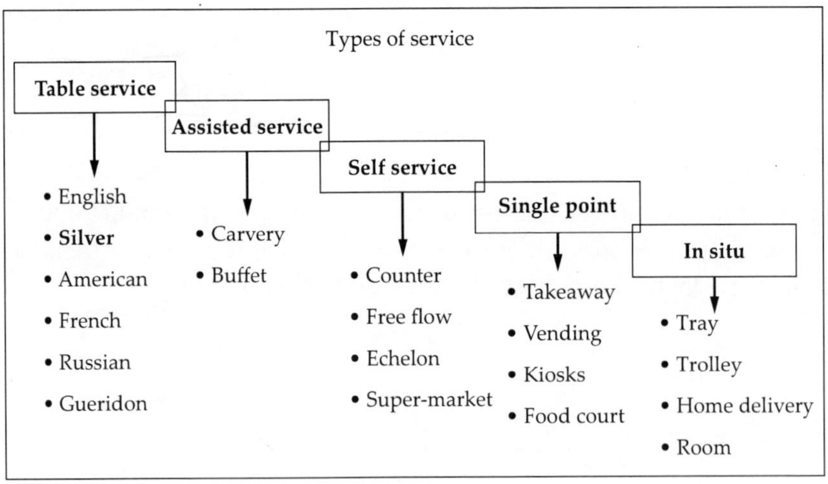

TABLE SERVICE

In this method of service, food and beverages are served to guests by waiters at the guest's table. Following services comes under table service:

- English
- Silver

- American
- French
- Russian
- Gueridon

ENGLISH SERVICE (À LA ANGLAISE)

Often referred to as the "host service" because the host plays an active role in the service. Food is brought on platters by the waiter and is shown to the host for approval. The waiter then places the platters on the tables. The host either portions the food into the guest plates directly or portions the food and allows the waiter to serve. The waiter may then take the dishes around for guests to help themselves or be served by the waiter.

Advantages

- Personalized service.
- Customer satisfaction.

Limitations

- Calls for high level of service skills, hence more labour costs
- More staff required
- Low seat turnover
- Slow service

SILVER SERVICE/PLATTER TO PLATE

Also known as platter-to-plate service or queen of all services. The table is set for hors d'oeuvres, soup, main courses and dessert. The food is portioned into platters at the kitchen itself which are placed at the sideboard with burners or hot plates to keep the food warm in the restaurant. Plates are placed before the guest. The waiter then picks the platter from the hot plate and presents the dish to the host for approval. He serves each guest using a service spoon and fork. All food is presented in an appropriate manner with elaborate dressing. Always remember to:

- Serve food from dish/platter on to guest's plate using service spoon and fork from the left-hand side of the guest.
- Conduct clearance from the right-hand side of the guest.
- Serve beverages from the right-hand side of the guest.

Advantages

- Quick, efficient service
- 'High class', sophisticated
- Individual attention

Limitations

- Skilled staff required
- Awkward at times
- May cause spillage
- Cannot be applied to delicate items
- Food presentation may be spoilt

AMERICAN SERVICE/PREPLATED SERVICE (À LA AMERICAINE)

The American service is a pre-plated service which means that the food is served into the guest's plate in the kitchen itself and brought to the guest. The portion is predetermined by the kitchen and the accompaniments served with the dish balance the entire presentation in terms of nutrition and colour. This type of service is commonly used in coffee shops where fast service is required. This is a simple and informal form of service. In this style, dishes are neatly plated in the kitchen by the kitchen staff and placed at the guest's cover from the right-hand side. This style of service is followed in restaurants where fast service is required. Always remember to:

- All plated food is served from the right-hand side to the guest.
- Beverages are also served from the right.
- Clearance is done from the right-hand side.
- Trays are used to carry cups, bowls, saucers, and under plates.
- Trays should not be used to carry full and half plates.
- Move clockwise when you work from the right-hand side and counterclockwise when you work from the left hand.

Advantages

- Service skill is not required.
- Low labour cost.
- Needs fewer waiters.
- Quick service.
- May be considered informal.
- High seat turnover as service is fast.
- Kitchen staff has scope for demonstrating their plating skills.

Limitations

- No personalized service.
- Chances of plate wastage.
- Skilled waiters do not have scope to show their service skills.
- Food may become cold.
- More of kitchen time and labour.

FRENCH SERVICE (À LA FRANÇAISE)

It is a very personalized service. Food is brought from the kitchen in dishes and salvers, which are placed directly on the table. The plates are kept near the dish and the guests help themselves. For a small party of two or three guests, dishes ordered by them are placed on the table with service implements and plates for the guests to help themselves. For larger parties of more than four guests, a side table or trolley can be used. The waiter keeps plates, service tools, and dishes on the trolley/sideboard. He/she places plates at guest's covers and then presents the dishes with service tools to each guest from the left-hand side to help themselves. Alternatively, all dishes may be placed on the table and the host may serve all his guests at the table first or assist them in service and serve himself finally. If assistance is required, the waiter may help the guest in passing and serving the dishes.

Advantages

- Service skills not required.
- Low labour cost.
- Seat turnover is more compared to silver service.
- Quick service.

Limitations

- Service staff will not be able to demonstrate their service skills.
- Food may go cold.
- Guest may spoil or burn himself.
- Needs more area on the table.
- Guest may feel neglected.
- Spillage may occur by the guest.

RUSSIAN SERVICE (À LA RUSSE)

This is a very elaborate service and may also be called sideboard service. In this style, large joints, roast poultry, whole fish, and so on that have elaborate garnish, are neatly arranged on a platter, presented to the host, taken back on the sideboard, portioned, are served to the guest with service spoon and fork or you can say it is a form of service in which large joints, whole roast meats, etc., are presented to the guest, then taken to sideboard for portioning and carving and then served to guest as platter to plate.

Advantages

- High level of guest satisfaction.
- Individual attention to guests.
- Eye appeal.

- Personalized service.
- Waiters have scope to exhibit carving, portioning and service skills.

Limitations

- Calls for highly skilled staff, hence higher labour cost.
- More wait staff required.
- Low speed of service.
- Low seat turnover, as time taken for service is more.

GUERIDON SERVICE (AU GUÉRIDON)

This is also called trolley service. In this style of service, dishes are prepared, carved, dressed, or flambéed on a trolley in front of the service and served with the service spoon and fork. It is a very effective tool for merchandising. Restaurant may have trolleys especially designed for various jobs such as carving, flambéing, and presentation. The design of the trolley varies according to its purpose. Carving trolley, flambé trolley, hors d'oeurve trolley, cheese trolley and liqueur trolley are some of the trolleys found in restaurants offering gueridon service. This type of service is practised is luxury, upmarket restaurants. However, one should not confuse this service with the trolleys for clearing dirty dishes and those facilitating service. For example, trolleys used in flight catering for carrying portioned food trays and trolleys used in casual dining restaurants for clearing soiled tableware do not constitute gueridon service.

Advantages

- Highly personalized and specialized service.
- Tremendous eye appeal.
- Showmanship.
- High level of customer satisfaction as the dishes are prepared, carved, or flambéed in their presence.
- Good merchandising device.
- Wait staff can exhibit their culinary, carving, and service skills.
- High average spending power (high revenue/cover).

Limitations

- Slow service.
- Low seat turnover.
- Expensive style of service as it requires more service area and highly skilled staff.
- Chances of accidents are more.
- Specialized equipment required.
- Cooking in the service area may leave odour.

ASSISTED SERVICE

- A combination of table and assisted service.
- Some parts of the meal and the clearance is done to the seated customer.
- Other parts such as food replenishment is done by the customer.

Buffet Service: A self-service where food is displayed on tables. The guest takes his plate from a stack at the end of each table or requests the waiter behind the buffet table to serve him. For sit-down buffet service, tables are laid with crockery and cutlery as in a restaurant. The guest may serve himself at the buffet table and return to eat at the guest table laid out. The waiter may serve a few courses like the appetizer and soup at the table.

SINGLE-POINT SERVICE

It is the service which is being done from various counters which is followed in the food service areas like fast food outlets, drive inns and kiosks.

Counter Service/Snack-Bar Service

Tall stools are placed along a counter so that the guest may eat the food at the counter itself. In better establishments, the covers are laid out on the counter itself. Food is either displayed behind the counter for the guests to choose from, or is listed on a menu card or common blackboard.

IN SITU/SPECIALISED SERVICE

It means to serve food and beverages in those areas also which are not primarily designated for food service. Example: room service, transport catering where tray service is done. Features of in situ service are as follows:

- Service to customers in areas not primarily designed for service like room service.
- Service is done on a tray, e.g., train , trolley (aircraft), home delivery.

Room Service/ In Room Dining/Eat In

It implies serving of food and beverages in guest rooms of hotels. Small orders are served in trays. Major meals are taken to the room on trolleys. The guest places his order with the room service order taker. The waiter receives the order and transmits the same to the kitchen. In the meanwhile he prepares his tray or trolley. He then goes to the cashier to have a cheque prepared to take along with the food order for the guest's signature or payment. Usually, clearance of soiled dishes from the room is done after half an hour or an hour. However, the guest can call room service for the clearance as and when he has finished with the meal. In this form of service, the dishes ordered by guests are neatly portioned and arranged on a tray with necessary cutlery and taken to their room/beds/ seats by waiters.

TYPES OF ROOM SERVICE

Centralized: Here all the food orders are processed from the main kitchen and sent to the rooms by a common team of waiters.

Decentralized: Each floor or a set of floors may have separate pantries to service them. Orders are taken at a central point by order-takers who, in turn, convey the order to the respective pantry.

Mobile Pantries: Some hotels have pantries installed in service elevators. Orders are received by a central point that convey it to the mobile pantry. The pantry has to just switch on the floor and give instant service. For the sake of information, in countries, which have a shortage of manpower, large hotels install mechanized dispensing units in rooms. The guest inserts the necessary value of coins into the machine, which will eject pre-prepared food and beverages for guest consumption.

9 TYPES OF MEALS

Various kinds of meals served in the catering organizations/hotels includes the following:

1. Breakfast
2. Brunch
3. Lunch
4. Dinner
5. Supper
6. Elevenses
7. High tea
8. Afternoon tea

BREAKFAST (PETIT-DÉJEUNER)

Breakfast is the first meal of the day, which literally means breaking the fast of the night. Before 18th century, breakfast was had in the morning and included food items such as cold meat, pate and cheese that provided immediate nourishment and energy. In Victorian era, it developed into a prolonged family meal, serving ham, omelette, roasted partridge, kedgeree, followed by fruits, honey, and biscuits, and served with tea. In France, breakfast was known as *petit déjeuner*, unlike the Britishers, the French had a light breakfast consisting of a cup of tea, coffee or *café au lait* or hot chocolate with buttered toast, croissant, bread or biscottes spread with jam or preserves or honey. Breakfast is the most important meal of the day for the customers as well as for the establishment. The in-house guests more often than not have breakfast in the hotel. The service provided during the first meal of the day can set the tone of the day for the guests. Any meal to be called breakfast must have any of two things:

- First meal of the day as it breaks the involuntary fast due to sleep.
- Must be consumed before 10:00 a.m.
- Must contain breakfast items.

In hotels breakfast may be served in the coffee shop or in the hotel restaurant in the form of buffet. Breakfast can also be served in the guest's bedroom or suite through room service. The current trend is that most of the hotels offer breakfast as complementary (bed and breakfast tariff).

TYPES OF BREAKFAST

In hotels nowadays following types of breakfast are being served:

- Continental breakfast
- English breakfast
- American breakfast
- Indian breakfast.

CONTINENTAL BREAKFAST OR CAFÉ COMPLET, THÉ COMPLET (IF TEA IS SERVED)

Light meal or light breakfast which includes the following:

Choice of fresh fruit juice or canned juice (freshly squeezed or canned)

Mango juice, pineapple juice, tomato juice, orange juice, grapefruit juice, watermelon juice. Sweet lime juice, tomato-depending on the season and many others.

> Jam can be made of any fruits whereas marmalade is made up of only citrus fruits especially oranges. Marmalades also have chunks in it.

Choice of breakfast rolls

Toast (white bread/brown bread), rolls, croissant, Danish pastry, doughnuts, brioche, muffins (jam, honey, marmalade and butter).

Beverage

Hot beverages such as tea or coffee.

Sometimes the continental breakfast may also include sliced cold meats, such as salami or ham, and yogurt or cereal.

CONTINENTAL BREAKFAST COVER

- B&B plate/B&B knife
- Napkin
- Teacup, tea saucer, teaspoon
- Preserve pots (jam, honey, marmalade)
- Butter dish
- Bread boat
- Salt & pepper cruet set
- Water goblet/tumbler
- Sugar sachet holder.

ENGLISH BREAKFAST OR FULL BREAKFAST

- Heavy breakfast—substantial in size and variety.
- Generally includes ten courses.
- With tea 'The Complet'.
- With coffee 'Café Complet'.
- Coffee alone 'Café Simple'.
- Takes alone 'The Simple'.

Full breakfast/ English breakfast comprises the following

Juice (Freshly squeezed or canned)

- Mango, pineapple, orange, apple fresh, stewed fruit, strawberries, lychees, melon, tomato juice, grapefruit (half or segments), figs, prunes (fresh and stewed).

Cereals (with hot or cold milk)

- Cornflakes, choccoflakes, weetabix, muesli, bran flakes, rice crispies, porridge, congee.

Yoghurts

- Natural or fruit, regular or low fat

Breads

- White toast/ brown toast, rolls, croissants, brioches, crisp breads.
- Plain sliced white or brown bread.
- Danish pastries, muffins.
- Spiced scones, tea cakes, doughnuts.

Preserves

Butter, jams, marmalade, honey

Fish

- Fried or grilled kippers, poached smoked haddock (sometimes with poached eggs), grilled herring, fried or grilled plaice, fried or grilled sole, kedgeree, smoked fish, marinated fish such as gravadiax.

Eggs (choice to order)

- Fried, poached, scrambled, boiled, plain.
- Savoury filled omelette and other various types of omlettes like Spanish, sunny side up, eggs benedict.

Meats

- Bacon in various styles, various sausages.
- Ham.

For vegetarian—potatoes and vegetables

- Hash browns, sauté potatoes, home fries,
- Mushrooms, baked beans fresh or frilled tomato.

Pancakes and waffles

- Regular pancakes or waffles, with maple syrup or other toppings, blueberry pancakes, whole meal pancakes, griddles cakes.

Cold buffet

- Hams, tongue, chicken, smoked cold meats.
- Salamis, various types of cheese.

Beverages

- Tea, coffee (including decaffeinated), hot chocolate, Ovaltine, milk.

English breakfast as we know is an elaborate meal consisting of many courses and takes a longer time to serve as compared to other types of breakfasts. In recent days, it has been made much simpler and shorter by clubbing courses or eliminating certain courses. This adaptation varies from one establishment to another.

COMPONENTS OF TRADITIONAL ENGLISH BREAKFAST

Choice of fresh fruit juice

(Orange, sweet lime, pineapple, pomegranate, mango, guava, papaya, tomato—depending on the season)

***

Choice of stewed fruits

(Prunes, apricot, plums, pear figs)

***

Choice of cereals

(Porridge, cornflakes (etc.), Muesli and served with hot or cold milk)

***

Choice of fish

(Poached finnan haddock, pan fried or grilled kipper, kedgeree)

***

Eggs to order

(Fried, poached, scrambled, boiled and omelette served with ham or bacon or sausages and black pudding and vegetable accompanied grilled tomatoes, creamed mushrooms on toast, baked beans breakfast potatoes, fried bread)

***

Choice of cold meats

(York Ham or Ox tongue)

***

Choice of breakfast rolls or toast

(Choice hard and soft bread rolls or toast served with preserves and butter)

***

Tea or coffee or hot chocolate

ENGLISH BREAKFAST COVER

- B&B plate/B&B knife.
- Napkin.
- Dessert spoon (stewed fruits): brought with the fruit.
- Dessert spoon (cereals): brought with the cereal or laid horizontally on cover.
- Fish fork/fish knife.
- AP fork/AP knife.
- Steak knife/AP fork.
- Hors'd oeuvre fork/knife: laid on the cover before cold meat is brought on the table.
- Teacup, tea saucer, seaspoon.
- Preserve pots.
- Butter dish/bread boat.
- Salt & pepper cruet set.
- Water goblet/tumbler.
- Sugar sachet holder.

AMERICAN BREAKFAST

Americans are known to have a heavy breakfast followed by a light lunch and a heavy and early dinner. American breakfast also consists too many courses, however, less elaborate than English breakfast.

- American breakfast derive's from the full English breakfast and features predominantly sweet or mild-flavoured foods, mostly hot.
- Menus based around egg dishes and meats such as sausage and bacon.
- Pancakes and waffles is popular.

AMERICAN BREAKFAST COVER

- B&B plate/B&B knife.
- Napkin.
- Teacup, tea saucer, teaspoon.
- Preserve pots/1 oz creamers for honey/maple syrup/melted butter.
- Butter dish/bread boat.
- Salt & pepper cruet set.
- Water goblet/tumbler.
- Sugar sachet holder.
- Dessert spoon (stewed fruits): brought with the fruit.
- Dessert spoon (cereals): Brought with the cereal or laid horizontally on cover.
- AP fork/steak knife or AP knife.

COMPONENTS OF AMERICAN BREAKFAST

Choice of fresh fruit juice

(Orange, sweet lime, pineapple, pomegranate, mango, guavas, papaya, tomato—depending on the season)

***

Choice of stewed fruits

(Prunes, apricot, plums, pear, figs)

***

(Porridge, cornflakes, cream of wheat, oatmeal, wheat flakes, muselie served with hot or cold milk)

***

Eggs to order

***

(Fried, poached, scrambled, boiled and omelette served with ham or bacon or sausages and hash brown potatoes and grilled tomato)

Waffle or hot pancakes

(Served with golden/maple syrup or honey and melted butter)

Baked beans on toast

Breakfast steak

Chicken liver on toast

Mushroom on toast

***

Choice of breakfast rolls or toast

(Choice of croissant, muffins, brioche, Danish pastry, donuts or toast served with preserves and butter)

***

Tea or coffee

INDIAN BREAKFAST

Indian breakfast is served in almost all the hotels in the form of buffet.

Cover

- B&B plate/ B&B knife.
- Napkin.
- Teacup, tea saucer, teaspoon.
- Salt and pepper cruet set.
- Water goblet/ tumbler.
- Sugar sachet holder.
- Dessert spoon accompaniment – curd/ sambhar/ potato.
- AP fork/ AP knife.

Components of Indian Breakfast

Choice of fresh fruit juice

(Orange, sweet lime, pineapple, pomegrante, mango, guavas, papaya, tomato —depending on the season)

***

Choice of fresh fruit

***

Puri Bhaji

Stuffed Paratha

Masala Dosa/Idli Sambhar/Uttapam

***

Lassi or masala tea or coffee

SERVICE OF THE BREAKFAST

- Breakfast menus are presented to each guest and the order is taken. Order must be taken carefully, guest's preference of type of preparation and choice of items must be noted carefully.
- As soon as the order is placed, tea/coffee is served.
- Breakfast is served course-wise.
- Cutlery/flatware is changed/refreshed as per the courses.
- Tea and coffee should be replenished.
- It must be ensured that toasts are served hot and should be replenished when finished.
- Breakfast is an important meal of the day, must be served quickly, without the guest having to wait for long and cheerfully.

Note: For foreigners tea/coffee shall be asked as soon as they sit whereas with Indians after they have done with their breakfast. Tea/coffee should be replenished time to time.

ELEVENSES

- It is generally less savoury than brunch, and might consist of some cakes or biscuits with a cup of tea or coffee. The name refers to the time of day that it is taken: around 11 a.m.
- The name refers to the time of day that it is taken around 11 a.m.
- In Australia and New Zealand it is known as morning tea or *smoko.*
- Choice of foods consumed at morning tea vary from cakes, pastries or lamingtons or biscuits to just coffee.

SUPPER

- Supper means evening meal in some dialects of English. Ordinarily, the last meal of the day, usually the meal that comes after dinner or supper is the name for the evening meal. The term derives from the French *souper,* related to soup.
- Originally, in the middle ages, it referred to the lighter meal following dinner which until the eighteenth century was invariably eaten as the midday meal.
- It is used to describe a less formal, simpler family meal, but also the fairly formal variety in others.
- It is common for social interest and hobby clubs that meet in the evening after normal dinner hours to announce that "a light supper" will be served after the main business of the meeting.
- Supper is usually lighter and often consists of bread with cold meat, cheese, soup, salads, fried potatoes, egg dishes and/or dairy products.

BRUNCH

- Brunch or bruncheon is a late morning meal between the typical time for breakfast and lunch.
- A combination of breakfast and lunch, usually eaten sometime between 11 a.m. and 3 p.m.
- The meal usually involves standard breakfast foods such as eggs, sausages, bacon, ham, fruits, pastries, and the like. However, it can include almost any other type of food served throughout the day.
- Buffets may have quiche, large roasts of meat or poultry, cold seafood like shrimp and smoked fish, salads, soups, vegetable dishes, many types of breadstuffs, and desserts of all sorts. Pancakes are not to be classified as brunch food, and are offered as an option to children who may be present at brunch.

Brunch usually involves standard breakfast foods such as

- Eggs sausages
- Bacon
- Ham
- Pastries
- Pancakes
- Fruits.

Buffets may have

- Alcoholic drinks like sparkling wine
- Quiche
- Large roasts of meat or poultry
- Cold seafood (shrimp and smoked fish)

- Salads
- Soups
- Vegetable dishes
- Breads and desserts.

In India Indian main courses are also available.

LUNCH (DÉJEUNER)

- Lunch is an abbreviation of luncheon, meaning a midday meal.
- In French the midday meal is called déjeuner and is the main meal of the day, taken between noon and 2 p.m.
- In English-speaking countries during the eighteenth century, lunch was originally called "dinner".
- In addition to its primary purpose, lunch can function as a form of entertainment, especially on weekends; a particularly fancy or formal lunch can be called a luncheon.
- Such lunches can be served at a restaurant, as a buffet or as a sit-down feast. Lunch, both simple and fancy, often includes dessert.
- Many nutritionists suggest that it is more appropriate to eat a large meal at lunch than it is to do so at supper, just before going to sleep, when the energy from the meal will not be properly used. An example of this style of meal can be found in the German, Brazilian and Scandinavian diet, whose lunch mostly is large.
- Cover size for all meals is generally 24″ × 18″.

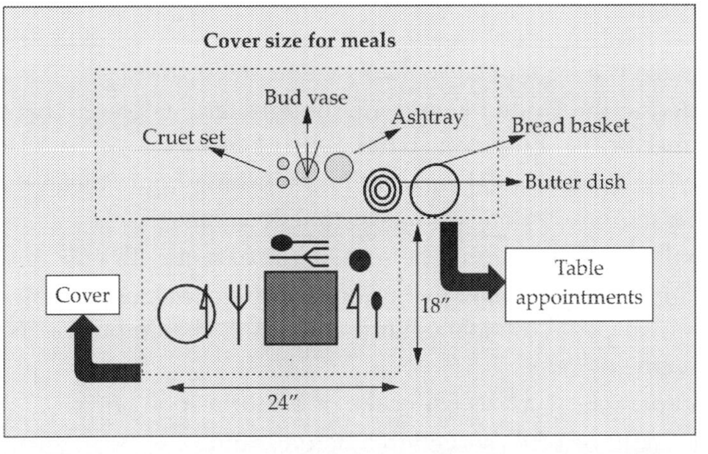

DINNER (DÎNER)

- The word dinner derives from the French word *diner*.
- Originally, dinner referred to the first meal of a two-meal day, a heavy meal occurring about noon, which broke the night's fast in the new day.
- The meal normally consists of a combination of cooked animals or vegetarian proteins (meat, fish or soy), vegetables, and starch products like rice, noodles, or potatoes.
- The term *dinner* has continued to refer to the largest meal of the day, even when this meal is eaten at the end of the day eaten from 5:30 p.m. onwards.

HIGH TEA

- High tea/meet tea is an early evening meal.
- Typically eaten between 5 p.m. and 6 p.m.
- Largely followed by a later lighter evening meal.
- Grills, toasted snacks, cold meats, eggs or fish (fried/grilled) cakes and sandwiches.
- It would be eaten as a substitute for both afternoon tea and the evening meal. The term comes from the meal being eaten at the 'high' (main) table, instead of the smaller lounge table. It is now largely replaced by a later evening meal.
- It usually consists of cold meats, eggs and/or fish, cakes and sandwiches. In a family, it tends to be less formal and is an informal snack (featuring sandwiches, biscuits, pastry, fruit and the like) or else it is the main evening meal.
- In recent years, high tea somehow became a word for exquisite afternoon tea.

AFTERNOON TEA

- Afternoon tea is a light meal typically eaten at 4 o'clock.
- It originated in the United Kingdom, though various places that used to be part of the former British Empire also have such a meal.
- However, changes in social customs and working hours mean that most Britons only take afternoon tea on special/formal occasions.
- Traditionally, loose tea would be served in a teapot with milk and sugar.
- This would be accompanied by various sandwiches (customarily cucumber, egg and cress, fish paste (bloater), ham, and smoked salmon), scones (with butter, clotted cream and jam.
- Cakes and pastries (such as fruit cake or Victoria sponge).
- The food would be often served in a tiered stand.

Note: Tea is served first in both high tea and afternoon tea.

SMORGASBORD

- Is a type of Scandinavian buffet.
- Multiple dishes of various foods on the table.
- Originated in Sweden.
- It is typically a celebratory meal and guests can help themselves from a range of dishes laid out for their choice.
- In a restaurant, the term refers to a buffet-style table laid out with many small dishes from which, for a fixed amount of money, one is allowed to choose as many as one wishes.

ACTIVITIES

- Prepare a power point presentation on different types of breakfast available in the hotel along with the cover required for them.
- Plan a five-course lunch menu for a French delegate.

10 FOOD SERVING TECHNIQUES

It is essential for any F&B personnel to know the various service techniques such as using service gears, placing plates and carrying trays/salvers, etc., while working inside the restaurant and serving food to the guest as it helps in smooth functioning of the food service.

USE OF A SPOON AND FORK AS SERVICE GEARS

Equipment Required

- Service fork
- Knives
- Service spoon
- Platter

Knowledge Required

- Type of fork and spoon used as service gear
- Hygiene and sanitation

Procedure

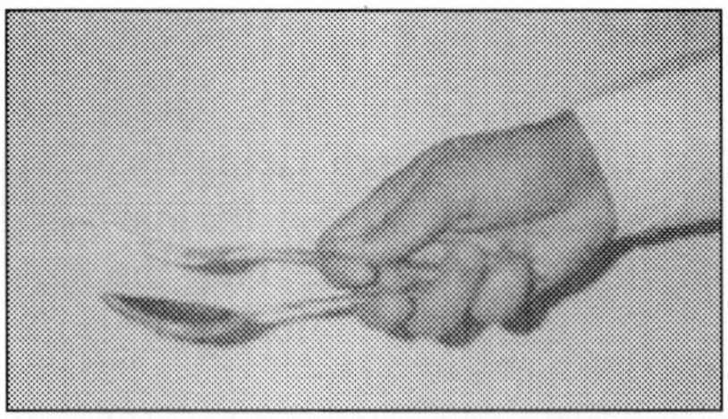

Service of meat items and snacks

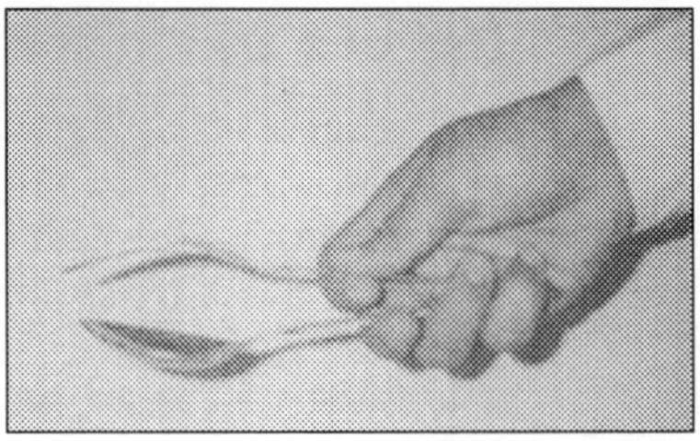

Service of round items

- Place a service fork over a service spoon in your right hand both facing up. They should rest across your middle, ring and little finger with the base of the gear resting in line with the bottom of the little finger, leaving the index finger and thumb free to move the gear. The handles should not protrude beyond your little finger.
- Slide your index finger between the service fork and the service spoon, and hold the service fork between the tip of your index finger and your thumb so that you can lift the service fork with your index finger and thumb.
- Holding the service fork between the tips of your index finger and your thumb raise the from the bowl of the service spoon, keeping the ends of the handles of the service fork and the service spoon together with your little finger.

- Lift food items with the service spoon and hold them firmly with the help of service fork while transferring food from platter to plate.
- To release the food item insert the tip of your index finger to separate the gear finger.

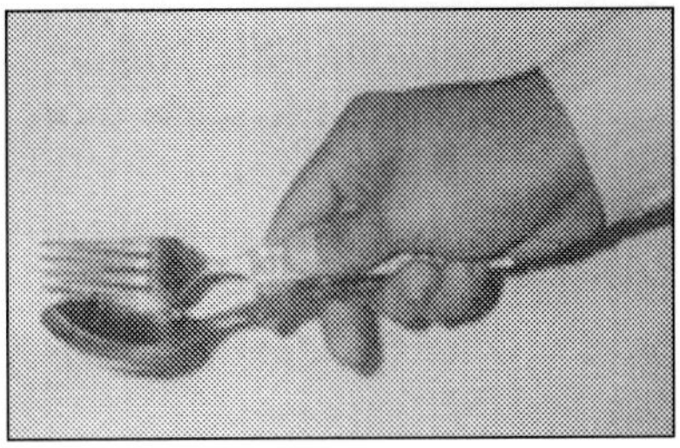

Service of rise

Standard

- Service fork and service spoon are collectively known as service gears.
- Service gear should be free from any stain.
- Do not allow the index finger and the thumb to slide more than half way up the handles of the gear.
- Pick the food up from the side, drawing the gear towards you as you lift it.
- For large and round items such as potatoes and egg turn the fork, enclosing the item.

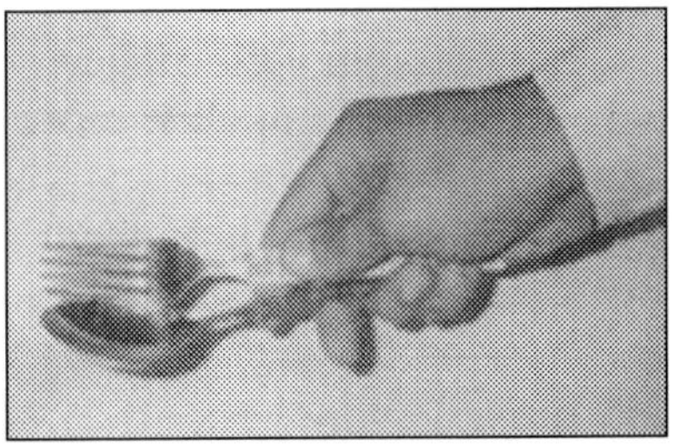

Using two knives

While Using Knives

- For service of soft or large items such as breads and omelets two knives (preferably fish knives) are used as it requires more support that can be given by a service spoon and fork.
- Hold the two knives in the same manner as service spoon and service fork.
- Place the knives under the food item supporting it while serving food to the plate from platter.

CARRYING TRAY/SALVERS (BEVERAGE ROUND)

Equipment Required

- Tray/salver

Knowledge Required

- Type of trays
- Hygiene and sanitation
- Safety precautions

Procedure

Correct Use of Salvers

- For laying cutlery at the table.
- For removing or replacing cutlery or glasses.
- For serving cocktail, mocktail, juices, wine by glass.
- For serving pies, soufflés, fresh fruits and petit fours.

CARRYING PLATES

Stack of plates	Wrap a clean napkin around the plates and carry them with both hands. Neither touch the plates nor hold the plates against your body.	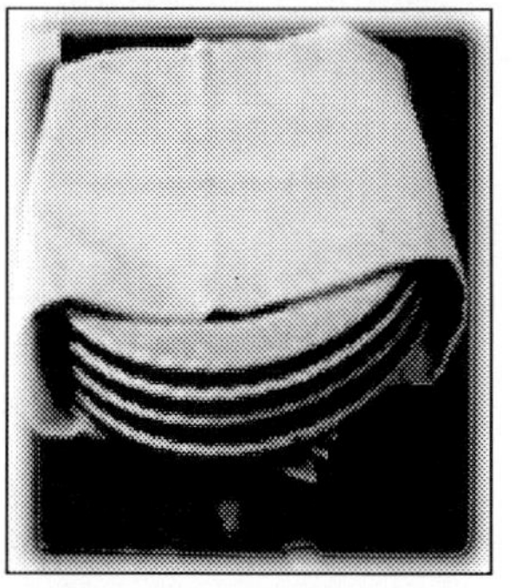
One plate	Hold the plate with the help of thumb and index finger. Make sure that the thumb should be flat on the rim of the plate, pointing towards the rim never into the plate.	
Two plates	• Held from below: Hold the first plate between the thumb and the index finger. The index finger is placed slightly behind the lower rim. Slide the support with the other fingers from beneath. • Held from above. The first plate is held with the thumb and index finger. With that hand turned slightly upward, balance the second plate on the lower forearm and the ball of the thumb. Support the upper plate with other fingers.	

PLACING MAIN PLATES ON GUEST TABLES

1. Hold pile of clean dry and hot plates resting on the palm of the left hand, which should be covered with one end of a service cloth.
2. As you approach the customer wipe the top plate with the other end of the service cloth and pick it by the rim. Keep the thumb well clear off the centre of the plate.

3. Keep the plate horizontal.
4. Lean forward slightly from the guest right and gently place the plate on the centre of the place seating in front of the customer.
5. Announce *"Plate for you Sir/Madam"* while placing the plate.
6. Place the plate with the monogram al 12 o' clock position.
7. Do not move the flatware on table while placing the plate.
8. Unrequired hand, i.e., the hand which is supporting the plates should be away from the guest when placing the plate.

Placing main plate

CLEARING OF PLATES

Equipment Required

- Soiled plates
- Soiled cutlery

Knowledge Required

- Hygiene and sanitation
- Eye for detail

Procedure

- Start with the person to the right of the host.
- Standing at the back right hand corner of the guest's chair, lean forward arrange the soiled cutleries in the plate and pick up the soiled plate along with cutlery by your right hand.

Step 1: Arrange the cutlery in plate

- Transfer the plate to your left hand, holding it between the thumb and the index finger.
- Place your thumb over the end of the fork handle.
- Use knife to move the leftover food to the front of the plate.
- Move anticlockwise round the table behind the next guest.
- Hold your left hand along with the first guest's soiled plate behind the guest.
- Lean forward to arrange the soiled cutleries in the plate and pick up the second soiled plate and its cutlery by your right hand.

Step 2: Clear the plate from guest table

- Transfer the second plate to your left hand. Position it on a platform above the first plate, supporting it with your ring finger, little finger and the base of your thumb and lower forearm.
- Place the fork alongside the other fork on the first plate and by using the knife push the leftover food down to the second plate on the first plate.
- Place the knife alongside the knife on the first plate.
- Move anticlockwise round the table and collect the remaining soiled plates and cutlery.

Step 3: Clear the side plates from the table

- Stack the plates on the second plate, push the leftover food down to the plates on to the first plate by using knife as before and arrange the cutlery on the first plate.
- Take the cleared plates and cutlery to the side station and place them on a tray in an appropriate manner to take it to the dishwash area or take them directly to the dishwash area.

Standard

- Do not touch the leftover food.
- All these activities should be done behind the guest so that it is invisible for the guest.
- The number of plates to be collected in this manner depends on the skills of the F&B associate.

- Upper deck of the sideboard should not be stacked with cleared plates and cutlery.

Step 4: Clear all bowl's using salver

CORRECT USE OF UNDERLINERS

Underliners (side plates) are used to enhance the presentation of certain dishes and should be used under the following items:

- Cereal bowls.
- Boiled eggs in egg cups.
- Cocktail coupes.
- Dessert bowl.
- Sweet coupes.
- When serving sauces, dressings from sauce boats or ramekins.
- When serving cream with dessert.
- When serving preserves such as jam, marmalade with a teaspoon.

Underliner

11 FOOD AND BEVERAGES SERVICE CYCLE

Food and beverages cycle is a sequence in which the service of food and beverages is to be followed. It helps in the smooth operation of restaurant. Each staff member should be aware of the right food and beverages service cycle.

GREETING THE GUEST

Procedure

- Address the guest by his name, if the guest is a regular one or the name of the guest is known *"Good Morning/Afternoon/ Evening, Mr./Ms.____* (guest name). Welcome back to the __________ . If name of the guest is not known then use *" Good Morning/Afternoon/evening, Sir/Madam. Welcome to the _________.*
- Inquire from the guest if there is a prior reservation made. (for lunch and dinner only) *"Are we holding a reservation for you Sir/Madam?"* For breakfast service request the guest for his room no.*"May I have your room number?"*
- If the guest is holding a reservation, check in the reservation diary, escort to the designated table. Use the standard phraseology *"May I have the name under which the reservation has been made? "Yes Madam/Sir we are holding a table reservation in the name of Ms./Mr. _____, for ____ (number of people). Allow me to escort you to your table".*

Greeting guest

- If a guest is not having a prior reservation, enquire about the number of guests in the party.*"May I know how many people would be joining you for breakfast/ lunch / dinner?"*
- The guests should be asked for their table preference. In case of a regular guest, with a preference for a particular table, offer the same.

- In case the table requested for is not available, request the guest to wait. *"I am sorry Madam/Sir; all the tables are occupied at the moment, would you like to wait at the lobby while we organize a table for you? It would probably take _____ minutes to arrange a table for you."*
- Make a note of the guest details in the reservation diary. The hostess/host should request the guest for her/his contact number. Ensure that time mentioned is as accurate as possible.
- When the table is ready, the associate contacts the guest either personally, or calls the guest on the mobile number. *"Sorry to have kept you waiting Madam/Sir. The table for you is ready. This way please."*

Standards

- Staff closest to the door to meet all guests at the entrance and greet as per the time of the day within 30 seconds of arrival.
- Guests will be asked their room number during breakfast service only, and it should be done in a discreet manner so as not to violate the privacy.
- All regular and long staying guests will be recognized and their preferences automatically accommodated.
- Guest should be seated only at a completely laid out table.

ESCORTING GUEST

Procedure

- The hostess/host should escort the guest to the table.
- If there are many guests at the entrance to be escorted to the tables, the hostess/host should ask the manager/ supervisor to assist the guest to the tables.
- Use the phrases "*This way please*".
- Show an open palm as an open and inviting gesture.
- The escort should walk at a steady pace and two steps ahead of the guest.
- The escort should walk to the right of the guest and in a manner that enables him/her to maintain eye contact.

Escorting guest

- Once reaching the table the escort should inquire from the guest regarding the table satisfaction, "*Madam / Sir would this table be fine?*". The hostess must point to the table with an open palm gesture of the right hand.

Standard

- All guests to be escorted to their table of preference using standard phrase while escorting.
- The hostess should walk in a right posture.
- Guest should be seated only at a completely laid out table.

SEATING THE GUEST

Placing a Chair – Procedure

Placing chair

- The escort should seat the guest by providing assistance with the chair.
- If the guests have infants accompanied with the F&B associate should offer a baby chair.
- Stand straight 9-12" behind the guest's chair.
- Keep the left leg behind and right leg forward, with the knee touching the wooden skirting of the seat in the middle.
- Hold the chair from both the hands from the sides of the back.
- Lift the chair about 1-1.5" from the ground and pull back. Ensure that there is adequate space for the guests to go between the table and chair.
- Always say "*Allow me Sir/Madam* and lift the chair and pull it back.
- When the guest proceeds to sit down, move the chair slowly towards the guest, till he is comfortable. Then rest the chair of the floor.
- The chair must not be dragged.
- The standard sequence is as follows:
  - □ Eldest lady
  - □ Children
  - □ Other ladies
  - □ Hostess
  - □ Eldest gentleman
  - □ Other gentlemen
  - □ Host

Seating the Guest on a Sofa

- If the space is not sufficient for the guests to move in, move the table outside and place it back in position when the guests have sat down.
- If the table is heavy then the waiter must ask for assistance from his colleagues. Under no circumstances should the guests' help be sought.

Don'ts While Seating a Guest

- Rapid movement of chair
- Incorrect handling of chair
- Ordering guests where to sit
- Show irritation due to indecisiveness of guests, as to where to sit.

OPENING NAPKINS

Procedure

- The hostess must confirm if anyone else will be joining the guest and turn down the napkin of the extra covers for the F&B associate to clear.
- Use the phrase "Madam/Sir, would anyone else be joining you?"
- The hostess/host should inform the station holder to remove the extra covers.
- The hostess to brief the guest about the choice of buffet or a la carte that is available. Use the phrase "for your convenience we have an extensive buffet. I will also be pleased to give you an a la carte menu should you wish so."

Placing napkins

- The hostess/associate to unfold the napkins and offer to place it on the lap of the guest.
- Pick up the napkin in your right hand from the right-hand side of the guest.
- Hold the napkin with the help of your thumb and finger.
- Place it across the guest's lap with the longest side of the triangle closet to the guest. Ensure that the arm is away from the guest's face.
- Move anticlockwise around the table opening the napkin, opening the host's last.
- The hostess to inform the F&B associate waiting at the table about the guest's arrival and his/her preference between buffet and a la carte.
- Hostess/host should note down the guest's name and room number (if applicable) on a piece of paper and hand it over to the station waiter.
- F&B associate to ask the guests for their preference of water (in case of lunch/dinner service). For breakfast service, offer the choice of hot beverages.

Standard

- Baby chairs or high cushioned chairs to be offered as required.
- Napkins should be properly starched, neat and clean.
- Once seated, the guests are asked if they are going to be joined by more people if there are empty chairs on the table. If not, then extra covers are removed.
- All guests will be oriented with the food and beverages offerings of the restaurant immediately.
- F&B associate/station waiter will give the menu cards to the guests after checking with the guests choice of buffet/à la carte. An open menu card to be presented open to the selection appropriate for the time of day.
- During breakfast tea/coffee to be served with in 3 minutes of the guest asking for the same.

WATER SERVICE

Procedure

- Ask the guest for choice of bottled water or regular filtered water.
- Use the phrases "Madam/Sir, would you prefer bottled water or regular filter water ".

  If the guest asks for regular water
- If the guest requests for regular filter water, the water jug should be wiped from outside with a wiping cloth before going on the table.
- In case the guest is apprehensive about regular water the F&B associate should assure the guest that regular water is also safe to consume.

Pouring regular water

If the guest requests for bottled water

1. The F&B associate should present the bottle of mineral water to the guest before opening the seal of the bottle. The bottle seal should be broken in front of the guest.
2. The F&B associate should serve the water from the right-hand side of the guest starting from the eldest lady at the table and ending with the host.
3. Water glasses should be filled up to 2 cm from the rim of the glass.
4. The label should face the guest when mineral water is being poured.
5. After serving water from the bottle the F&B associate should place the bottle in the centre of the table.
6. Water to be topped when 1/3rd empty.

7. In case of mineral water F&B associate should check with the host before placing a new bottle on the table.
8. Replenish water regularly.

Standard

- Water to be poured within 3 minutes of the guest order.
- The F&B associate should ensure that the water goblets are refilled whenever the glass is one-third empty. While pouring the F&B associate should ensure that the jug/bottle does not touch the rim of the glass.

Presenting mineral water

Pouring mineral water

Mineral Water		
Name	**Type**	**Country**
Appolinaris	Naturally sparkling	Germany
Contrex	Still	France
Perrier	Naturally sparkling (or in fruit flavours)	France
Royal Farris	Naturally sparkling	Norway
San Pellegrino	Carbonated	Italy
Spa	Still, naturally sparkling (or in fruit flavours)	Belgium
Spa Monopole	Still or sparkling	Belgium
Vichy Celestine	Naturally sparkling	France
Vittel	Naturally sparkling	France
Volvic	Still	France
Ashboure	Still or sparkling	England
Evian	Still	France
Highland Spring	Still or carbonated	Scotland
Himalayan	Still	India

PRESENTING MENU

Procedure

Presenting menu

- The hostess/host after seating the guests comes back to the hostess desk and picks up the menus and approaches back to the table. Menu to be presented within 1 minute of sitting the guest.
- Present the beverage menu to the guest, ladies first. Then present the beverage menu to the gentleman/host at the table. This menu is to be presented irrespective if the guest chooses to have buffet or à la carte.
- The hostess/host should take the order if the guest is ready to order immediately.
- If the guest does not order at the same time the hostess/host should inform the guest that the F&B associate would be at the table shortly to take the order.
- If the guest orders the beverages, the hostess/host/associate should collect back the beverage menus, "May I clear the drinks menu, Madam/Sir?"
- If the guest is not having the buffet, present the lunch/dinner food menu.

Standard

- Menu to be presented within 1 minute of sitting the guest.
- The menus should be clean and stain free.
- The number of food menus should be the same as the number of adult guests.
- There should be at least 1 beverage menu for every 2-3 guests at the table.
- The hostess should hold the menu firm, from the right hand. The thumb should be on the upper side and four fingers should support the base.
- The menus should be offered from the right-hand side of the guests.
- The menu should not be presented to a group/guests with a pre-fixed menu.
- The menu should be handed over in the sequence:
  - □ Eldest lady
  - □ Other ladies
  - □ Hostess
  - □ Eldest gentleman

- □ Other gentleman
- □ Host

- In case the guest is occupieds; the hostess should wait.
- Standard phrase for presenting the menu, "*Menu card for you Madam / Sir*".
- The hostess/host/F&B associate should know the "*not available*" beverages and the other "*off the menu*" cocktails possible.
- F&B associate/station waiter will give the menu cards to the guests after checking with the guests his/her choice for buffet or à la carte. An open menu card to be presented for selecting appropriate items for the time of the day.
- All restaurant associate staff members should be courteous and competent in their knowledge of the food, beverage and cooking times of all items being served.

ORDER TAKING

Procedure

- The station associate should proceed to take the order from the guest table after 5 minutes of giving the menu card or when the guest has left the menu on the table after reading, whichever is earlier. The F&B associate should pick up a KOT pad from the side station and go to the guest table to take the order; the associate should have a working hotel pen.
- The F&B associate should observe the non-verbal signals of the guest's uncertainty or readiness to order. These signs include a confused look, placing the menu aside and looking around the restaurant. At the table, the associate should excuse himself, maintain eye contact and ask if the guest would like to order. "*Excuse me Madam / Sir, may I take your order?*"
- The F&B associate to note down the cover numbers on the KOT as per the order.
- The F&B associate should listen carefully while taking the order.
- Should stand at a distance of two feet from the left-hand side of the host.
- Stand erect, shoulders straight and should have a pleasant expression on the face.
- The F&B associate should write down the specifications the guest gives for the particular item.
- Use the phrase *Madam/Sir, may I repeat your order? You have ordered for _____ (repeat the order). Would that be all?*
- The F&B associate should suggest and up-sell while taking the order.
- When the beverage order is taken, the F&B associate repeats the order.
- Use the phrase "*Madam/Sir, may I repeat your order? You have ordered for _____ (repeat the order). Would that be all?*"
- After the beverage order is placed, the beverage menu should be removed and the food menu should be handed over with the relevant page open
- Use the phrase "*May I clear the drinks menu*"?

- The F&B associate should approach the table to take the food order within 3 minutes of serving the beverage order.
- Use the phrase "*Madam/Sir would you like to have some starters or soup?*"
- "*Madam/Sir, may I repeat your order? You have ordered for ______ (repeat the order). Would that be all?*".
- The F&B associate should repeat the food order in the course-wise and collect the menus back.
- Use the phrase "*May I clear the food menu?*"
- The lunch/dinner order should be taken course-wise as follows:
  - □ Starters
  - □ Soup
  - □ Main course
  - □ Desert
  - □ Coffee
- Intimate the time of service of the guest. "*It would take approximately ..... minutes of time for your .... (State the item/course) to be served.*"

Standard

- All restaurant associates should be courteous and competent in their knowledge of food, beverage and cooking times of all items being served.
- Guests' orders will be taken and served as per the standards.
- Every attempt should be made to accommodate off-menu requests and if not possible an alternative, that is acceptable to the guest, to be offered.

Children's orders

Special attention should be given to children. Parties with children should be taken care of as soon as possible, since it is the nature of children to be restless. Parental consent should be given before offering the following:

- Any "games" or drawing materials which the restaurant might have available.
- A booster chair or high chair (offered to the guests by the hostess when seating the party, although other service associates may be asked to bring the chair to the table).
- A bib for small children.
- Special children's menus (chalkboard, lollipop and so on).
- Advise the parents that a children's menu is available.
- When taking an order from a young child, it is always advisable to repeat the order to the parents for approval.
- The server can offer to serve the children's orders prior to bringing out the other orders.

Suggestive Selling

- Order taking will be done professionally, courteously and warmly. Order taking staff will be knowledgeable and will be able to make recommendations as per guest preferences.
- The F&B associate asks for the guest's preferences for vegetarian or non-vegetarian food.
- The F&B associate asks for the guests' preferences of spicy or non-spicy food.
- Use the phrase "Would you like to order for vegetarian or non-vegetarian food?", "Would you like your food to be spicy or non-spicy?".
- The F&B associate recommends items based on the preferences stated by the guest. *"I would recommend you to try our _____ or _______ (based on guest's preferences for cuisine and spice level)."* Also explain the dish, like the sauce, method of cooking.
- The F&B associate should recommend not more than 2 items to narrow down the guest's opinion. The F&B associate should make the guest feel that the dish is customized to his/her taste.
- The F&B associate recommends a wine to go with the meal. He should attempt to sell a wine bottle if the guests have not placed a beverage order.
- The wine recommended should complement the food.

For order taking/suggestive selling and up-selling a F&B associate should have the following knowledge:

- Complete knowledge of the menu.
- Principles of wine and food pairing.
- Description and brief history of all the items on the menu.
- Knowledge of the wines available.
- Knowledge of the hidden menu.
- Price of various food and beverages items.

Up-Selling

- The F&B associate suggests some alcoholic and non-alcoholic cocktails to the guest and other house specialties if the guest asks for simple aerated drinks or juice.
- Use the phrase *"Sir/Madam, I would recommend you to try our _________ (name of the drink and a brief description)"*.
- The F&B associate suggests wine to accompany the food and provokes impulse buying.
- Use the phrase *"Sir / Madam, I would recommend you to try _____ (name of the wine). It will complement with your meal really well."*
- The F&B associate recommends the house specialties to the guest.

- Use the phrase *"Sir/Madam, I would recommend you try our specialty ________."* The F&B associate should give a brief description about the dish and its spice level. Example *"May I recommend the Lobster _______ instead of the Chicken?*
- The guest should not feel like he is being forced.
- The F&B associate asks the guest for tea/coffee after the dessert course.
- Use the phrase *"Sir/Madam, would you like to have some tea or coffee?"*

REMOVING EXTRA COVERS

Procedure

- Once the hostess informs the associate of the extra cover, the associate proceeds with the same.
- The F&B associate should remove the covers from the table onto the salver and carry to the side station.
- The F&B associate should first flatten the napkin on the plate and then pick-up the plate with the napkin and place onto the salver. Never let the napkin touch the base of the salver.
- Remove the fork and knife. The cutlery should be handled from the neck only.
- Remove the water goblet, holding it from the stem of the glass. The F&B associate should stack these items back in the side station in their respective places and not leave on top of the station.

Removing extra covers

- When the extra covers are removed, the F&B associate should rearrange the table appointments in a manner that the table appears to be balanced well, providing space on the table.

SERVICE OF SOUP

Procedure

- If the guest has ordered for a continental soup, place butter and a bread basket. Bread basket to contain – 3 rolls (2 soft and 1 hard) for one portion. Bread basket to be placed immediately after the guest orders the continental soup.
- If the guest has ordered for a Chinese soup, place chilly, vinegar, soya sauce.
- Chilly vinegar and soya sauce to be served in sauce bowls with an underliner and teaspoon.

- The food pick-up incharge collects the soup from the kitchen counter on a salver and takes it to the side station.
- The section holder collects the soup spoon from the side station, places it on the underliner and proceeds to the table.
- The soup should be placed on the table from the right-hand side of the guest at the centre of the cover and according to the cover numbers ensuring the arrangement is as mentioned on top.
- The soup should be served by gripping the underliner firmly with the right hand.
- The station F&B associate places the soup on the table and announces the name *(name of the soup), Sir/Madam."*
- The F&B associate notices the amount of bread in the breadbasket and replaces the same if necessary.

Standard

- The standard time for service of soup is 8 minutes.
- The soup bowl should be clean and free from spillage on the outer surface.
- The soup should be piping hot with no film formed on the surface.
- The bowl should be placed on an underliner.
- The soup spoon should be clean.

For a continental soup, place butter and a bread basket

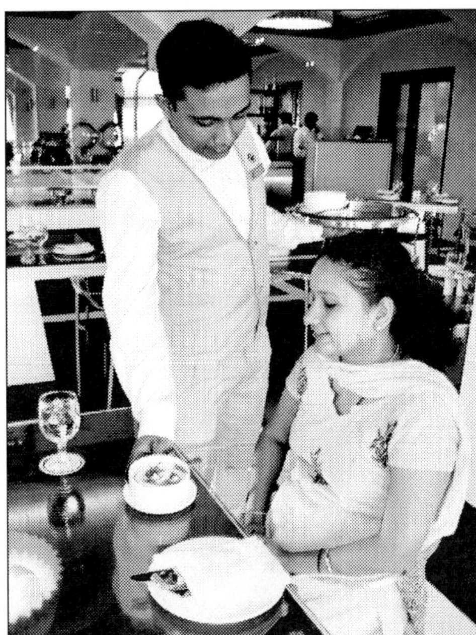

Place soup on the table and announce the name

SERVICE OF STARTER

Procedure

- The food pick-up incharge collects the starter from the kitchen counter on a salver and takes it to the side station.
- The starter plate should be clean and free from any stains on the outer surface. The salad should look fresh and not limp and soggy.
- The section holder collects the service tongs from the side station, places it on the underliner and proceeds to the table with the accompaniments.
- The service tong should be scrupulously clean.
- The station F&B associate places the starter on the table and announces the name.
- The starter should be served by gripping the underliner firmly with the right hand. The salad should be placed on the table from the right-hand side of the guest at the centre of the cover and according to the cover numbers.
- The garnish must be at the 12 o'clock position.
- Announce the name of the salad/starter "____ *(name of the salad), Sir/Madam.*"
- The standard time for service of salad/appetizer is 10 minutes.
- The standard sequence is as follows:
  - □ Eldest lady
  - □ Children
  - □ Other ladies
  - □ Hostess
  - □ Eldest gentleman
  - □ Other gentlemen
  - □ Host
- In case of pre-plated starter, place it from the right-hand side of the guest.
- In case the starter has to be served from platter to plate, serve it from left-hand side.
- Chinese orders to be accompanied with chilly, vinegar, soya sauce.

Standard

- Cold food will be served below 15°C & hot food above 65°C.
- F&B associate should know the appropriate crockery and cutlery for all salads, menu knowledge, proper accompaniments and garnishes.

Note: Use cover numbers to avoid confusion while serving food and beverages to the guest. Cover no. 1 is assigned to the person with his back towards the service entrance, and the numbers progress clockwise. Cover numbers are assigned to vacant chairs as well.

Placement of the starter and accompanying sauces

Service the starter from left-hand side of the guest (platter to plate service)

SERVICE OF MAIN COURSE

Procedure

- Immediately after the order has been taken the food pick-up incharge collects the bread basket/accompaniments from the kitchen counter on a salver.
- The associate should place the bread basket and butter at the centre of the table in case of continental orders. In case of Chinese orders chilly, vinegar and soya sauce to be placed.
- The F&B associate to pick up the food from the kitchen as per the KOT.
- The standard time for service of main course is 20 minutes. The only exception is the well-done steak, which takes 25-30 minutes.
- The F&B associate will not try and find out as to who is having what.

Pre-Plated Service

- All pre-plated main course should be placed on the table from the right-hand side of the guest according to the cover numbers.
- The item should be served by gripping the plate firmly with the right hand.
- Announce the name of the dish "____ *(name of the dish), Sir/Madam.*"
- The main course item should be at 6 o'clock position and the garnish to be at 12 o'clock position.

- Pre-plated food to be placed in the centre of the cover.
- Serve the ladies first followed by the guest and then the host.
- If there are children on the table, the children to be served first.

Platter-to-Plate Service

- Place the large/full plate on the table.
- The food pick-up incharge collects the food from the counter on a salver and places it on the table.
- In the meantime, the station associate picks up the service cutlery and approaches the table.
- The associate to serve the food on to the plate from the left-hand side.
- The station associate should wish the guest and leave the table. *"Enjoy your food"*
- The station associate to check with the guest on the quality of food served.
- If the guest is not happy with a particular food item, apologize and offer to replace the dish with either a fresh portion of the same item or another item from the menu. Use the phrase *"I apologize for the ________, would you like me to replace the dish* or *would you like to choose something else from the menu?"*
- The station associate to keep an eye on the table for replenishment.

Standard

- High levels of hygiene should be maintained in the restaurant at all times. Side-boards to be neat and clean at all times.
- Dirties to be cleared immediately and not allowed to pile on the sideboard.
- The hot food to be served above 65°C and cold food below 15°C.
- Bowls to be given in case of dal preparations.
- For all grilled meats, extra sauce should be provided in the sauce boat.
- The F&B associate/station holder should ascertain the guest's satisfaction within 5 minutes of serving the main course.
- If the dinner plate is marked like a clock, the main dish is served at 6 o' clock position, and the potatoes and vegetable accompaniments are served at 2 o' clock and 10 o'clock positions respectively.

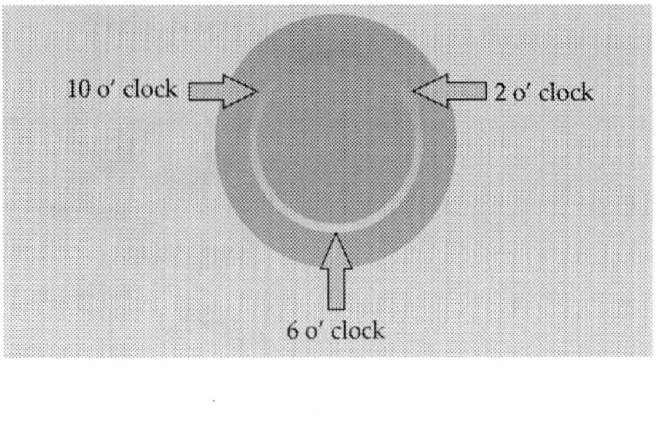

CLEARANCE AFTER MAIN COURSE

Procedure

- Clear the dirty dinner plates from the table and place them on the sideboard.
- With the help of a salver, place the toothpick.
- Clear all the leftover food bowls on to the salver and keep it on the sideboard.
- Clear empty glasses, cruet set, sauce sets and unused cutlery.
- Crumb the table with a crumbing set.

Standard

- To be done when everyone on the table has completed his meal.
- Guest plates to be cleared after all have finished eating and only after checking with the guest.
- Move clockwise when crumbing.

Arrange the cutlery properly in the plate and clear the plate from the table

Arrange the plates in your left hand at the back side of the guest

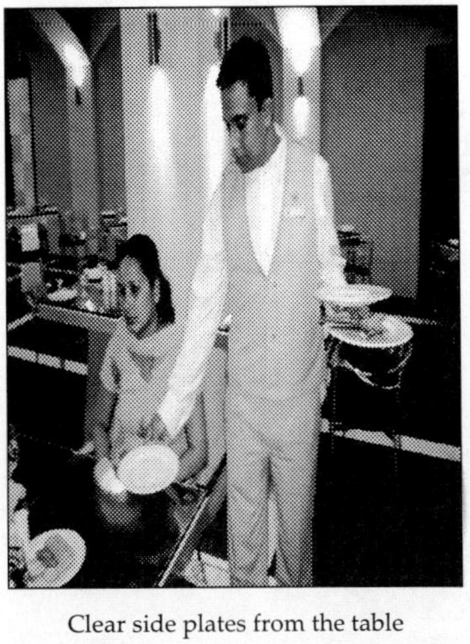

Clear side plates from the table

Clear all the bowls using salvar

Crumb the table using napking

Crumb the table from both sides of the guest

SERVICE OF FINGER BOWL

Procedure

After completion of meal especially after Indian meal it is necessary to provide finger bowl to the guest before serving dessert. Procedures for serving finger bowl are as follows:

- Cut a lemon slice and put it in the soup bowl.
- Pour lukewarm water in the bowl to the half.
- Serve finger bowl to the guest with an under plate from the right-hand side of the guest.

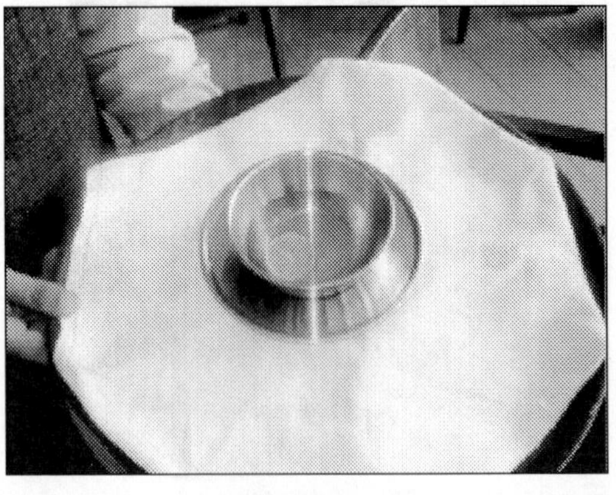

Placing finger bowl

Serving finger bowl

PRESENT DESSERT MENU

Procedure

- All guests will be offered a dessert and coffee menu.
- Positive and knowledgeable descriptions are necessary when answering questions about the various selections.
- Only puddings, sorbets and ice cream type selections do not require a fork, but only a dessert spoon.
- The proper dessert setting is a dessert/appetizer fork to the left and a dessert spoon (not coffee spoon) to the right of the guest.
- This flatware is placed prior to the delivery of the dessert. Serve the dessert.

PRESENTING A BILL

Procedure

- The associate keeps the bill ready when the guest has been served his last course.
- All bills should be presented to the guest within three minutes of being requested in a clean bill folder with a pen. Bill to be cleared within five minutes of collection from the guest table.
- When the guest requests for the bill the associate to place feedback card. Request for guests feedback by saying *"We request you for your valuable feedback on our food and service"*.
- While the guest is filling in the feedback cards, prepare and print the final bill. Tally the contents on the bill along with the manual KOTs before printing the bill.
- The steward presents the bill in a closed leather bill folder.
- Collect the bill folder for settlement.

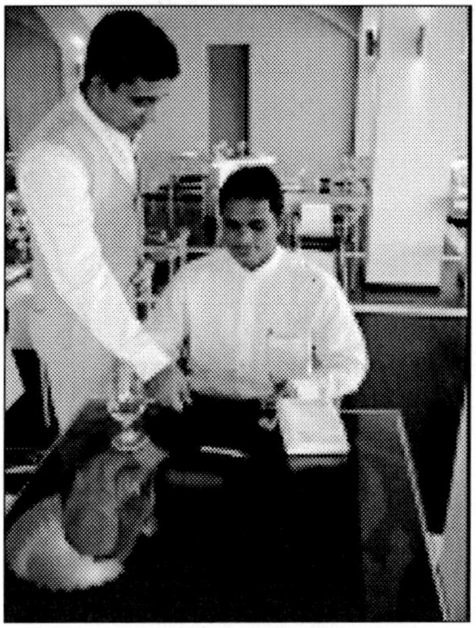

Presenting bill

BID FAREWELL

Procedure

- Assist the guest with the chairs when they get up to leave the restaurant.
- All staff even in passing will engage the guest with a smile, eye contact and acknowledgement.
- If a guest is leaving and station holder is not available then it's the duty of the other staff to bid farewell, using the guest's name, if possible.

- It is important to thank them for choosing our restaurant. It is just as important to bid them a good day as they leave, as it is to greet them when they enter the restaurant, using their name if known.
- Use the phrase "*Thank you for coming. We look forward to seeing you again. Have a pleasant day/Goodnight*".

Thanking a guest

CLEARING AND RESETTING TABLES

Procedure

- Remove all the cutlery, crockery and glassware on a salver.
- Remove all the table mats and the table must be carefully wiped.
- Whether the table is reset or not, ensure that all the chairs are returned to their original positions round the table.
- Do not forget to check the chairs for crumb.
- Workstations are restocked with cleaned, polished equipment immediately after the completion of service in preparation for the next service.

Clear and resetting tables

12 FOOD SERVICE SEQUENCE FOR MEALS

Food service sequence is to initiate and maintain a sense of friendly awareness of the guest's needs for quick and anticipative meal service, with excellent cuisine. It is the specific order in which food and beverages service will be provided to the guest. Each sequence is created to consistently meet the standards and to ensure efficient and effective service or completion of tasks. The only person who can change the service sequence is the guest—not the manager or any employee. Always remember that service sequence is developed to meet the guest's needs and not the employee's needs. All guests should receive the sequence of service/tasks, regardless of:

- What the guest requests.
- The time of day.
- Any staffing, personnel or personal problems.

In this unit you will learn about the service sequence for breakfast and other meals which are generally followed in most of the five-star hotels. This service sequence differs from establishment to establishment.

BREAKFAST SERVICE SEQUENCE

Action of Sequence: Breakfast	
1.	Greet the guest, ascertain table preference.
2.	Offer newspaper.
3.	Escort guest and assist with seating.
4.	Present menu and mark the table.
5.	Greet guest and offer morning beverages.
6.	Make recommendations and explain specials.
7.	Pick-up and serve any necessary beverages.
8.	Remove extra place settings.
9.	Take order.
10.	Open, check and post order to the point of sale.
11.	Print check and hold.
12.	Prepare table for food selection.
13.	Pick-up and serve food and condiments, inquire about further needs.

14.	Detail table.
15.	Quality check by manager.
16.	Review and place check.
17.	Clear and detail table.
18.	Settle check.
19.	Follow-up and continue service.
20.	Assist with leaving.
21.	Bid farewell.

LUNCH / DINNER SERVICE SEQUENCE

Action of Sequence: Lunch/Dinner Service Sequence	
1.	Greet the guest, ascertain table preference.
2.	Escort the guest and assist with seating.
3.	Present menu and mark the table.
4.	Serve bread and butter, remove extra place settings.
5.	Open check and post order to point of sale.
6.	Pick up and serve beverage.
7.	Make recommendations and/or answer questions.
8.	Take food order.
9.	Post order to the point of sale.
10.	Prepare table for food selection.
11.	Pick up and serve food and condiments, inquire about further needs if main course.
12.	Detail table.
13.	Quality check by manager.
14.	Clear and table.
15.	Present dessert tray or menu, take order and offer coffee service.
16.	Post dessert and coffee order to point of sale.
17.	Prepare table for dessert selection.
18.	Pick up and serve coffee and condiments.
19.	Print and review check.
20.	Clear and detail table.
21.	Place check.
22.	Settle check.
23.	Follow-up and continue service.
24.	Assist with leaving.
25.	Bid farewell.

POINTS TO REMEMBER

Breakfast

- The greeter will actively greet guests, smile, make eye contact and speak clearly in a friendly manner.
- Guests will be greeted within 30 seconds of arriving at the restaurant, and may be asked their name preferably during seating unless a reservation is indicated.
- If there is a delay of several minutes, waiting guests will be offered a newspaper and a second dining option suggested (if available in hotel), but in no event will a guest wait more than six minutes.
- In situations where guests must wait for seating, coffee will be offered, or a self-service coffee station will be available.
- Juice and coffee/tea will be offered and served within two minutes of guest seating.
- Coffee service will consist of staff pouring a first cup, then placing a pot on the table for guest's convenience.
- Guest orders will be served exactly as requested, and with no confusion about which items were ordered.
- When presenting the main course, staff will inquire as to further needs before leaving the table.
- Guests will easily get attention within sixty seconds.
- It will be possible to have a complete continental breakfast on the table eight minutes after seating; fifteen minutes for a cooked breakfast.
- Service will always be prompt, including soiled plates cleared within two minutes of all guest's finishing; bills will be automatically presented; payment will be collected within two minutes.
- Service will always be attentive, including condiments preset or provided at time of food service; no water glass empty more than two minutes before offer of refill; silverware always appropriate; table kept neat and tidy.
- Service will be discreet; glasses will be topped up only when less than one-third full; the number of visits to the table will be combined and minimized.
- Service will not be interruptive, including the staff will not interrupt with questions or make excessively long descriptions or conversation.
- The staff will be able to answer basic questions about the property, will take ownership of simple requests, and not simply refer guests elsewhere.
- All staff, even in passing will engage guests with a smile, eye contact and acknowledgement.
- Staff will create a sense of recognition by using the guest's name, if known, in a natural and discreet manner.

- Staff will speak to guests in an attentive, natural and courteous manner, avoiding pretensions.
- Staff will always appear clean, crisp, polished, and well fitted.
- Guests who are alone in our restaurants and bars will receive special attention, and be actively offered reading material.
- Food & beverages staff will be well informed about food and beverages products, and able to discuss them effectively with the guests.

Additional Lunch and Dinner

- If reserved, guest's tables will be ready within four minutes of the appointed time, and set for the correct number of guests.
- Initial drink orders will be served within five minutes of guest seating.
- Daily specials must be available except during buffet presentations.
- If more than two specials are offered they must be printed on the menu. No more than two specials will be verbally described.
- Avoid lengthy descriptions. Verbal specials must be offered at the presentation of menu or when taking drink order.
- It will be possible to complete lunch within fifty minutes (including appetizer, main course and coffee or main course, dessert and coffee). In lounges a two-course meal may be completed within 30 minutes.
- Bills will be automatically presented after guests decline further service.
- Glass wine will be poured at the table after the label is displayed.

BREAKFAST SERVICE SEQUENCE

Greet the Guest

- The greeter will actively greet guests, smile, make eye contact and speak clearly in a friendly manner.
- Guests will be greeted within 30 seconds of arriving at the restaurant, and may be asked their name preferably during seating unless a reservation is indicated.
- When a guest arrives at the door, move towards the guest and out from behind the reservation desk/table to greet him/her.
- Staff will create a sense of recognition by using the guest's name, when known, in a natural and discreet manner.
- Use the guest's name, if known, and welcome him/her. If you do not know the guest's name, it is still important to welcome him/her. DO NOT ask the guests their room number, or if they are staying in the hotel.
- If reserved, guest's tables will be ready within four minutes of the appointed time, and set for the correct number of guests. At breakfast, generally reservations are only taken for parties of six or more.

- If there is a delay of several minutes, waiting guests will be offered a newspaper and a second dining option suggested (if available in hotel), but in no event will a guest wait more than six minutes.
- At breakfast in situations where guests must wait for seating, coffee will be offered, or a self-service coffee station will be available.
- Paperwork regarding the guest's name and/or table number where he/she is seated is completed after the guest(s) has/have been escorted to their table.

Table Preference

- If the guest has a reservation confirm the information in the reservation book by saying; "Mr. Smith, I have a table for four in the non-smoking section." At breakfast, reservations are not accepted unless for a table of 6 or more.
- Confirm the number in the party. If a single guest is dining, do not ask, "*Are you alone?*", or "*Are you by yourself?.*"
- All guests in our restaurants, cafes and lounges are offered a choice of seating preference. Generally, the options will be "*smoking* or *non-smoking*" or "*inside* or on the *terrace*."
- Tables in the smoking section will be set with ashtrays and matchbox.
- If a guest requests a seating preference that is unavailable, let them know the length of the wait. All waitlist guests will have their names listed on the reservation sheet, to ensure sequential accommodation. Also, note where the guest is waiting, so that when the table becomes available the guest can be quickly informed.
- Should a guest request for a no-smoking table and a member of the party begins to smoke, inform the Manager, so he/she can handle the situation.
- Cigar smoking is to be restricted to designated areas within the hotel.

Offer Newspaper

- Newspapers will be available and actively offered.
- At breakfast a selection of newspapers is available for guests, at no charge. The guest may take the newspaper when he/she leaves the restaurant. If the used paper is left and it is in good condition, it should be refolded and reused.
- Newspapers are for the guests only, and not for employees.
- The guest may pick-up the paper himself or herself or the host can carry it for them to the table, and hand it to him/her after he/she is seated.
- Throughout the day, if a guest should requests a newspaper, it should be available, but not offered unless the guest is a single diner.
- If a newspaper is requested and is not available, we should go to the gift shop to purchase one for the guest. Each hotel is to establish guidelines as to whether a guest should be charged for particular newspapers purchased in the gift shop. Such charges may be added to the bill.

Escort Guests and Assist With Seating

- Guests are always escorted only to fully prepared tables.
- Be sure that you know the table where you plan to seat the guest(s), and that it is prepared to accommodate the party, i.e., wheelchairs, special requirements or children.
- When escorting the guest(s) to the table, take the shortest route and walk at a speed that is comfortable for the guest. Seat a guest at a table that is appropriate for them. For example, do not seat a guest who has difficulty walking to a far table.
- Assist the guest(s) with chairs and packages, giving initial attention to ladies and children, but also assisting men when possible, by moving the chair out from the original location.
- Guests with reservations should be seated at tables pre-set for the exact number in the party.

Whenever Possible

- Offer table options to single diners; do not seat two or more single diners next to each other.
- Do not seat a single lady guest next to a group of men.
- Give a lady a seat that allows her to sit with her back to a wall, for comfort and privacy.
- Do not seat any single diner near the exit or kitchen doors.
- Naturally, if all other tables are full, or if the guest requests a particular table in this location, his/her request will be accommodated.
- A guest should have at least one table between himself and another party, until such time that business does not allow for this type of seating. If there are 4 tops available and a party of 2 arrives, try to seat them at the larger table.
- If there is a buffet during the meal period, it is to be mentioned as we take the guest to their table or described by the server when they greet the guest at the table.

Present the Menu

- Generally, menus are presented at the time of seating.
- When possible, menus are presented open, from the right side, with the right hand, moving in a clockwise movement around the table.
- Begin with a lady and continue in a clockwise movement, ending with the host/hostess of the party, when possible. If prefer, you may do all ladies first and then present to the men.
- Menus must always be clean and in perfect condition.

- Do not present menus that are torn, dirty or marked. If there is a mistake on the menu or an item is unavailable, do not mark on the menu with a pen or white-out. Inform the Manager immediately of the unavailable items or mistakes on the menu.
- If a server finds a "bad" menu, do not put it back into circulation, give it to the manager or put it in the designated place.

Mark Table

- Marking the table is the way for the hostess to inform the staff of the number of people planning to sit at the table, regardless if all guests are seated at the same time.
- By moving the napkin from the plate position on to the bread and butter plate, the staff has been informed that this place setting can be removed, as no one will be sitting in this chair or joining the party later.
- If you see this mark, do not ask the guest *"Is someone joining you?"* The mark tells you to clear this extra place setting.
- Should you see the napkin has been left in the plate position, this is a mark that informs you that a person will be joining the party at some point.
- If there are no more than two place settings to remove and if time permits, the hostess should immediately remove extra place settings.
- After marking the table the hostess will leave with an appropriate comment using the guest's name if known; i.e., *"Enjoy your breakfast Mr. Brown"*. Under no circumstances will the hostess tell the guest the name of their server.
- Guests that arrive late for the party will be escorted to the table, and not pointed the way to the table.

Greet the Guest

- Servers and bussers will actively greet guests, smile, make eye contact and speak clearly in a friendly manner.
- The approach should be done within one minute of the guest seating.
- An appropriate salutation for the time of day may be used; *"Good morning, may I start you with some coffee or orange juice? We also have fresh squeezed papaya juice today."* Use the guest's surname when known. Never introduce yourself to the guests.

Offering Beverages

- Juice and coffee will be offered and served within two minutes of guest seating.

Serving Coffee and Tea at Breakfast

- The table should be pre-set with coffee cups and juice glasses. Either a server or a busser may approach the table with a full pot of regular coffee, orange juice, doilies and a filled milk pitcher (if it is not pre-set) on a clean and lined tray.
- Two-fisted pouring is never allowed, regardless of what beverage is being served.
- When serving coffee or any beverage poured tableside, do not approach the table unless you have enough beverages to completely serve or refill the cups for the entire table.
- Milk may either be pre-set or placed in the centre of the table during approach.
- Begin by offering coffee and suggest espresso drinks: "Good morning, may I start you with a cup of coffee, espresso or cappuccino?" If the guest requests another beverage, such as espresso, hot tea or hot chocolate, say "certainly", verbally offering the selection available and offering the choice of condiment, if appropriate.
- Do not stop at that time to get the special selection. Continue the offering of coffee to the remaining guests.
- Beginning with a lady, offer from the right side, with the right hand, the regular selection of coffee. Pour slowly and carefully, filling the cup approximately 4/5 full, leaving room for condiments. Do not splash or spill.
- It is important to note that in every room there are tables that do not permit serving the guest from the right side, with the right hand.
- For safety reasons, when serving a guest who is seated with their back or right shoulder to a wall, in a banquette or near a pillar or piece of furniture, you will need to serve the guest from the left side, or from across the table.
- You can also pick up the guest's empty cup, place it on the table near yourself and fill the cup carefully. You then replace the filled cup to its original place.
- Foremost, we do not disturb a guest or risk injury to the guest or yourself when completing service.
- If the guest refuses coffee, leave the cup and saucer and proceed to the next guest, unless you have enough room on your tray to remove. Do not turn the cup upside down on to the saucer.
- If the guest requests decaffeinated coffee, place a paper doily under the edge of the saucer to indicate (when refilling this cup later) that this is decaffeinated coffee.
- If the guest says he/she will have coffee later, do not turn the cup upside down on the saucer. Remove the cup and saucer if there is room on your tray.
- When all coffees are served at this initial offering, proceed to the pantry to retrieve beverages not served tableside, speciality coffees, tea and/or hot chocolate.
- Serve all the additional beverages at the same time; do not take partial orders to the table.

- At this time pick up all unused cups, saucers and spoons that were not removed previously and place on your beverage tray.
- Coffee service will consist of staff pouring the first cup, and then placing the pot on the table for guest's convenience. If the table has three to four guests and all of them have coffee, you will need to return with a full pot of coffee to place on the table.
- Even though the pot of coffee has been placed on the table, the staff should offer to refill coffee for the guests when the cup is no less than one-third full.
- Replenishing coffee is not automatic, always ask the guests if they would like more coffee poured in their cup. Approach the table with a thermal pot, pour the refill for the guest and place the pot on the table next to the cup and saucer. If everyone at the table is having coffee, place the pot in the centre of table.
- At breakfast a freshly brewed pot of tea is brought to the guest. Tea service should be established and served according to beverage modes of service guidelines.
- Original servings and refills of hot chocolates and all espresso drinks are made fresh, served in a fresh pot or cup and charged accordingly. See beverage modes of service for service and condiments.

Offering Juices

- Orange juice may be brought to the table on a tray with regular coffee during initial offering of beverages.
- The server will verbally offer a selection of fresh juices available, as well as any speciality offered that day.
- Juice is to be offered to all guests regardless if there is a breakfast buffet where juice is provided. This is non-negotiable.
- Other juices such as grapefruit juices and juice of the day may be either attractively displayed or in the side station for efficient service.
- Begin taking the order from a lady, continuing around the table in a clockwise movement.
- At this time the server will explain the menu, simply describe the buffet and offer any special selections, mentioning items that may be unavailable.
- The server will prepare and serve the juices according to the beverage modes of service.

Water Service

- Water service guidelines are established at each hotel based on local circumstances and customs.
- Ice water is water with ice poured from a pitcher.
- Bottled water is served chilled and normally is not served with ice unless the guest requests ice. Bottled water is charged accordingly.

- At breakfast water is served on request. At lunch and dinner bottled water is suggested when taking the pre-meal beverage order. When guest requests water, they will be asked, *"Would you prefer our ice water or bottled water? We have Evian or Perrier."* The bottled water should be mentioned by brand name.
- If one guest asks for ice water at the table, serve ice water to everyone.
- When a water glass is not pre-set, ice water is poured into the glass in the pantry and then served to the guest at the table. Refills are poured at the table.

When Serving the Bottled Water

- The bottle is opened in the service area/bar and not at the table.
- If the individual bottle cannot be emptied completely into the glass, the bottle is placed on the table, with the label facing the guest.
- If a large bottle is poured for many guests at the table, but is not emptied, then place the remaining water on the table or put in an ice bucket near the table.
- If the bottle can be emptied completely, without making it difficult for the guest to drink from a too-full glass, do so, and remove the empty bottle from the table.
- Service will always be attentive. No water glass is to be empty longer than two minutes before offer of refill.
- For safety reasons, we do not pick-up the guest's glass and hold it in the air to refill, regardless if it is bottled or regular water. If we cannot reach a guest's pre-set glass, pick it up and move it to a position closer to you and place it back on the table for filling. The glass remains on the table near the server as the glass is filled. Then you may gently push the glass towards the guest.

Make Recommendations

- At this time the server will explain the menu, simply describe the buffet and offer any special selections, mentioning items that might be unavailable.
- At this time the server will anticipate the guest who is in a hurry by asking, *"Have you made a selection at this time?"* or, *"Do you have any questions about the menu?"*
- Recommendations must be positive. Do not make uncomplimentary remarks about one item to make another item sound more appealing. Descriptions should not be lengthy.
- If the guests ask "What dishes do you like?", do not make comments about personal preferences. Anticipate the guests' needs and refer to their preferences. An example would be; rather than saying *"I love the mango pancakes"*, or *"I don't eat meat, so I've never tasted the sausage"*, say *"The guests that have ordered the pancakes really seemed to enjoy them"*, or *"It is our most popular breakfast meat."*

Prepare and Serve Additional Beverages

- Speciality coffees, tea and hot chocolate should be served within 5 minutes of guest seating. See your beverage modes of service for information on preparing and serving beverages.

- The server will serve the beverage, beginning with a lady, and continue in a clockwise movement around the table. Specialty coffees, tea and hot chocolate should be served within 5 minutes of guest seating.
- All stemware and glassware are to be served from a clean and lined tray.

Remove Extra Place Settings

- If there are no more than two place settings to remove and if time permits, the hostess should immediately remove extra place settings when times permits. This should be done after the menus are presented.
- Place settings should be removed as quickly as possible once the mark has been made. If there is only one unrequired place setting at the table, it can be removed by hand if appropriate. For two or more extra place settings, a clean, lined tray is required.
- Place setting removal must be quiet and unobtrusive. When the removal is complete, the table appointments are adjusted to maximize the space for the guests.
- A demonstration on the correct method of clearing extra place settings will be given.

Take Order

- Determine if the guests are prepared to order by questioning; for example, *"May I answer any questions about our menu?"* or *"May I make a few recommendations for you?"*
- To take an order, position yourself to the right side of the guest, so that the guest can easily see you.
- If there is more than one guest at the table, try to position yourself so that you will require limited movement around the table when taking the order.
- Guest orders will be served exactly as requested, and with no confusion about which items were ordered. Writing the order according to standards will prevent confusion during serving. Begin with a lady, when possible.

The following order taking system is required for all servers: this system is non-negotiable. The chair nearest the entrance is seat number 1. Tables such as banquettes or against the wall may have exceptions. As long as there is a chair in the position nearest the door, it will be seat number 1, regardless of whether:

- there is a lady in the seat
- there is a man in the seat
- there is a child in the seat, or
- the seat is empty! It is still seat number 1.

If you are looking at the front of seat number 1, then moving clockwise, the chair to the right of seat number 1 is seat number 2, continuing around the table. If a chair has been removed, the position at the table retains a number. When taking an order you can begin at any seat number, it does not have to be seat number 1. The order does not have to be sequential, as long as the correct chair number is placed next to the item ordered. If there is only one lady at a table of 4 people, and she is seated in seat number 3, begin taking the order there. Her seat number remains number 3, and does not become seat number 1.

Seat numbers indicate positions at the table only; they do not indicate which order is taken or served first. Every table will also have a number. Accuracy of the seat numbers and table numbers is important, so that an order can be served to the correct person, without asking. Food and beverages abbreviations should be consistent with the printing of menu items on the kitchen printer at the point of sale system. The information can be found on the modes of service sheets. Never place a tray or order pad on a guest table, regardless if the table has guests, or is empty. Be prepared to offer "positive" suggestions. Collect and remove the menu from the guests after taking their order. When taking an order you will take both the first and second course selections from the guest at the same time, before starting to take an order from the next guest. This complete order taking makes the horizontal line on the order pad, separating the courses, very important. At breakfast it is important to ascertain if the guest would like their breakfast served in courses. If the order consists of grapefruit and cereal then ask the guest; *"Would you care for the grapefruit before your cereal or would you like them served together?"* This is non-negotiable. At times a guest may ask to order only the first course, and after eating the first course, they will then order their second course. Service will not be interruptive—staff will not interrupt with questions or make long descriptions or conversation. Food & Beverage guest contact staff will be well informed about food and beverages products, and able to discuss them effectively with guests. Staff will speak to guests in an attentive, natural and courteous manner, avoiding pretensions. Remember that not all guests will recognize or understand the menu. If they ask you a question, ensure your reply does not make them feel stupid or bad.

Pass Food Order to Back Server

This step is used for team service. If the runner position is used in the restaurant, passing the order to the back waiter is unnecessary. The order is to be posted by the front waiter and the runner uses the duplicate ticket from the expeditor printer in the kitchen. The information on the ticket will direct the runner to table number, seat position, females and all food to be delivered. The order dupe is put in a designated place at the line for the back server to pick up, ensuring that it is complete and accurate. Moving the dupe to designated placement, correctly, throughout service, is important. This placement is a mark so everyone knows what the table has or has not been served and what course they are on. At this time the back server begins to plan the management of the table, including the condiments needed, timing and any assistance that may be required for service.

Open, Check and Post Order to Point Of Sale

- When the order is complete, it is posted to the point of sale system immediately.
- Establish who is going to post the order based on the responsibilities in the sequence of service and the layout of the restaurant. At breakfast, since most guests are particular with their orders, the front waiter generally does posting.
- Regardless of who posts the orders, the orders should not be held until there are 2 or 3 orders to post. This delay will prevent timely service of the first orders and create problems for the guest, the kitchen and the servers.
- Posting in the point of sale must be complete and accurate, to prevent the kitchen from incorrectly preparing the order, requiring re-cooking of the selection and a delay in service.
- Guest orders will be served exactly as requested, and with no confusion about which items were ordered. Posting orders into the POS accurately, including seat numbers and location of female communicates to everyone and prevents confusion.
- Guests who are alone will receive special attention, and be actively offered reading material. Special attention consists of placing a rush on the food order so the kitchen will cook a single diners meal quickly.

Print Check and Hold

At breakfast most guests order all the items they will eat or drink when the initial order is taken. Usually, no dessert or additional items are ordered at the breakfast. To save time for the guest and the server, we print the check immediately (when placing the order to the point of sale by the server or the cashier). This is done so that the check can be placed quickly for the guest at the proper time, as per the sequence of service. By printing the check at this time, it will not require the server to print the check at a later time, when he/she may be busy with another guest.

Prepare The Table for The Food Selected

After the order is taken and posted, the table needs to be prepared for the items ordered. To prepare the table means that the server will remove any items/equipment not needed and add any items/equipment required. At breakfast, unnecessary silverware and china may be left on the table in order to expedite service. The priority at breakfast is to serve quickly, ensuring hot food is hot and cold is cold. If the table at breakfast is set for buffet and the guest is having à la carte breakfast, the server may remove unnecessary silverware immediately after taking the order so as not to interrupt the table any additional time. Preparing the table for the food to be brought to the guest must be completed before (not after or at the same time) the food is brought from the kitchen. However, do not set for more than 2 courses at one time.

Example

If a guest orders sliced papaya starter and fried eggs as the main selection, a starter fork and knife are added to the outside of the place setting and the cereal spoon is removed. Guest orders will be served exactly as requested, and with no confusion about which items were ordered. Preparing the table according to the order will prevent confusion and ensure guests are served exactly as requested. When clearing or adding equipment, it is important that a set plate, lined beverage tray or small tray be utilized. Flatware should never be carried in your hands. Most condiments that are needed for the items ordered can be pre-set prior to the delivery of the food, or they can be delivered with the food. They cannot come after the delivery of the food. Examples: catsup for eggs, or cold milk for cold cereal. If, however, the condiment is served hot or warm, it must come with the food item. For example, you cannot pre-set warm maple syrup for pancakes, it must be served with the pancakes.

Pick-up the Food and Condiments

Only when all the food for the course of a table is ready, can you begin the pick-up procedure. Remember no partial orders!! The kitchen has a procedure in place to designate when all items have been prepared.

- The server should ascertain that all dishes are complete with garnish prior to removing them from the line.
- When picking up food in the kitchen, cold items must be picked up before hot items. This is non-negotiable. If toast is served with breakfast, it is essential that the toast is prepared prior to the main items.
- Hand service is to be used whenever possible in cafes and restaurants. If you are unable to pick up and serve all the food at the table at the same time, you must find someone to assist you. Communicate to the person assisting, which plates to pick up, what positions and what table is being served. Carry no more than 3 plates at one time.
- For small side plates and condiments a clean lined tray may be used to serve.
- Make sure you pick up the food so that it can be served from the right side of the guest, with the right hand, in sequential order around the table. (There are exceptions to the rules according to table layout in the dining room.)
- The food is to be picked up backwards in accordance to the seat numbers. If you want to serve the guests in seat numbers 1, 2 and 3, in that order.
- Service will always be attentive, including condiments preset or provided at time of food service; no water glass empty more than two minutes before offer of refill; silverware always appropriate; table kept neat and tidy.

Serve the Food and Condiments

- It will be possible to have a complete continental breakfast on the table eight minutes after seating, fifteen minutes for a cooked breakfast.

- Remember the person who picks up the food, serves the food.
- Orders will be served exactly as requested, and with no confusion about which items were ordered. Order pads and the point of sale provide this information. Accuracy of order taking and communication between servers is essential.
- We never ask a guest, "*Who gets what*?" This is why we use a chair numbering system and an order pad. This is non-negotiable!
- Serve from the right and serve ladies first, continuing in a clockwise movement around the table. Children should be served first, if possible.
- Condiments and side dishes should be served on the left side of the guests above the fork. Do not cross the guest mid-line to place an item on the left, in this case serve on the left side.
- If two servers are utilized to serve at one table, the proper starting point at the table for each server must be established before the food is picked up in the kitchen and brought into the restaurant.
- This decision is important to ensure smooth service for the guest and prevent waiting and crossing each other's pathway. (Example: Server Sue takes seats 2, 3 and 4 and Server Bill takes seats 5, 6 and 1.)
- When serving, announce the dish with a one/two word description: "Banana Pancakes."
- When presenting main course, staff will inquire as to further needs before leaving the table. They may do this by asking a question like, "*May I get you anything else at this time?*" or "*Would you like some more coffee?*" Staff should anticipate the guests' needs by observing the table.

Detail the Table and Anticipate Needs

Service will be discreet; glasses will be topped up only when less than one-third full; the number of visits to the table will be combined and minimized. If a guest is having buffet the server will ascertain the guest's needs by approaching the table immediately after the guest has returned from the buffet to his table. The server will inquire, "*Is there anything else I might bring you at this time?*" Minimal conversation should take place at this step. We never ask the guest, "*Is everything alright?*" or "*Are you enjoying your breakfast?*" We do not want to solicit compliments. The only person who is allowed to ask the guest if they are enjoying their meal is the manager. By being present and establishing eye contact, the server should easily be able to anticipate the guest's needs during service. At all times a staff member should be present on the floor during service. Guests will be able to easily get staff attention within sixty seconds at any given time in the restaurant. Service will always be attentive, including condiments preset or provided at time of food service; no water glass empty more than two minutes before offer of refill; silverware always appropriate; table kept neat and tidy. Detailing the table means that you look at the table carefully and remove any item(s) not needed by the guest.

Example

- empty side plates,
- empty juice glasses, and
- empty water/beverage bottles.

Detailing also means offering items by anticipating guests' needs.

Examples

- checking for coffee levels and offering refills if necessary,
- changing ashtrays,
- a fork that was dropped and needs replacing, or
- additional syrup if the pitcher is empty and the guest is still eating his/her pancakes.

Detailing continues throughout service, each time a server approaches the table.

Quality Check

Manager, to ensure product and service control, completes a quality check at every table. This also creates the sense of presence in the room during times of service. Managers: this is non-negotiable. Checking does not always require a manager and guest to have a conversation, but may be completed by quietly detailing the table or making eye contact. When a manager does elicit conversation, they may ask the question to the guest; *"Are you enjoying your breakfast this morning?"*Guests who are alone in our restaurants and bars will receive special attention, and be actively offered reading material. A manager should make an effort to make conversation with single diners to ensure special attention.

Review and Place Check

Service will always be prompt, including soiled plates cleared in two minutes of all guest's finishing; bills will be automatically presented; payment will be collected within two minutes of guest payment or signature. Guest checks will be reviewed and inspected for accuracy. When we have offered all courses, and have ascertained that no additional items will be ordered, the guest check is placed on the table in a check folder, always with a working, designated pen for the guest's convenience. It is proper to say, *"I'll leave this for your convenience Mr. Stewart."* Do not interrupt a guest's conversation during this step. Staff will create a sense of recognition by using the guest's name, when known, in a natural and discreet manner. Servers are to use the guest's name when presenting a check. The check must be clean, neat and accurate. We never write anything on a check. Check covers must be clean and in excellent condition. The pens we give with the check must be those supplied by the hotel. Guest checks are laid flat on the table near the host. Pens are placed on top of the check presenter at an angle. This is used as a mark to signal when a guest has touched his check without having to ask them.

Never

- ask the guest to settle the check,
- wait at the table to hurry the guest to make payment,
- stand next to the guest while he/she reviews the charges,
- tell the guest you are leaving at this time and you would like to close out, or
- tell the guest that you will be his/her cashier.

Clear Table and Detail

Service will always be prompt, including soiled plated cleared in two minutes of all guests' finishing. For à la carte breakfasts, tables are cleared:

- when all guests have finished their meals,
- if they move the empty plates to the side,
- if they mark their plate with the flatware, or
- if they leave the table permanently.

How to Clear

- Ensure the table is ready to be cleared.
- Know if you can clear the table completely by yourself, or you require assistance, get the assistance before you begin to clear.
- Know where you will begin the clearing process, so that you can begin with a lady (when possible), and move in a clockwise movement around the table, if everyone has completed her/his course at the same time.
- Whenever possible, we will clear plates in our hands and not to a tray. The exception to clearing to a tray is clean or dirty glassware to a beverage tray, and removing small items such as bread and butter plates or salt and pepper from tables to beverage trays.
- When clearing the main selection course, we will first remove the course plates and used flatware left on the plate and try to work clockwise, from the right side of the guest, working with your right hand for removal. The plates are then carried in the left hand. No scraping of plates!! Plates are taken directly to dish breakdown station.
- We return to the table with a beverage tray to remove remaining small items, such as bread and butter plates, remaining flatware, empty glasses and condiments.
- For tables of one or two, if you can easily collect the bread and butter plate (only) with the entrée plate, it is acceptable to do so. However, it is not acceptable for three or more plate settings.
- The last item to be removed and carried from the table, in the right hand, is the bread basket.
- Do not build or un-build at the table in front of a guest.
- Do not cross the guest's middle line.

- Salt and pepper/shakers and mills and the sugar bowl will remain at breakfast, during the clearing process.

Settle Check

Payment will be collected within two minutes of guest payment or signature. It is important to close a check to the point of sell system as quickly as possible so as not to delay charges to a room. Process the credit card, cash or signature, following the guidelines listed in the manual, and as instructed by your manager and accounts department. If appropriate, explain to the guest, which copies, are for him and which copies he will need to sign to verify correct payment. It is the server's responsibility to ensure correct payment from a guest prior to their leaving the restaurant. A server should always monitor payment collection and the check presenter should be removed from the table prior to departure of the guest.

Remember

- All change is returned to the guest in a guest check folder and is never assumed to be a gratuity.
- Add no gratuities, unless instructed by the guest or manager.
- Do not offer to add the gratuity.
- Return the credit card and properly imprinted voucher in a guest check folder and remind the guest not to forget the credit card.
- Ensure a pen is included with the credit card voucher.
- All guests are thanked, using their names, if known, when the settlement is complete.
- If the credit card is denied, do not tell the guest, inform the manager immediately and he/she will discretely handle the situation.

Continue Service

To "continue service" means that throughout the time the guest is in the restaurant or cafe, he/she will continue to receive attention from the service staff. For example, ensure that water glasses and coffee cups are filled, items no longer needed are removed, where necessary stains are covered with a fresh napkin, ashtrays changed, etc. "Continuing service" happens as long as the guest is in the restaurant, regardless:

- of what has been ordered,
- if the check has been settled,
- the time of day,
- if it is the last table of guests,
- if there is side work to complete, or
- if you would like to go home or on break.

Assist with Leaving and Bid Farewell

When your guests are ready to leave it is important for all employees to assist with chairs and packages, regardless if the party is in your station. Help ladies with coats and packages and then assist the men. If a package or umbrella has been stored, retrieve it and assist the guest. It is the responsibility of the other staff to assist the guest with leaving, if necessary.

Bid Farewell

Staff will create a sense of recognition by using the guest's name, when known, in a natural and discreet manner. The hostess should bid the guest farewell using their names. All staff even in passing will engage guests with a smile, eye contact and acknowledgement. Remember, at all times as you walk through the restaurant, reflect a positive attitude. When a guest leaves the restaurant it is important to thank her/his for choosing our restaurant. It is just as important to bid them a good day as they leave, as it is to greet them when they enter the restaurant, using their name if known. If a guest is leaving the table and the server is not available, it is the responsibility of the other staff to bid farewell, using the guest's name, if possible. The host and/or manager will also bid the guest farewell, coming from behind the desk whenever possible.

ADDITIONAL LUNCH & DINNER HOW TO'S

Offering Pre-meal Beverages

The server will verbally offer a selection of wines by the glass, mineral waters or beers that are available, as well as any specialty selections offered that day. Example: "*May I start you with a beverage this evening? We are pouring a Hess Select Chardonnay by the glass, or perhaps a special martini or Coca Cola?*" and wait for the response. Continue to sell bottled water to the entire table: "*Would you care for mineral water with your dinner? We have (brand names) Evian or Perrier?*"

Initial drink orders will be served within five minutes of guest seating.
The bottled water is a suggestive upsell in addition to the pre-beverage they order. The written order will be taken using the system outlined in the manual, under order taking. Also, the designated abbreviations for beverage orders will be used, as listed in the modes of service. This is non-negotiable. Begin taking the order with a lady, continuing around the table in a clockwise movement.

Water Service

At lunch and dinner, bottled water is offered at the time the server ascertains a pre-meal beverage. House water is served upon request. When a guest requests water, they will be asked, "*Would you prefer mineral or our house water? We have Evian or Perrier.*" The bottled water should be mentioned by brand name. If the guest requests house water consider: do you serve house water from a tap? Is the water pre-poured in the back and carried on a tray? Does the back server or busser complete the job? Is it automatically poured at the table by the front server, back server, or busser, in pre-set water glasses?

If you serve bottled house water?

- What is the size of the bottle?
- Is the bottle used only once?
- Is the original bottle refilled from a larger container?
- Is the water taken from a larger container and put into a pitcher or decanter?
- Is the water pre-poured in the back and carried on a tray?
- Does the back server or busser complete the job?
- Is it automatically poured at the table by the front server, back server or busser, in pre-set water glasses?
- Guests are charged accordingly for bottled water.
- The bottle is opened in the service area/bar and not at the table.

When Serving the Bottled Water

If the individual bottle cannot be emptied completely into the glass, the bottle is placed on the table, with the label facing the guest. If a large bottle is poured for many guests at the table, but is not emptied, then offer to place the remaining water on the table or put in an ice bucket near the table. If the bottle can be emptied completely, without making it difficult for the guest to drink from a too-full glass, do so, and remove the empty bottle from the table. Service will always be attentive. No water glass is to be empty longer than two minutes before offer of refill. For safety reasons, we do not pick up the guest's glass and hold it in the air to refill, regardless if it is bottled or regular water. If we cannot reach a guest's pre-set glass, pick it up and move it to a position closer to you and place it back on the table for filling. The glass remains on the table near the server as the glass is filled. Then you may gently push the glass towards the guest.

No paper napkins on linen tablecloths. This in non-negotiable.

MAKE RECOMMENDATIONS

At this time the server will explain the menu, simply describe and offer any special selections, mentioning items that might be unavailable. At this time the server will anticipate the guest who is in a hurry by asking, *"Have you made a selection at this time?"* or, *"Do you have any questions about the menu?"* Daily specials must be available except during buffet presentations. If more than two specials are offered they must be printed on the menu. No more than two specials will be verbally described, avoiding lengthy descriptions. Verbal specials must be offered at the presentation of menu or when taking drink orders. Recommendations must be positive. Do not make uncomplimentary remarks about one item to make another item sound more appealing. If the guests ask *"What is your favourite dish?"*, do not make comments about personal preferences. Anticipate the guests' needs and refer to their preferences. An example would be; rather than saying *"I love the burgers"*, or *"I don't eat meat, so I've never tasted the steak"*; say *"The guests that have ordered the burgers really seemed to enjoy them"*, or *"the NY steak is our most popular item"*.

TAKING A BEVERAGE ORDER

To take an order, position yourself to the right side of the guest, so that the guest can easily see you. If there is more than one guest at the table, try to position yourself so that you will require limited movement around the table when taking the order. Begin with a lady, when possible. Review order taking procedures listed under "food order".

Serving a Beverage Order

Glass wine will be poured at the table after the label is displayed. Refer to modes of service for beverage on how all beverages are served.

PICK-UP AND SERVE BREAD AND BUTTER

Bread and butter are served prior to the order taking of food. The amount of bread served per person is listed in the modes of service, and will be followed. Chilled, non-salted butter is served when the bread is placed on the table. Other spreads or oils may be used instead of butter. A variety of breads are served in a basket, and placed in a convenient location on the table. While the person serving the bread will not announce the types of breads available in the basket, it is necessary that he/she knows all the types of breads available, should a guest have a question about the selections. When replenishing bread, it is best to do so before the basket is empty. When you see that additional bread will be needed, leave the first basket with the last pieces still in the basket on the table. Go to the pantry and get another basket. Bring additional butter (oil) with the second basket, only if needed. Place the butter (oil) from the tray, pick up the first basket and place the new basket. If you notice that the first basket is completely empty, remove the empty basket (and empty butter/(oil) dish) and take it with you when you go to the pantry for the second basket. Then replace the basket on the table with the additional butter (oil).

PREPARE THE TABLE FOR THE FOOD SELECTED

After the order is taken and posted, the table needs to be prepared for the items ordered. To prepare the table means that the server will remove any items/equipment not needed and add any items/equipment required. Preparing the table for the food to be brought to the guest must be completed before (not after or at the same time) the food is brought from the kitchen. However, do not set for more than 2 courses at one time.

Examples

If a guest orders only soup, the original place setting is removed and a soup spoon is placed on the right side. If a guest orders a salad as a starter course, and veal as their main selection, a salad fork and knife must be placed to the outside of the original place setting. If a guest is having only salad as a starter and clam chowder as his main selection, the original place setting flatware is removed, a soup spoon is placed, and to the outside of this new place setting, a salad fork and knife are added.

Present Dessert Menu

All guests will be offered a dessert and coffee menu. Positive and knowledgeable descriptions are necessary when answering questions about the various selections.

Prepare the Table for Dessert

The proper dessert place setting is a dessert/appetizer fork to the left, and a dessert spoon (not coffee spoon) to the right of the guest. This flatware is placed prior to the delivery of the dessert. Now remove that imaginary plate so you can place the real dessert. Only puddings, sorbets and ice cream type selections do not require a fork, but only a dessert spoon.

Presenting Check

Follow the procedures as outlined for breakfast. In addition, it will be possible to complete lunch within fifty minutes (including appetizer, main course and coffee or main course, dessert and coffee). Bills will be automatically presented after guests decline further service.

CLOSING THE MEAL PERIOD

1. The captain/supervisor to check the system for any unsettled bills.
2. The F&B associate should settle all the checks in the system and end the meal period.
3. If there are any unsettled bills ascertain the mode of payment and settle the bill accordingly in the system.
4. Arrange the checks/folio according to the serial numbers to ensure there are no missing folios.
5. Take the sales summary for the day which would give you the breakup of cash/credit/NCK/discounts/room postings and city ledger postings
6. Cash and credit postings are tallied with the cash collection and credit card summary sheet along with the respective tip collection.
7. If actual and the summary don't tally then check the bills for error of amount posting and the mode of payment.
8. After tallying, the bills are to be kept along with the summary sheet. Cash is arranged as per denominations and the same is put in the cash deposit envelope.
9. Do the "day end" on the system and shut the computer off.
10. Get cash receipt for the cash from the cashier and submit the same along with the tallied bills, shift summary sheet and credit card summary sheet to the night auditor.
11. Put the cash envelope with the cash as per the denominations into the drop box at the front office.
12. Fill the sales book details.

13 WRITING A KOT AND BILLING METHODS

KOT (kitchen order ticket) is a written document which is provided to the kitchen before picking up the food from the kitchen whereas BOT (bar order ticket) is given in the bar before collecting any beverages from the bar. It helps in establishing a coordination between the kitchen and F&B department.

KOT serves the following purposes:

- Helps to avoid chaos at the pick-up counter.
- Facilitates proper control system.
- Helps in controlling cost.
- Avoids fraud and wastage.
- Helps in raising the bill for settlement.
- Helps in menu engineering that is by knowing highest selling items and lowest selling items.
- Record guests' choice from the menu.

Writing order in KOT

- Inform the guest order to the kitchen, along with the special requests, if any.
- Serve the right order to the right person.

Normally, KOT is prepared in triplicate:

- Original, for the kitchen to prepare the order.
- Second copy, for the cashier to prepare the bill.
- Last copy, retained at the side station, used at the time of serving the order.

The details recorded on the KOT are the meal time, date, table number, number of guests, waiter's name, time of the order taken and section. In modern restaurant service KOT is used only to take order from the table, which is fed on the MICROS or other installed restaurant software, and a copy of it gets printed to the respective kitchen from where the food is to be picked up.

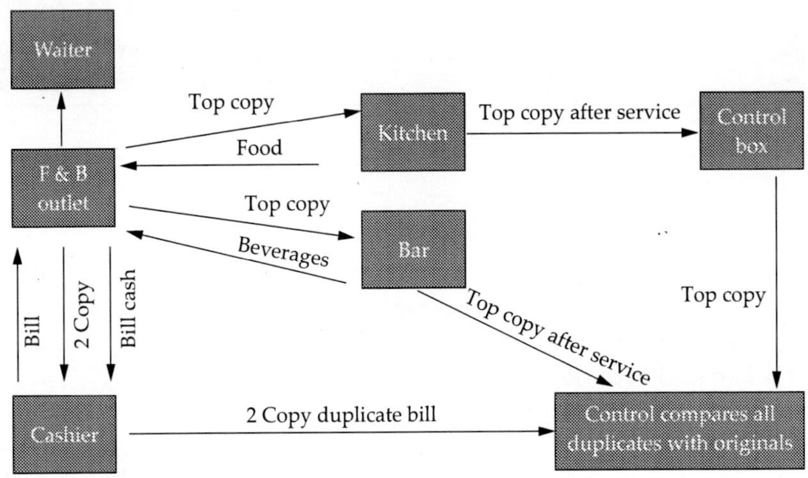

Triplicate KOT system

KOT/BOT

Date__________ Table No.__________ KOT/BOT No.____001

Room No.__________ No. of pax__________ Time__________

S. No.	Items	Quantity
1.		
2.		
3.		
4.		
5.		
6.		
7.		
8.		
9.		

Waiters name__________ Signature__________

Format of KOT

WRITING A KOT

- Items must be noted course-wise, with the first course in the beginning followed by the other courses in a sequential order.
- Each course must be separated by a dotted line or a space.
- Cover numbers must be recorded on the right side of the item.

- First cover is the one closest to the entrance of the restaurant and then continued in the clockwise direction.
- After the order has been taken then the order quantity (e.g., 2 salad) must be recorded on the left side of the item.
- Beverage orders must be recorded in a separate KOT.
- If a new KOT has to be made for the same guests, 'continued' is written on top. All other details are mentioned except for the number of covers.
- As and when the order is served, it must be ticked on the KOT.

Micros-point of sale

Generating KOT

PLACING AN ORDER

- Order is placed in the kitchen by the restaurant staff, which is further called out to each section by an aboyeur.
- Waiter must ensure that he lets the chef know of any special requirement that the guest wants.
- Menu items must be written clearly to eliminate confusion.
- Food that does not meet the order specifications must not be picked up.
- Waiter must ensure that he is clued on to the guests' table, and picks up the order on time.
- The steward must let the chef know 5-7 minutes before the order has to be picked up so that neither the guest is kept waiting, nor is the food left on the pick-up counter for longer than necessary.

BILL GENERATION

Equipment Required

- Integrated computer system with installed restaurant software such as SHAWMAN, MICRO, IDS or so on.

Knowledge Required

- Operating restaurant software
- Discounts prevailing in hotel
- Accuracy in work
- Eye for detail

Procedure

- F&B associate asks the supervisor/cashier for bill.
- The supervisor/cashier prints the bill and checks it for accuracy.
- The supervisor/cashier hands over the bill to the F&B associate for payment.
- The associate hands over the bill to the supervisor/cashier after getting the payment.

Standards

- Ensure that the bill is raised on the correct table number and the guest.
- Ensure that the all chargeable items are posted in the bill.
- Ensure that the quantity of each item charged is accurate.
- Ensure that the bill is generated in triplicate.
- Ensure that the bill is accurately itemized and totalled.
- Ensure that the bill is legible.
- All bills to be machine imprinted.
- Ensure that the time stamp and date is accurately printed on the bill.
- Bill is presented in clean bill folder, with a clean hotel pen in good working condition.
- Ensure that the cash and bill is handed over back to the supervisor/cashier.

PRESENTING A BILL WITH COMMENT CARD

Equipment Required

- Bill folder
- Pen
- Check

Knowledge Required

- Right body language
- Eye for detail
- Discounts prevailing in restaurant
- Standard phrases

Procedure

- The associate keeps the bill ready when the guest is served his last course.
- All bills should be presented to the guest within three minutes of being requested in a clean bill folder with a pen. Bill to be cleared within five minutes of collection from the guest table.
- When the guest requests for the bill the associate to place feedback card. Request for guests feedback by saying *"We request you for your valuable feedback on our food and service."*
- While the guests is filling in the feedback cards, prepare and print the final bill. Tally the contents on the bill along with the manual KOTs before printing the bill.
- The steward presents the bill in a closed leather bill folder.
- Collect the bill folder for settlement.

Presenting bill

Cash Settlements

1. Count the cash at the cashier's desk.
2. Stamp "cash paid" on the bill and signed by the associate.
3. Return the exact balance along with the top copy of the bill.
4. The denominations to be of good quality and should not be worn or torn.
5. Place the cash in the drawer with proper segregation.

Credit Card

1. Check the credit card for expiry date , signature and swipe it on the EDC machine.
2. If accepted, enter the exact amount and press "Enter". Wait for approval.
3. Tear the charge slips and attach the customer copy to the guest bill. The merchant copy to be attached to the second copy of the bill.
4. Place the customer bill copy on the left-hand side of the folder and the merchant copy on the right-hand side.
5. Present the folder to the guest for signature on the merchant copy.
6. Signature to match the signature on card.
7. Once signed, collect the folder and leave behind the customer copy, customer charge slip and credit card.

Bill to Company

1. Obtain the signature of the host and his visiting card. Also ensure that the hotel has received a fax or any written communication from the company on its letterhead about the same.
2. Make sure that the company is on the credit list of hotel.
3. Attach the visiting card to the account copy (second copy).

City Ledger

- This facility to be extended only to those who are regular guests to the hotel and have been authorised by the General Manager, Sales Manager or F&B Manager.
- The guest signs the bill copy.
- The copy to be authorised by the concerned HoD along with the ad hoc credit form.
- To be sent to the accounts.

Room Posting

- When guest signs on his/her room number, verify with the restaurant software to ensure that the right room number has been stated.

Non-Chargeble KOTs

- Extended to executives working in hotel.
- Raise a bill without tax and present it to the executive for signature.
- Settle the bill on the HoD's name.
- Executive to be charged liquor and smokes as per hotel policy.
- The bills to be sent to the F&B Manager for authorization.

Entertainment Slips

- The HoD to fill in the details on the entertainment slip and get it authorised by the General Manager prior to the invitation.
- Bill is not presented to the invited guest. The bill is sent to the concerned HoD.

Staff Discounts

- Discounts to be offered as per hotel's policy, if staff is dining with his family and friends, provided the booking have been authorised by the concerned HoD.
- The bills to be settled against the ticket number.
- Once the bills have been settled, thank the guest.
- Assist the guest with the chairs when they get up to leave the restaurant.
- Thank the guest for coming by using phrases *"Thank you for coming. We look forward to seeing you again. Have a pleasant day/evening/good night."*

Standards

- The software should be updated with orders at all times to ensure that no order is missed.
- The feedback card folder should not be torn or frayed.
- The bill is presented from the right-hand side of the host.
- The bill folder should not be stained or frayed.
- Offer the bill with the hotel pen.
- The steward should not stand there and solicit tips. The steward should not stand while the guest is checking the bill.
- The restaurant feedback card will be presented to the guest using the standard talk lines. The card may be presented with the bill or while the bill is being presented.
- If the credit card is declined, the guest should be intimated discreetly through a credit card decline slip.

14 CLOSING MEAL PERIODS

Knowledge Required

- Restaurant software operations
- EDC machine operations

Procedure

- The captain/supervisor to check the system for any unsettled bills.
- If there are any unsettled bills ascertain the mode of payment and settle the bill accordingly in the system and close the meal period.
- Arrange the checks/folio according to the serial numbers to ensure there are no missing folios.
- Take the sales summary for the day which would give you the break-up of cash/credit/NCK/discounts/room postings and city ledger postings.
- Cash and credit postings are tallied with the cash collection and credit card summary sheet along with the respective tip collection.
- If the actual and the summary don't tally then check the bills for error of amount posting and the mode of payment.
- After tallying, the bills are to be kept along with the summary sheet. Cash is arranged as per denominations and the same is put in the cash deposit envelope.
- Do the "day end" on the system and shut the computer off.
- Get cash receipt for the cash from the cashier and submit the same along with the tallied bills, shift summary sheet and credit card summary sheet to the night auditor.
- Put the cash envelope with the cash as per the denominations into the drop box at the front office.
- Fill the sales book details.

EVENING SHIFT CLOSING

- Close the buffet and set the breakfast buffet.
- Set the tables for breakfast.
- Set the side station.

Coffee Machine Cleaning

1. Remove the perforated tray for washing.
2. Empty the inbuilt plastic drawer.
3. Empty the milk container, wash it and clean with hot water.
4. Refill the milk container with hot water and liquid solution for rinsing.
5. Clean the machine as per the manual.
6. Switch off the machine.

Logbook Updating (Supervisory Function)

- Update the logbook.
- Send the updated logbook to F&B Manager's office.

Bar and Lounge Closing

1. Switch off all electrical equipment.
2. All liquor bottles from the display counter to be placed back in the shelf.
3. All soiled glassware, ashtray and cutlery to be sent for washing.
4. Clean the entire bar equipment.
5. Empty the bottle chiller, clean and dry with wiping cloth.
6. Follow the HACCP guidelines for juices and syrups.
7. Restack the chiller with beer/aerated beverages/soda/juices and wines
8. Wipe the cleaned glassware and stack in respective cupboards
9. Lock all the liquor cupboards and chiller.
10. Clean all bar table tops and bar counter with a wiping cloth and cleaning solution.
11. Check the bar once again before switching off the lights.
12. Deposit the liquor cupboard keys to security.

Back Area Closing

1. Wipe all washed cutlery, crockery and glassware with wiping cloth.
2. Segregate all varieties of crockery, cutlery and glassware and stack it inside the restaurant in allocated cupboards and sideboards.
3. Portion bowls and soup cups to be stacked in the designated back area shelves.
4. Ensure all glass racks and crockery racks are cleaned and dried by kitchen stewarding.
5. Ensure dishwash counter is thoroughly washed and cleaned with warm water and disinfectant.

15 ACCOMPANIMENTS

Accompaniments are offered separately or with the main dish of food. It is provided by the kitchen department. F&B personnel must know the right accompaniments of foods. Accompaniments are served with food for the following purposes.

- To give balance to the food.
- To improve the flavour of the food.
- To give eye appeal to the food.

Accompaniments and cover for some food dishes are given below.

S. No.	Food Items	Cover on the Table	Accompaniments
1.	Tomato juice	• Juice glass. • Teaspoon.	Worcestershire sauce.
2.	Fruit juice	• Juice glass. • Underliner, teaspoon.	Caster sugar.
3.	Grape fruit cocktail	• Underliner, teaspoon.	Caster sugar.
4.	Melon frappe/ Chilled melon	• Small fork.	Caster sugar and ground ginger.
5.	Potted shrimps	• Shrimps placed on a bed of lettuce on a cold fish plate, fish knife and fork.	Cayenne pepper, pepper mill, lemon segments.
6.	Grape fruit Cocktail	• Coupe with a doily on side plate, grape fruit spoon or tea spoon.	Caster sugar in a bowl with doily and side plate.
7.	Oyster	• Served in a pony tumbler placed on a doily on a quarter plate and teaspoon.	Oyster cruet: Cayenne pepper, pepper mill, tobasco sauce, chili vinegar, brown bread and butter, lemon wedges.
8.	Caviar (Roe of Sturgeon fish)	• Caviar knife or fish knife on the right-hand side of the cover. Cold fish plate.	• Segments of lemon. • Hot breakfast toast or blinis with butter. • Finely chopped shallots, parsley. • Sieved hard boiled eggs, (yolks and white separately). • Served in glass bowl placed on a bed of ice in welled dish.

			• Each portion of caviar is around 30 gm
9.	Smoked salmon	• Fish knife and fish fork cold fish plate.	Red pepper, pepper mill, brown bread and butter.
10.	Pate de foie gras	• Small knife and fork. foie gras is served in from the box in which it is available onto a cold fish plate.	Paste or flattened goose liver.
11.	Asparagus	• Asparagus tong on the right of the cover. • Asparagus is served on a dinner plate which is kept tilted to one side with the help of a joint fork placed under the dinner plate either on a asparagus grid or rack serviette.	Hot asparagus served with hollandaise or melted butter. Cold asparagus served with vinaigrette or mayonnaise.
12.	Corn on the cob	• Corn on the cob holder, side plate.	Served with beurre fondue.
13.	Avocado	• Avocado is cut on half is served in an avocado dish. A teaspoon is placed on the table in this arrangement.	Brown bread and butter.
14.	Omelette	• Joint fork and joint knife.	Grilled tomatoes. Hash brown.
15.	Petit Marmite	• Served in a container called petit marmite, which is placed on a doily on a quarter plate. The cutlery is a dessert spoon.	French bread. Grated parmesan cheese and poached beef bone marrow.
16.	French onion soup	• Soup plate with fish plate as underliner. Soup spoon is laid on the right.	Grilled flute, grated parmesan cheese.
17.	Potage St. Germaine	• Green pea soup. • Soup plate with fish plate as underliner. • Soup spoon is laid on the right.	Fried croutons.
18.	Cream of tomato soup	• Soup spoon, soup plate/cup underliner plate with doily.	Fried croutons.
19.	Consommé	• Dessert spoon, consommé cup and saucer.	Depend on ingredients and vegetable.
20.	Minestrone soup	• Soup spoon • Soup plate • Underliner	Grated parmesan cheese grilled flutes.

21.	Bouillabaisse	• Dessert spoon, soup plate, underliner, fish knife and fork.	Thin slices of French bread, dipped in oil and grilled.
22.	Borscht	• Dessert spoon on the right of the cover soup plate with fish plate as the underliner.	Sour cream, Beetroot juice and bouchees filled with duck paste, served in the same order.
23.	Crumb fried fish	• Fish knife and fork, hot fish plate.	Tartar sauce served in a sauceboat on a side plate and doily, lemon slices served along with the fish as garnish.
24.	Roast lamb	• Large knife and fork. • Hot dinner plate.	Mint sauce, roast gravy, barbeque sauce.
25.	Roast mutton	• Large knife and fork hot dinner plate.	Onion sauce if shoulder is served. Red current jelly if saddle is served, roast gravy.
26.	Roast pork	• Large knife and fork. • Hot dinner plate.	Sage and onion stuffing. Apple sauce. Roast gravy.
27.	Roast beef	• Large knife and fork. • Hot dinner plate.	French and English mustard in mustard pots on aside plate with doily. Yorkshire pudding comes with the meat, horse radish sauce and roast gravy are served in a sauceboats.
28.	Pasta	• Joint fork and joint spoon. • Joint fork on right-hand side for the spaghetti pasta and joint spoon is on left-hand side.	Grated parmesan cheese. Oregano (kind of herb). Crushed chilly flakes. Olive oil and peppermill.
29.	Mixed grills and grilled steaks	• Large knife and fork. • Hot dinner plate.	French and English mustard in a mustard pot. Maitre d'hotel butter. Straw potatoes.
30.	Roast chicken	• Large knife and fork. • Hot dinner plate.	Bread sauce in a sauce boat roast gravy in a sauce boat. Parsley and thyme stuffing comes with the meat. Bacon rolls come along with the meat. Game chips. Watercress.
31.	Cheese	• Side plate. • Side knife. • Dessert fork (optional).	Cruet (salt, pepper, mustard) Butter in butter dish celery, radish, and assorted cream crackers, olives.

		• Cheese knife is used only to cut the cheese and place it on the guest's plate.	
32.	Fresh fruit and nuts	• Dessert plate. • Fruit fork and knife interlocked on the fruit plate. • Finger bowl and spare serviette for the guest to rinse his fingers is placed on the right, top of the cover nut cracker and grape scissors. • Spare side plates for peels and shell.	Sugar bowl with caster sugar on a side plate. Salt for nuts.
33.	Savouries	• Half plate (hot). • Side knife and dessert fork.	Cruet set. Cayenne pepper placed on a side plate. Pepper mill. Worcestershire sauce: Shake the bottle and remove the lid, keep it on a side plate on the table.
34.	Sandwitch	• Side plate. • Side knife.	French fries. Tomato ketchup. Mustard sauce.

Did you know?

CAVIAR is a roe (mass of eggs) of sturgeon fish.

The three species of sturgeon fish that supply caviar are the Beluga, Osetra, and the Sevruga. These three give us 90 per cent of the world's production. And only 30 gm of caviar is served.

Types of caviar are :

- Beluga
- Osetra
- Sevruga

Butter:

Butter is a byproduct of milk obtained from churned cream. It is full of fat and gives glaze, flavour, texture and richness to the food. Butter is widely used in many forms.

Butter chip lets / Moulded butter

- Butter block is cut into suitable thickness and then cutting them into different shapes and sizes.
- Butter for portion control and to prevent wastage is served in small chiplets.
- Butter curls are obtained by running a jagged edged curved knife on a hard block of butter.

CONDIMENTS

Condiments are food substances used to heighten the natural flavour of the food, to stimulate the appetite, to aid digestion, or to preserve certain products. The word condiment derives from the Latin word "condire", which means to preserve. Condiments are generally for the whole cuisine and are set on the table whereas accompaniments are for particular food. Many condiments are nowadays available packaged in single-serving packets (sachets), like mustard or ketchup, particularly when supplied with take-out or fast food meals. Condiments are provided by the F&B personnel and it should be placed on the table before the food comes. Condiments are used to harmonize the food. Most of the condiments are of vegetable origin. They are prepared from herbs, spices aromatic vegetables. Condiments vary from one country to another.

S. No.	Name	Description
1.	HP Sauce	Steak sauce from UK. Main ingredients in this sauce are malt vinegar, tomato extract, malt vinegar, sugar, raisins, salt, spices, tamarind and onion extract. This sauce is an excellent accompaniment to all red meats, especially steaks.
2.	Tabasco Sauce	This famous sauce made with vinegar, red pepper, salt and vinegar is made in Avery Islands, USA. This sauce is used to spice up juices, sauces, soups and cocktails. Comes in different flavours such as Green jalapeno peppers. Habanero, Garlic Pepper, Sweet and spicy and many others.
3.	French Mustard	French mustard in sold in the form of a paste. The main production is Dijon. It is prepared with white wine or vinegar. It is used as a condiment with meat and charcuterie.
4.	English Mustard	English mustard is prepared with milk, mustard powder and cream. Goes in breakfast. Preferred with poached fish, charcuterie and meat products.
5.	Cayenne Pepper	Cayenne pepper is prepared by coarsely grinding dry pepper, which is a long thin variety of red pepper grown in south America and France. Preferred with pizzas and pastas.
6.	Grated Parmesan Cheese	A hard cheese from Italy. It has a granular texture and yellow colour. It is offered with pastas and many soups.
7.	Mango Chutney	It is an Indian condiment of worldwide repute. It is made by cooking mangoes with sugar, spices, and vinegar. It is a standard accompaniment to Indian food.

8.	Pickles	An Indian condiment consisting of vegetables or fruits (or both), preserved in spiced vinegar or oil. A standard accompaniment to Indian food.
9.	Tomato Ketchup	A sweet or sour condiment made from tomato puree, vinegar, sugar and spices. It is served with fried fish, burgers, omelettes and pizzas.
10.	Vinegar	Vinegar is an acidic liquid that comes from a variety of sources. Balsamic - a fruity, mild vinegar Cider - made from apples Distilled - made from other vinegars, usually malt Malt - made from barley Wine - made from wine that is allowed to age and sour French vinegar is made by French wine and ageing it in an oak casks.
11.	Soya Sauce	A basic condiment with Chinese and Japanese food. It is called shoyu in Japan and jiangyong in China. The sauce is made from soy beans, wheat, water and salt. Soya sauce comes in light and dark varieties and has the same nutritional value as meat extract. Soya sauce improves with age.
12.	Worcestershire Sauce	This dark sauce imparts a rich, tangy flavour to the dish. It consists of barley malt vinegar, spirit vinegar, molasses, sugar, salt, anchovies, tamarind extract, onions, garlic, spices and other flavourings. Used in Bloody Marry cocktail also.
13.	Maple Syrup	This is classical accompaniment to pancakes and waffles. This thick syrup is obtained from the fruit of the maple tree. At times corn syrup, sugar and water is added to enhance the sweetness.
14.	White Pepper Powder	This is suited for both, the nutritional and digestive qualities.
15.	Orange Marmalade	This is a bitter preserve placed as part of centre table accompariment during breakfast. It is prepared from oranges, sugar, citric acid and pectin is added as the gelling agent. It takes approximately 35 g of fruit & 60 g of sugar to produce 100 g of marmalade.
16.	Jams/Fruit Preserves/ Jellies	Sweet condiments usually made from fruit that are used on toast and other bread items. It is placed as part of centre table accompariment during breakfast.
17.	Honey	It is the sweet product made by bees. Served in small jars for control purpose. Served in preserve tray during breakfast.

18.	Barbecue Sauce	It is a spicy tomato based sauce used for chicken and other meats before grilling.
19.	Teriyaki	Teriyaki is a mixture of soy sauce in sweet rice wine. It is good in many oriental dishes.
20.	Aioli	It is a garlic flavoured mayonnaise.
21.	Capers	
22.	Bearnaise	Another French sauce, Béarnaise is a rich accompaniment to grilled meat and fish.
23.	Salsa	Salsa is a fresh Mexican sauce that is made of fresh chopped tomatoes and other vegetables in an acidic base such as lemon juice or vinegar.
24.	Horseradish	Horseradish is a uniquely flavoured hot herb that is ground into a paste. It is good with roast beef and many other meats.

BREADS

- Breads are made from flour and water dough with yeast that is fermented, kneaded and baked in oven.
- Good bread must have a crispy crust, an attractive golden colour and a soft crumb.
- Bread must be served warm.
- Breads are served in a silver basket lined with a clean white napkin. The breads are offered from left-hand side of the guest so that the bread of the guest's choice can be served on side plate, which is placed on the left-hand side of the guest.
- Bread is always served with butter either in butter dish or butter plate.
- A B&B knife should be used to serve the bread on to the plate.

KINDS OF BREAD USED IN HOTELS

Pita Bread: Flat, oval or round wheat bread made from flour, water, yeast and salt. The "pocket" in some breads is made by resting the flattened pieces of dough under dry conditions so that both sides become slightly drier than the centre. During baking at high temperature, the steam produced inside the dough is trapped by the baked, drier outside layers. The pocket can also be stuffed with various fillings such as chicken, meat, fish, vegetables, eggs and salads. This bread is used as an accompaniment with Hummus, Baba Ganush (made from aubergine).

Gluten-free Bread: Gluten-free bread is usually based on cornflour to which flour from gluten-free grains (such as rice and maize), potato or pulses is added. Gluten-free bread has a denser, more crumbly texture than traditional bread, since the presence of gluten is essential for the typical structure and texture of bread.

Rye Bread: Made from a combination of rye flour and wheat flour. Dark rye bread contains a higher proportion of rye flour and rye meal than light rye and is consequently more dense, heavy and has a stronger flavour. Pumpernickel is a heavy, dark bread made from rye flour, rye meal and kibbled or cracked rye grains.

Bread Brown: In the process of making brown bread, the bran and germ of the wheat flour are not removed and left intact. The bread retains all its essential nutrients, along with the much healthy fibre.

White Bread: The most common variety of bread is white bread. It is made from wheat flour (extraction rate of 77%) and is made in many different sizes, shapes and textures. Ingredients such as other cereal or vegetable flours, seeds, herbs or a mixture of these can be added.

Focaccia Bread: Thick, leavened, aromatic, doughy and flavourful bread from Italy. It comes in various variations.

French Bread: The ultimate dinner-bread, and what a shape; between baguettes and the Eiffel Tower, it's no wonder Paris is thought of as the city of love. Types of breads:

Multigrain bread: Multigrain breads are made of multiple grains. Among the most popular are oats, wheat, flax, barley and buckwheat. Anywhere from 3 to 12 different kinds of grains are typically included in a loaf of multigrain bread.

Ciabatta: Flat and soft bread from Italy is used for preparing sandwitches.

Baquette: Hails from France having crispy crust and crispy texture.

Lavash: Very thin bread used as an accompaniment with soups, dips and main course. Apart from all these there are many other types of breads used in hotels and restaurants.

ACTIVITIES

- List down all the accompaniments/condiments required for serving the following:
  - □ Pasta
  - □ Sandwich
  - □ Indian cuisine
  - □ Chinese cuisine
  - □ Cheese
  - □ Roast chicken
  - □ Roast lamb
  - □ Melon frappe
  - □ Grilled fish
  - □ Juice
- Survey the nearby bakery shops at your place and make a list of all the kinds of breads available and their uses.

16 TABLE MANNERS

HANDLING CUTLERY

- Use cutlery on the outside first and work your way inward with each new course that is served.
- If not sure which cutlery to use, wait to see what is being served.
- Or, watch others at the table and follow their lead.
- Hold your fork in your left hand, tines downward.
- Hold your knife in your right hand low to the plate, an inch or two above. Extend your index finger along the top of the blade.
- Use your fork to spear and lift food to your mouth.
- If knife is not needed, it remains on the table. Hold your fork in your right hand, tines upward.
- Never lick the knife.

Two Cutleries

Using two cutlery as opposed to one is preferred because food is easier to manipulate with two utensils. In formal dining, two utensils are used for the appetizer course, main course, salad course, dessert course, and fruit course.

RESTING CUTLERY

Soiled cutlery is laid on the plate or bowl it is provided with (not on the table). Never rest cutlery half on a plate and half on the table. You can rest your utensils in one of two ways when taking a break from eating:

1. Put your fork and knife in the centre of your plate with the tips facing each other in an inverted V (slightly angled); or
2. Rest your knife on the top right of your plate (diagonally) with the fork nearby (tines up).

These two resting positions, recognized by trained staff, signal that you're not ready to have your plate removed. At most restaurants, used utensils are replaced with clean ones for the next course.

- If, however, a waiter asks you to keep your dirty utensils for the next course, it's okay to ask for clean ones.

Soup Spoons

- **Soup Bowl:** If soup or dessert is served in a deep bowl, cup, or stemmed bowl set on another plate, place your utensil(s) on this underplate when you finish. If the underplate is too small to balance the spoon, the spoon is laid in the bowl.
- **Soup Plate:** If the bowl is what is called a soup plate (shallow and wide), leave the spoon in the bowl.

FINISHED WITH A COURSE

When each course is finished:

1. Place the knife and fork parallel with the handles in the four o'clock position on the right rim of the plate.
2. The tips rest in the well of the plate in the 10 o'clock position.
3. The blade of your knife should face inward.
4. The fork tines may be either up or down.
5. This position signals to the server that you're finished. It also decreases the chance that the utensils could fall to the floor when the plates are cleared.

TEMPORARY PLACEMENT DURING A CONVERSATION

For temporary placement of the fork and knife in conversation:

Continental Style

- The fork is laid on the side of the plate with the tines downward and the handle in the 8 o'clock position.
- The knife handle is laid in the 4 o'clock position.
- If space permits, the tines rest over the blade of the knife.

Resting position

Finished position

American Style

- The knife is kept on the right rim of the plate with the handle in the 4 o'clock position.
- The fork is laid near the knife.
- Fork tines upward.

Temporarily Leaving the Table

When leaving the table temporarily, put the napkin on the chair. If the chair is upholstered, place the napkin soiled side up.

PASSING FOOD

- Traditionally, food is passed to the left—but the point is for the food to be moving in only one direction.

- One diner either holds the dish as the next diner takes some food, or he hands it to the person, who then serves herself.
- Any heavy or awkward dishes are put on the table with each pass.
- Cream pitchers and other dishes with handles should be passed with the handle towards the person receiving them.
- If a platter for sharing is present it is passed around the table, with each diner holding it as the person next to him serves himself, using only the serving utensils provided.

SALT AND PEPPER ETIQUETTE

Be sure to taste the food before putting salt or pepper on it. That way one can be sure it needs the seasoning or not .Always pass salt and pepper together. If a person asks for just one anyway pass both.

BREAD AND BUTTER ETIQUETTE

Bread is most often placed on the table in a basket that everyone shares.

- If the bread is placed in front of you, feel free to pick up the basket and offer it to the person on your left.
- If the loaf is not cut, cut a few pieces, offer them to the person to your right, and then pass the basket to your left.
- Do not touch the loaf with your fingers, instead use the cloth in the bread basket as a buffer to steady the bread as you slice it.
- Place the bread and butter on your butter plate – yours is on your left – then break off a bite sized piece of bread, put a little butter on it, and eat it.

ACTIVITIES

- Practise the above-mentioned table manners at home while having meal.

17 HANDLING EMERGENCY SITUATIONS

Handling emergency situations is a gigantic task. To handle an accident or emergency situation in a hotel, restaurant or a bar you must have precautionary arrangements or some policy. In big hotels many house rules are made to face all kinds of situations. Any situation should be faced by the proper decision, intelligence and according to the house rules. Some important emergency situations which take place in hotels are as follows;

- Fire
- Death
- Accidents
- Drunken guest
- Damage to the hotel property
- Theft

FIRE

It is one of the major threats faced by hotels and restaurants. Many hotels around the world have faced this threat. For such situation hotels form a firefighting team or an emergency/rescue management team to face any emergency situation. Orientation programmes are conducted where the employees are informed about how to face the emergency situation like fire and others. Employees are chosen from every department for these team. During fire all employees assemble at the assembling area located near the Time Office. Any person who notices fire should inform the telephone operator first. The telephone operator has to call the nearest fire brigade station and every station of the hotel. The trained personnel of emergency/rescue management team will start fighting with the fire with fire extinguishers, fire axe and with all other arrangements like water sprinklers at service. Every guest and all staff have to come out through the emergency exit or the normal way if it is safe. Make sure that no one uses the elevator and should use only fire exit staircase as shown in EXIT AREA. The hotel emergency/rescue team should research all the rooms including bathroom to make sure that no guest is left behind. The front office and other management should look after the whole property so that the miscreants could not do any harm.

DEATH

If any death occurs in the hotel premises or in the guest room then the front office department should inform the general manager, chief security officer and the hotel doctor. If necessary the general manager can call the police if the death is accidental. The dead body must be removed through the staff entrance and room should be sealed till the police formalities are done. As per the guest registration card address or information the concerned personnel are to be contracted to hand over the body. It is not necessary to inform other guests in the hotels.

ACCIDENTS

In case of any injury or fracture received by a guest or staff, the house doctor should be called immediately informing him of the nature of accident and the condition of the patient. But until the doctor arrives the first-aid treatment should be given.

DAMAGE BY GUEST

If anything is broken or damaged by a hotel guest then a damage report has to be prepared by the concerned department. As per the damage report the shift duty manager has to determine the amount (more than the cost price) and instruct the front office cashier to charge the amount to guest's account.

DRUNK GUEST

The bar manager has to handle the guest—better not to argue with the guest at all. The guest must be politely taken away from the bar/public area to the office or to his room. If he is quite imbalanced or behaves very badly then the matter should be handled by the security officer. If a guest is drunk and is not able to drive his own car then call his family members and arrange for the drop facility.

THEFT

If any loss and damage slip comes from housekeeping department saying that a certain article is missing from a certain guest's room that means the guest has taken the item from his room without informing anybody then the value of the item has to be charged on concerned guest folio. By doing this you are serving two purposes one is, you are getting the value of the item back and also the guest is being informed of his misdeed. The thing is to be handled by the shift duty manager. But before doing that, you must make sure whether the guest has done it or not. Sometimes it is also found that guest items are being are stolen by the hotel employees. In such cases all the security points have to be informed specially the staff in-coming and out-going area and staff should be checked physically while going out. If it is established after proper investigation that the money has been stolen by the hotel staff then it should be compensated by the hotel for the greater interest of the hotel's future business. But while checking-in the guest should be informed by the receptionist that valuables should be kept in safe deposits box at the cashier counter.

The following precautions can be taken to protect thefts:

- Safe deposit box for guest's valuables.
- Self-locking room doors.
- Keeping an eye on walk-in guests and light baggage guests.
- Do not to let any unrecognized person or the telephone caller know the guest's room number unless he/she tells the guest's name.
- Reception, while giving the room key to the guest, must make sure that he/she is giving the right key to the right person.
- Strictly controlling the grand master key. For the slept out guest, the room should be double locked with security officer. Only after guest's arrival, the room should be opened by the shift duty manager.
- Posting of security personnel at all possible corners and all the floors.
- All the areas should be well lighted.
- Report to security about any suspicious person.

CASE STUDY FROM A HOTEL IN JAPAN

This accident occurred during dishwashing work in a hotel kitchen where a gas water heater was installed. Three workers started dishwashing work at 8:30 a.m. As the amount of dishes was several times more than that on a usual day due to the large banquet held on the previous day, a total of eleven workers including eight supporting workers were carrying out dishwashing work in the kitchen from 1:00 p.m.

The procedures taken in the dishwashing work consisted of:

1. Pre-rinsing the dirty dishes by hand in a water tank.
2. Washing the pre-rinsed dishes in the automatic dishwasher.
3. Draining the washed dishes, and placing them in cupboards.

Starting around 2:00 p.m., however, workers began complaining of such symptoms as headaches and dizziness one after another. As all workers showed the same symptoms by the time they stopped work around 2:30 p.m., two seriously affected workers were taken to the hospital by ambulance and the other nine workers were also taken to the hospital for treatment. All the workers were diagnosed as suffering from carbon monoxide poisoning. Although two systems were installed in the kitchen as ventilation facilities—a suction type hood (two units) for the kitchen and a local ventilator for the gas water heater – neither of these systems was in operation. Only two fans attached to the ceiling above the automatic dishwashing machine were being used at the time. Causes supposed to be the following:

- Carbon monoxide gas generated by incomplete combustion in the gas water heater gradually accumulated.
- Ventilation was insufficient, and the following can be cited as the causes for such insufficient ventilation.
    1. The room was closed to outside air as the windows were shut because of rain, and the two fans that were in operation simply circulated the polluted air.
    2. The local ventilator to discharge gas such as carbon monoxide gas generated by the gas water heater was not in operation.
    3. The exhaust ventilator for the kitchen was not in operation either.
- Work supervision was not conducted. In particular, the workers were odd-jobbers. As a majority of these workers were part-timers, they did not know how to operate the ventilation facilities.

HANDLING DIFFICULT SITUATIONS IN A RESTAURANT

When an unforeseen incident happens it must be coped with promptly and efficiently without causing any more disturbance to guests. Quick action very often soothes the irate customer and a return visit to your establishment is possible.

Listed below are some situations that might happen and the suggested steps that should be taken in order to correct any fault.

Spillage

During Course of Service

1. Check immediately that something has fallen on the guest being served. Apologize to the guest.
2. If something has fallen on the guest's clothing, allow the guest to rub over the dirtied area with a clean damp cloth. This will remove the worst of spillage.

3. If it is necessary for the guest to retire to the cloakroom to remove the spillage then his/her meal should be placed on the hot plate until s/he returns.
4. Depending on the nature of spillage the establishment may offer to have the garment concerned cleaned.
5. If there is spillage on the tablecloth, the waiter should first remove any items or equipment that may be dirtied or in his/her way.
6. S/he should then mop or scrape up the spillage with either a clean damp cloth or knife.
7. A clean rolled serviette should then be brought to the table and rolled completely over the damaged area.
8. Any items or equipment removed should be retuned to its correct position on the tabletop.
9. Any meals taken to the hotplate should be returned and fresh covers put down where necessary.
10. Again apologies should be made to guests for the inconvenience caused.

Spillage by the Guest

1. Ensure none has gone on the guest.
2. If some water has fallen on the guest's clothing, then follow steps 2 & 3 above.
3. If possible, as it usually happens, change the tablecloth. The party of guests should be seated at another table and allowed to continue their meal without delay.
4. If they cannot be moved to another table then they should be seated slightly back from the table so that the waiter can carry out the necessary procedures to rectify the fault speedily and efficiently.
5. The guest meal should be placed on the hot plate/hot case to keep warm.
6. All dirty items should be removed.
7. All cleaning items should be kept on sideboard.
8. The tablecloth should be mopped with a clean absorbent cloth.
9. A clean tablecloth should be placed with new cutlery.
10. Now guest should be reseated and served.

Lost Property

1. A check should be made immediately as to whether or not the guest has left the service area. If s/he is in the area, the wallet must be returned to him/her.
2. If the guest has left the service area, the waiter should hand the wallet to the supervisor or manager in charge.
3. The supervisor should check with the reception and the doorman should see if the guest has left the building.
4. If the guest concerned is in house, then reception must ring his/her room, stating the wallet has been found and can be collected at a convenient time.
5. If the guest is a regular customer, it is possible that the manager may know where to contact him/her to call for the wallet.
6. If the guest is a regular customer and cannot be contacted, the wallet should be kept in the lost & found section.

Alcohol Over Consumption

1. If difficulty is found in handling this type of guest then assistance in removing the person from eating area may come from the staff members or a bell boy.
2. If a guest is suspected of being drunk this must first of all be ascertained by the manager.
3. The guest should then be asked to leave rather than be allowed to become objectionable to other guests later.
4. On finishing, the guest should be watched until s/he has left the premises.

Lost Children

- Take a complete description of the child lost:
  - ☐ Male/female
  - ☐ Age
  - ☐ Where last seen
  - ☐ Clothing
  - ☐ Any predominant feature
  - ☐ Colour of hair
  - ☐ Any accessories, i.e., handbag/doll, etc.
- Immediately inform the supervisor/security.
- Constant watch on entrance and exit.
- Check all cloakrooms/rest areas.
- If nothing results from taking the above action, immediately inform the local police.

Timid Guest

Genuine interest and patient understanding will put this type of guest at ease. Even a comment on the weather can make him feel at home whereas the aggressive guest must be handled in a courteous and business-like manner. Kindness and politeness can often change him into a steady and appreciative customer.

Fussy Guest

This is one of the most difficult guests to please. Try to stay one step ahead of him by learning the things that irritate him. Be sure to have everything just right, before serving the fussy guest. Remember all of the little things the fussy guest especially likes, even when they may seem peculiar to the average person.

Over-Familiar Guest

Be courteous, dignified, and avoid long conversations. Stay away from the table, except when actual service is needed. Never try to give a wise crack answer to a smart remark. You will only cheapen yourself and lower yourself to the same level as the rudeness of the guest.

Guest Who is Alone

Don't call attention by asking if he is alone. Seat him where he can see what is going on. The guest may be lonely and want someone to talk to. Be friendly, but don't neglect other guests. With nobody to talk to, time seems long, so serve as quickly as possible. This could be your most critical guest.

Noisy Trouble-Maker Guest

Don't be drawn into arguments. Speak softly. Don't antagonize. Refuse to participate in criticism of management, the establishment, or other personnel.

Blind Guest

Seat blind people with a dog so that the dog will not be noticed. Never hover over blind customers. Always stand near enough to help if needed. Issue menus in Braille to the blind guest. Always appreciate and make a blind customer feel important.

Handling a Challenging Guest Request

We will attempt to accommodate any reasonable request that a guest makes. Remember to answer always with a yes. No matter what a guest or colleague asks of you, or whether you can meet the demand or not, acknowledge the request and provide a positive attitude. When a guest asks for something you do not have or is difficult to provide, follow these basic steps:

- Listen carefully to what the guest is saying.
- Begin with a positive attitude, empathize.
- Ask questions when appropriate.

- Offer options.
- Let guest select himself.
- Involve your manager.

Below are examples of the steps listed above:

- A guest requests salmon, which is not on the menu:

  "I apologize, unfortunately we do not have salmon today. What we do have is halibut or trout which our chef will be pleased to prepare for you."

- A guest complains to you that he has waited too long for his dinner:

  "I apologize. I can see you are upset with the length of time you have waited for your dinner. It will be approximately three minutes more. May I bring you something else immediately or would you mind waiting a moment?"

- A guest orders an item that you have not been informed that the restaurant does not temporarily have:

  "My apologies. Unfortunately we are temporarily out of the wine you requested. May I recommend some other excellent choices that would go with your meal, the ..... and the ......are very similar. May I bring you a bottle of either one?" Ensure the options you provide are comparable in price. Remember to involve your manager about a complaint you have received within three minutes.

In the event of a specific complaint, the employee receiving it will listen carefully, sympathetically, apologize and advise the guest what actions will be taken, and when. If a problem involves a response by other employees, all details will be carefully relayed, so that it is never necessary for the guest to repeat himself. Managers are involved in each complaint to ensure satisfaction. If guests experience food quality problem, the offending dish will be immediately substituted, and there will be no cost for the new item. During pre-meal briefing, all staff members should be well informed of menu items temporarily unavailable and any substitute available to offer guests. If you are uncertain about a food item, always ask the chef. You should explain to the guest, "**Please let me check with our chef to see if salmon is available.**" When checking with the chef about the availability of a food item, inquire about alternatives and preparation time. Clear communication with the chef is important to meet the guest's needs.

FOOD ALLERGIES

If the guest has a food allergy or a dietary need, ask questions to ensure you understand the request such as, *"Mr. Smith, you are allergic to walnuts. Are you allergic to any other kind of nuts?"* Asking questions will clarify for you what the guest can and cannot eat. With any allergy or dietary need you must explain to the chef personally the request. Inform your manager of the special request. Food and beverages staff should be know all items on the menu and be prepared to handle any dietary request. If you are uncertain, explain to the guest you will check with the chef and return with the answer by saying, *"Mr. Smith, I am not certain whether the sauce for the salmon has butter. Please let me check with the chef and I will return with the answer for you."*

INTERACTING WITH A GUEST

When interacting with a guest, appropriate and professional communication skills should be used. All employees should be aware of that their body language, tone of voice and the words they use when communicating. Words that are service positive and make a guest feel comfortable include:

- Please
- Thank You
- Excuse Me
- May I help you?
- Yes Sir/Madam, and
- Certainly.

Avoid the use of slang expressions, specifically those associated with eating in a restaurant. An example of restaurant slang is, *"That item is 86'd" or "Would you like decaf?"* Instead say, *"Unfortunately we are out of the glazed salmon,"* and *"Would you prefer decaffeinated coffee?"*

It is inappropriate to express to guests any negative opinions you may have about the food, hotel or other guests. You should always speak with a positive attitude when sharing information with the guests. An example is if a guest asks you about a menu item, a positive answer would be, *"All the items on the menu are delicious. May I recommend some of our most popular items."* Avoid making comments such as, *"Many guests complain about the glazed salmon."* Every effort is made to learn and use the guest surname. It is appropriate to use the guest's name 3 times when they are dining in a restaurant; upon greeting, presenting the guest check and bidding the guest farewell. This also applies to a server in room service delivering food. When on the telephone, the guest's name should be used minimum 2 times. There are words or phrases we avoid using to prevent a guest from becoming angry or upset with service. Choose other words that are appropriate.*"No"* – There are times we are unable to meet a guest's request, however we should not use the word 'no." Instead you may say, *"I apologize Mr. Smith, unfortunately salmon is unavailable. What I can offer you is either halibut or swordfish."* The phrase *"I don't know"* will make you appear that you are not knowledgeable. A better phrase to say is, *"I will find out for you."* Ensure that the information you give the guest is accurate.*"That is not my job,"* or *"This is not my table."* – When a guest asks a simple a request, you are to take ownership and not refer the guest elsewhere. You should say, *"Let me check for you and I will come back with the answer."* If you know you can meet the request say, *"It will be my pleasure to do that for you." "We do not do that."* – Guest will request something that we cannot do, however select the words and phrases that are appropriate to the situation. A positive phrase is, *"I apologize Mr. Smith. I would like to be able to give you what you have requested however we are unable to do so. Would you be interested in ......"* When possible provide two options to give the guest a choice. When interacting with a guest, always give them your full attention. Establish good eye contact and listen carefully. Paraphrasing and asking questions will demonstrate to the guest that you care and understand what they are saying.

Do not say, "yes" if you do not understand the guest. This will cause further embarrassment for you and frustrate the guest who may have to explain or repeat a request to another employee. If you do not understand, it is better to say, *"I apologize, I do not understand. Let me get my manager."* When a guest asks for directions, do not point the way with your finger. When you gesture a direction, use an underhand motion pointing with hand. If time permits, walk with the guest in the direction he/she has asked. Avoid giving an excuse to the guest, even if it is true. An example would be if the restaurant is busy and a cook has called off sick you are not allowed to say, *"Mr. Smith, I apologize for the delay of your breakfast. It is very busy today and a cook is sick."* The guest will not care about what is causing the delay. What they want is his breakfast. It is more appropriate to say, *"I apologize for the delay of your breakfast Mr. Smith. I will have it served to you in a few moments."*

PROPER BEHAVIOUR FOR ALL STAFF

While working, interacting with guests, or even when you are in the kitchen, smile, make eye contact and speak friendly. Treat internal and external guests the same way you would want to be treated. We do not touch guests unless administering CPR (respiratory first aid). Even if the guest appears familiar and you want to handshake or hug them, the only time you may do this is when the guest initiates the movement. Body language makes the first impression when a guest sees you. Avoid poor body language such as leaning on walls or furniture, hands in your pocket, touching your face or hair and not yielding the right of way when you cross paths. The guest may perceive you as lazy, rude and not caring.

ACTIVITIES

It is a Saturday night and there is crowd in the bar situated in the fivestar hotel of your city. Lights, music and alcohol is making the crowd out of control. Bar is full and now no more spaces are available to give entry to further guests. Suddenly three friends fully drunk come in the bar and try to enter the bar without any pass. Bouncer at the entrance stops them and asks them politely to leave as there is no more spaces available inside but they started shouting and screaming over the bouncers asking them to allow them inside the bar. You, as a bar manager heard the discussion between the bouncer and the guests and approach the guests to make them calm. Bouncers, in the meantime call the security to handle the situation. You, while asking the guest and trying to make them understand that no spaces are available inside the bar observed that one of the guests is carrying a gun with him. As a manager, how will you handle the situation?

18 NAPKIN FOLDING TECHNIQUES

A napkin is a small piece of table linen that is used to wipe the mouth and to cover the lap in order to protect clothing. Napkins are used for various functions in banquets and restaurants in the form of napkin folds as it adds decor to the table. Cloth napkins are used to make various napkin folds that have a flowing design. Crisp, freshly laundered napkin folds are an essential feature of every well set table. The fanciest napkins are those made from damask cloth.

Napkin Size

- Lunch napkin: 18 square inch.
- Dinner Napkin: 20 square inch.
- Tea Napkin: 12 square inch.
- Cocktail Napkin: 9 square inch.
- Paper Napkin: 14-17 square inch.

Did You Know?

Damask takes its name from the city of Damascus, Syria, used to refer to a method of weaving cloth in which threads of one type of fabric would be woven with threads of another like silk with flax. This is still done, though the term damask nowadays also applies to textiles with just the look of this type of weave. This is something that can now be achieved using a single type of thread such as cotton or linen.

Simple napkin folds are used in the lunch whereas elegant napkin folds are generally used in the dinner service. Some commonly used napkin folds are as follows:

PURE AND SIMPLE

Step 1: Fold the napkin diagonally to form a triangular shape and then fold the bottom corner up to meet the top.

Step 2: Fold the bottom left and bottom right corners up to the top corner.	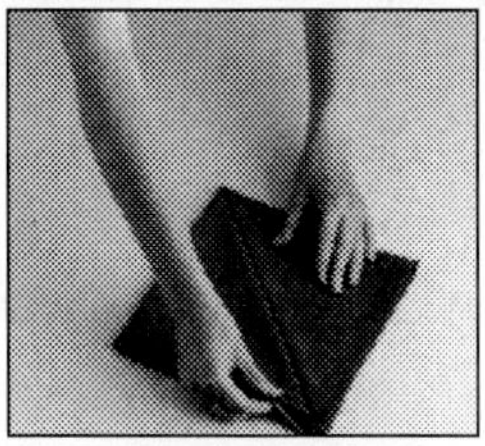
Step 3: Turn the napkin over horizontally, from left to right and fold the bottom of the napkin up about 2 inches.	
Step 4: Carefully tuck both the sides under the napkin.	
Step 5: A beautiful napkin fold is ready for lunch service.	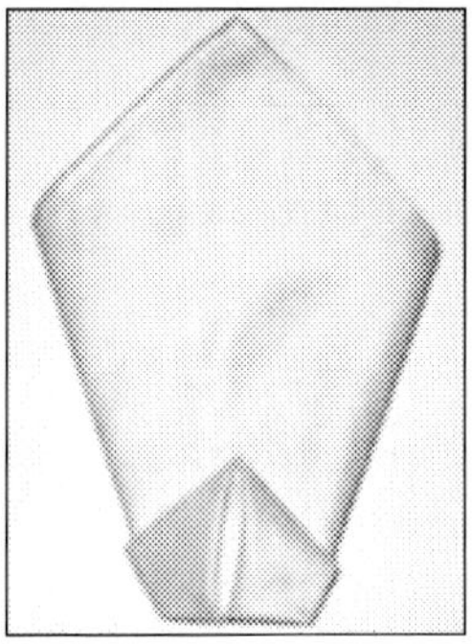

CANDLE FOLD

Step 1: Fold the napkin diagonally to form a triangle shape and fold up base 1/3rd.	

Step 2: Turn napkin over and roll from bottom to top.	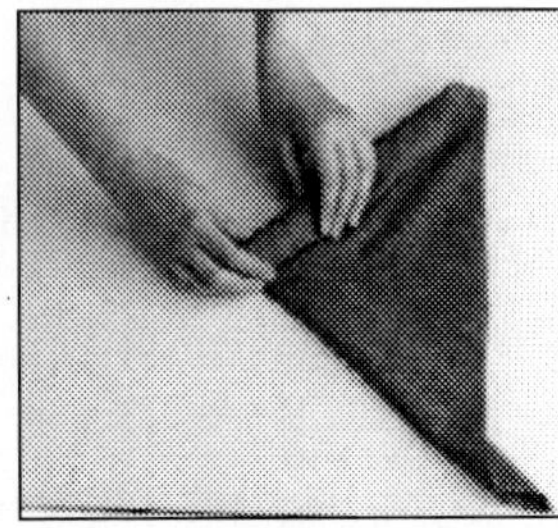
Step 3: Tuck corners inside cuff at base of fold.	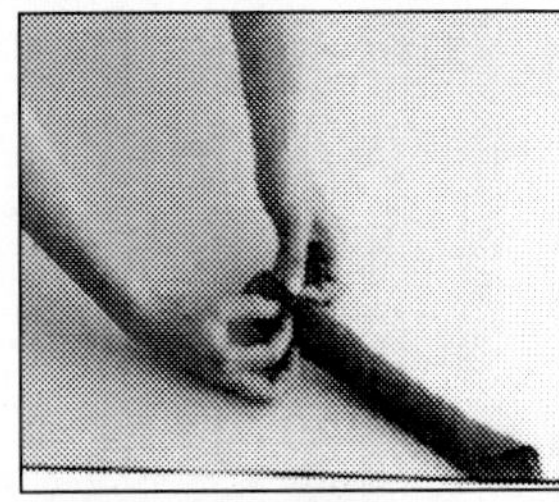
Step 4: One layer of point down and set on base.	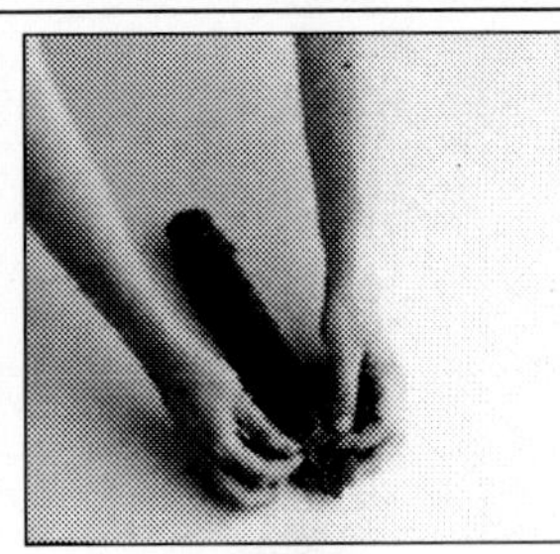
Step 5: Candle fold is completed.	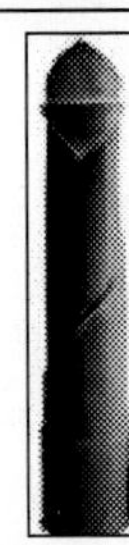

PYRAMID

Step 1: Fold napkin half diagonally.	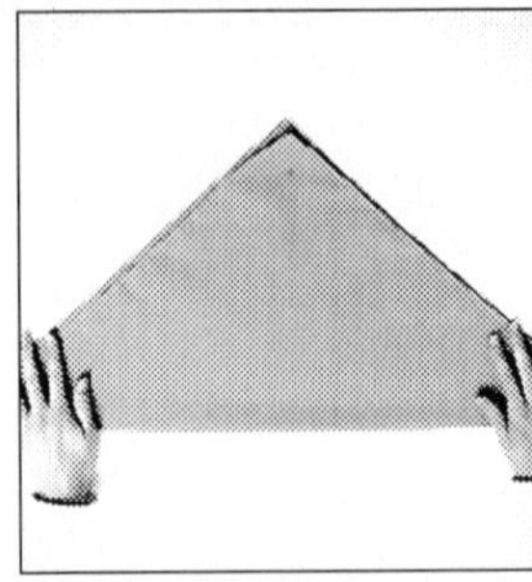

Step 2: Fold corners to meet the top point.	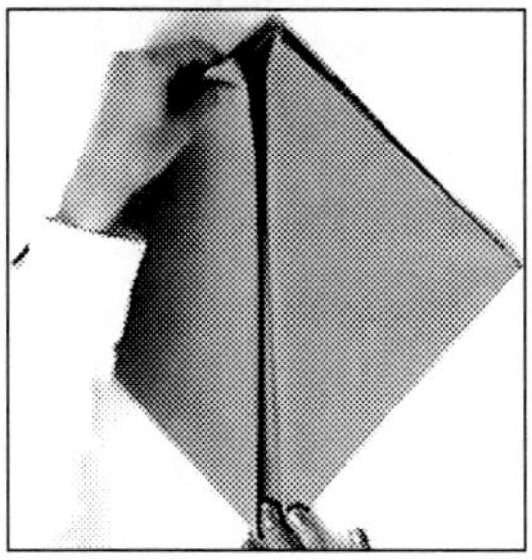
Step 3: Turn napkin over and fold in half.	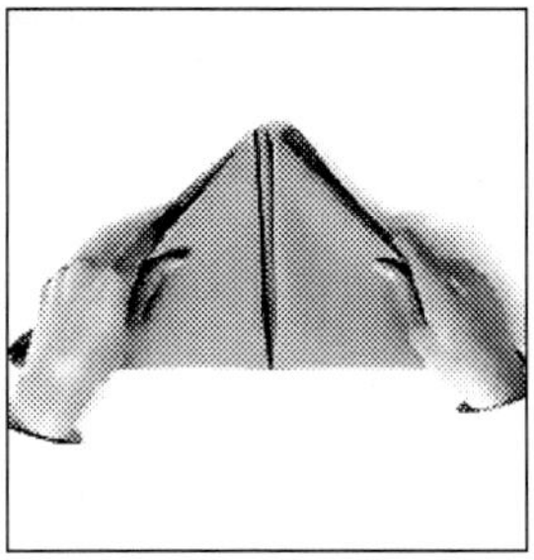
Step 4: Pick up at centre and stand on base of triangle.	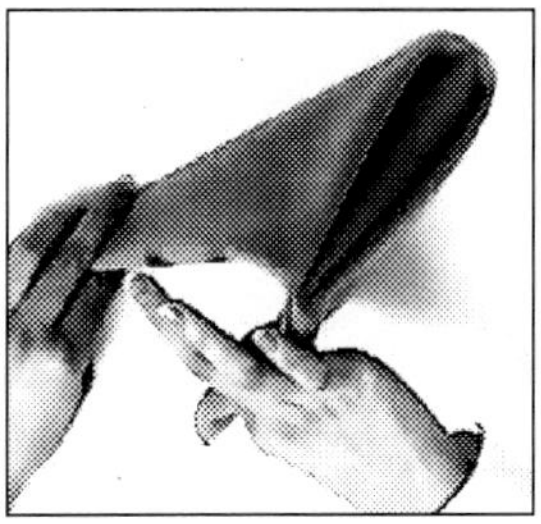
Step 5: Completed pyramid.	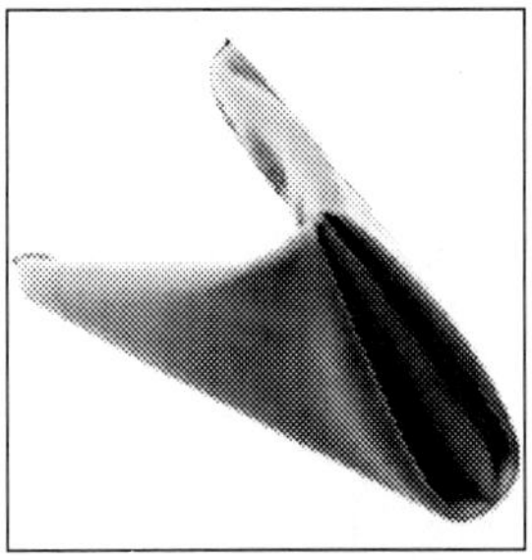

LEAF

Step 1: Fold the napkins diagonally to form triangle.	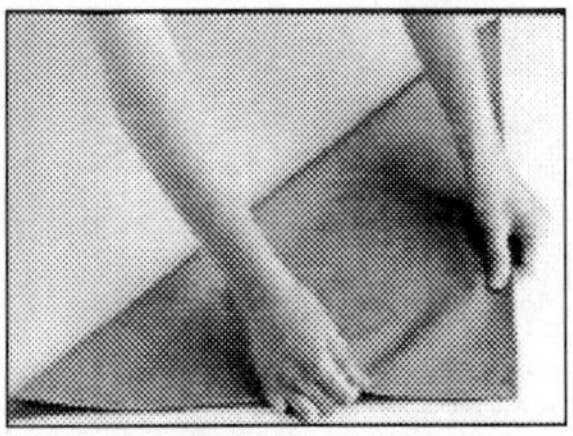

Step 2: Make accordion pleats from the bottom to top.

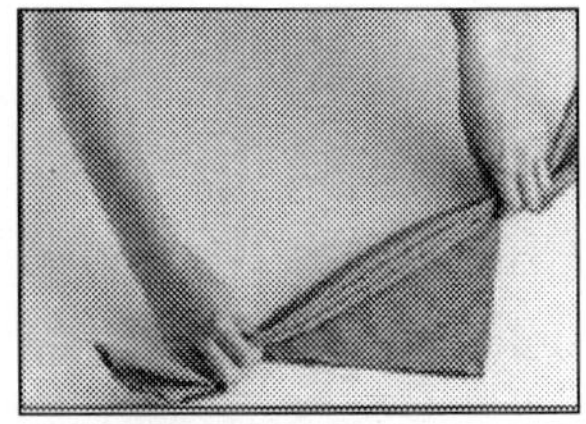

Step 3: Fold the pleated napkin in half from left to right.

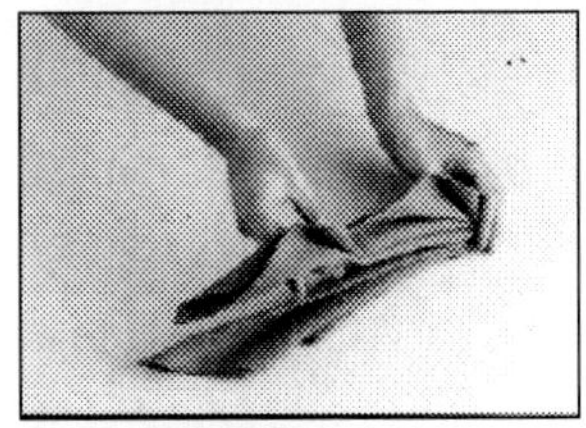

Step 4: Pinch at the fold to hold the shape. Leaf fold is ready to lay on the plate.

STANDING FAN

Step 1: Place the napkin flat on the table.

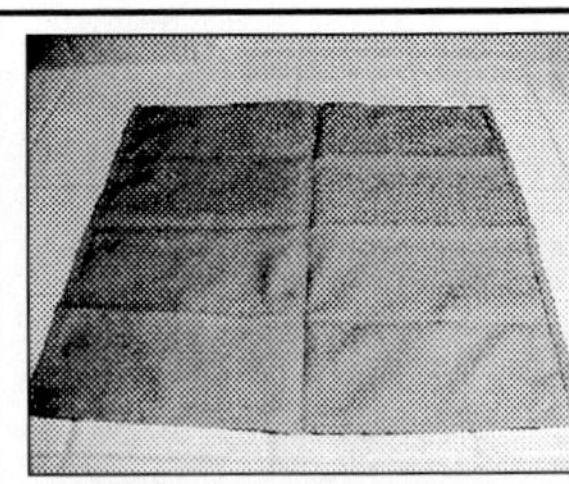

Step 2: Fold the left half over to form a rectangle.

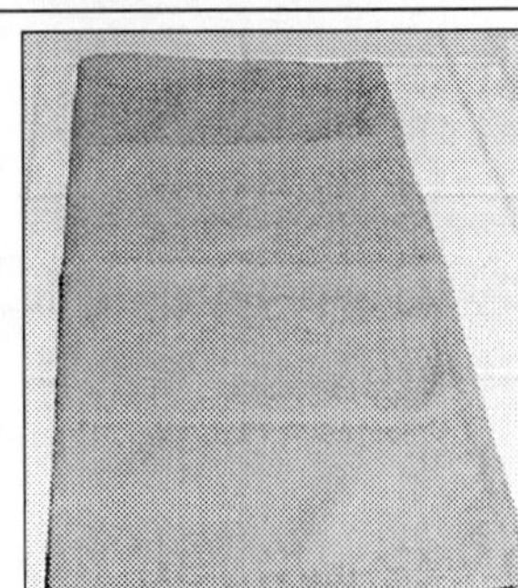

Step 3: Starting at the edge nearest to you start making accordion pleats till two-thirds of the rectangle. Make each pleat about 3/4″-1″ and also press each pleat.	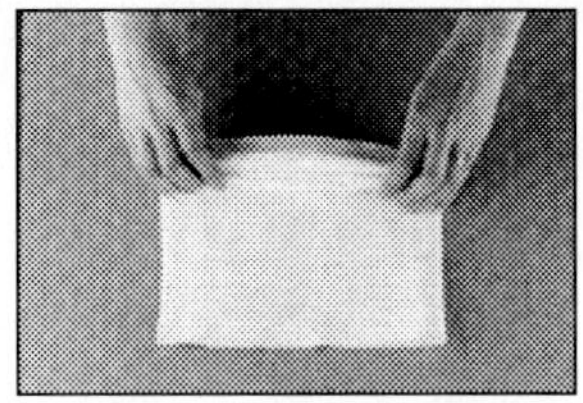
Step 4: Fold the napkin in half with the accordion folds outside.	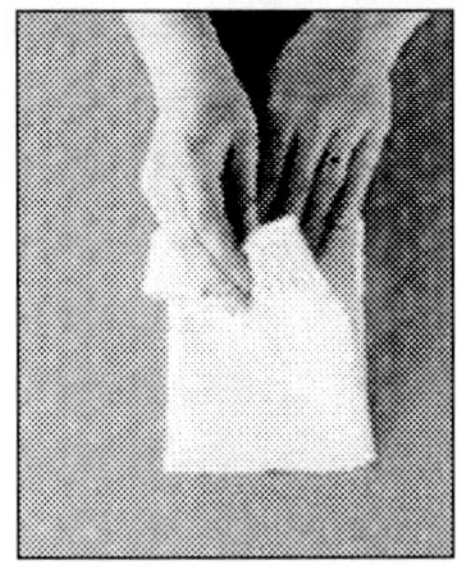
Step 5: Grasp the unfolded corners where they meet on the open end and fold them in diagonally, tucking them under the accordion folds.	
Step 6: Let go of the pleats and let the fan out.	

CABLE BUFFET

Step 1: Fold the napkin in half so that the bottom edge meets the top edge and then fold the top layer down to meet the bottom edge.	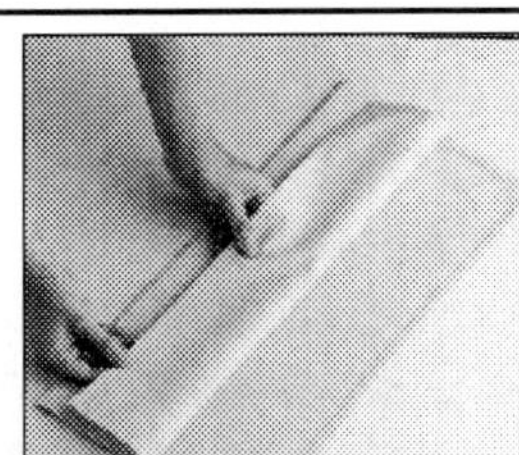

Step 2: Fold all the bottom layers back up a little way and turn over the napkin.	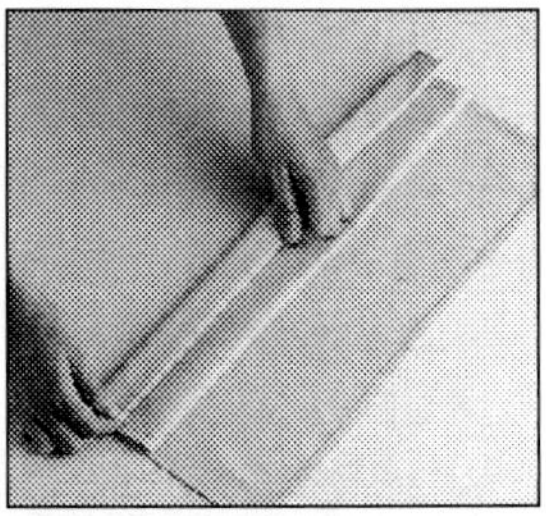
Step 3: Fold the right side to the centre.	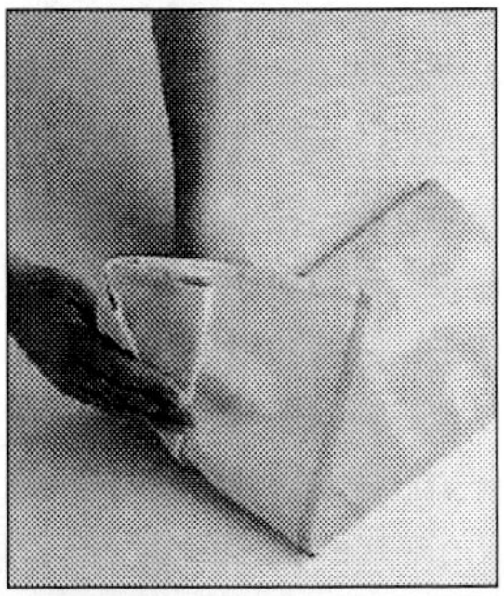
Step 4: Also fold the left side to the centre.	
Step 5: Tucking one half into the other half.	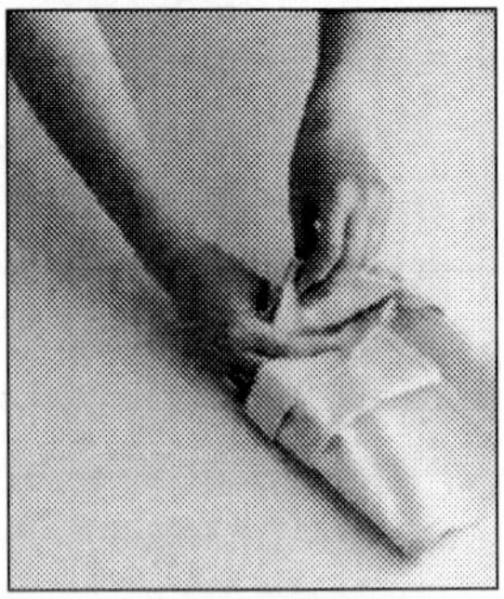
Step 6: Beautiful table fold is ready for IRD and buffet.	

BISHOP CAP

Step 1: Fold napkin in half.	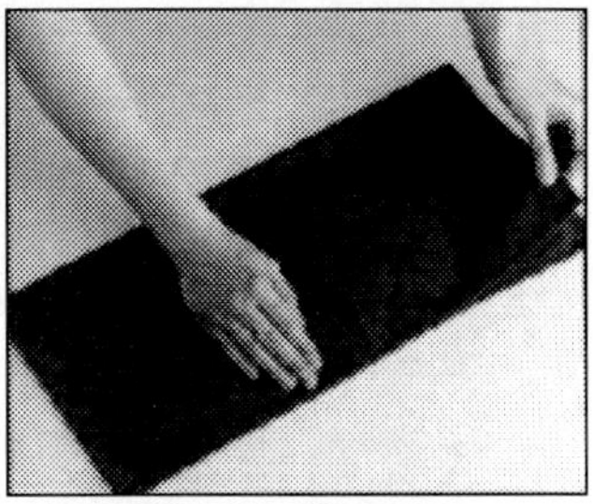
Step 2: Fold napkin in half and fold right corner to top.	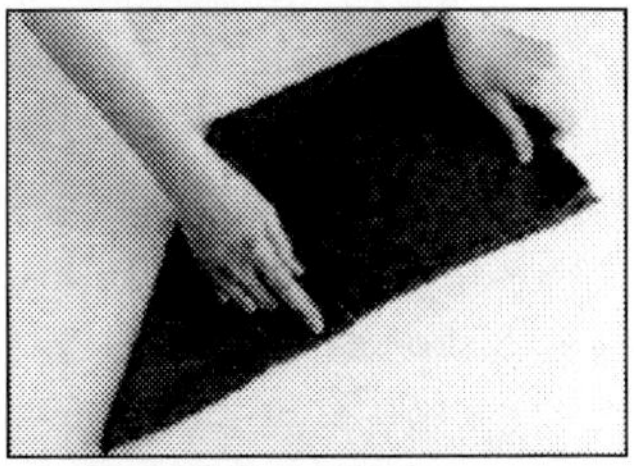
Step 3: Fold left top open sided corner to bottom. Fold back onto itself, bring corners together tucking one into the other. Open base of fold and stand upright.	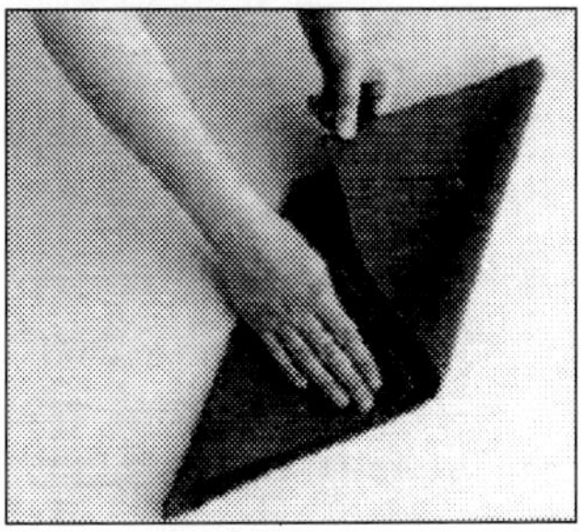
Step 4: Turn napkin over and make sure that the long folded edges are directly facing you top and bottom. Fold over the top edge farthest from you to meet the edge nearest to you.	
Step 5: Release the second point which is still tucked under so that there are two triangles at the top.	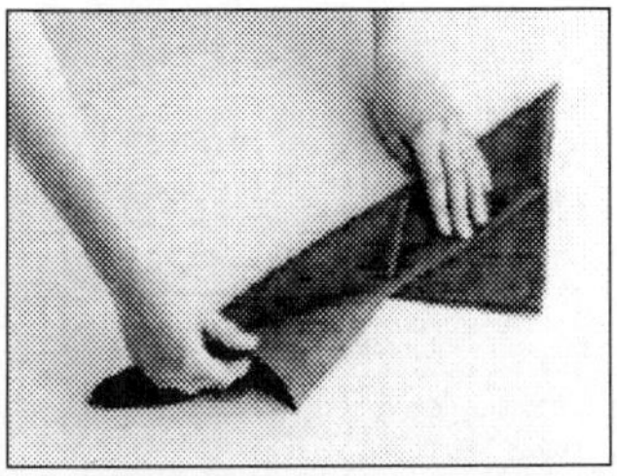

Step 6: Bring corners together tucking one into the other.	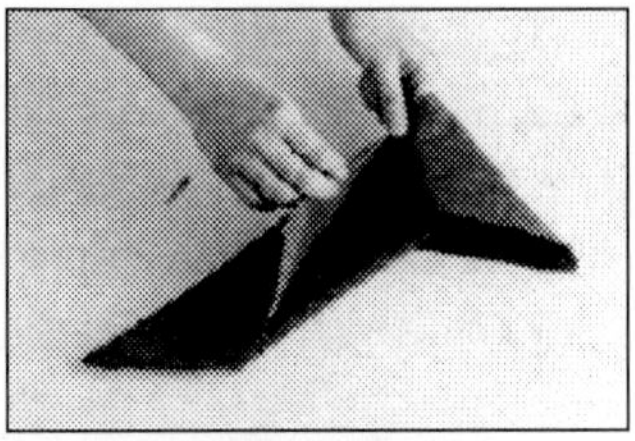
Step 7: Open base of fold and stand upright.	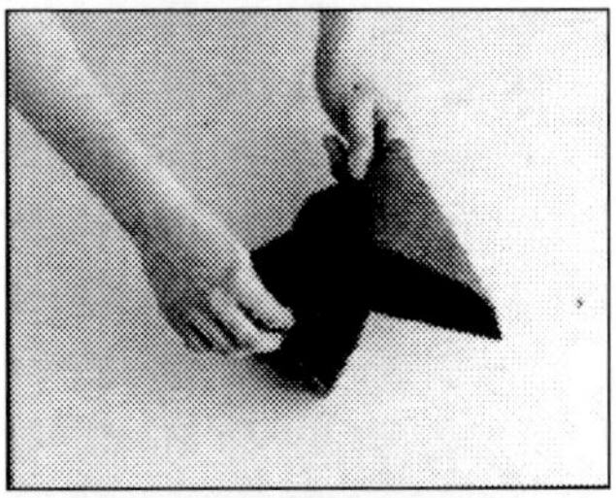
Step 8: Bishop cap is ready.	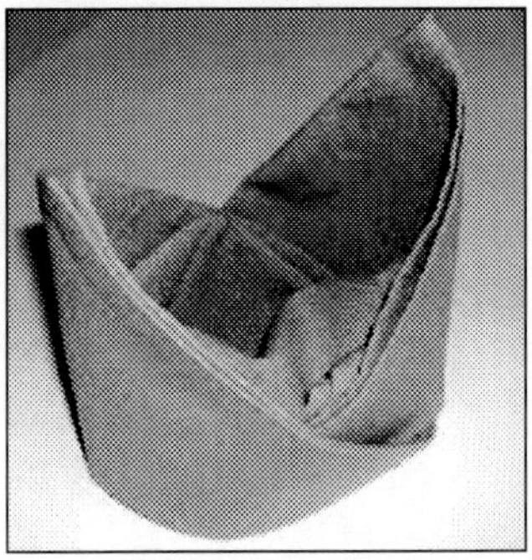

THE CROWN

Step 1: Fold napkin half diagonally.	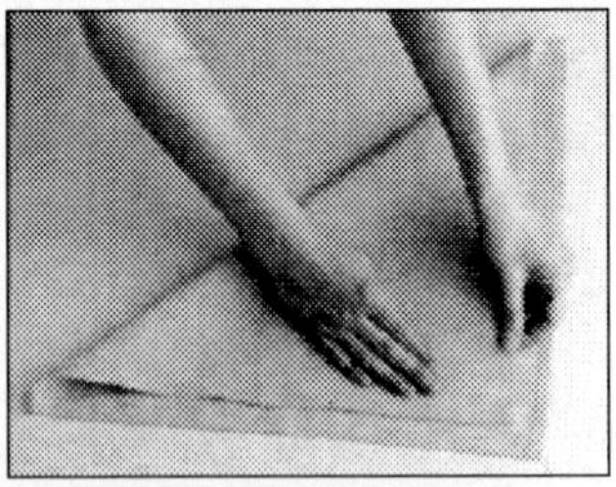
Step 2: Fold corners to meet at the top point.	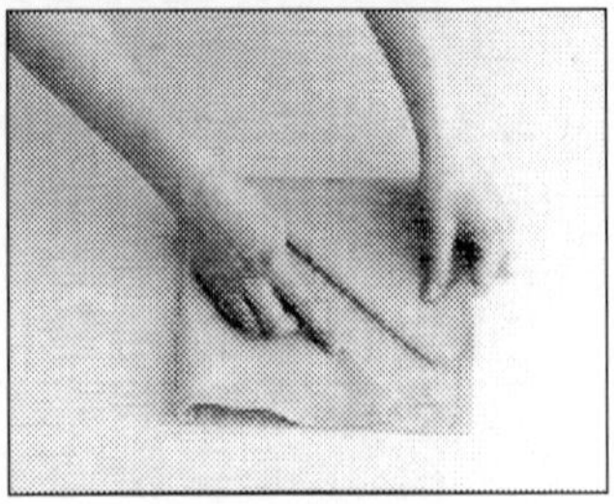

Step 3: Fold bottom point 2/3 way to top. Fold back onto itself.	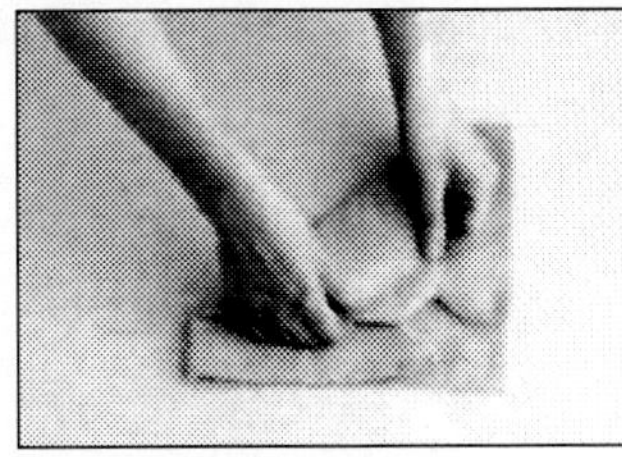
Step 4: Fold back onto itself.	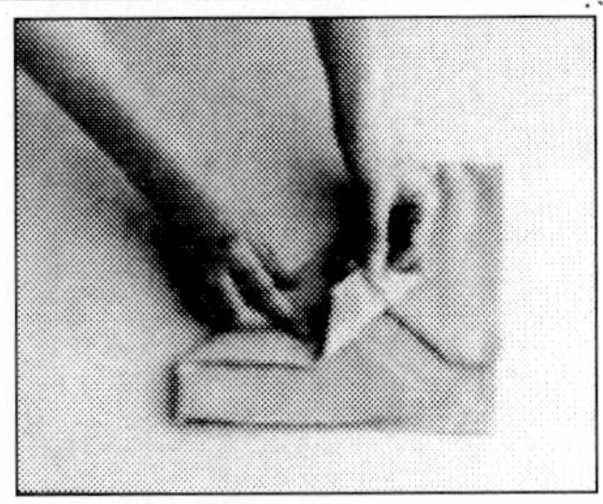
Step 5: Turn napkin over bringing corners together, tucking one into the other.	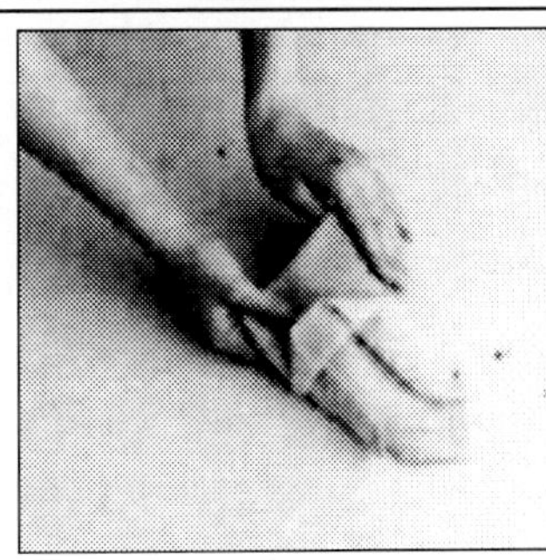
Step 6: The crown fold is ready.	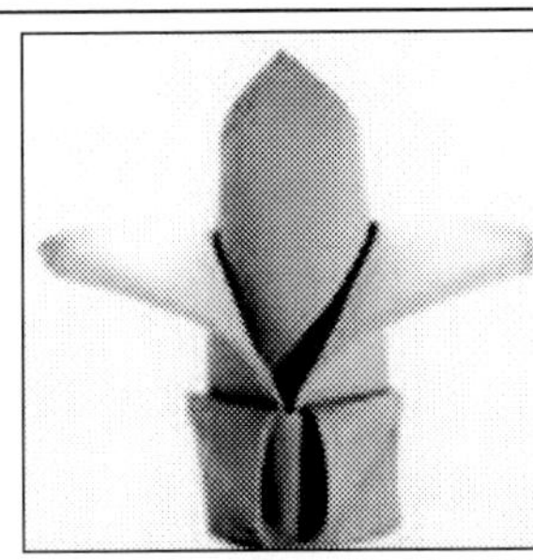

WATER LILY

Step 1: Open the napkin and fold all the corners to the centre. Fold the corner of that square to the centre as well.	

Step 2: Turn the napkin over and fold all the corners to the centre once again.	
Step 3: Hold the napkin in the centre and lift the corners up from underneath the napkin so that they look like petals.	
Step 4: Use that petal as it is or you pull the side sections from underneath as well. To do this lift the corners up from underneath again.	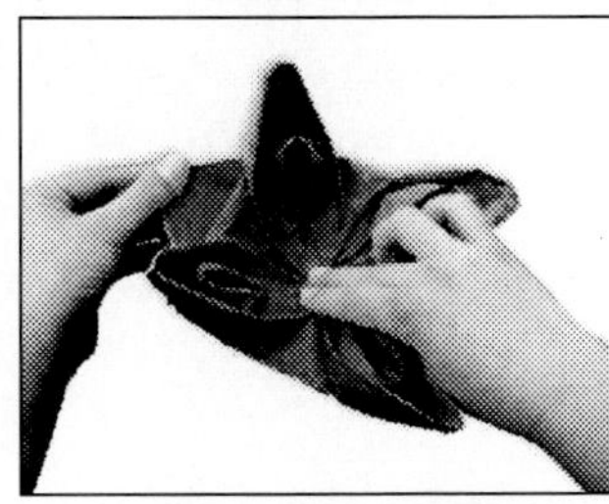
Step 5: Water lily is now ready to lay on table.	

STAR

Step 1: Open the napkin up and place it in front of you. Fold the upper and the lower edges at an horizontal line to the centre.	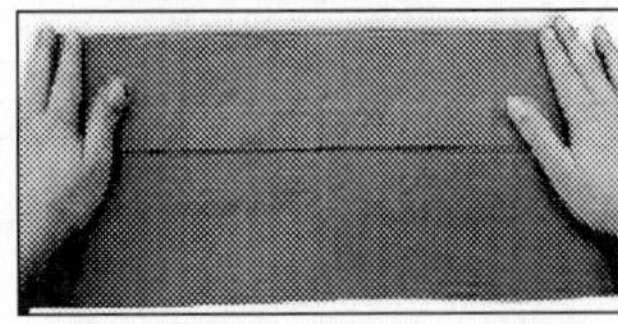

Step 2: Fold the napkin at the horizontal centre line and turn the napkin so that the long side with the two layers is on the left.	
Step 3: Fold the napkin using accordion folds. Hold the napkin in your hand like a fan. The side with the 2 layers needs to face up.	
Step 4: Pull down the inner layer of the fan of each pleat so that small triangles evolve at the top edges. Do that on one side first and after that on the other one.	

SOME TIPS

1. Heavy linen is best as it becomes firm and crisp when starched. Starching napkins during washing and iron not only makes them easier to fold but also helps repel stains the next time they are used.
2. Glycerin removes lipstick stains.
3. To remove wine stains wash napkins with water as soon as possible, then mound salt on both sides of the stain.
4. Used and soiled napkin should be washed as soon as possible.
5. Treat the stains with a prewash stain remover, then wash promptly.
6. Wash napkins in warm or hot water using a powdered oxygen bleach and an enzyme-boosted detergent.
7. When all else fails, soak white napkins in strong bleach solution.

19 CHEESE

Cheese is made from coagulated milk, cream or a mixture of these, drained in a mould, fermented and cooked. Different degrees of heat and pressures are applied to produce different types of cheese. The longer the cheese is pressed, harder the texture. Cheese is a valuable product in terms of nutrients. It has roughly $1/3^{rd}$ of protein, $1/3^{rd}$ fat and $1/3^{rd}$ of water. Cheese is also available in processed form. Processed cheeses are made by grinding the cheese and then cooking in a vacuum cooker. They are then moulded and packed. Natural cheese is categorised into:

- Soft or cream cheese
- Semi-hard cheese
- Hard cheese
- Blue cheese: The blue colour is imparted by skewering the cheese with copper wires and then introducing a type of penicillin mould into the cheese.

Cheese should be stored in cool and dark place to avoid drying or sweating. It should be wrapped in greaseproof paper and kept away from foods of strong flavour otherwise it absorbs flavour. Cheese is used in salads, soups, sandwiches, canapés, hors d'oeuvres and desserts. They are also served at the end of the meal. Indian cottage cheese (paneer) is used in curries, pagodas and so on.

CHEESE MAKING PROCESS

- **Milk:** It is the base product from which cheese is obtained. It has all ingredients which are essential for cheese making like protein, fat, lactose and minerals. The composition of milk varies from animal to animal—the reason for different tastes and textures of various cheeses.
- **Curdling of milk:** Cheese making starts from curdling of milk, which is usually done by adding a starter, which converts milk sugar into lactic acid. Rennet was traditionally added which is an enzyme found in the calf's bladder, which separates the milk into curd and whey. Nowadays rennet is no more used.
- **Removal of whey and pressing of curd:** The curd is cut into small pieces and is allowed to heat slowly which turns the curd into tiny grains and starts to settle at the bottom and the remaining whey is drained off.
- **Salting:** The curd is salted now to help in preserving and flavouring the cheese.
- **Pressing:** The final step is to press the cheese for packing in various forms and shapes.

TERMS RELATED TO CHEESE AND CHEESE MAKING

- **Fresh cheese:** Cheese that is not ripened like cottage cheese, cream cheese.
- **Holes:** Also known as eyes. These are basically openings in the structure of cheese. These holes occur due to the bacterial activity as found in the Swiss cheeses like *Gruyere* and *Emmenthal.*
- **Moulds:** They are added purposely to the cheese to give blue veins in the cheese. They can be external and internal.
- **Nutty:** Refers to the flavour of nuts like hazelnut or any other nut aroma in the cheese.
- **Paraffin:** A wax coating, which is given to certain types of cheese like *Edam* to protect the cheese from drying.
- **Rind:** The external surface of the cheese. They can be natural or artificial, thick or thin, hard or soft and sometimes washed, also parrafined as described above.

FAMOUS CHEESES WITH THE TYPE AND COUNTRY OF ORIGIN

Cheese	Country	Texture
Boursin	France	Cream
Mascarpone	Italy	Cream
Ricotta	Italy	Soft
Feta	Greece	Soft
Mozzarella	Italy	Soft
Brie	France	Soft
Camembert	France	Soft
Bel Paese	Italy	Soft
Cheddar	England	Semi-hard
Gouda	Holland	Semi-hard
Emmenthal	Switzerland	Semi-hard
Parmesan	Italy	Hard
Edam	Holland	Hard
Gruyere	Switzerland	Hard
Stilton	England	Blue veined
Gorgonzola	Italy	Blue veined
Roquefort	France	Blue veined

CHEESE ACCOMPANIMENTS

- Cheese is best accompanied with the crusty bread, cheese crackers and sour cream.
- It is also accompanied with olives, fresh fuits like garpes, berries, apples or pears, dried apricots, fresh crunchy vegetable crudités, dry fruits like almonds and walnuts.

PRESENTING CHEESE BOARD

Cheese comes in different containers, wrappers, coatings and in different shapes and sizes. It is a great addition to any meal. Presenting cheese board is an art. A great bonus of serving cheese is that it can be arranged an hour in advance before meal. Always cover cheese with a plastic wrap until taking it out from the refrigerator for serving. Cheese must be stored at 4-6 degree centigrade. Let cheese come to room temperature so that

Roquefort

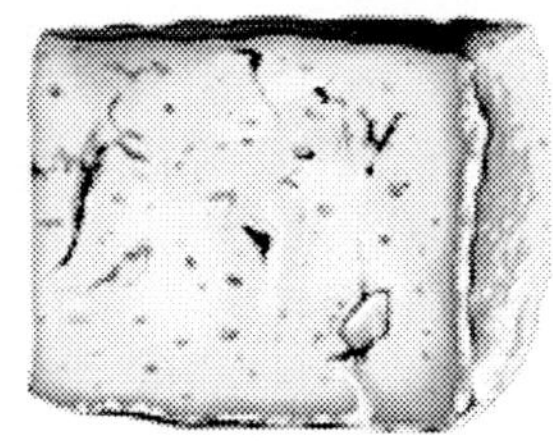

Gorgonzola

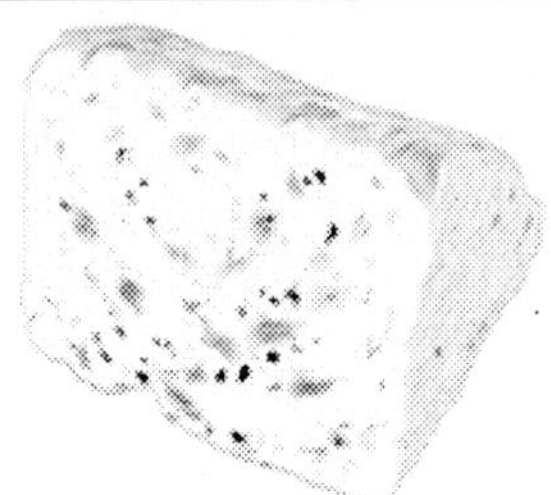

Danish blue

Stilton

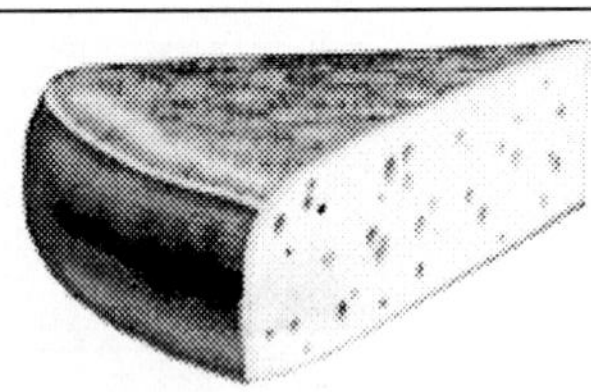

Gruyère

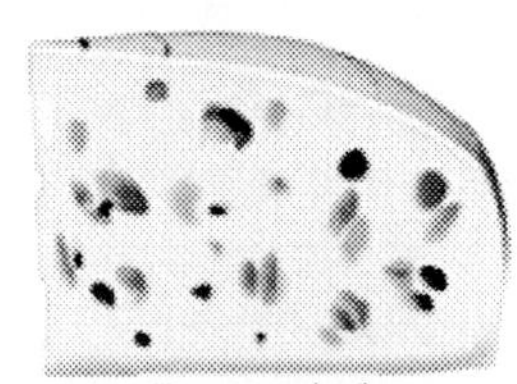

Emmenthal

Romano

Parmesan

it softens a bit and its flavour does not get masked by cold. Make sure that the cheeses are served at their peak conditions and full flavour. Depending on the hardness of cheese, this could take about an hour in cool weather and in hot weather as little as thirty minutes to give it full flavour. Always remember hard cheese takes longer time to come to room temperature than soft cheese. Cheese dries up easily so always wrap the cheese and unwrap it just before the service. It is very important that the first appearance of cheese board should be impressive so the shapes, sizes, textures and colours reflect balance and harmony. A well presented cheese board is the first step in making the meal a memorable experience. Once cheeses have been selected place them on the plates in an artistic manner. Make sure that cheese must be fresh and appetizing. It is also important to remember that

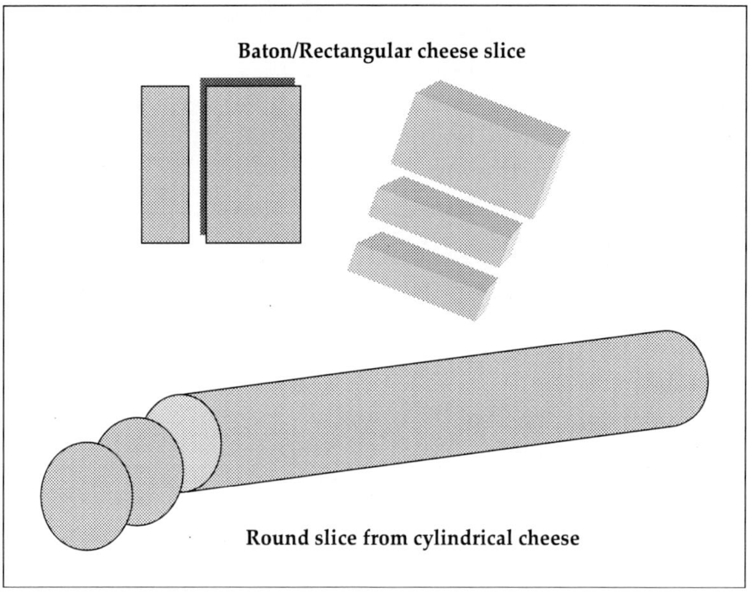

no cheese board is complete without the Trinity of the Table which comprises cheese, bread and wine. Cheeses also marry well with the crusty exterior and the soft interior of the bread. Cheese crackers, olives and dry fruits also give it a perfect company. As for wine each cheese has its own ideal partner. Not more than five cheeses should be kept in one big platter, otherwise the soft cheese may run into each other which will not only intermingle their aromas but will also become difficult to differentiate. For cheese board flat plate should be used as cheese must lie flat in order to easily cut. Arrange cheese from mild to strong. Select cheeses that have different flavours like one made from goat's milk, sheep's milk and another from cow's milk. You can also arrange according to the texture like soft, hard and semi-soft or choose that follow theme so such as cheese from Spain, England and other places. Many hotels use wooden plates for cheese board. Marble plates can also be used. Cutting cheese is also an art. Cut a Roquefort cheese in such a way that one takes all the blue part and leaves only the white part which is not as tasty. Every portion of cheese should be cut in the manner that the part of rind is distributed with the cheese portions and every cheese has its own knife. For instance the Roquefortaise is a wire butter knife that allows the cheese to be cut without damaging its fragile texture. Hard cheese such as Parmesan will require a knife where one uses both hands whereas soft cheese requires a small knife with a slightly bent blade with the point of the knife divided into two which will enable one to correctly handle the cheese. Put the knife in hot water, as this will make it easier to cut, particularly the blue cheese. If you do not possess the ideal knife choose a knife with a long rigid blade. Also be prepared to use a cheese fork. Cut the cheese with one strong stroke, which will prevent the cheese from being crushed. Try to make the portions of cheese equal and cleanly sliced. Keep the knife clean. Round cheese should be cut in wedges like a cake and sliced cheese should be cut lengthwise.

Cheese board

SERVICE OF CHEESE/FRUIT

Equipment Required

- Cheese board
- Cheese knife
- Accompaniments for cheese
- Fruit basket
- Fruit knife

Knowledge Required

- Types of cheese
- Using cheese knife
- Accompaniments for cheese
- Hygiene and sanitation

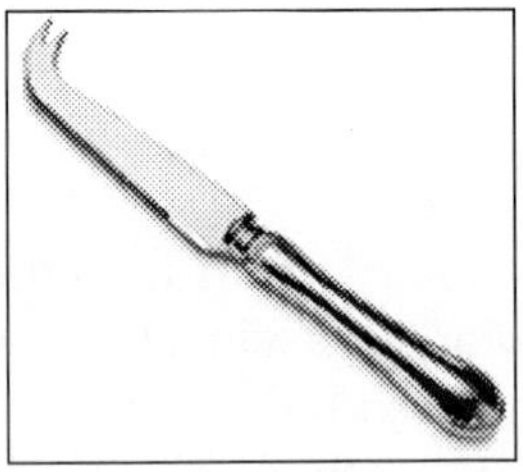

Cheese knife

Procedure

- Ensure that the guest has a clean side plate and side knife.
- Ensure that cheese board is in presentable condition and the cheeses can be identified.
- Present cheese board to the guest.
- Serve cheese from the left-hand side of the guest.
- Balance a corner of the cheese board on the edge of the table.

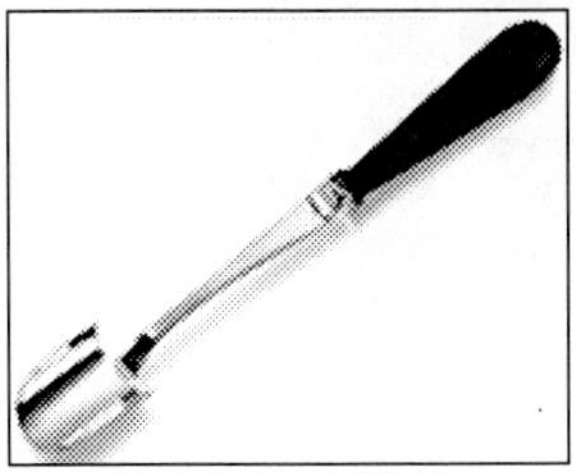

Stilton scoop

- Use a separate cheese knife for blue cheese. Ensure there are two knives on the board when you pick it up.
- Cut a portion of cheese to suit the guest and it onto their side plate.
- Use a stilton spoon for serving stilton cheese.
- Offer a selection of cheese accompaniments such as cheese biscuits and dry fruits.
- Ensure the fruit basket contains a selection of fruits. If the fruit basket has been depleted during service then it must be replenished before offering it to the other guests.
- Silvers serve the fruit onto a clean side plate and give them a fruit knife or side knife.

ACTIVITIES

- Visit a nearby departmental store in your city and find out the various types of cheese available.

20 PASTRY COUNTER SETUP

Equipment Required

- Functional pastry counter

Knowledge Required

- Menu knowledge
- Bakery items available

Procedure

- Switch on the counter lights, report any fused lamps to the concerned department.
- Check for cleanliness of the counter.
- Switch on the chiller.
- Fresh bakery and confectionery delicacies to be picked from the bakery according to the day's requirement.
- The same needs to be brought on a tray inside the restaurant and stacked.
- Place the name tags in front of each bakery/confectionery product.

Standard

- Counter to be free from debris and stains.
- Outer glass to be free from fingerprints and watermark stains.
- Chiller to be maintained at temperature of 4-5°C
- Bakery items to be transported from the bakery to the pastry counter in a covered trolley.
- All food to be covered with plastic food covers.
- There should be no spelling mistakes in the names of the dishes.
- All vegetarian items will be in green tag and non-vegetarian in red.
- Cold food to be served below 15° Celcius and hot food above 65° Celcius.

Well stacked pastry counter

21 PRACTISING TROLLEY SERVICE

HORS D'OEUVRE TROLLEY SERVICE

Hors d'oeuvre trolley

- Most cold hors d'oeuvres can be served from the trolley.
- Vegetarian and non-vegetarian items can be included.
- Meat and fish items are best in salad form: although items like sardines can be served whole and sausages like salami can be served in slices.
- Other items include egg mayonnaise, Russian salad, potato salad, green beans, tomato salad, red beans, asparagus, and host of other salad items.
- All these hors d'oeuvres are placed in small containers of equal size, usually fitting in compartments.
- They should always be kept clean and frequent refilling is necessary.

Procedure

- The waiter brings the hors d'oeuvre trolley to the guest table.
- The guest selects from the assortment of starters placed on the trolley.
- The waiter takes the order.
- The waiter takes the half plate from the underrack of the trolley.
- The waiter places correct cutlery on the guest table.
- The waiter places the starter from the trolley to the guest plate.
- Takes the plate to the guest table.
- Serves pre-plated from the right-hand side.

DESSERT TROLLEY SERVICE

- This trolley is a visual aid to selling desserts.
- Guests are more likely to order a dessert if they can see what is available, particularly if it is well presented.

- Some dessert trolleys are refrigerated.
- Gateaux, pastries, jellies, tarts, pies, flans and soufflés can be served from a dessert trolley.

Dessert trolly

Procedure

- The waiter brings the dessert trolley to the guest table.
- The waiter clears cruet set and crumbs the table if required.
- The guest selects his choice from the assortment of starters placed on the trolley.
- The waiter takes the order.
- The waiter takes the half dessert from under rack of the trolley.
- The waiter places correct cutlery on the guest table.
- The waiter places the dessert from the trolley to the guest plate.
- Takes the plate to the guest table.
- Serves pre-plated from the right-hand side.

BEVERAGE/LIQUOR TROLLEY SERVICE

- The beverage trolley holds the liquor that a restaurant wishes to serve to the guest.
- It is multi-tiered to aid storage of appropriate glassware necessary for liquor service.
- The liquor is placed segregated as per their classification.

Procedure

Liquor trolley

- Liqueurs (sweetened and flavoured spirits) are generally offered from a liqueur trolley.
- The Sommelier brings the liquor trolley to the guest table.
- The Sommelier should present the trolley immediately after the sweet course is finished to ensure that any liqueurs required will be on the table by the time the coffee is served.
- The guest selects his choice from the selection of liquor placed on the trolley.
- The sommelier takes the order.
- The sommelier presents/exhibits the bottle for guest's approval.
- The sommelier brings forth the appropriate glassware to be used for service.

- Normally, all liqueurs are served in an Algin-shaped liqueur glass which holds one measure.
- If a person asks for a liqueur to be served frappé, then it is served on crushed ice.
- A larger glass will then have to be used. The glass should be two-thirds filled with crushed ice and then 60 ml of liqueur poured over. Two short drinking straws should be placed into the glass and then served, for example, Crème de Menthe frappé.
- If a liqueur is requested with cream, then the cream is slowly poured over the back of a teaspoon to settle on the top of the selected liqueur, without mixing with it. Under no circumstances should the liqueur and cream be mixed together. For example, TiaMaria with cream.
- The basic pieces equipment required on the liqueur trolley are:
    - □ Assorted liqueurs
    - □ Assorted glassware
    - □ Liqueur/brandy/port
    - □ Standard measures
    - □ Service salver
    - □ Creamer with double cream
    - □ Teaspoon
    - □ Drinking straws
    - □ Cigars
    - □ Matchbox
    - □ Cigar cutter
    - □ Wine list and check pad
- Other items served from the liqueur trolley may be brandy and port (a fortified liqueur wine). For service, brandy requires a small measure and port a large measure.

22 IN ROOM DINING/ ROOM SERVICE/EAT IN

In room dining (IRD) also known a room service or eat in is the oldest and first activity of hotels apart from renting rooms. In earlier days concept of IRD was *"Small meal prepared in the pantry and served in the room to avoid the various rules & laws required for running a full-fledged restaurant"*. In the present scenario IRD is one of the most essential features of F&B department. It means serving of food and drinks to a guest in his or her room in a hotel. IRD department or section, as at a hotel is responsible for rendering this service. Round-the-cloak room service facility is expected in all star categories hotels – classified and unclassified – to satisfy customers needs. IRD works on a shift system to provide 24 hr room service facilities except resorts situated in hill stations. IRD is located near the still room, service elevator and kitchen for a speedy service. IRD cabin has a glass partition which makes it possible for the room service order taker or captain to monitor the work in progress in kitchen and still room and also the movement and activities of room service waiters. The cabin is equipped with room service menu cards, telephone, room service kitchen order ticket, room list, integrated computer system, room service order docket, waiter's card, status of the guest staying and so on.

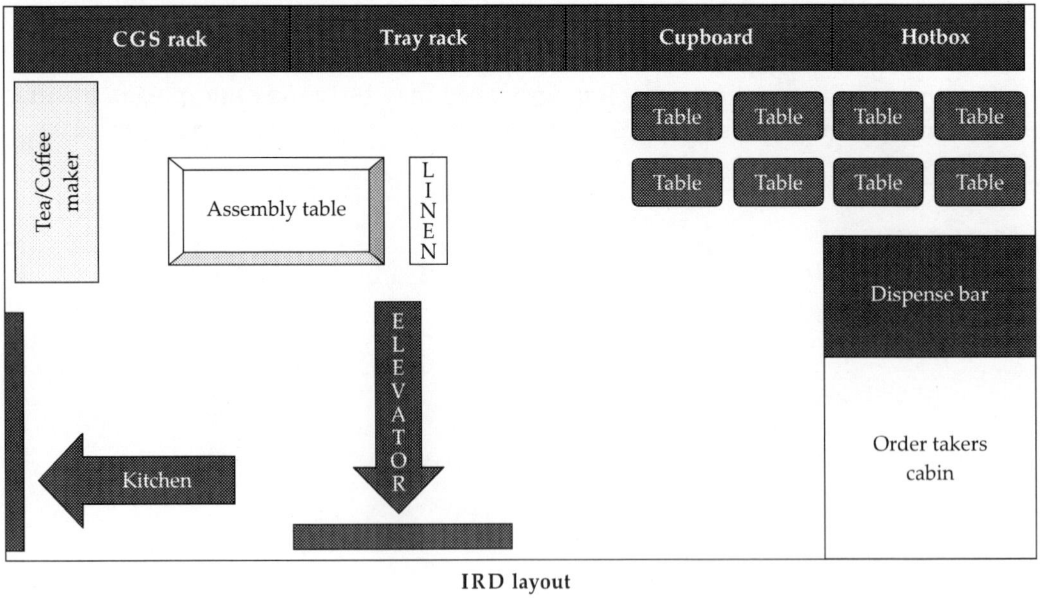

IRD layout

Room Service trolley: To place large order in the room generally for two or more than two persons or when order is large. It has two extendable flaps which makes room service trolley a round table.	 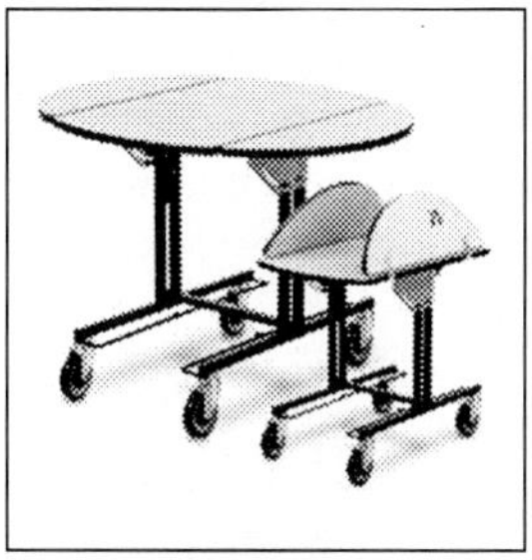
Tray: Two type, i.e., tea tray and continental tray are used to serve tea/coffee orders or for small orders.	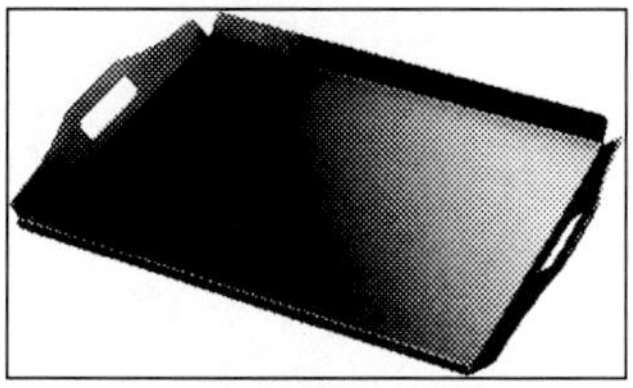
Cloche: Used to cover the food. Mostly used in the orders of cakes and ice cream.	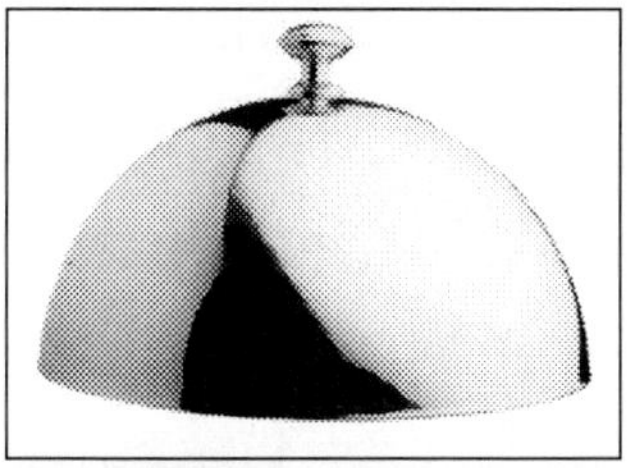
Food Cover: Used to cover the food.	

Hot Case/ Hot Box / Warmer: Used to carry food when orders are to be served from trolley. Hot case keeps the food warm. It is placed in the cabinet incorporated beneath the room service trolley.	
Tray Rack: Used to stack trays in room service department.	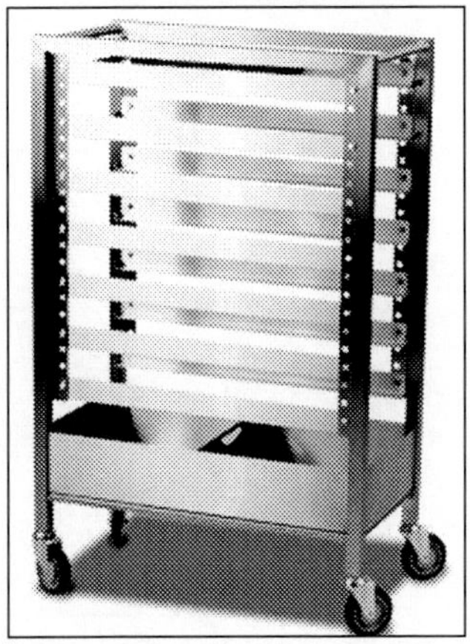

ANSWERING THE CALL IN IRD/ROOM SERVICE/EAT IN

Equipment Required

- Telephone
- Headset

Knowledge Required

- Telephone etiquette
- Basic etiquette and manners

Procedure

- Greet the caller in a clear and audible voice.
- All telephone calls to "eat in" must be answered within 3 rings.
- Wear the headset before answering the call.
- Ensure that the initial greeting to be clear and audible. *"Good morning / afternoon / evening, this is ________ (tell your name) from Eat In, how may I assist you?"*
- Voice to be low-pitched, well modulated and of the right volume.
- Guest's surname to be used during initial telephone greeting or immediately thereafter if available.

- Guest's surname to be used at least once and not more than twice during interaction.
- Always smile while talking on the phone; the guest can sense it.
- No jargon to be used while talking to guests.
- Ensure there is no background noise while speaking to guests.
- Place the caller on hold if he/she would like to speak to someone specific in "eat in" or the information required is not readily available after taking his/her permission by saying. *"May I place you on hold Sir/Madam?"*
- Transfer the call if the caller would like to speak to someone in another department. While transferring the call: *"Certainly Sir/Madam. Allow me to transfer your call."*
- If the transferred extension is busy, offer to take down the message from the caller or ask whether the caller would like to be placed on hold again.
- In case of multiple calls take permission from the current caller to place him on hold and attend the next call using standard phraseology.*"May I place you on hold for a moment Sir/ Maam?"*
- Inform the caller that you are on another call.
- Offer to call back within a stipulated time.
- Return to the first caller apologizing for having kept him on hold. *"I am sorry to have kept you on hold Sir/ Maam.........".*
- Telephone conversation is closed with a pleasant final remark by staff. *"Thank you for calling Eat In. Have a pleasant day Sir/Madam.*

Standard

- Answer all telephone calls within 3 rings. A clearly spoken standardized greeting will be used at all times.
- All conversation should be in polite and courteous.
- Make sure that there is no noise.
- No caller will be kept on hold for more than 15 seconds.
- Never bang the telephone, first let the guest put the telephone.

ORDER TAKING IN IRD/ROOM SERVICE/EAT IN

Equipment Required

- Telephone
- Headset
- Menu knowledge
- Availability of dishes
- Knowledge of wines and food accompaniments.
- Knowledge of standard delivery time of all items.

Knowledge Required

- Telephone etiquette
- Basic etiquette and manners

Procedure

- Guest calls Eat In.
- Greet the caller in a clear and audible voice.
- Voice to be low-pitched, well modulated and of the right volume.
- Guest greeted according to the time of the day addressing him/her using surname if displayed in the telephone monitor.
- Good morning/afternoon/evening, Ms./Mr.________ (use guest's name) this is ________________ (your name) from Eat In, how may I assist you?
- Guest's surname to be used during initial telephone greeting or immediately thereafter if available.
- Guest's surname to be used at least twice during the conversation.
- Always smile while talking on the phone; the guest can sense it.
- No jargon to be used while talking to guests.
- The order taker must have a clear diction and must be fluent in English.
- Ensure there is no background noise while speaking to guests.
- The associate to assist the guest while taking the order.
- If the guest requests for assistance while ordering the order taker should suggest food and beverages matching the guest preferences and as appropriate for the meal period. *"Would you prefer to have Cornflakes with cold skimmed milk and a glass of fresh orange juice at room temperature Mr./Ms....?*
  - □ Whenever appropriate, the order taker must try and do suggestive selling in order to give the guest a complete meal experience.
  - □ *"Would you like to order a starter/drink/wine/dessert?"*

    or
  - □ *"May I suggest our chef's special (dish name) to go along with your (dish name)"*.

    or
  - □ *"May I recommend a glass of Red Wine to go with your steak Sir/Madam?*
- If the guest is asking for something you can provide say, *"Certainly, Sir/Ma'am, we would be more than happy to serve you... (dish name)."*
  - If the guest has any special requests or specific requirements for his food and beverages orders, ask questions to clarify the exact requirements.
  - *"Would you like your lassi sweat, salted or plain Sir/Madam?"*

    or
  - *"Would you like your food without salt Sir/Madam?*

- A record of the menu items to made and compiled monthly.
- If the guest is asking for something you are not sure you can provide:
  - ☐ If not possible: *"May I check with the chef and revert?"*
  - ☐ If "Yes" by chef: *"The chef is delighted to prepare (dish name) for you."*
  - ☐ If "No" by chef: *"I am sorry we are unable to serve you the item you have requested for. May I offer you _________ instead"* Sir/Madam?
- Order taker to repeat order with the specifications if any, *"May I repeat your order? Mr./Ms. (use guest's surname)______you have ordered for (dish name/s) with (special instructions/requests/preferences)."*
- Write everything down on dedicated pads or dupes and later on in room service order docket.
- In case of alcoholic beverages, snacks and desserts, check with the guest if he/she would like the same to be served along with their main meal or they prefer to have it served at different times. Example:
  - ☐ *"Would you like me to send the (drinks/starter) first?"* or
  - ☐ *"Would you like me to send the desserts later?"*
- In the case of straight drinks.
- The order taker should always confirm whether the guest would like the spirit with or without ice.
- The order taker should also confirm the mixer guest would prefer to have with the spirit.
- Order taker to confirm the number of covers. Use phraseology ,*"How many guests would this meal be for?"*
- Order taker to provide the estimated delivery time.
- *"The time now is 09.10 a.m. Your order will reach you by 09.25 a.m."*
- While providing the estimated delivery time order taker should keep in mind items that take longer preparation time or items which has to be picked up from different kitchens to conform to guest specifications.
- Follow the estimated time for delivery as per the standards of hotel.
- In case of any service delays due to unforeseen circumstances the guest must be informed about the same in advance .Use phrases, *"Good morning/afternoon/evening, Mr./Ms. Use guest's surname, this is (use your name) speaking from Eat In. I am sorry for the inconvenience caused; would you allow me another 10 more minutes to deliver the order Sir/Maam"?*
- Telephone conversation is closed with a pleasant final remark by staff.
- Use phrases, *"Thank you for calling Eat In Mr./Ms. ...use guest surname, have a pleasant day".*

Standard

- All phone calls to be answered within 3 rings with a clearly spoken standardized greeting in a polite and courteous manner.
- Wear the headset before answering the call.
- Order taking will be done professionally, courteously and warmly. Order taking staff should be knowledgeable and should be able to make recommendations as per guest preferences.
- Sincere attempt must be made to accommodate all the guest's request. If that is not possible, an alternative that is acceptable to the guest must be offered.
- The order taker will state the time the order is being placed and should inform the guest as to what time the order would reach the room.
- Delivery time not to exceed
    - □ Tea/coffee 10 min
    - □ Beverage and ice 10 min
    - □ Continental breakfast 15 min
    - □ Indian/English breakfast 20 min
    - □ Snacks 15 min
    - □ Lunch/dinner 30 min
    - □ Lunch/dinner (from specialty restaurant) 40 min
- All guests will be called back within a stipulated time in the case of any delay.

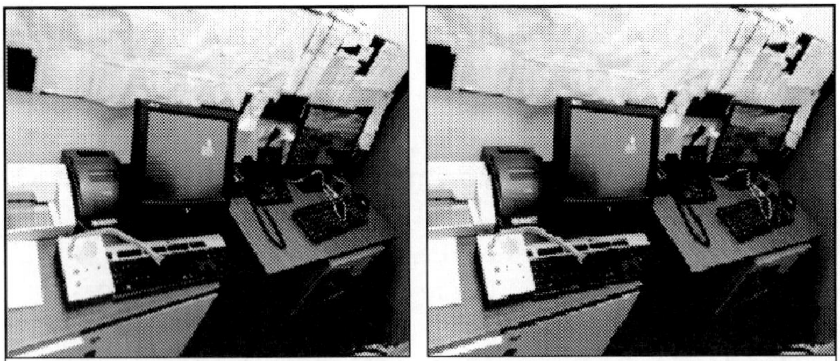

Room service order taker cabin

MINI BAR REPLENISHMENT

Procedure

- Staff to use service lift and not guest elevators.
- Staff to knock on door, or ring door bell and announce 'Room Service'. Staff to knock again after 10 seconds, if no response. If no reply, staff to open the door, enter and announce themselves again.
- If DND on door, the staff to mark on the placement chart.

- If DND on door post check-out time the Front Office cashier to be contacted.
- Room service manager to be informed unless late checkout has been indicated.
- Door of the room to be kept ajar while in the room for replenishment. If guest is present, to be thanked and asked if any other service is required.
- Staff to check and note usage or consumption advice, if not entered by guest. A copy of the consumption advice to be left for information to the guest.
- The bar to be replenished and cleaned thoroughly.
- All stocks to be checked for expiry date: Products to have an expiry of at least 3 months.
- All cans and bottles placed on the mini bar to be wiped clean and rust free with labels properly affixed.
- The bar accessories to be replaced as per requirement.

Mini bar in the room

FORMATS USED IN IRD – IRD CHECKLIST

S. No.	Job responsibility	Status	Handover
		Incoming	
1.	Morning briefing		
2.	Going through the logbook		
3.	Discuss all day arrivals		
4.	Check for stock.		
5.	Check for all keys.		
6.	Check for the mise en place.		
7.	Check working condition of		
8.	Take handover from the night		
9.	Check all the pending night work		
10.	Check for all the VIP in house		
11.	Check all the early arrival blocked		
12.	Arrange for welcome drinks		
13.	Check for rest of the days VIP		
14.	Preparation of trays for breakfast		
15.	Arranging amenities accordingly		
16.	Check for the status of tray		
17.	Requisition of stores		
18.	Checking for tray clearance		
19.	Preparation for lunch orders.		
		Outgoing	
1.	Arrange for handover for the		
2.	Check for the status of trays stuck		
3.	Check for the days follow-ups		
4.	Inform incoming shift for any		
5.	Check for the next day arrivals		
6.	Make note for any preferences of		
7.	Inform concerned departments for		
8.	Make note of next day's follow		
9.	Give proper handover of stocks to		
10.	Clearly inform incoming shift about		
11.	Check for any pending guest bills.		
12.	Debriefing		
			Room Service Manager

R/S Errand Card

Name:__________________Date:__________

Shift:________________________________

S. No.	Room No.	Time out	Time in	Clearance	Captain's sign
1.					
2.					
3.					
4.					
5.					
6.					
7.					
8.					
9.					
10.					
11.					
12.					
13.					
14.					
15.					
16.					
17.					
18.					
19.					
20.					

KOT NO. 9305 **Park Prime** JAIPUR ROOM SERVICE

Date	Time	PAX	Table No.	Steward

Quantity	Particulars

SIGNATURE

ROOM SERVICE

NO RESPONSE SLIP

Room No.______________

Date:_________________ Time:____________a.m./p.m.

STEWARD WAS UNABLE TO:

I. Serve your order
II. Replenish your amenities
III. Clear your tray

AS THERE WAS:

I. A do not disturb sign
II. No response

KINDLY CALL US ON EXTENSION FOR SERVICE:

Thank you

Room Service Captain

DATE
SHIFT
ORDER TAKER

Park Prime
JAIPUR

ROOM SERVICE ORDER CONTROL SHEET

CAPTAIN
STEWARD
STEWARD

S. No.	ROOM NO.	TIME IN	ORDER	BILL NO.	SERVER	TIME OUT	CLEARNANCE	REMARKS

23 FOOD SERVICE IN IRD

Food service in "In Room Dining (IRD)/Room Service/Eat In" requires lots of skills, eye for detail and techniques. IRD gives an opportunity to the IRD associate to interact with a guest in a friendly manner but always remember, be friendly but not over familiar with the guest. Do also note to fill the Room Service Errand Card before delivering the food in the guest room.

PRESENTING A TRAY

Equipment Required

- Room service tray
- Types of linen used in IRD
- Types of cutlery used in IRD
- Condiments
- Types of plates used in IRD
- Paper mat/tray mat

Knowledge Required

- The various types of cutlery and crockery used in IRD
- Tray accompaniments
- Standard accompaniments during breakfast/lunch/dinner
- Carrying tray

Procedure

- The IRD associate checks the tray.
- The IRD associate should ensure that the tray has no sharp edges or protrusions.
- The tray top should not be chipped or cracked.
- Tray top to be clean, free from dust, food stains and spots.
- The IRD associate wipes the tray clean.
- In case of heavy stains or spots the tray is given to IRD associate to wash.

Indian breakfast tray setup

- Tray to be clean, free from dust, food stains and spots.
- The IRD associate places a clean paper tray mat on the tray.
- The paper tray mat used to be clean and not be frayed at the edges, torn or marked worn or damaged.
- The paper tray mat and tray should be aligned.
- Arrange the trays in the racks in the "Eat In" preset area.

Continental breakfast set-up

- The tray racks should be arranged in a manner that they are easily accessible and do not disturb the work flow.

Indian lunch/dinner setup

Continental lunch/dinner tray setup

MIS EN PLACE FOR BREAKFAST SERVICE IN IRD

- Wiping breakfast cups and saucer, side plates, cereal bowls and full plates.
- Wiping and polishing all cutlery and flatware like teaspoons, forks, spoons, butter knifes, toast racks, teapots, milk pots, coffee pots, preserve boat and others.
- Cleaning and checking cruet set. Filling up the preserves in preserve boat like jam, honey and marmalade.
- Cleaning butter dish and filling butter in butter dish.
- Wiping and filling sugar bowl with sachets of white sugar, brown sugar and "sugar free" as per hotel policy.
- Cleaning and polishing coffee pots, tea pots, tea strainer and slop basin.
- Lining bread baskets with cloth napkins.
- Polishing food cover and cloche.

- Switch on the hot box.
- Wiping and polishing trolley and trays.
- Exchanging linen from housekeeping, i.e., napkins, moultons, trolley cover, etc.
- Getting newspaper to be sent with breakfast.

TROLLEY SETUP

Equipment Required

- Room service trolley
- Types of linen used in IRD
- Types of cutlery used in IRD
- Trolley appointments
- Plates
- Hot box

Indian breakfast trolley setup

Knowledge Required

- The various types of cutlery and crockery used in IRD
- Tray appointments
- Standard accompaniments during breakfast/lunch/dinner.

Procedure

- The IRD associate checks the trolley.
- The trolley should be clean, free from dust, spots and not wobbling.
- The IRD associate should ensure that the trolley has no sharp edges or protrusions.
- Ensure that the trolley wheels are running freely and without any threads/rugs wound on it.
- The trolley top should not be chipped or cracked
- The IRD associate cleans the trolley with a damp, clean wiping cloth.
- Trolley top to be clean, free from dust, food stains and spots.
- The trolley should be clean and free from dust, stains or spots.

Continental breakfast trolley setup

- The IRD associate covers the trolley with a clean trolley cover and then places an overlay over.
- The trolley cloth and overlay should be clean, ironed, colour-resistant and not torn, frayed, worn, damaged or stained.
- The trolley cover and overlay should be aligned so that the fall is even and regular on all sides.

Indian lunch/dinner trolley setup

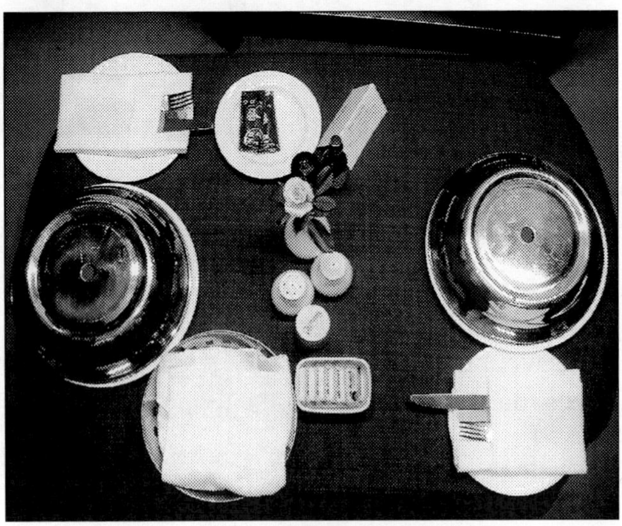

Continental lunch/dinner trolley setup

PICK-UP FOOD FROM THE KITCHEN

Equipment Required

- Room service trolley
- Types of linen used in IRD
- Types of cutlery used in IRD
- Trolley appointments
- Plates
- Hot box

Knowledge Required

- Reading a bill.
- Placement of food on tray/trolley
- Temperature at which food should be placed.

Procedure

- After the IRD supervisor checks for adherence to standard tray/trolley setup the IRD associate will do the beverage pick-up first followed by the food from the kitchen.
- In case of trolley it is pushed to the pick-up counter and kept in a convenient manner so that it is easy to pick up and place the food.
- All alcoholic beverages should be picked up in appropriate glassware covered by glass covers except for champagne, beer and wines which are ordered by bottle.
- Any non-alcoholic bottled beverages like aerated water, soda, soft drinks and mineral water should never be taken after pouring into the glass.
- All hot orders will be served on a trolley. All food served is covered to ensure that the guest receives a hygienic meal.
- The food pick-up will be done against the bill. The IRD associate double checks each food and beverages item placed on the tray/trolley against the bill for conformance.
- Confirmation of special request/instructions is done by checking both verbally and visually.
- Pick up the cold food first followed by the hot food.
- Food and beverages to be served at room temperature/chilled are picked up first.
- Ensure that the ice tong is not out of shape, tarnished, spotted, worn, damaged or dented.
- The food pick-up from the hot counter to start once all the hot food is ready at the counter.

- The food must be picked up from the kitchen counter at 65°C temperature and delivered to the room immediately.
- Once the food is picked up, it is arranged on the tray/trolley.
- The positioning of items on the tray should be such that all items should be easily accessible to the guest with least inconvenience.
- Place heavy items in the centre of the tray/trolley, as this will facilitate easy balance.
- Place flatware and light items towards the edge of the tray/trolley.
- Any bottled beverages like aerated water, soda, soft drinks, mineral water or beer should be laid flat on the tray/trolley to avoid accidents while taking it to the room.
- Cold food should never be stacked over hot food since heat travels upwards.
- The IRD associate takes the tray/trolley to the supervisor to check for nonconformance on items against the bill.
- The supervisor checks the food and beverages items on the tray/trolley against the bill.
- If the supervisor notices a non-compliance on order it is immediately rectified.

Standard

- All hot food will be served above 65° C and cold food below 5° C.

Once the food is picked up it is arranged in the tray or trolley

Supervisor checks for nonconformance on items against the bill

TAKING THE TRAY IN THE ROOM

Equipment Required

- Room service tray
- Types of IRD cutlery
- Types of chinaware
- Bill folder.

Carrying room service tray

Knowledge Required

- Reading a bill.
- Placement of food on tray/trolley
- Temperature at which food should be placed.

Procedure

- In one motion bend the knees and lift the tray using both hands and keep it in the flattened palm of your left hand.
- Release the right hand once the tray sits steadily and firmly on your left hand.
- The weight of the tray should rest on the hand and not on the shoulder.
- Grip the edge of the tray with the free hand and keep it there if the tray is heavy.
- Shoulders must be straight and not slouched.
- The trays are carried at the shoulder level.
- Press switch and hold the elevator door open using your free hand while entering with the tray.
- Step inside the elevator carefully.
- Switch off the elevator fan.
- When going through doors use your free hand or shoulder or back to open the door in order to protect and balance the tray.
- The IRD associate should ensure that the way is clear with no obstacles in his path.

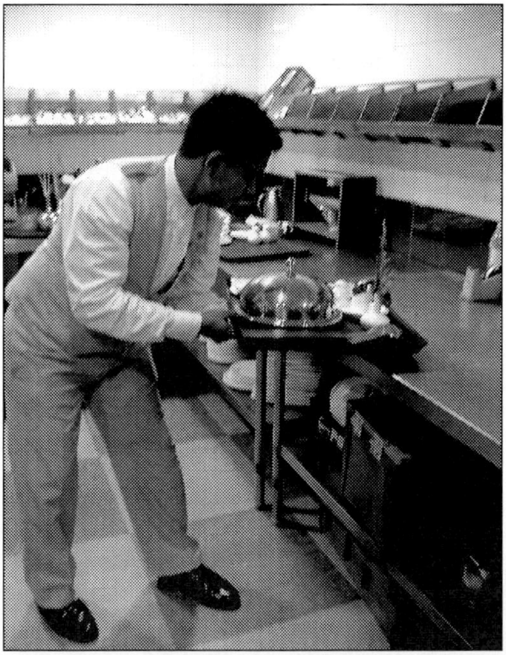

In one motion bend the knees and lift the tray using both hands and keep it in the flattened palm of your left hand

- Always check for other people coming through the door to avoid a collision or loss of balance.
- At any point of time the tray should not wobble and the items on the tray should not be displaced.
- Ensure that the door is held open firmly and that there are no obstacles in the path.
- Entering floor corridor.
  - Maintain silence.
  - The trolley should be rolled carefully and smoothly through the corridors.
  - Walking in the floor corridor.
  - Walk erect and maintain poise.
  - Walk at an even pace.
  - Avoid any sound of the footsteps.
  - Do not run in the floors.
  - Move aside if a guest is approaching and give the guest the right of way.
  - Walk to the right of the guest while escorting.
  - Walk on the left-hand side.
- Standing in the guest area
  - Stand erect, at ease but not casually
  - Weight balanced on both feet
  - Shoulders straight
  - Chest out
  - Stomach in
  - Keep your hands if free on the sides or behind your back.
  - Not in the pockets or on the hips.

When going through doors use your free hand to open the door in order to protect and balance the tray

Walking is the floor corridor

TAKING TROLLEY TO THE ROOM

Equipment Required

- Trolley
- Types of IRD cutlery

- Types of chinaware
- Hot box
- Bill bolder.

Knowledge Required

- Reading a bill
- Placement of food on trolley
- Temperature at which food should be placed.

Procedure

- Press switch and hold the elevator door open using your free hand and gently pull the trolley carefully into the elevator.
- Step inside the elevator carefully.
- Switch off the elevator fan.
- After reaching the respective floor depress switch and hold the elevator door open using your free hand and gently pull the trolley out carefully out of the elevator.
- The trolley should be rolled carefully and smoothly through the corridors.
- When going through doors use your free hand or shoulder or back to open the door in order to protect and balance the trolley.
- When going through doors to the corridor the associate must be careful to ensure that the trolley passes through smoothly without disturbing the trolley setup.
- The IRD associate should ensure that the way is clear with no obstacles in his path.
- Always check for other people coming through the door to avoid a collision or loss of balance.
- At any point of time the trolley should not wobble and the items on the trolley should not be displaced.
- Ensure that the door is held open firmly and that there are no obstacles in the path.
- Before entering the guest room make the final adjustments in the arrangement of the items in the trolley.
- Entering floor corridor.
  - □ Maintain silence.
  - □ The trolley should be rolled carefully and smoothly through the corridors.
- Walking in the floor corridor.
  - □ Walk erect and maintain poise.
  - □ Walk at an even pace.
  - □ Avoid any sound of the footsteps.
  - □ Do not run in the floors.

- ☐ Move aside if a guest is approaching and give the guest the right of way.
- ☐ Walk to the right of the guest while escorting.
- ☐ Walk on the left-hand side
- Standing in the guest area
  - ☐ Stand erect, at ease but not casually.
  - ☐ Weight balanced on both feet.
  - ☐ Shoulders straight.
  - ☐ Chest out.
  - ☐ Stomach in.
  - ☐ Keep your hands if free on the sides or behind your back.
  - ☐ Not in the pockets or on the hips.

TRAY/TROLLEY CLEARANCE FROM THE ROOM

Knowledge Required

- Aware of clearance procedure.
- Knowledge of where soiled equipment is to be placed.
- Knowledge of how timely clearance helps in smooth operations.
- Eye for detail.

Procedure

- Check with the guest about clearance.
- Timely clearance is exceedingly important as it prevents shortage of operating equipment and furthermore it reduces breakage and pilferage.
- If the guest has not mentioned any specific clearance time or If the guest had said clearance can be done later, guest should not be disturbed by calling for clearance.
- If the guest has mentioned a specific clearance time then as per the time instructed by the guest, the IRD associate should go to the room and clear the tray/trolley.

Check for clearance in the corridors, housekeeping pantry while going back to IRD

- Clear all used cutlery/crockery/glassware/linen and other F&B items in the room including any item from the previous order if left in the room.

- Eye for detail is necessary while doing clearance not to miss out on anything.
- A floor check must be carried out every 2 hours to ensure that no clearance is lying around.
- Check in front of all rooms where the guest has informed that he will keep the tray outside.
- The trolley must be brought in carefully so that all crockery, cutlery and glassware are intact.

Standard

- Floor clearance of trays and trolleys will be carried out every 2 hours. This will ensure that the corridor remains free of obstruction and no trays are left in guest rooms.

CUSTOMIZING THE PRESET TRAY AND TROLLEY AS PER THE ORDER

Equipment Required

- Room service tray/trolley
- Types of linen used in IRD
- Types of cutlery used in IRD
- Tray/trolley appointments
- Plates
- Hot box

Knowledge Required

- Knowledge to set up a tray
- Knowledge to set up a trolley
- Correct sequence of setup
- Eye for detail

Procedure

- The IRD associate to set a tray/trolley as per the guest's order.
- The IRD associate to select appropriate food and beverages containers and hand it over to the food production areas as per the guest's order.
- The stewarding department stacks the kitchen counters with only plate, platters and flatware in order to prevent misuse and avoid breakage by kitchen staff.
- The remaining food and beverages containers have to be given by the IRD associate immediately after and as per the order placed by the guest.
- Platters, plates and serving pieces to be clean.
- Flatware clean and not tarnished, spotted, worn, damaged or dented.
- Glassware, china, platters, plates not worn or damaged.

- The covers, meal plates, service gears, underliners, coasters, glass covers and accompaniments like sauces, salads, pickles, butter, etc., are placed on the tray/trolley as per the guest's order.
- Condition of crockery, cutlery, glassware and linen should be clean and in impeccable condition.
- Coasters and napkins to be clean and neat.
- Equipment, if used, not to be worn or damaged.
- The supervisor to check for adherence to standard tray/trolley setup.
- If there is a non-adherence it is immediately rectified.

Standard

- Chinaware, cutlery, flatware and glassware should be neat and clean.

FOOD SERVICE IN THE GUEST ROOM

Equipment Required

- Room service tray/trolley
- Types of linen used in IRD
- Types of cutlery used in IRD
- Condiments
- Types of plates used in IRD
- Paper mat/tray mat

Knowledge Required

- Cutlery and crockery used in IRD
- Tray/trolley appointments
- Standard accompaniments during breakfast/lunch/dinner
- Carrying tray and trolley
- How to announce oneself
- Standard polite phrases
- Sequence of service

Procedure

- Check the indicator panel on the door of the guest room before ringing the bell.
- If the "Guest Inside" light is OFF use the floor pantry phone and inform the order taker to check with the reception about the whereabouts of the guest.
- If both "Guest Inside" light and "Privacy Please" light is ON use the floor pantry phone and inform the order taker to inform the guest that his/her food is ready.

- If the "Guest Inside" light is ON and the "Privacy Please" light is OFF ring the door bell once and announce "IN ROOM DINING".
- Reconfirm the room number and name of the guest from the bill and then ring the bell and announce "IN ROOM DINING".
- IRD associate rings door bell once, announces self, pauses for 10 seconds, rings again.
- Wait for 10 seconds (count from 1 to 10) before ringing the bell again and once gain announce "IN ROOM DINING".
- If there is NO RESPONSE after waiting for 10 seconds more use the floor pantry phone and inform the order taker to inform the guest that his/her food is ready.
- When the guest opens the door, wish the guest and ask for permission to enter the room.
- Wish the guest by saying, *"Good morning/afternoon/evening, Mr./Ms. (Use guest's surname) I am (tell your name) your steward. May I come in Sir/Maam".*
- Check with guest as to where s/he would like her/his tray to be placed.
- Check with guest as to where s/he would like her/his tray to be placed by saying *"Where would you like me to place the tray Sir/ Maam".*
- Move smartly inside the room and place the tray as indicated by the guest.
- In case if you have any guest articles hand it over to the guest.
- In case of newspaper open it and place it neatly on the writing table.
- If any of the guest items are lying on the space required to keep the tray, seek guest's permission to remove it.
- Place the tray taking care to balance it properly. Ensure that the tray is placed on even surface. *"May I move these items so as to place the tray Sir/ Madam".*
- Take extreme care when handling guest's items.
- As you place the tray at the desired place you could find out if you could draw the curtains if they are not drawn especially during service at day time Use phrases *"Would you like me to draw the curtains Sir/Maam/Name of the guest – Mr/Mrs. ......".*
- The IRD associate should also offer to serve the dishes to the guest. Use phrases *"Would you like me to serve you your meal?* or *"Would you like me to make the coffee/ tea for you Sir/Madam".*
- If the guest says "NO" when the steward offers to serve the dishes to the guest, seek guest's permission to show and explain the dishes on the tray/trolley.
- The steward will offer to explain the dishes on the tray/trolley with the specifications if any. Use phrases *"May I explain the dishes for you Sir/Maam?*
- If the guest says "YES", the IRD associate will remove the covers of the dishes one by one and announce the potions and the dish names taking care to include the special instructions/requests/preferences if any. For example, *1 portion of Paneer Makhani without cream, 1 portion of Dal Tadka and 4 phulkas without oil."*
- The IRD associate to offer to remove the cling wraps on food containers.

- Any cling wraps removed to be placed in the steward's coat pocket and not to be left on the tray/trolley.
- If the guest says "YES" then only the IRD associate offers to serve the dishes to the guest and lay the cover on the table in a manner which is convenient for the guest to have his meal.
- Check whether the guest would prefer to have some water served to him.
- The IRD associate then serves the food course-wise after announcing the dish name/s taking care to include the special instructions/requests/preferences if any.
- Any bottle caps or cling wrap removed while serving to be placed in the IRD associate's pocket and not to be left on the tray.
- Obtain the signature of the guest on the bill by saying *"May I have your signature on the bill Sir/Madam?*
- Offer the bill folder with the hotel pen to the guest for signature.
- Maintain an erect posture with a smile while presenting the bill to the guest.
- No attempt to be made to solicit tips.
- Check with guest for clearance by saying, *"When would you like me to come back to clear the tray Sir/Madam/."*
- If there is any clearance left in the room from the previous service the same also has to be cleared while leaving the room.
- Check if the guest would like to order for anything else.
- In case the guest says "yes", take down the order correctly in the scribbling pad and then convey the same to the order taker at IRD using the pantry phone if the order has to be delivered immediately. If it is an advance which needs to be delivered after a while go to IRD and place the order directly with the order taker.
- Before leaving the room thank the guest by saying, *"Thank You Sir/Madam/Name of the guest – Mr/Mrs. ...... Enjoy your meal"* or *"Thank You Sir/Madam/Name of the guest – Mr/Mrs. ......Have a pleasant day."*
- Close the door slowly but firmly while leaving the room.
- Close the door without turning the knob so that the guest can confirm that the door is locked on hearing the door closing sound.

Standard

- The In Room dining tray must be placed on the coffee table or at an appropriate place as desired by the guest. The steward must always enquire time of clearance after serving the meal and ascertain if there are any additional requests.
- All bills will be presented with a hotel pen and in a clean folder.
- The steward must always enquire time of clearance after serving the meal and ascertain if there are any special requests.

Food Service in Guest Room	
Step 1: Check the indicator panel on the door of the guest room before ringing the bell.	
Step 2: Associate rings door bell once, announces self, pauses 10 seconds, rings again.	
Step 3: When the guest opens the door, wish the guest and ask for permission to enter the room.	
Step 4: Check with guest as to where s/he would like her/his tray to be placed.	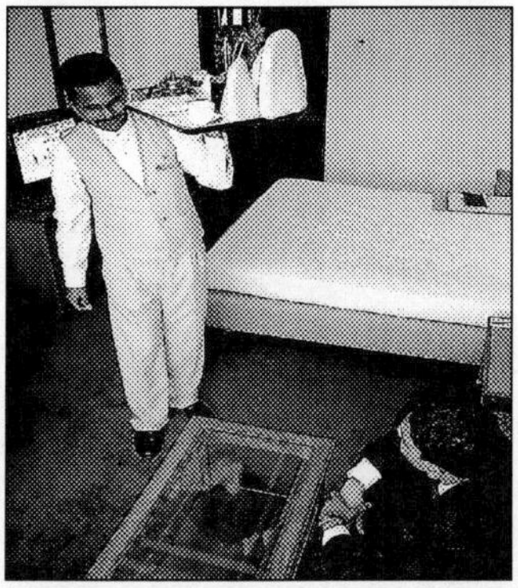

Step 5: Move smartly inside the room and place the tray as indicated by the guest.	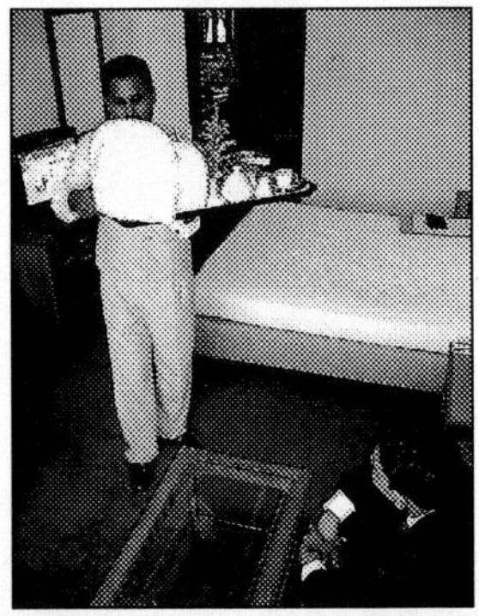
Step 6: Move smartly inside the room and place the tray as indicated by the guest.	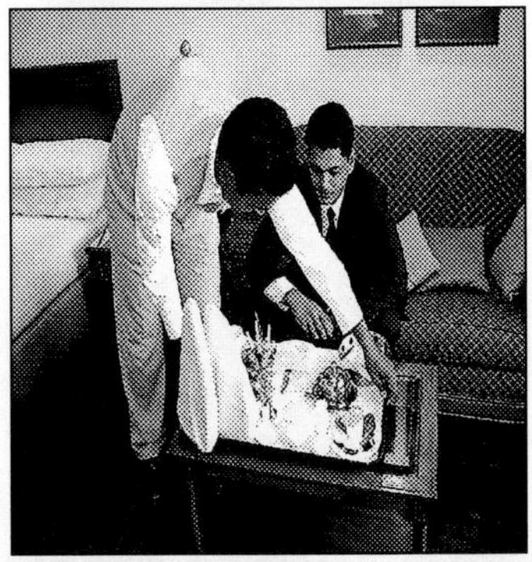
Step 7: Explaining the dishes.	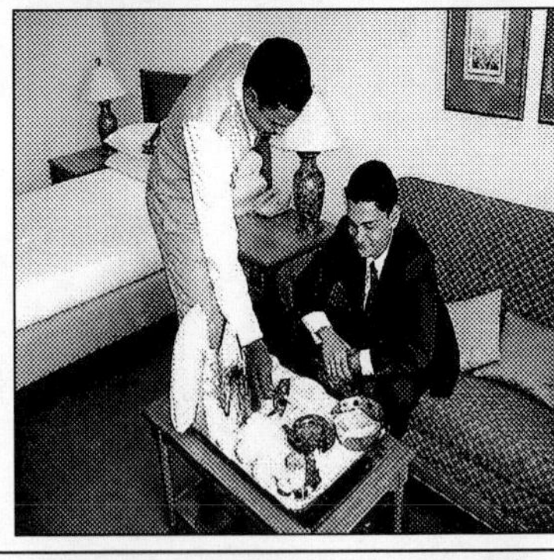
Step 8: Obtaining the guest's signature.	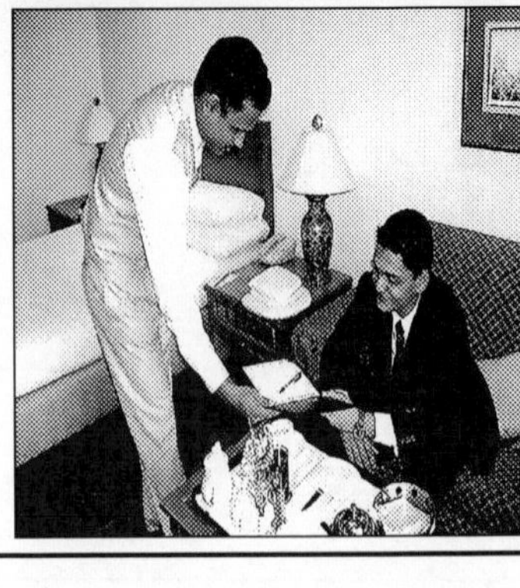

TROLLEY SERVICE

Step 1: Move smartly inside the room with trolley.	
Step 2: Check with guest as to where he would like his trolley to be placed.	
Step 3: If any of the guest items are lying on the space required to keep the tray, seek guest's permission to remove it.	

Step 4: Move smartly inside the room and place the trolley as indicated by the guest.	
Step 5: Open the flaps of the trolley.	
Step 6: Set the covers on the trolley.	
Step 7: Organise the chairs for the guest.	

Step 8: Seat the guest, explain the dishes and offer to serve.	
Step 9: Obtain the signature of the guest on the bill.	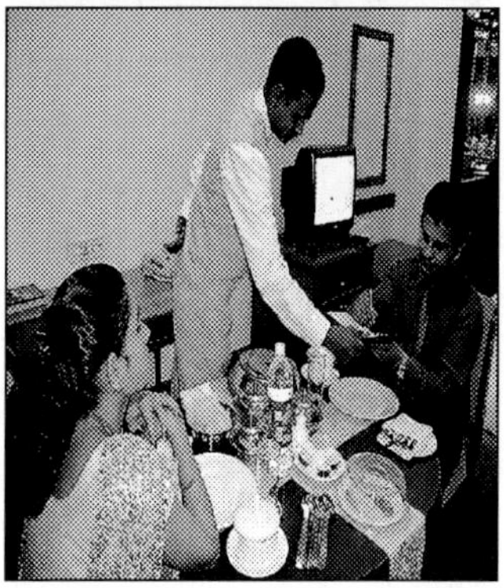

SERVICE OF MORNING TEA AND COFFEE

Equipment Required

- Room service tray
- Crockery for tea/coffee service
- Cookies

Knowledge Required

- Procedure for service
- Standard phraseology

Procedure

- IRD associate picks up the tea/coffee from the IRD pantry or kitchen depending on the order.
- Select crockery and other equipment appropriate to the drink portion, style and as per the menu specifications.
- In the case of morning coffee/tea service 3 cookies are offered along with the coffee/tea for one person.
  - For 2 people = 5 cookies

  - For 3 people = 7 cookies
  - For 4 people = 9 cookies

- Check the indicator panel on the door of the guest room before ringing the bell.
- Ensure that the crockery is without any food stains, spots, chip or cracks.
- If the "Guest Inside" light is OFF inform the order taker to check with reception about the whereabouts of the guest.
- If both "Guest Inside" light and "Privacy Please" lights are ON use the floor pantry phone and inform the order taker to inform the guest that his/her food is ready.
- If the "Guest Inside" light is ON and the "Privacy Please" light is OFF ring the door bell once and announce "Eat In".
- If DND (Do Not Disturb) card is on the door knob then do not ring the bell but use the floor pantry phone and inform the order taker to inform the guest that his/her food is read.
- Ring the door bell and at the same time check to see whether the newspaper/any articles are still seen in the rack. If yes, take it and place it on the tray if there is space or hold it carefully in your right hand.
- Wait for 10 seconds (count from 1 to 10) before ringing the bell again and once again announce "IRD".
- If there is NO RESPONSE after waiting for 10 seconds more use the floor pantry phone and inform the order taker to inform the guest that his/her tea/coffee is ready.
- When the guest opens the door, wish the guest and ask for permission to enter the room. Use phrases, "*Good Morning Name of the guest – Mr/Mrs. ......*".
- Ask for permission to enter the room by saying "*May I come in Sir/Madam/Name of the guest – Mr/Mrs. ......*".
- Check with the guest as to where he would like his tea/coffee placed by saying "*Where would you like me to place the tray Sir/Madam/Name of the guest – Mr/Mrs ......*".
- In case of any articles hand it over to the guest saying "*Sir/Madam/Name of the guest – Mr/Mrs. ......*".
- In the case of newspaper open it and place it neatly on the writing table.
- As you place the tray at the desired place you could find out if you could draw the curtains if they are not drawn. Use phrases. "*Would you like me to draw the curtains Sir/Madam/Name of the guest – Mr/Mrs. ......*".
- If the guest says "yes", draw the curtains gently.
- Ask the guest whether you could pour the coffee/tea by saying "*Would you like me to make the coffee/tea for you Sir/Madam/Name of the guest – Mr/Mrs. ......*".
- If guest says "yes". Check with him by saying, "*Would you like your tea/coffee light or strong*".
- Make the tea/coffee according to guest's preference.

- Check for the amount of sweetness preferred by the guest by saying, *"May I add one/two sachets of sugar or would you like low calorie sweetener Sir/Madam/Name of the guest – Mr/ Mrs. ......".*
- In the case of tea/coffee with separate milk, the associate should pour the tea/ coffee till three-fourths of the cup is full and then add 4-5 drops of milk or as desired by the guest.
- In case of tea/coffee without milk or readymade tea/coffee, the IRD associate should pour the tea/coffee till four-fifths level.
- The IRD associate should pour with a steady flow so as to avoid any spillage in the saucer or on the table.
- Obtain the signature of the guest on the bill by saying, *"May I please have the bill signed Sir/Madam/Name of the guest – Mr/Mrs. _____________".*
- Offer the bill folder with the hotel pen to the guest for signature.
- Check with the guest about clearance
- Check for clearance by saying, *"When would you like me to come back to clear the tray Sir/Madam/Name of the guest – Mr/Mrs. ......".*
- Thank the guest before leaving the room before leaving the room by saying, *"Thank You Sir/Madam/Name of the guest – Mr/Mrs. ...... Enjoy your tea/coffee"* or *"Thank You Sir/Madam/Name of the guest – Mr/Mrs. ......Have a pleasant day".*
- Close the door while leaving the room without turning the knob so that the guest can confirm that the door is locked on hearing the door closing sound.

Tea tray setup

Coffee tray setup

HANDLING AMENITIES

Amenities are the gestures provided to the guest for which he/she need not to pay. It reflects the standard of the organization, the cost involved comes under room division management. There are various grades that have been set by the corporate world, for example, Grade A, B, C.

Depending upon the type of room sold and guest the amenity chart is prepared by the front office department and then accelerated ahead to F&B Department, in which IRD is the section who takes care of it and places it before the guest arrives and on daily basis in case of occupied room. In many organizations this assignment is taken care by housekeeping department.

Equipment Required

- Fruit basket
- Cover-fruit knife, fork, plate, napkin
- Cookies jar
- Bottle of wine
- Wine glass
- Wine opener
- Glass finger bowl
- Coasters/glass covers
- Welcome letter

Amenitties provided in room by IRD

Knowledge Required

- Procedure for service
- Standard phraseology

Procedure

- Collect the amenity request from the front office.
- Punch no charge for the same.
- Provide chef with fruit baskets for arrangements and other necessary accessories for the amenities.
- Prepare the amenity chart for different floors and according to the grades.
- Pick up the prepared baskets and other relevant stuff, wrap them with clean film and load them in the buggy/cart.
- Pick up the master keys of assigned floor, make entry of the same in the master key movement book.
- Pick up the amenity card (Example: It is used when the room is on privacy or no response, it says we are unable to replenish your amenity as you are on privacy at 12:30 kindly contact IRD at Extension XYZ, Thank you}.
- Start placing the amenities in the arrival room first in coordination with housekeeping department.
- Amenity is always placed in the clean room.

Placing the Fresh Amenity

- Before entering in a room weather it is occupied or vacant all the standard need to be followed.

- Knock the door thrice, announcing yourself wait for some time and then again re-do it.
- Apply the master key, open the door wide open for security reason while you are inside the room.
- Pick up the amenity to be placed as per the requisition from the front desk.
- Remove the clean wrap, wipe the fruits if required.
- Place the basket on the coffee table with cover and glass finger bowl, three-fourths full with water and a flower floating in it.
- Wipe the bottle of wine place it on the side table underneath the table lamp with label facing the entrance and coaster underneath and glass covered with glass cover.
- Place the wine opener on the napkin in between the wine glasses.
- Place the welcome card on the top of the cover next to fruit basket.
- Move out of the room, check for anything suspicious or dirty, inform the concerned department.
- Move out of the room and close the door, mark entry in the amenity chart with time.
- In case of VIP room inform the concerned supervisor.

Replenishing Amenity

- In case of occupied room, follow the standard procedure of entering the room.
- Inform the guest why you had approached.
- Carry the amenity in a clean tray with relevant accessories, remove the old ones and replace with fresh ones
- Remove all the clutter and if required inform the housekeeping department for cleaning
- Thank the guest and move out of the room and close the door softly
- Mark the entry in your amenity chart with time, and move to next room.

TAKING ADVANCE PACKING ORDERS IN IRD

Equipment Required

- Telephone
- KOT
- RSOT
- Pen

Knowledge Required

- Awareness on how to take a packed order
- Knowledge of packed order items
- Standard phraseology

Procedure

- Request for an advance packed order—may be received from resident or non-resident guests.
- In case of non-resident guests the mode of request is usually through telephone, fax or email.
- In any case the order taker has to call back the guest and confirm the details.
- Greet the guest in a clear and audible voice identifying yourself.
- Wear the headset before answering the call.
- Ensure that the initial greeting to be clear and audible. "*Good morning/afternoon/evening, this is (tell your name), from Eat In how may I assist you?*".
- Voice to be low-pitched, well modulated and of the right volume.
- Guest's surname to be used during initial telephone greeting or immediately thereafter if available.
- Order taker to clarify the specifications of the order.
- If the guest has any special requests or specific requirements on his advance orders, ask questions to clarify the exact requirements by saying, "*Would you like your cake to be egg less Sir/Madam?*" or *Would you like your Indian, Continental or Chinese food Sir/Madam?*
- In case of if the guest is asking for something you are not sure you can provide:
  - If not possible say, "*May I check with the chef and revert?*'
  - If "Yes" by chef say, "*The chef is delighted to prepare (dish name) for you.*"
  - If "No" by chef say, "*I am sorry we are unable to serve you the item you have requested for. May I offer ______ instead sir/madam?*
- Order taker to repeat order with the specifications if any. Use phrase "*May I repeat your order? Mr/Ms (Use guest surname) ______ you have ordered for (dish name/s) with (special instructions/requests/preferences).*
- Inform the guest about the rates and the delivery charges if any in case of transportation by IRD.
- Ensure that the following details are collected like the name of the guest, contact number, date and time packed order required, mode of payment and delivery is confirmed.
- Raise an advance requisition for the order.
- The advance requisition is done in duplicate of which the first copy is given to the kitchen and second copy is retained in the department for reference.
- The bill is generated and settled as per the mode of payment on delivery of the order.
- Cross-check and ensure that the rates printed in the bill tally with the rates agreed upon with the guest at the time of placing the order.

Standard

- No jargon to be used while talking to guests.
- Ensure there is no background noise while speaking to guests.

- Always smile while talking on the phone; the guest can sense it.
- Guest's surname to be used at least once and not more than twice during an interaction.
- Order taking will be done professionally, courteously and warmly. Order taking associate will be knowledgeable and will be able to make recommendations as per guest's preferences.
- Sincere attempt must be made to accommodate all guest's requests. If that is not possible, an alternative that is acceptable to the guest must be offered.
- All guest's orders/requests will be repeated to ascertain accuracy.

BILL GENERATION AND SETTLEMENT

Equipment Required

- Printer
- Restaurant software, POS
- Bill folder with hotel pen

Knowledge Required

- Knowledge of how to operate restaurant software such as showman
- Knowledge on different modes of bill settlement

Procedure

- Order taker feeds the order into the POS while the guest is ordering.
- Ensure that the bill is raised on the correct room number.
- Ensure that the all chargeable items are posted in the bill.
- Ensure that the quantity of each item charged is accurate.
- Ensure that the bill is generated in triplicate.
- The IRD supervisor double-checks the bill for accuracy.
- Ensure that the bill is accurately itemized and totalled.
- Ensure that the bill is legible.
- All bills to be machine imprinted.
- Ensure that the stamp of time and date is accurately printed on bill.
- The IRD supervisor hands over the bill in triplicate to the IRD associate to obtain the signature of the guest on the bill after delivery/service of the order.
- Present the bill in a clean bill folder, with a hotel pen in good working condition.
- Guest has to sign on the original copy of all bills except for the ones he is settling by cash.
- The associate hands over the bill to the IRD supervisor after delivery/service of the order.
- Ensure that the bill is handed over back to IRD supervisor in triplicate.

- The bill is posted into the correct room account immediately.
- In the case of room settlement check for any discrepancy in the room number printed in the bill and the room number written by the guest if any while signing the bill.
- In the case of cash payment.
    - □ Ensure that the cash paid bill is cleared within 5 minutes of guest making payment.
    - □ The original copy of the bill along with excess cash paid by guest if any is returned to the guest.
    - □ Guest's copy of all cash paid bills to be presented after stamping "C A S H P A I D" with ink seal.
- In the case of credit card payment:
    - □ The credit card is swiped in the EDC machine.
    - □ Accurate bill amount is posted into the account.
    - □ Charge slip is generated in duplicate.
    - □ The customer copy of the bill and credit card charge slip are attached together.
    - □ The second and third copies of the bill and the merchant copy of the charge slip are attached together.
    - □ Associate gets the merchant copy signed by the guest.
    - □ The customer copy is handed over to the guest along with his credit card
    - □ The merchant copy is given back to the IRD supervisor for settlement.
- In case of party settlement.
    - □ This kind of credit settlement is done only on instruction from the concerned party.
    - □ Associate gets the bill signed by the guest in the original copy.
    - □ The bill is handed over in triplicate to the IRD supervisor.
    - □ The supervisor settles the bill into party account.
- If the party is the host of a banquet function happening in the hotel at that time, the original copy of the bill is handed over to the concerned banquet supervisor to be included in the final bill/challan.

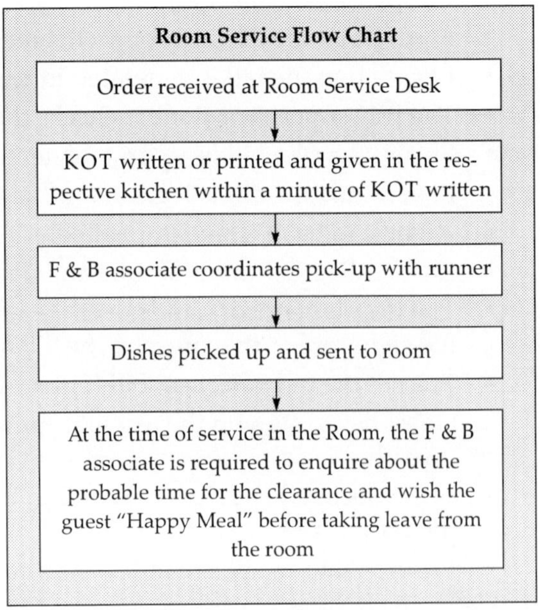

Standard

- All bills will be presented with a hotel pen and in a clean folder.

Order Taking for Lunch/Dinner

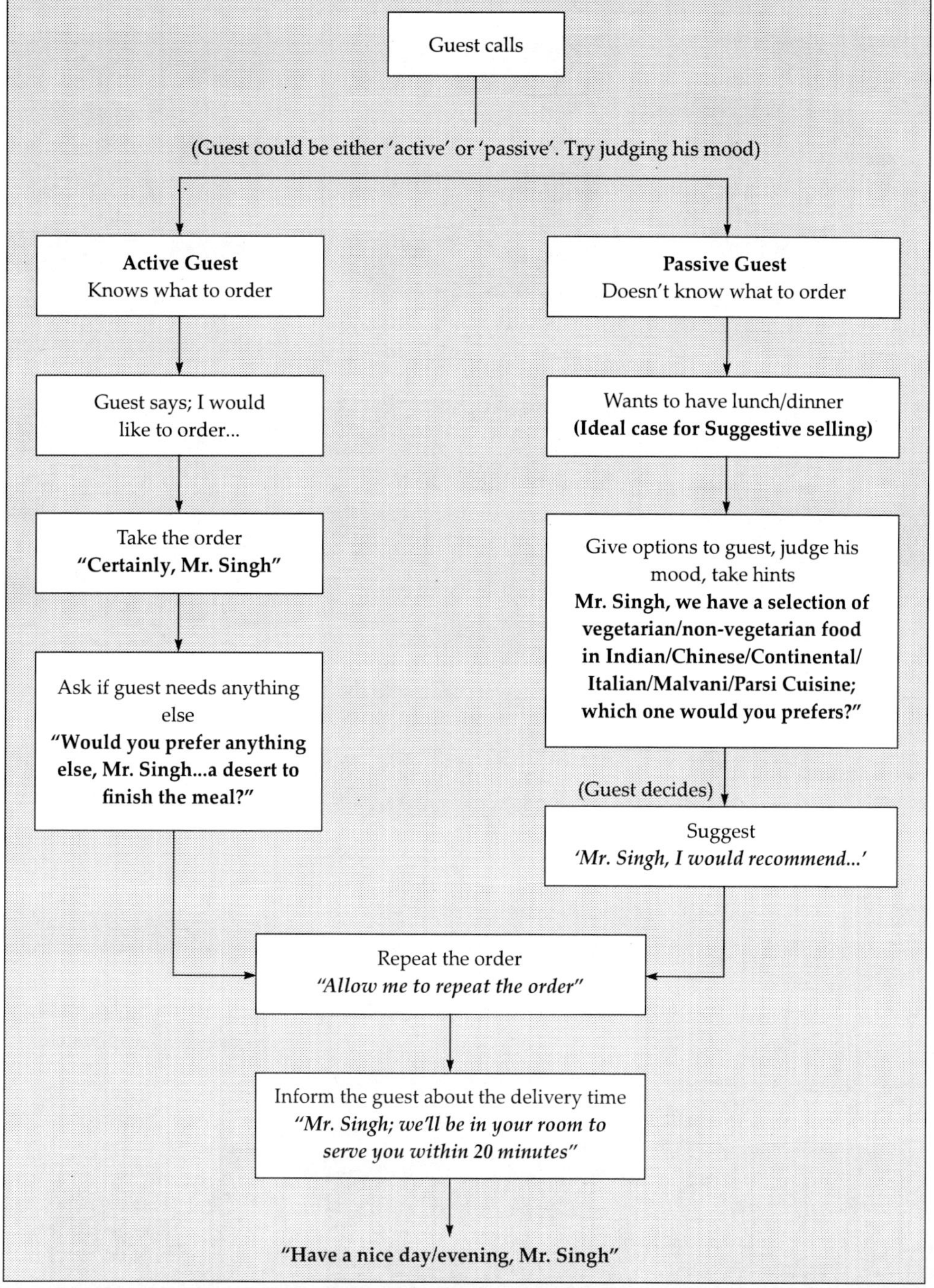

STEP-BY-STEP ROOM SERVICE PROCEDURE

Switch on the hot case.

Enter the order in micros and print the check/bill.

Put the bill in bill folder along with a hotel pen.

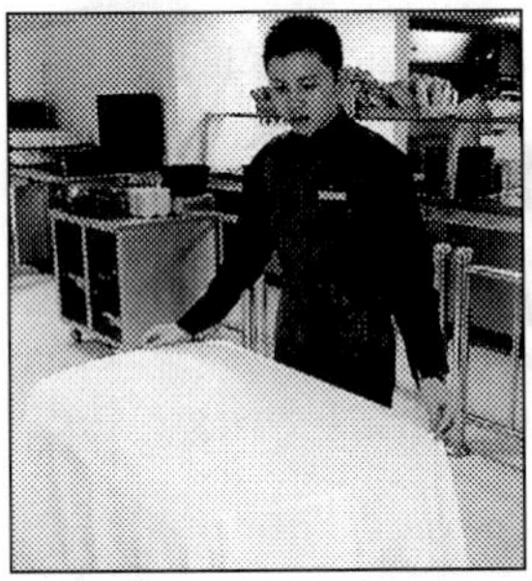

Prepare the trolley.

Place cutlery according to the food.

Prepare water goblet.

Prepare bread basket if applicable.

Prepare condiment setup, if applicable.

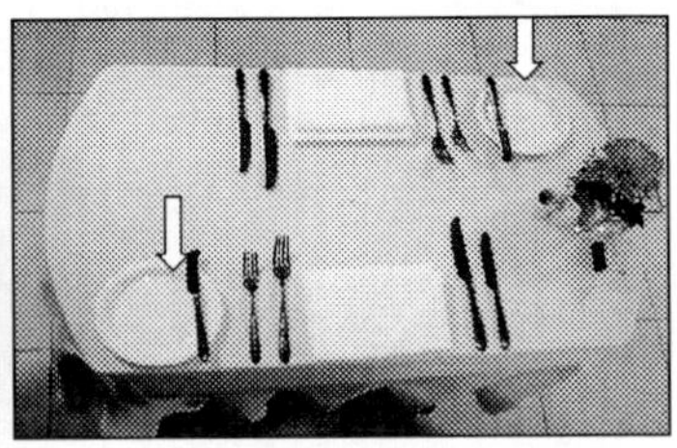

Set the B&B plates and butter knives, if applicable.

Prepare beverages, if applicable.

Prepare tea/coffee setup.

Switch off the hot case.

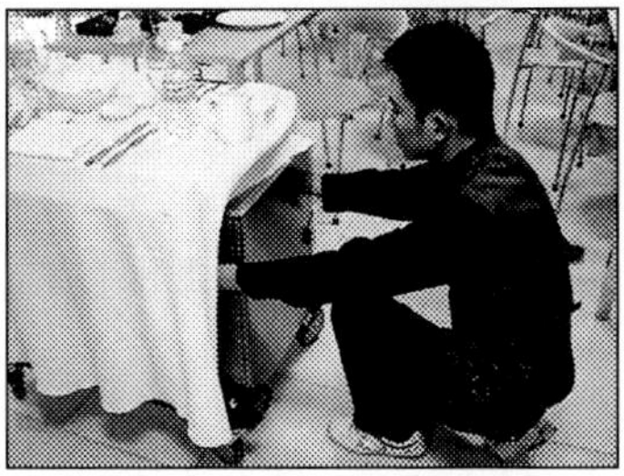

Place warmer beneath the trolley in the cabinet.

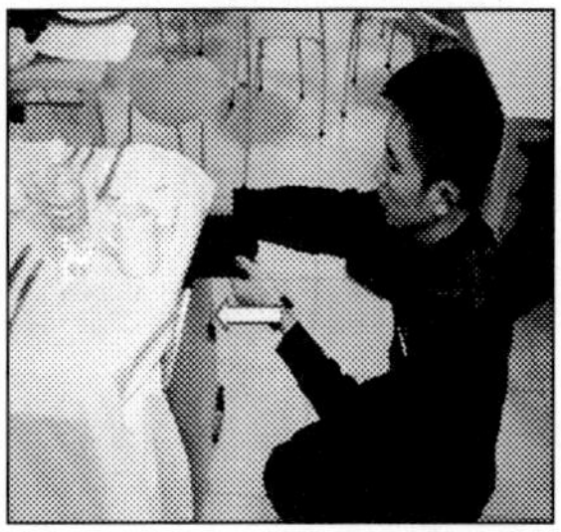

Place service cloth on top of the hot case.

Bread pick up.

Pick up cold food first.

Pick up hot food.

Pick up tea/coffee/ice cream last.

Double-check all the dishes, collect check /bill and put it inside the bill folder before leaving the I.R.D.

Push the trolley with both hands. Never pull the loaded trolley.

Press the service elevator button and wait.

Turn your back and carefully pull the trolley into the service elevator.

Be careful as the door closes suddenly.

Different levels between floor level and elevator level.

While loading the trolley in service elevator, avoid hitting the door as well.

Press the floor number of room to be served the guest.

Check the floor number before leaving the elevator.

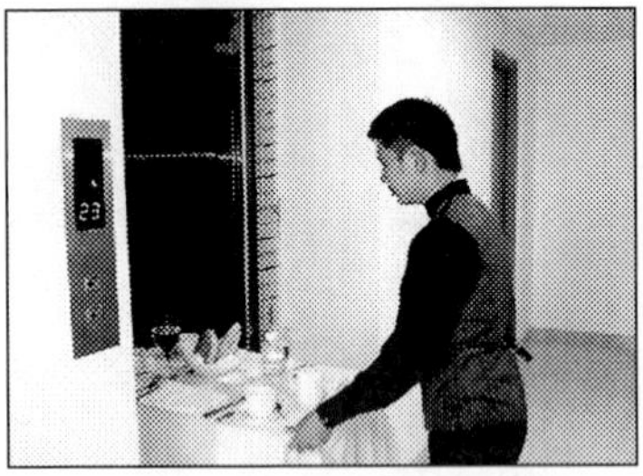

Turn your back and pull the trolley gently out from the service elevator.

Check the room correct with the room number on the check and knock at the door, introducing your name and department and wait for guest's response.

Double-check the food setup in trolley before entering the guest room.

Ask the guest where to put the food.

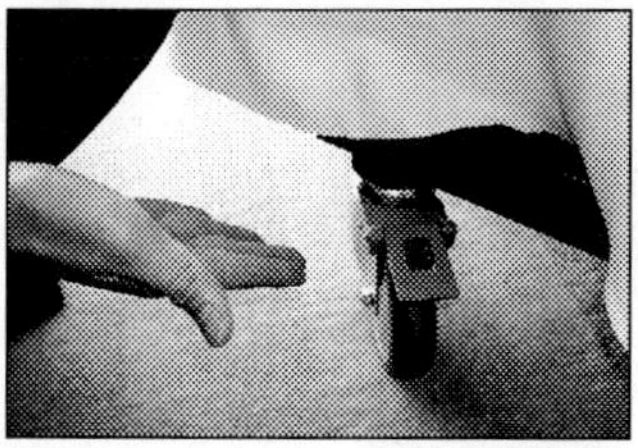

Wheel is easy to lock if you pull the trolley 45 degree on the right side.

Lock the wheel first and open the trolley's wing.

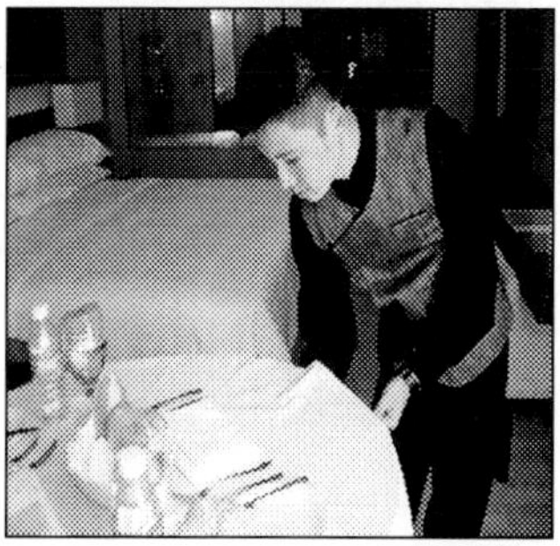

Open the trolley's wing.

Take food from the warmer and place in the trolley.

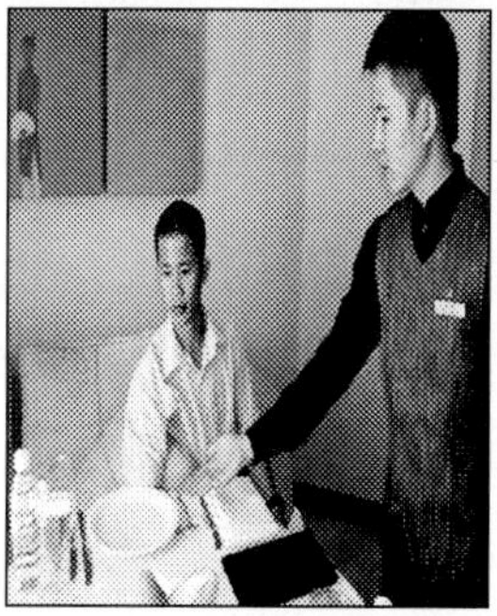

Announce the food to the guest and ask for service.

Present the check/bill to the guest.

Offer further assistance.

Thanks the guest and close the door politely.

On the way back to IRD check the corridors, housekeeping floor pantry for clearance.

Carrying room service trays.

24 FUNCTIONS IN BANQUET

Banquet can be described as a large gathering of people where arrangements are done for service of food and beverages. The word banquet means a sumptuous feast or meal. In the hotel industry it refers to all kinds of functions.

BOOKING A FUNCTION

Equipment Required

- Pencil
- Pen
- Diary
- Telephone
- Specimen lunch and dinner menu
- Photographs of various table layouts
- Booking sheet

Knowledge Required

- Types of functions
- Sense the requirement of guest
- Various policies of booking a function
- Detail about facilities provided in functions

Procedure

- Request for booking the function may arise either through telephone, fax or in person.
- At the initial meeting of the banquet manager and the client a file must be opened recording all points pertaining to the particular function and to hold all the correspondence receipt.
- If it is an enquiry only then the provisional details should be only penciled in until the booking is confirmed.
- After confirmation all the details should be written with ink.
- An initial non-refundable deposit for all catering events should be received by the banquet manager. Full payment for private and social events should be made at least a week prior to the date of function.

- The banquet manager should have specimen luncheon and dinner menus with the cost per head and photographs of the various table layouts for different numbers and occasions. This gives the client a clear picture of the facilities available in the price range he/she can afford.
- After the initial meeting the booking having been confirmed the following basic points should be noted:
  - □ Type of function
  - □ Date
  - □ Time
  - □ Number of covers
  - □ Price per head
  - □ Menu and method of service
  - □ Wines - inclusive or cash
  - □ Type of organization
  - □ Table plan

After this the final points should be decided upon:

- Toastmaster
- Music
- Place cards
- Seating plan
- Types of menu for printing - formal, humorous
- Specialist information - vegetarian, non-vegetarian, special meals.
- Any special requirement.

Depending upon the nature of a particular function, its requirement may vary and it is useful for the banqueting manager to have a checklist of these possible requirements. Other than those points listed above, the following should also be considered.

- List of toasts - who will propose and who will reply?
- Flower decoration for the tables, room, reception area, etc.
- Audio-visual equipment required.
- Special licencse - licence and number.
- Car parking.
- Cloak rooms.
- Artists.
- Changing rooms.
- Cigar and cigarettes.
- Accommodation.
- Telephones.
- Special light, refreshment.
- Secretarial facilities.

- Syndicate room.
- Photographer.
- Sign-posting.
- Private bar facilities.
- Function cancellation fee amount and dead line date.
- Date for final details.

When the booking is confirmed note down all the above-mentioned items in the booking sheet.

FUNCTION PROSPECTUS

Menu and other requirements are usually finalized two weeks in advance of the date of function. A copy of the banquet prospectus will be sent to the client for the review and approval. After all this information is confirmed the necessary details should be circulated well in time to the concerned departments to take care of the requirements which have to be procured from their end.

- Simultaneously/time to time the banquet manager may update the client about the progress of the arrangements being made for the function.
- During the function the banquet manager needs to interact with the client as well as the important guests to ensure them for the smooth operation of the function from their end and to build liaison with the people for future business with them.
- After the function is over it is the duty of the banquet manager to discuss the feedback of the services, bill with the client and he should collect the remaining payment that has to be made by the guest.
- Later a thanks letter should be sent by the banquet manager to the client for opting their venue for the function and to discuss future prospects for the business.
- Letter to all the coordinating departments and fellow employees should be sent by the banquet manager or the person responsible for their support to make the function successful and for future support and coordination.

Organizing the Function

After confirming the booking with all the necessary requirements and passing the information to various departments, the following should be done.

- Finalizing the seating plan with the host which tells who will sit where and the table number.
- Working out the staff requirement and hiring them.
- Checking the availability and other requirements and their working conditions. Hiring them, if necessary.
- Setting up the table plan as required.
- Setting up the rostrum, podium, dance floor, screen, etc., as required.

- Setting up the dining area – formal dining, buffet, etc., as per the host's requirement.
- Conducting service rehearsal for very formal service.
- Inviting the host for final check-up and adjusting the plan according to his/her requirement.
- Food and beverages in-charge and the supervisors should closely monitor the preparation for the function.

On the Day of the Event

- Check the personal grooming of the staff engaged.
- Allocate the mise en place and mise en scene activities to the service staff.
- Inspect the mise en place and mise en scene thoroughly.
- Check the bar counter, if required and ensuring it is equipped with adequate stock and other supplies.
- Assign the tables to the service staff.
- Give adequate briefing to the service staff on the menu, service procedures of food and drinks, toast, etc.
- Count the number of plates placed, if banquet service is organized in the presence of the host's representative and a person from the control department.

During the Service

- Ensure that food and beverages are served according to the instructions given.
- See that the guests receive the food and beverages on time.
- If plated, food reaches the guests quickly at right temperature. If buffet, head count is made and the dishes are replenished quickly.
- Fuel containers of the chafing dishes are frequently topped up with chemi-fuel.
- Clearance of soiled cutlery and crockery should be done quickly.
- Water glasses are filled frequently.
- The temperature of the function hall is at comfort level.
- Monitoring the service of alcoholic beverages.
- If toast is proposed, all wine glasses are filled with wine – normally, it is done in formal functions.
- After the toast, coffee is served.

After the Function

- The tables are cleared.
- The soiled service equipment are sent for washing.
- A/C is switched off.
- Food containers on the buffet tables are sent back to the kitchen.
- Buffet counters are dismantled and tables are stacked.
- Banquet chairs are arranged properly or stacked and kept aside.

<table>
<tr><td colspan="3">Function Prospectus Conferences</td><td>FP No.:</td></tr>
<tr><td>Day Date</td><td colspan="2">Time Type of function</td><td>Venue</td></tr>
<tr><td>Name of the guest</td><td colspan="2">Contact Tel. No.
Office:
Res:</td><td>Address</td></tr>
<tr><td>No. of guests
Guaranteed:
Expected:</td><td colspan="2">Plate: Rs.
Hall rent: Rs.
Board to read</td><td>Pick up time
Soup:
Sancks:
Lunch dinner:</td></tr>
<tr><td colspan="2">Special instruction</td><td colspan="2">Kitchen</td></tr>
<tr><td colspan="2" rowspan="5">Engineering
Air conditioning On at:
Microphone
• Podium Nos. @
• Collar Nos. @
• Cordless Nos. @
• Table Nos. @
• LCD Nos. @
•Overhead Nos. @
• Carousel Nos. @
• Screen Nos. @
• Electronic pointer Nos. @
• TV Nos. @
• Video scoop Nos. @
• Channel music Nos. @
• Special lighting Nos. @
Housekeeping
• Cloakroom attendant
• Flower type
Set-up
• No. of buffers
• Ice carving
• Banquets
• Theatre style
• U-shape
• Boardroom
• Classroom
• Informal
• Fish bone
• White board
• Dias
• Pads
• Pencils
• Entertainment
• Photographer
Videographer</td><td colspan="2">Arrival time:
AMT:
Menu</td></tr>
<tr><td colspan="2"></td></tr>
<tr><td colspan="2">PMT:</td></tr>
<tr><td colspan="2">End time</td></tr>
<tr></tr>
<tr><td>Beverages</td><td>Rates</td><td colspan="2">Billing instructions</td></tr>
<tr><td></td><td></td><td colspan="2">Advance paid Rs.
Date:
Balance amount
Cash ☐ Cheque ☐ Bill to company ☐</td></tr>
<tr><td colspan="4">Distribution: GM/Chef/Dis bar/EHK/Stores/BQTS/ENGG/ Banquet manager acounts/controls</td></tr>
</table>

- Soiled linen are sorted, counted, and kept aside for laundry.
- Bar counter is closed and the closing stock of the bar is taken.
- Bar cash is tallied with the consumption of alcohol, if drinks are not inclusive.
- Returning the empty, full, and partly used bottles to the bar.
- Settling the bar cash to the control department.
- Giving feedback to the service staff.
- Paying off the hired staff and terminating their services.
- Switching off the lights and other electric gadgets.
- Closing the banquet suits and locking.
- Preparing the bill for settlement.
- Entering the bill amount in the banquet sales record.
- During the function, generator backup, additional fuse cartridges, fire extinguishers, and first aid must be kept ready.

STAFF ALLOCATION FOR FUNCTION

Equipment Required

- Pencil
- Pen
- Diary
- Telephone

Knowledge Required

- Types of functions
- Details of banqueting function

Procedure

- The banquet supervisor to review the staffing requirements based on the function for the next three days.
- Banquet supervisor to identify the number of additional manpower that will be required based on the current manpower status.
- If additional manpower is not required then the banquet supervisor plans the duty allocations on the hall-wise duty allocation sheet one day prior to the event.
- If additional manpower is required the banquet manager sends an email to the HR manager requesting for the same.

Standard

Guest to staff ratio is as follows:

- **Conferences:** 15-25 guest: 01 F&B associate.

For every 20 additional guest 1 associate.

- **Banquet Events:** 15-25 Guests: 2 F&B associates

For every 20 additional guests 1 F&B associate.

- Duty allocation to be done by 5.00 p.m everyday.
- Request for additional staff to be provided should be forwarded to the HR department a minimum of 48 hrs. notice.

BANQUET TABLE SETUP – ROUND AND RECTANGULAR TABLES

Equipment Required

- Banquet tables
- Crockery, cutlery and glassware and linen

Knowledge Required

- Conference amenities
- Eye for detail
- Types of setup
- Hygiene and sanitation

Procedure

- Check that the tables are in good condition.
- The associate to now frill the table.
- A right handed F&B associate may start frilling the tables in an anticlock direction and vice versa.
- While frilling the F&B associate to ensure that there are no visible creases on the table.
- The F&B associate to now place the chairs as per the setup.
- The F&B associate to now place the chair covers on the chairs.

For Conferences

- The F&B associate to place the note pads, pencil, hi-ball glass, stationery box, Flower vase (only on request), mints, 1 litre mineral water bottle on the table.
- Arrange the tables as per the conference requirement.

For Banquets

- The associate to place the cutlery, crockery, glassware, flower arrangement, candle, linen, etc., on the table.

Standard

- Table should not be wobbling.
- The table's leg locks should be functional.
- The edges of the table are intact.
- The moulton should not be torn.
- Fall on the guests' side should not be more than 6 inches.

- The frill to be clean, free from stains; well ironed.
- The frill should not be torn.
- No pins to be used for frilling.
- The chair should not be wobbling.
- The chairs should not have any protruding parts.
- All the chair legs should have rubber shoes.
- A six-feet table to accommodate not more than 3 chairs.
- The front edge of the chair cushion to be in line with the fall of the felt.
- All chairs to have chair covers irrespective of the type of function.
- The chair cover should be free from any visible stains and tears.
- The chair cover should cover the chair completely.
- The note pad to be placed on the table in line with the center of the chair, 1 inch from the inner edge of the table.
- Stationery box to contain:
  1. 1 stapler filled with the staples.
  2. Staple box.

Banquet set ups

Buffet layout

Event setup

Theatre setup

Boardroom setup

Round table setup

Classroom setup

U-Shape setup

Banquet layout

Round table setup

3. 4 white board markers (two black, one each of red and green.)
4. 10 "U" clips.
5. 1 eraser.
6. 1 Pencil sharpener.
7. 5 Rubber bands.
8. 1 Ruler – 6 inches.

FORMAL SIT-DOWN BUFFET

Equipment Required

- Banquet tables
- Crockery, cutlery and glassware and linen

Knowledge Required

- Conference amenities
- Types of formal setup
- Eye for detail
- Hygiene and sanitation

Procedure

For Rectangular Tables

1. Check that the tables are in good condition.
2. The F&B associate to now place the green felt on the table top, after checking that it is in good condition.
3. The F&B associate to lay the tablecloth on the table.
4. The F&B associate to now frill the table.
5. While frilling the F&B associate ensures that there are no visible creases on the table.
6. The F&B associate to now place the chairs as per the setup.
7. The F&B associate to now place the chair covers on the chairs.
8. The F&B associate to place the cutlery, crockery, glassware, flower arrangement, candle, linen, etc., on the table.

For Round Tables

9. Check that the tables are in good condition.
10. The F&B associate to now place the round felt on the table.
11. The F&B associate to now place the tablecloth on the table.
12. The F&B associate to now place the net overlay on the tablecloth.
13. The F&B associate to place the cutlery, crockery, glassware, flowers, candle, linen, etc., on the table.

For State Banquets (Brigade Service)

14. All the steps from step 1 to step 13
15. A light fixture with three lights of three colors (red, green, orange) to be fixed inside the banquet hall and in the back area of the hall.
16. The controls of the light board to be arranged for on a podium near the service entrance.
17. The light controls to be operated by the banquet manager/F&B manager.

Standard

- All equipment should be checked for their functionality and hygiene factor.
- Table should not be wobbling.
- The table leg locks should be functional.
- The edges of the tables to be intact.
- The moulton should not be torn.
- The felt should not be torn and should be free from stains.
- The tablecloth to be clean, free from stains, well ironed, and should not be torn.
- Chair should not be wobbling.
- Chair should not have any protruding points.
- Chair legs should having rubber shoes.
- All chairs should have chair covers irrespective of the type of function.
- Chair covers should be neat, clean and free from any visible stains.
- Frill should be neat and clean, free from any stains.
- A six feet table to accommodate not more than three chairs.
- Frills to be clean, free from stains, ironed and should not be torn.
- No pins to be used for frilling.
- The front edge of the chair cushion to be just touching the frill of the table.
- Chair cover should cover the chair completely.
- The felt should not be torn and must be free from stains
- Tablecloth to be clean, well ironed and free from stains.
- Tablecloth should not be torn.
- Tablecloth should fall evenly on all sides.
- The net overlay to be clean, free from stains.
- The net overlay to be well ironed.
- The net overlay should not be torn.
- The net overlay should fall evenly on all sides.
- The lights in the hall to be fixed directly above the service entry in the hall facing the guest area.

- The lights in the back area to be fixed directly above the service entry in the hall facing the back area.
- One switch each for red, green, and orange light.
- The lights mean:
    - □ **Red:** Stop (service or clearance)
    - □ **Green:** Start (service or clearance).
    - □ **Orange:** be prepared (for service or clearance)

HANDLING PLATES IN BANQUETS

Equipment Required

- Plates
- Wiping sheet
- Trolley

Knowledge Required

- Physical location of banquet stores
- Eye for detail
- Safety
- Hygiene and sanitation

Procedure

- Pick up the washed crockery from the dish washing rack in the stewarding counter/wash-up area.
- Arrange and sort the crockery by type and size.
- Wipe the crockery using a clean wiping cloth.
- Hold one side of the crockery in the left hand using one corner of the wiping cloth.
- Hold the remaining cloth in the right hand and wipe using a circular motion first the top part of the crockery and then the bottom side.
- Check completion by ensuring no visual stains or marks are seen.
- The crockery is stacked in the designated racks .

Standard

- There should be no food deposits, oil stains and soap deposits in the plates. Any such items should be given for rewashing.
- The crockery should be without any chips or cracks, any such items to be kept in breakage items stock.

- The crockery is placed on the trolleys according to the type and size, i.e., all B&B plates together, saucers together and so on.
- The crockery should be stacked firmly and safely on top of one another with larger plates at the bottom and the smaller ones on the top.
- The crockery should be carried in trolleys to ensure that there is no slippage.
- The discarded tablecloths are to be used as wiping cloths.
- The wiping cloth should not be damp.
- The wiping cloth should not smell.
- The wiping cloth should be changed regularly.
- Hands should never be in direct contact with the crockery.
- The crockery must be dry and unchipped and lint free.
- Follow the marking on the racks while stacking.
- Each stack to have 25 pieces of crockery.

HANDLING CUTLERY IN BANQUETS

Equipment Required

- Cutlery
- Wiping sheet
- Salver

Knowledge Required

- Physical location of banquet stores
- Eye for detail
- Safety
- Hygiene and sanitation

Procedure

- Pick up the washed cutlery from the rack in the stewarding counter/wash-up area.
- Arrange and sort the cutlery by type and size.
- Carry the cutlery back to the banquet area carefully.
- Dip the cutlery in hot water before wiping it.
- Wipe the cutlery using a clean cloth.
- Hold the base of the cutlery in the left hand with one corner of the wiping cloth.
- Wipe with the left hand using with front and back motion.
- Check completion by visual observation for stains or marks and dryness.
- Carry the cutlery to banquet store on a salver.
- The cutlery is placed in the banquet store in their respective slots.

Standard

- There should be no food deposits, oil stains and soap deposits. Any such items should be given for rewashing.
- The cutlery should be in good condition, i.e., not bent or out of shape.
- The cutlery is placed on tray according to the type, all knives together, all spoons together and so on.
- The cutlery should be stacked firmly and safely in bundles flat on the tray.
- Hands should never be in direct contact with the cutlery.
- The discarded tablecloths are to be used as wiping cloths.
- The wiping cloth should not be damp.
- The wiping cloth should not smell.
- The wiping cloth should be changed regularly.
- Ensure minimum handling of cutlery.
- VIP cutlery if used to be wrapped in bundles of 100 with a cling wrap.

HANDLING GLASSWARE IN BANQUETS

Equipment Required

- Glassware
- Wiping sheet
- Salver
- Glass rack

Knowledge Required

- Physical location of banquet stores
- Eye for detail
- Safety
- Hygiene and sanitation

Procedure

1. The glassware is placed in the racks above the stewarding counter.
2. The person deputed for rinsing glasses brings the rack to the rinse basin located near the kitchen stewarding area.
3. Wipe the glasses with the wiping cloth.
4. Warm the glass using hot water before it is wiped.
5. Hold the base of the glass in the left hand using one corner of the wiping cloth.
6. Insert the remaining cloth in the glass using the right hand.
7. Insert the index, second and ring finger in the glass and use the thumb as support on the outer side.

8. Wipe the glass with the right hand using swift clockwise motion.
9. Invert the glasses and place them in the racks.
10. Carry the racks to the banquet store and place them in the designated area.

APPLYING FRILLS ON THE TABLES

Equipment Required

- Frill
- Banquet tables
- Thumb pin

Knowledge Required

- Eye for detail
- Various patterns of pleats

Procedure

- Select the frill which suits your theme.
- Make the fall up to the table's height to cover the legs.
- Pin it at one corner.
- Start forming the pleats as per the requirement of the function and pin it to retain the pleats.
- Pleats should be made at equidistance or should follow certain sequence.
- Pleats may run either to one side or to both the direction, it depends upon the type of frill arrangement whether it is single sided or double sided, with closed ends or open ends.
- For box type setups straight frill can be applied to cover all the corners of the table to form a box.

Standard

- Frill should be well ironed, neat, clean and free from any stains.
- While frilling ensure that there are no visible creases on the table.
- A right handed F&B associate may start frilling the tables in anticlock direction and vice versa.
- Thumb pin should not be visible.
- Pleats should be of same size and in same manner.
- Frill should hang evenly from all sides.

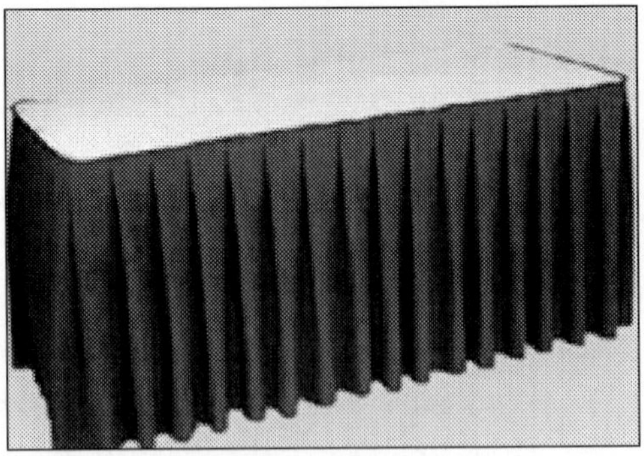

Frill applied on a table

LIGHTING FUEL

Equipment Required

- Fuel lamp
- Aluminium foil
- Scooper
- Matchbox

Knowledge Required

- Safety

Procedure

- Fill the fuel into the fuel lamps with the help of a scooper.
- Cover the lamps with the aluminium foil so that it is not exposed.
- During the time when the fuel lamps have to be lighten up. Prick the foil with the help of a folk at the centre forming a small mouth.
- Light a matchstick and bring it near to the fuel to lighten up the fuel lamps.

BANQUET FORMATS

Banquets Ammendment Note

To: All concerned Date: FP No. Venue: Name of party:	Subject: Date of function:
Original No. of Pax Min. Max. Menu items 1 2 3 4 5	**Changed to** No. of Pax Min. Max. Menu items 1 2 3 4 5
Rate (Reference of Decrease)	
Addition	
General	

Note the above and make necessary changes
Thanks and Regards

Authorised signatory

Function comment card

We would appreciate if you please take the time to complete the questionnaire, as we very much value your comments

	Excellent	Good	Average
Service			
Courtesy	☐	☐	☐
Efficiency	☐	☐	☐
Food			
Quality	☐	☐	☐
Presentation	☐	☐	☐
Variety of menu	☐	☐	☐
Ambience			
Decor	☐	☐	☐
Set-up	☐	☐	☐
Music	☐	☐	☐
Audio/visual	☐	☐	☐

Additional comments

____
____
____
____
____
____
____
____

FP No.
Name :--------------------------------
Designation :--------------------------------
Company :--------------------------------
Address :--------------------------------
:--------------------------------
PHN :--------------------------------
E-mail :--------------------------------

Is it your first banquet at Park Prime Jaipur?

Yes ☐ No ☐

Would you host future banquets/functions with us?

Yes ☐ No ☐

If not, please tell us why?

____
____
____

How often do you host banquet functions?

☐ More than once a month
☐ Once a month
☐ Every three months
☐ Every six months
☐ Others

How would you rate our product?

☐ Value for money
☐ Expensive

Thank you for your time

COCKTAIL LUNCH/DINNER SETUP IN BANQUETS

Equipment Required

- Setup requirement as per function prospectus

Knowledge Required

- Types of functions
- Types of setup
- Types of services
- Service etiquettes
- Eye for detail

Procedure

- Post the pre-event briefing, the associates to begin the setup as per the requirements stated on the FP.
- The supervisor to coordinate the procurement of items that need to come from another departments or external vendors.
- The associate to set up the tables as per standard.
- Following are the possible seating arrangements for a cocktail dinner.
  (a) Casual seating
  (b) Round table seating
  (c) Theatre style
  (d) "Gadda" seating in case of ghazal night.
- Seating arrangement for casual and round table to be two-thirds of the guaranteed numbers. In case of theatre equal number to be provided.
- Bed sheet to be stain and torn free.
- Mattress to be in good repair.
- Bar to be set up as per task standard mentioned below.
- Buffet set to be done as per standard mentioned.
- The snack counter to be set as per task mentioned below.
- The back area to be set very well so that the flow of food and at the end clearance is done properly with minimum breakage.
- No furniture in the passage to the wash-up area.
- Glass racks for glasses to be kept ready.
- A stainless steel tray with liquid soap and water to be kept ready for dirty cutlery.
- Back area to be free from any spillage.
- If the function is being held on the poolside area, garden court or halls which are away from the wash-up area, a plate trolley and 4 garbage bins to be placed in the back area closest to the venue.

- Hall checklist to be strictly followed.
- In case of an outside decorator the person to be briefed about the policies of the hotel and the decorations should suit the theme of the function.
- Set-up to be explained to the host for any further changes that may be requested.

Standard

- Standard operating procedures will be followed for set-up and service to ensure that the guest receives seamless and flawless service.
- A trained technician will be present for assistance during the function depending on the equipment used.
- The banquet hall should be at the standard temperature prior to guest arrival / scheduled to start of the function. The hall to be at a temperature of 22°C ± 1°C in summer and at a temperature of 23°C ± 1°C in winter before arrival of the host.
- All equipment will be checked for its working condition.

BAR SETUP FOR BANQUET

Equipment Required

- Setup requirement for bar as per function prospectus

Knowledge Required

- Types of beverages.
- Types of bar setups.
- Types of glassware.
- Types of equipment.
- Knowledge of cocktails and mocktails.

Procedure

- The size of the bar depends on the number of people attending the function, convenience of service and manpower.
- Generally, above 400 people 2 bars are given
- Width of the bar: 6 feet for up to 100 covers and above 300 covers it is 12 feet.
- Mobile bar counters can be used if available since they have in-built facilities but the commonly used one is the built up and elevated bar.
- The bar counter should be away from the seating and the catering area so that there is no crowding at the counter for buffet and drinks in the same area.
- The bar is laid in U shape. The distance between the back end of the bar and the back end of the front table should be 8 feet minimum and 10 feet if a separate display is made
- Ideal table size is for the vertical arms of the "U" are 6 feet × 2 feet. For the horizontal arm of the U is 6 feet × 2.5 feet. The table used for the elevation of the

horizontal counter should be 6 feet × 2 feet in size so that at the base table on the service side 0.5 feet of space is left which can be used as work area.

- The elevation should be minimum 1 foot. Two racks are enough for giving the elevation.
- The glass racks should be of equal height and placed in such a way that the elevation table balances evenly on top of the racks. The total number of glasses should be double the number of the expected persons for the function.
- In case of a bar setup in a banquet hall the floor area should be covered with rubber sheets to avoid carpet from getting damaged.
- Put the glasses on the counter.
- Before setting up the bar soft drinks, beers and juices are required to be chilled.
- While chilling the soft drink start putting layers of the 1.5 litre bottles. Water to be 1½ times the amount of ice.
- Preferably beer, tonic water, mineral water and canned juices should be chilled separately.
- For larger functions a partitioned chilling trolley should be used in which beer should be chilled in one part and soft drinks, juices, mineral water in the other.
- Add ice and water to the dry chilling.
- Keep the following bar items ready before service:
  - □ Swizzle sticks in a Tom Collins
  - □ Plain straws in a Tom Collins
  - □ Cocktail napkins (for VIP events)
  - □ Paper napkins for all other event's
  - □ Ice bucket with tongs
  - □ Sauces – Tabasco, Worcestershire sauce
  - □ Angostura bitters
  - □ Khus, rose, pomegranate and strawberry crush
  - □ Blue Curacao (non-alcoholic)
  - □ Freshly squeezed lime juice, sugar syrup, lime cordial
  - □ Salt on a saucer
  - □ Garnishes: lime wedge, lime slice, pineapple triangles, canned cherry, mint leaves.
- Keep salvers ready with two decanters, one ice bucket with a tong, 5 old fashioned glasses with swizzle stick, paper/cocktail napkins.

Procedure of service from the bar

1. When the guest approaches the bar ask the guest his preference of drinks.
2. Check whether ice is required and also the mixer. If he likes cocktails inform him about the cocktails that can be made.
3. Make the drink as desired by the guest.

Standard

- Standard operating procedures will be followed for setup and service to ensure that the guest receives.
- Place two ice buckets on the bar counter and one on each salver.
- Minimum one hour before the function beer, soft drinks and juices should be chilled in a chilling trolley or chilling tub.
- The total number of glasses should be double the number of the expected persons for the function.
- The bottles to be placed vertically.

SNACK COUNTER SETUP FOR COCKTAIL/DINNER IN BANQUET

Equipment Required

- Setup requirement for bar as per function prospectus
- Platters
- Types of cutlery and crockery
- Condiment bowl
- Hot case
- Tissue paper

Knowledge Required

- Types of snacks
- Hot case and its working
- Types of crockery, cutlery and glassware

Procedure

- In cocktail parties, service of snacks is a very important component in the initial phase with the cocktails.
- This counter is set up at the back area of the hall where snack service is to be done.
- Ideal table size is 6 × 2 feet or 6 × 2.5 feet.
- The location of the table should be decided in such a way that proper proximity is maintained with the service door of the venue and the kitchen area and the hot cases but still not block any passage or disturb the workflow.
- Items required for the snack counters are: salvers, snack platters (4 portion platter), sauce boats, cocktail sticks or toothpicks, toothpick stands, paper napkins, doily papers, fish bowls for sauces.
- Arrange the platters on the table.
- If the quantity of snacks to be served is up to 10 dozens then the snacks can be directly picked up from the kitchen. If the quantity is above 10 dozens then it is ideal to use a hot case.

- Every platter should have a doily on which the snacks will be placed.
- The sauceboat should be placed towards the guest side.
- The snack platters must be well presented and easy to carry.
- The salver to be set with the snack, paper napkins, cocktail napkins, toothpick or cocktail sticks, a plate for debris.
- The end of the platter should have paper napkins, tent card which displays the name of the snack and if it is vegetarian or non-vegetarian and the toothpick stand.
- Every snack platter should have a tent card with the name of the dish and a one liner explaining the dish should on the back of the tent card for the server to see.
- If the vegetarian and non-vegetarian snacks have common sauces then they should be kept separate in separate sauce boats and care should be taken that the sauce boats are not mixed up.
- In case of large quantities of snacks it is advisable to pick up the snacks in batches and not the whole lot.
- In larger banqueting the stewards who rotate the snacks are allotted particular area so that the entire guest's enjoy the starters, because it happens that the starters get stuck in a particular group or area and some guests don't get it at all.
- In case of snacks like chicken drumsticks, the steward should carry a cheese plate in the right hand to collect the bones.
- The platter must be free from crumbs, stains from sauces and chutneys and left-over toothpicks and swizzle sticks and garnishes.
- The number of persons on snack service depends on the number of snacks ordered, quantity of snacks ordered and number of covers. Appropriate sauces to be used for the snacks.
- After every round of service the snack platter should be wiped of, doily to be removed and fresh doily should be placed. If there is any carved garnish (e.g., carrot, radish, beetroot, etc., then a bowl of water should be placed on the snacks counter. Once the platter comes out the garnishes should go in the garnish bowl.
- After one round is finished and the platter comes in the remaining pieces of snacks should be put back in the hot case so that they get reheated.
- Once the snack service is over make sure that the snack counter is immediately cleared so that the space can be used to station clearance trolley before the meal starts. The hot case should also be cleared and switched off. Leftover snacks must be reheated and look fresh on the platter each time. Cold snack need to be placed din chillers and cold cases so that they look fresh and not wilted. Condensation and moisture must be avoided on cold starters.
- Counter must be cleared and dismantled quietly. No banging and loud movement of furniture. Relay the tablecloth and tables.
- The snacks tray can be decorated according to the theme of the event; the most common is putting a candle in a cut tomato, or floating it in a small bowl of water.

- In some parties banana leaves, or spices or some vegetables are used as the base of the platter to give the snacks an authentic look.

Standard

- Standard operating procedures will be followed for setup and service to ensure that the guest receives seamless and delightful service.
- Non-vegetarian and vegetarian tags to be used for all buffet presentations.

BUFFET SETUP FOR BANQUET

Equipment Required

- Setup requirement as per function prospectus

Knowledge Required

- Types of buffet setup
- Types of tables used
- Types of chaffing dishes
- Types of service equipment
- Eye for detail

Procedure

- Before the setup the supervisor has to read the FP thoroughly and brief the staff accordingly.
- The standard for the number of counters is
  - One buffet counter for every 75 people
  - Two counters for more than 100
  - One bar counter for 100 pax, which is big enough to dispense drinks to the crowd.
  - Indian breads have to be given live for more than 75 people.
- Lunch buffets are not very elaborate and are set in the pre-function area where the guests break out for lunch.
- The salads and the accompaniments are well elevated so that the food looks well presented during the function.
- The buffet is set for the guest at least 15 minutes before the scheduled break time.
- Make sure that all the food is kept ready except the Indian breads to serve the guest at one go.
- Buffet layout to be continuously refreshed throughout the service time.
- Buffet to be very well laid and the buffet tables to be well presented.
- The buffet is kept clean all the time, the ladles and side plates changed when they become soiled.

- In sit-down luncheons the buffet is set in the back area and side stations are made in the hall itself to serve the guests promptly.
- Buffet tags to be placed in front of every dish.
- The vegetarian and non-vegetarian dishes are to be marked clearly on the name slips.
- There should be no spelling mistakes in the dish names.
- Demarcation to be done as per the standards, in case vegetarian and non-vegetarian buffets to be separately laid (green and red dots).
- The required food pans to be kept ready in the hall back area.
- Three fuel pots to be kept below each chafing dish.
- Ensure that the fuel pots are filled properly.
- Pour water in water pan of the chafing dish. Water to be filled in one-fourth of the water pan.
- A water counter to be set close to the buffet counter.
- A soft bar can also be set apart from the water counter as per the requirement.

Standards

- Standard operating procedures will be followed for setup and service to ensure that the guest receives seamless service.
- Buffet to be ready in the night itself in case of lunch conferences.
- All outsourced food should only be procured from certified supplies as per the prevention of food adulteration norms.
- Hot food to be served above 65°C and cold food below 4-5°C.
- Non-vegetarian and vegetarian tags to be used for all buffet presentations.
- Buffet tables should not wobble.
- Chafing dish should be neat and clean and without any watermarks.
- Fuel should be lighted properly.

25 BUFFET SETUP

Buffet is displayed in the restaurant/coffee shop for the in-house guest as well as for walk-inns. Guest can have breakfast, lunch and dinner from the buffet available in the restaurant and coffee shop. Buffet helps in serving large number of people at a time as the guests can easily see the dishes displayed in the buffet and can choose what to eat and in what quantity? Refilling of buffet is done by kitchen and F&B staff together.

Equipment Required

- Buffet tags
- Cutlery/crockery for buffet
- Food pans
- Wiping cloth

Knowledge Required

- Items available for the buffet
- Cyclic buffet menu
- Signature dishes
- Safety precautions while lighting fuel
- Hygiene and sanitation

BREAKFAST BUFFET SETUP PROCEDURE

Evening Shift

1. Wipe the buffet counter tops with wiping cloth.
2. Place the chafing dishes along with the ladles, fuels, dip bowls and full plates.
3. Set the fresh fruit and juice counter.
4. Place cereal bowls and juice glasses on the counter. The toaster to be placed on the on-site counter.
5. The hot plate and the waffle maker places on the onsite counter (live counter). Place half plates for the egg/waffles and pancakes.
6. Fill cereal dispensers and cover with a cling film. These jars to be placed on the buffet counter along with cereal bowls.
7. Arrange the jam bar next to the bread counter.

8. Arrange the coffee machine as per task. Arrange the hot plate for tea/coffee.
9. Place the buffet tags.
10. The F&B associate to place plates on all the counters.

Morning Shift

11. Put hot water in the chafing dishes and light the fuel.
12. Collect ice from the ice cube machine. Crush the ice using the ice crushing machine. Put this ice in a glass bowl and place the chutney and yoghurt bowls.
13. Pick up the cold food from the designated kitchen.
14. Pick up the hot food from the designated kitchen.
15. Place the appropriate service gear for each item on the buffet.
16. Pick up hot and cold milk in a flask from the pantry.
17. The chef to be ready with the live counter – eggs, waffles, dosa and pancakes.

Breakfast Buffet Clearance

18. Inform all guests in the restaurant before clearing the buffet.
19. Place the buffet closed sign board
20. Switch off the chafing dish heater
21. Remove the service gears and the dip bowls
22. Return the hot and cold food to the kitchen
23. Clear the juice counter by removing the fruits, the juicers, juice glasses, cereal bowls and glass elevation. Clean the juice counter top.
24. Clean the toaster with a damp cloth and place it under the counter.
25. Remove the buffet tags.

Standard

- The counter should be cleaned thoroughly to ensure that there are no food stains or fingerprints on the glass.
- Chafing dishes to be free from finger or water marks.
- Dips bowls should be free from marks, crack or chips.
- Full plates should not be cracked or chipped.
- The glass block should be properly aligned, spotlessly clean and shining.
- Juice glasses should not be cracked or chipped.
- Toaster should be free from crumbs and in working condition.
- Plates should not be stained, cracked or chipped.
- Cereal jar to be washed and wiped dry after the end of every breakfast session.
- Cereal jar should be free from all stains.
- Cereal bowl should not be chipped or cracked.
- Place jam bar on an underliner and teaspoon.

- There should be no spelling mistakes in the names of the dishes.
- The buffet tag to be colour coded – vegetarian (green)/non-vegetarian (red).
- The F&B associate should place 50 plates on the buffet counter, 30 plates (cold) at the cold counter, in 2 stacks of 15 each.
- The water poured in the water pan of chafing dishes should be hot so that the temperature of the item remains constant. Pour water till 1 inch level.
- Do not use cutlery or paper to light the fuel.
- To be picked up as per the menu.
- Buffet temperature should be checked by digital thermometer twice in an hour.
- Food to be picked up as per menu.
- The hot items should be placed 10 minutes before the commencement of the buffet.
- Flask to be washed and cleaned before pouring the milk.
- Cyclic menu to be followed for lunch and breakfast buffets to reduce menu fatigue.

Live Counter

Fill cereals jar and cover it

Place appropriate service gear for each item

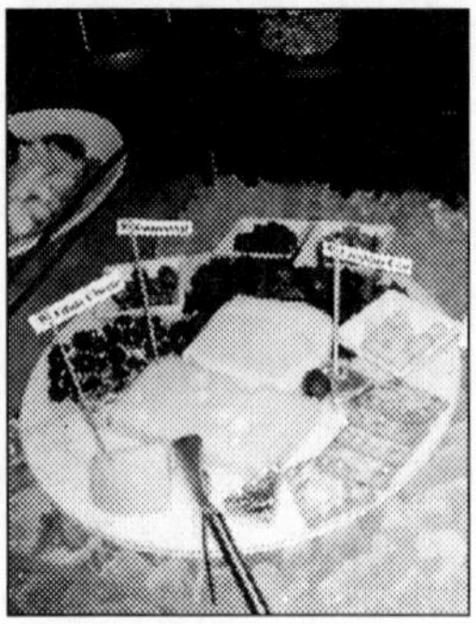

Cheese counter

Bread counter

Fresh fruit counter

Juice counter

- Chef to conduct random checks of buffet to ensure that temperature of food is maintained. Cold food served below 5°C and hot food below 65°C, soups to be served at 80-90°C.
- Food pans never to be more than one-third empty.

While Clearance

- Cereal bowl and juice glasses to be collected on a salver and taken to the wash-up area.
- The counter to be debris free and dry.
- The chafing dishes to be cleaned and free from debris.
- There should be no debris on the counter.
- Place the tags in their respective storage areas.

LUNCH/DINNER BUFFET SETUP

Procedure

Lunch

1. Wipe the buffet counter with a wiping cloth.
2. Place the chafing dishes, ladles, dip bowls and full plates.
3. Place the buffet tags.
4. Set up the elevations for the salad counter and dessert counter. Place half plates for the dessert counter.
5. Set the hot plate for the live counter.
6. Set up the soup counter along with soup tureens, the soup cups, underliners and half plates.
7. Set up the pickle counter.

Buffet layout

Pick Up

8. Pour piping hot water into the chafing dishes.
9. Pick up the desserts from bakery and *halwai* and cold and hot food from respective kitchens.
10. Place appropriate service gears and ladles.

Dinner

11. Dinner buffet to be set up as per the process enumerated above.

CLEARANCE TO BE DONE

Standard

- The counter should be cleaned thoroughly to ensure that there are no food stains or fingerprints on the glass.
- Chafing dishes to be free from finger or watermarks.
- Dips bowls should be free from marks, crack or chips.
- Full plates should not be cracked or chipped.
- There should be no spelling mistakes in the names of the dishes.
- The buffet tag to be colour coded – vegetarian (green)/non-vegetarian (red).
- The glass block should be properly aligned, spotlessly clean and shining.
- Plates to be free from cracks, chips and stains.
- Soup cups, underliners and half plates should not be stained, cracked or chipped.

While explaining buffet to a guest you should always open the food cover and explain all the dishes with proper ingredients.

- Soup tureens should be in working condition.
- Jars to be free from stains and crackers.
- Lip of the jar should be wiped.
- The water poured should be hot so that the temperature of the item remains constant.
- Pour water in water pan of chafing dishes till 1 inch level.
- Pick up the food as per the cyclic menu.
- Cold food will be brought covered in a cling wrap, this cover to be removed before opening the buffet counter.
- Service gears to be stain free.
- Indian breads not to be displayed but to be served on the table by F&B associates.

Salad counter

Hot food counter

Bread counter

Dessert counter

26 FUELS USED IN RESTAURANTS

Calorific Value: *Number of heat units produced by complete combustion of unit quantity of fuel.*

- Wood : 2500 (kcal/kg)
- Peat : 3500 (kcal/kg)
- Charcoal : 6903
- Lignite coal : 3000 (kcal/kg)
- Bituminous coal : 7000 (kcal/kg)
- Gasoline : 11,200
- L.P.G : 10,882

Any source of heat energy is called fuel. A fuel is a substance which when once raised to its ignition temperature continues to burn if sufficient oxygen or air is available. The material which is burnt to produce heat is known as fuel, for example, wood, coal, domestic gas (LPG), kerosene oil, diesel, and petrol are used as fuels in home, industries and for transport. You can also say that fuel is any substance capable of chemical combustion with oxygen producing heat and light. When a fuel is burnt, it combines with oxygen in the air to form carbon dioxide and water vapour. A lot of energy, heat and sometimes light is also produced during this process. Fuel can be classified as primary fuel, found in abundance in nature and used in natural form like coal, wood and so on and secondary fuel which requires some refining or processing or mixing like petrol, kerosene, diesel and so on. Fuels can also be classified as:

- *Solid:* Coal, wood, peat, anthracite, bituminous.
- *Liquid:* Petrol, diesel, kerosene, spirit, coal tar.
- *Gaseous:* LPG (liquified petroleum gas), CNG (compressed natural gas), methane and compressed butane.
- *Electricity*
- *Conventional fuel:* Solar energy, biogas.

PROPERTIES OF IDEAL FUEL

- Low ignition point and high calorific value.
- Produces minimum amount of smoke.
- Should be easy to store and convenient for transportation and economical.
- Has moderate rate of combustion.
- Has low content of non-volatile material.

- Is readily and available.
- Produces no poisonous products on combustion.

SOLID FUEL

- **Wood:** Used for boiler furnace and sometimes to make wood oven pizza. Contains large amount of moisture, has low thermal value.
- **Coal:** Extensively used solid fuel, used for both industrial and domestic purposes. Mainly used in tandoors in kitchen.
- **Coke:** Mainly used for domestic purpose. Has higher calorific value.

Classification of Coal

- **Anthracite:** Low sulphur content & high heat value.
- **Bituminous:** High in sulphur & with a high heat value.
- **Brown Coal:** Very low in sulphur & with medium heat content.
- **Lignite:** Low sulphur & a low heat value.

Advantages of Solid Fuel

- Low maintenance cost.
- Easily available.
- Thickest type of fuel.
- No expert required to take care.
- Easy to transport.

Disadvantages of Solid Fuel

- Requires space.
- Heat cannot be controlled.
- Pollutes the environment.
- Causes health hazard.
- Ignition time is high.
- More labour required to operate.
- Not ecofriendly.

LIQUID FUEL

Liquid fuels: Most of the liquid fuels in use are the hydrocarbons which exist in the liquid phase at room temperature. The liquid fuels and their calorific values are given below.

Advantages of Liquid Fuel

- Requires less storage space.
- Relative cleanliness.

- Flow can be regulated.
- Production of energy is instant.
- Readily available.
- Not as dirty as solid fuel.
- More friendly.

Disadvantages of Liquid Fuel

- Requires space.
- Lot of care to be taken.
- Releases pollution.
- Sources are not reliable in terms of purity.
- Bad odour.

GASEOUS FUEL

Gas energy resources include natural gas, liquid natural gas, liquefied petroleum gas (LPG), and synthetic natural gas (SNG). Liquefied petroleum gas (LPG) contains methane, propane, butane, etc., gases as constituents. On applying pressure to this mixture of natural gas, a liquid mixture of gas obtained and this liquid is known as LPG. Calorific value of this is higher than that of natural gas obtained from oil walls. Therefore, it is a better gaseous fuel. Combustion control is also easy.

Advantages of Gaseous Fuel

- Can be easily transported.
- Combustion control effective.
- Smoke and ash eliminated.
- Easy to handle.
- Saves a lot of labour.
- Controllable through regulators.
- Very little pollution.
- Instant fuel.

Disadvantages of Gaseous Fuel

- Transportation cost is high because of high volatility.
- Regular check of equipment and supply line required.
- Lot of care by an expert required.
- Very large storage tanks are needed.
- Highly inflammable.

GEL FUEL

Gel fuel is an alcohol-based product that doesn't give off smoke or odour, or at least no odours that are toxic or noxious. Its primary use is in fireplaces, but nowadays it is used in indoor catering. Gel fuel is mainly used by caterers and hotels for food warming purpose, i.e., heating chafing dish/containers, hence the word dish warmer. Its availability in disposable cans is not only safe but economical also.

Advantages of Gel Fuel

- It burns with controlled fire, hence it warms the food and does not burn the food.
- It burns with pleasant blue flame (also known as blue flame gel fuel).
- It does not leave soot, smoke, and does not blackens the utensils.
- It is odourless and transparent.
- It burns completely without any physical residue.
- It burns without noise (splutter free).
- It can be ignited by opening the lid and lighting off with matchstick, it is simpler to handle compared to other wick fuels, hence the term wick-less gel fuel. It can be put off easily by covering with lid.

ELECTRICITY

It is a source of fuel generated from electric power, which is supplied through the electrical mains. It is the cleanest fuel, controllable, with easy heat adjustment and requiring no storage space. It can be used efficiently for roasting, baking and toasting than for boiling and frying. However, it is often plagued with power cuts and interruptions. Insulation costs for electric equipment are higher than gas, owing to the costly switchgears required. Stove/cookers are connected to the mains and the knobs of the stoves are turned onto supply the heat.

Advantages of Electricity

- Easy to operate
- Fuel is clean
- No storage required
- Efficiency is good
- Ecofriendly.

Disadvantages of Electricity

- Expert required to handle the equipment.
- Chances of fire if short circuit.
- It is costly.
- Risk of shock.
- Maintenance cost is high.

CALCULATION OF FUEL AMOUNT AND ITS COST

In hotels, various fuels are required. Amount of solid fuels is measured by their weight and liquid fuels, gaseous fuels and electric energy through meter. By knowing the amount of fuels used during a period, say a month and then by knowing the unit cost of fuels the fuel cost for a month may be found and thus average expenditure on fuels can be calculated. Let us take an example regarding cost of fuel in the catering section of a hotel. Suppose in a small hotel 120 gas cylinders are used per year in its restaurant and cost per cylinder is Rs. 400 then the average cost of gas fuel per month for said restaurant will be:

- Number of gas cylinders used per year: 120.
- Cost of one gas cylinder: Rs. 400.
- Cost of gas fuel for one year: 120 × 400 = Rs. 48,000.
- Cost of gas fuel per month: 48,000/12 = Rs. 4000.

Therefore, the cost of gas fuel used per month will be Rs. 4000.

ACTIVITIES

- Research about various fuels used in restaurants and nearby catering institutions along with their advantages and disadvantages.

27 PLANNING DUTY ROSTER

Duty rosters specify the allotment of jobs, hours of duty, and off day for the staff. To make for an even share of duties, the roster should be rotated every five weeks. Duty roster must be simple in format, easy to interpret, clearly written, and displayed on the staff notice board at least a week in advance. Before planning duty roster it is important to consider certain points such as:

- Room occupancy for that particular week.
- Any application or request of an employee for off day on a certain day(s).
- Events to be held on that particular week in the hotel.
- To cross-check with the last planned duty roster.

ADVANTAGES OF DUTY ROSTER

- Helps to ensure the exact number of staff required to be on duty at any given occupancy.
- The staff working hours are as per their employment contract.
- That regular off days are availed for enhancing productivity.
- Information of employees who are present on the premises in instance of emergency.
- Accuracy in attendance and payroll reports.

STEPS FOR MAKING A DUTY ROSTER

- **Step 1:** Ascertain occupancy levels and events expected in the hotel. This information is provided by the sales and marketing department at the beginning of the financial year. On a daily and weekly basis, more specific reports of occupancy are available with the front office department. The overall forecasts of occupancy must be considered before scheduling the employees' annual leave. These forecasts also help the restaurant manager to follow the staffing guide to ensure sufficient staff at peak periods and avoid excess staff during slack periods.

- **Step 2:** Ascertain the spread of duty hours to be scheduled in the duty rosters, whether 12 hours, 16 hours, or 24 hours. Decide whether the positions will work for 5 or 7 days per week.

- **Step 3:** Ascertain the type of shift – straight shift, break shift, rotating shift, or any other alternative scheduling – to be used.
- **Step 4:** Ascertain the number of full -time and part- time staff on the payroll.
- **Step 5:** Ascertain the number of labour hours per day and per week required for various positions.
- **Step 6:** Incorporate coffee breaks and meal time allowances in the roster.
- **Step 7:** Ascertain that each employee gets a weekly off day after 6 working days. Provide for compensatory offs. Schedule one reliever per six employees.
- **Step 8:** Ascertain closed days and restricted holidays, and any contingencies planning that may be needed.
  - □ All duty rosters will be generated and approved by the outlet manager concerned. Copies of the duty roster will be placed on and forwarded to the following areas.

    Original : Outlet manager's file.

    Copy : Outlet staff notice board.

    Copy : F&B office file.
  - □ All duty rosters will cover a one week period, beginning on Monday and ending on Sunday.
  - □ Staff who are on leave, (annual, extended sick leave, maternity, etc.) will be marked on the duty roster.
  - □ Staff, who is on sick leave during any week, will have the days on the duty roster marked as "off sick".
  - □ The duty roster is to be kept for recording purposes, and is not to be destroyed or thrown out, and will be used in conjunction with the sign-in and sign-out records, to record the monthly attendance of all staff.

Code	Shift Time
M	7 a.m. to 4 p.m.
A	3 p.m. to 12 mid-night
N	11 p.m. to 8 a.m.

Name of the Employee	Mon	Tues	Wed	Thurs	Fri	Sat	Sun
Employee 1	M	**Off**	M	M	M	N	M
Employee 2	M	M	**Off**	M	M	M	M
Employee 3	**Off**	A	A	A	A	A	A
Employee 4	A	A	A	**Off**	A	M	A
Employee 5	N	N	N	**Off**	N	A	N
Employee 6	N	N	N	N	**Off**	N	N

Sample Duty Roster of a Restaurant

28 BAR SETUP

OPENING A BAR

1. Staff must report in duty on time.
2. Uniform must be clean and staff must be well groomed.
3. Use shift checklist to check the bar.
4. Condition of chairs and tables must be examined.
5. Condition of music player and speed pourer must be checked.
6. Check the table setup done in the bar before the shift starts.
7. Table setup includes the cleanliness of the ashtray.

Bar

8. Exchange dirty linen at the housekeeping linen room based on trolley exchange system.
9. Check for the bar counter setup as per the stacking sequence.
10. All bar station settings have to be completed before the end of each shift.

MIS EN ECENE FOR BAR SETTING

- Carpet and tiles to be free from any stains and debris.
- Light fixtures to be fully illuminated.
- Air condition to be working properly.
- All walls to be clean and free from any chips or marks.
- All mirrors/glass to be polished and free from any smudge.
- All windows to be clean and free from any streaks.
- All plant and floral decorations should be fresh.
- Side stations to be stacked properly and must be neat and clean.
- Tables and chairs to be steady.
- Tables and chair legs to be free from any scuffs and scratches.
- Chair/couch upholstery to be clean, matching and in good condition.

- Appropriate music to be played at pleasant level.
- Hotel tissue box to be available at the bar on request.
- Hotel pad, pen and matchbox to be available at the bar on request.

MIS EN PLACE TABLE SETTING IN BAR

- Bar and table setup are to be completed before the opening time of the bar.
- All tables in the bar to be consistently laid and cleared within five minutes of guest departure.
- Tables to be set as per the bar design specifications.
- Beverage list to be placed on each table.
- Napkins and coaster to be free from any creases and stains.
- Correct cutlery as per bar design specifications to be used for its intended purpose.
- Glassware as per bar design specifications to be clean and unchipped.
- Crockery to be clean and unchipped.
- Cutlery, crockery and glassware to be stored in designated areas.
- Beverage round to be cleaned.
- Ice bucket to be clean and well polished.
- Salt and pepper cruets to be made available on request.
- Sugar caddy selection to include white, brown and sugar substitutes.
- Salt rimmer to be ready.
- Bar caddy to be well arranged.
- Sugar crystals, if used to be presented with sugar tongs and spoons.

BAR SETUP PROCEDURE

Equipment Required

- Functional bar
- Wiping cloth/sheet

Knowledge Required

- Standard recipe of cocktails/mocktails
- Types of glassware
- Handling glasses
- Par stock of beverage
- Beverage cost control
- Eye for detail
- Hygiene and sanitation

Procedure

1. F&B associate to check if the floor has been cleaned the previous night.
2. Bar area to be cleaned (inside and outside area as applicable).
3. Check the temperature of all the chillers and place the requisite items in the same. Call engineer if it is not working.
4. Collect the fruits/lemon from the kitchen to make garnishes.
6. Ensure that the straws, swizzle stick, cocktail sticks, coasters and napkins are placed at the bar in bar caddy.
7. Check the cordials, mixers and other cocktail ingredients and replace or replenish, if necessary.
8. Prepare sour mix, squeeze lemon for lime juice, sugar syrup and fill them in thoroughly cleaned store and pour containers.
9. Wash the muddler, cocktail shaker and other bar equipment used for cocktail making.
10. The bar steward ensures that the bottles at the display are well laid and free from dust.
11. Check if the required number of glassware is placed in the shelves inside the bar.

Standard

- All nooks and corners to be checked for cleanliness.
- All surfaces and areas should be free from stains, water marks and other sticky substances.
- The surfaces should be cleaned with soap solution and wiped dry with a clean red duster.
- The temperature of the chiller should be 4-7°C.
- Display all the bottles in the sequence of whisky, vodka from front, liqueur and tequila at last country-wise.
- Store and pour container should be labelled accordingly.
- The steward should ensure that the muddler, cocktail shaker, shaker glass, bar spoon, chopping board, paring knife, blender, ice crusher and peg measure are free from any deposits and spotlessly clean.

Step 1	Inspect the bar from inside and outside.	

Step 2	Take out all bottles from the cupboard carefully. Clean and wipe the bottles with a duster.	
Step 3	Clean and wipe the counter with a damp duster.	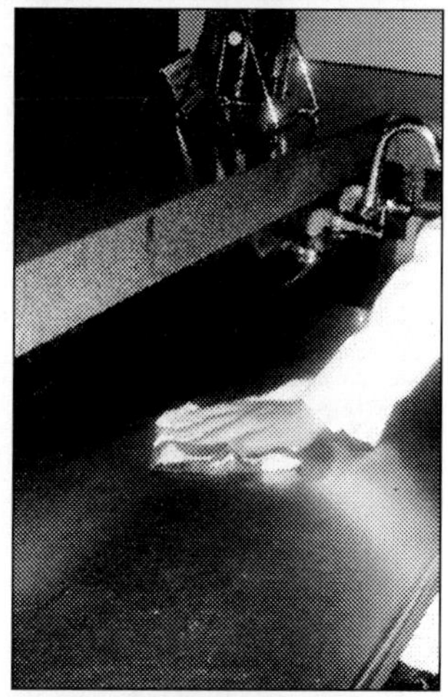
Step 4	Stack the beverage and juices in the chiller situated in underbar.	

Step 5	Cut and organize fresh garnishes in the garnish tray.	
Step 6	Organize straws, swizzle stick, muddler, coasters, paper napkins for the meal period.	
Step 7	Clean the cocktail shaker thoroughly with the help of a long brush.	

SETTING SERVICE BAR COUNTER

- Clean the bar counter using a clean cloth with sanitizer.
- Put ashtrays in between every two chairs.
- Put four bar mats on the counter on first bar station. Keep cocktail shaker on it.
- Fill the ice-bin with ice on left-hand side and crushed ice on right-hand side of the sink. Keep juices in the right sink.

- Two bar rails to be set on each counter, i.e., first rail to be set with white spirit and 2nd with dark spirit. Lime cordial and sugar syrup to be kept in the 2nd rail.
- All the ingredients of the cocktails like salt, pepper, angostura, honey, etc., to be kept on by the side table.
- Prepare standard beverage garnishes like lemon wedges, lemon slices, lemon rings, lemon twists and mint sprigs.

PREPARE GARNISHES

Equipment Required

- Chopping board
- Bar knife
- Fruits and vegetables
- Garnish tray
- Wiping cloth/sheet

Knowledge Required

- Types of garnishes used in bar
- Hygiene and sanitation
- Safety

Procedure

- Prepare yourself for cutting the garnishes to be used in bar.
- Put on a disposable glove to avoid cross-contamination.
- With a clean bar knife cut according to the specific garnishes using the green colour cutting board.

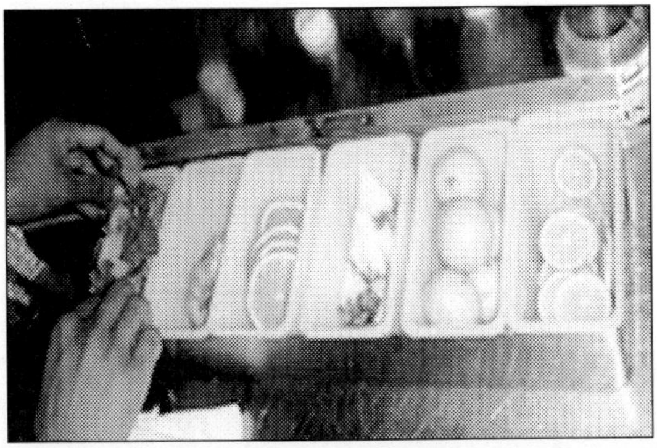

Placing garnishes

- Keep all garnish separately in the garnish tray in a bed of ice or refrigerator to keep them fresh.

Standard

- Thickness of garnishes and size should be standard.
- Garnish tray should be neat and clean.
- Never leave the garnish tray uncovered.
- Do not mix the garnishes together.

BAR SNACK SERVICE

Equipment Required

- Menu card
- KOT/BOT pad
- Pen

Knowledge Required

- Types of snacks available
- Non-available items in menu
- Food pairing with various beverages
- Up-selling and suggestive selling techniques

Procedure

1. Observe the guest if he is ready for ordering.
2. Approach the table to take order and stand in a position that allows you to have eye contact with the guest. Use standard phrases such as "Mr. Smith, May I take your order."
3. Guide the guest by suggesting the snacks according to the drink.
4. Repeat the order to the guest after writing in the order pad." Mr. Smith may I repeat your food order?"
5. Speak to the guest slowly, clearly and politely.
6. Punch the order in restaurant software and check for that order is received by kitchen department.
7. Pick up the snack and present to the guest in an appealing manner.
8. Snacks to be served at a right temperature.
9. Appropriate condiments and accompaniments to be offered.
10. Plated items to be served with a little disruption as possible.

Standard

- The texture and colour of the snack to be acceptable.
- The portion to be as per the hotel/bar policy.

- Snacks should resemble its description on the menu.
- Snacks to be served within ten minutes of placing order.
- Guest to be informed of any unexpected delay.
- When guest leaves temporarily, napkin to be folded neatly by F&B associate and placed appropriately.
- Order to be correct and complete.
- Condiments to be placed in an appropriate container.
- Tables to be visited to ascertain satisfaction on the level of service within five minutes of service of the snack.

29 BAR GLASSWARE AND EQUIPMENT

INTRODUCTION

Glassware is a term used for all types of glasses used for the purpose of drinking beverages. These are of two types: stem glass and flat bottom glass. Small stem glass is known as *footed glassware* like brandy balloon. Capacity of glassware is measured in fluid ounce and 1 fluid ounce is equal to 30 ml. Glassware is an essential part of cocktail and should be dust free, neat and clean. Glasses vary in shape and size according to the cocktail.

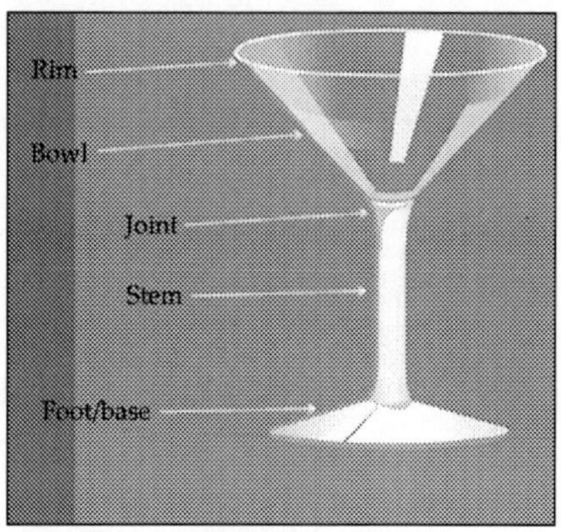

Parts of a Glass

ESSENTIAL BAR GLASSWARE

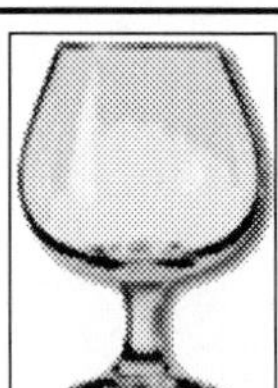	**Brandy Snifter/ Brandy Balloon** **Uses:** To serve brandy and cognac **Capacity:** (8 fl oz)
	Large Martini Glass: 300 ml (10 fl oz)

	**Martini Glass** **Uses:** To serve Martini (Cocktail) **Capacity:** Small Martini Glass: 150 ml (5 fl oz)
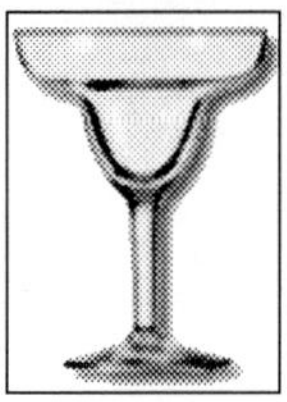	**Margarita** **Uses:** To serve Margarita (Cocktail) **Capacity:** 425 ml (14 fl oz)
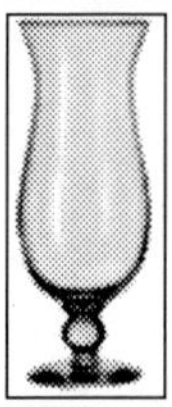	**Hurricane** **Uses:** To serve blended cocktails or cocktails built over ice, e.g., Mai tai **Capacity:** 450 ml (14 fl oz)
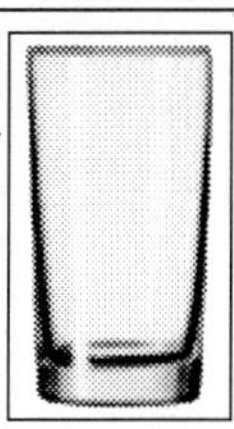	**Highball Glass** **Uses:** To serve long or double spirits as Gin, Vodka **Capacity:** 8 fl oz
	**Irish Coffee Mug** **Uses:** To serve Irish Coffee **Capacity:** 300 ml (20 fl oz)
	**Rock Glass** **Uses:** To serve whisky on the rocks **Capacity:** (9 fl oz)

	**Sherry Glass/ Capita** **Uses:** To serve Sherry and fortified wine **Capacity:** 90 ml (3 fl oz)
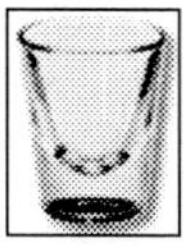	**Shot Glass** **Uses:** Used as a shooter glass. To drink Tequila. Used for straight spirit shots. **Capacity:** 30 ml (1fl oz)
	**Red Wine Glass** **Uses:** To serve Red Wine **Capacity:** 7 fl oz
	**White Wine Glass** **Uses:** To serve White Wine **Capacity:** 5.5 fl oz
	**Pitcher** **Uses:** To serve beer
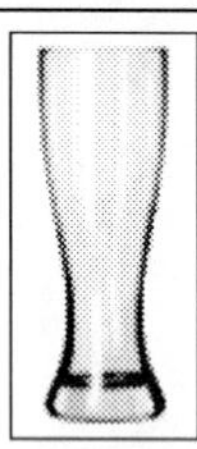	**Pilsner Glass** **Uses:** To serve Pilsner Beer **Capacity:** 425 ml (14 fl oz)
	**Champagne Flute** **Uses:** To serve Champagne **Capacity:** 6 fl oz

<table>
<tr><td>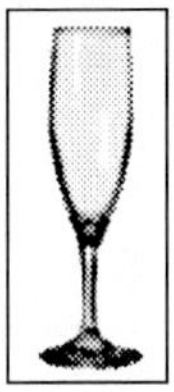</td><td>Champagne Tulip
Uses: To serve Champagne
Capacity: 6 fl oz</td></tr>
<tr><td></td><td>Champagne Saucer/ Coupe
Uses: To serve Champagne
Capacity: 6 fl oz</td></tr>
<tr><td>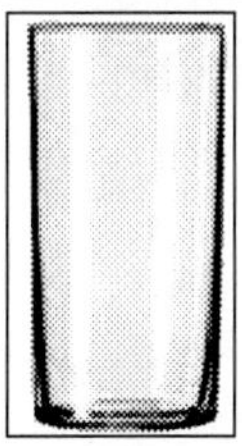</td><td>Tom Collin
Uses: To serve long drinks
Capacity: 12 oz</td></tr>
<tr><td>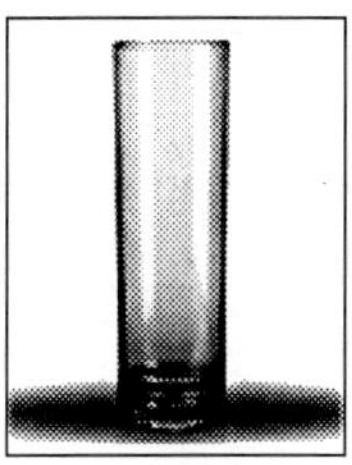</td><td>Slim Gim
Uses: To serve long drinks
Capacity: 16 oz</td></tr>
<tr><td>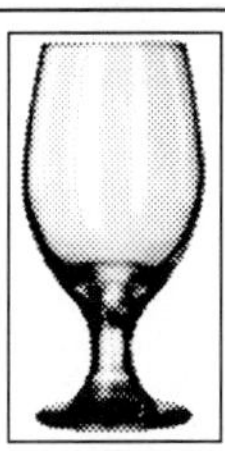</td><td>Beer Goblet
Uses: To serve beer
Capacity: 10-12 fl oz</td></tr>
<tr><td></td><td>Rolly Polly
Uses: To serve Bloody Mary (cocktail)
Capacity: 9 fl oz</td></tr>
</table>

Liqueur glass
Brandy snifter
Port glass
Alsace glass
Bordeaux glass
White wine glass
Burgundy glass

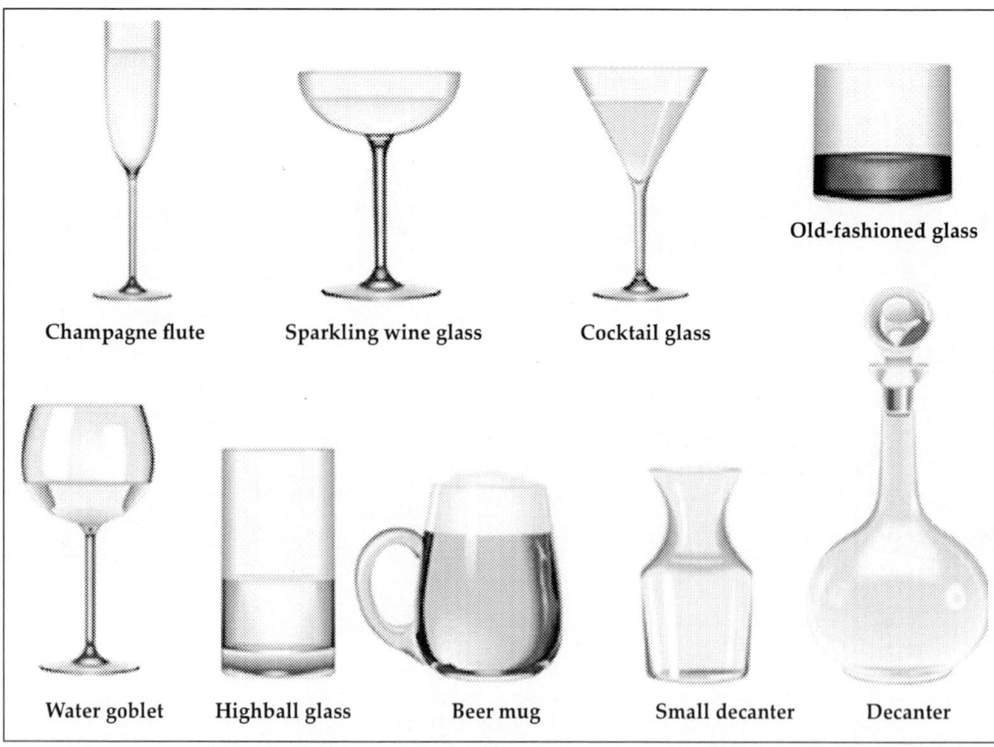
Champagne flute
Sparkling wine glass
Cocktail glass
Old-fashioned glass
Water goblet
Highball glass
Beer mug
Small decanter
Decanter

DAILY CARE AND CLEANING

- Glassware is cleaned in the dish washing machine and goes through the process of washing, rinsing and sterilizng.
- To polish glass, hold glass over-boiling hot water until steam condenses on glass. Using a waiter's cloth, the glass is wiped or polished.
- A little lemon juice or white vinegar may be added in water to remove any white marks on the glasses due to chlorination.
- Always check for brilliance and any spots against the sunlight.
- All glasses should be held at the base. Those with a stem should be inverted and then held at the stem.
- Any chipped glass should be discarded at this stage.
- Always use an ice scoop to fill the glasses with ice. Never use the glass to scoop ice. It can break in your ice.
- If you break glass in your ice, throw away all the ice and make sure that there are no pieces of broken glass.
- If a glass is hot, do not put ice in it. The glass can break with the change of temperature.
- If the glass is cold, do not pour anything hot in it.
- Don't carry more glasses than what you can handle with your hands. Use a tray to carry them.
- Glasses must be checked for any lipstick marks.

Storage

- Stored in single rows on paper-lined shelves. Each shelf should be labelled with the names of the items that it holds.

- Should be stored upside down to prevent any dust settling in them.
- Ideally, plastic coated wire racks should be used for stacking, storing and transporting.
- Glasses should never be stacked inside each other. Do not stack the glasses too high.
- Do not stack two different glasses together. They can get stuck together and if you try to separate them, they might break.

Did you know?

Hock (German White Wine) glasses have brown stems same like the colour of the Hock bottle and Moselle glasses (German white wine) have green stems, the same colour as the Moselle bottle.

Except in certain specialty restaurants or first class establishments where either coloured glassware or cut glassware may be used, hotel and bar glassware is usually plain. However, many restaurants and bar use a clear stemmed glass for all wines to cut the cost and quantity. A good wine glass should be clear and plain so that the colour and brilliance of a wine can be clearly seen. It should have a stem for holding the wine glass so that the heat of one's hand does not affect the taste of wine. Wine glasses always have a curving lip to hold the aroma and it should be large enough to hold the wine being tasted. Some of the major brands of glasses used in hotels and major bars are:

- Schott Zwiesel (German)
- Imperial Ocean (Thailand)
- Somiya (India)
- Cisterna (Thailand)

BAR EQUIPMENT

Can Opener: Useful for opening cans of fruit and syrup.	
Corkscrew: For opening wine and champagne bottles.	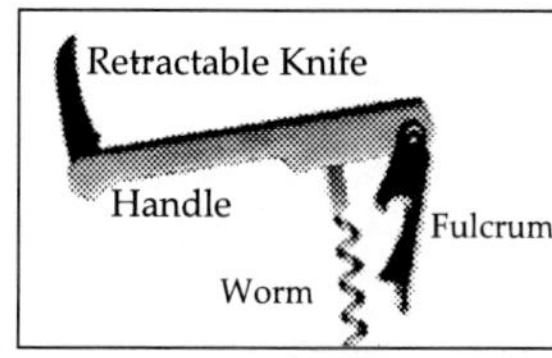
Cloths: For wiping surfaces and equipment. These should be damp and not wet.	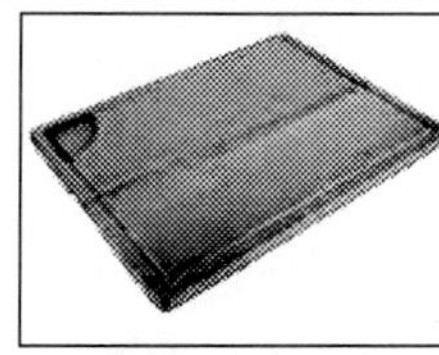
Cutting Board: For slicing fruit and other garnishes. This should be heavy and laminated.	
Bar Towels: These are 100% cotton and have sewn edges for durability. Use these along with cloths to keep things clean. Make good use of times where you have no guests to clean bottles and wipe surfaces.	
Cocktail Napkin: To be served with drinks.	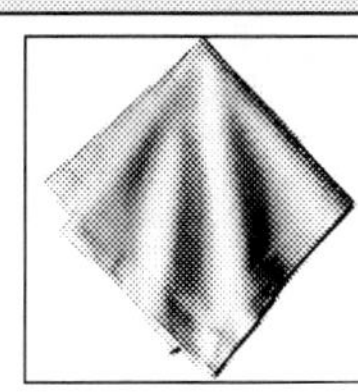
Bottle Opener: For opening screw top bottles.	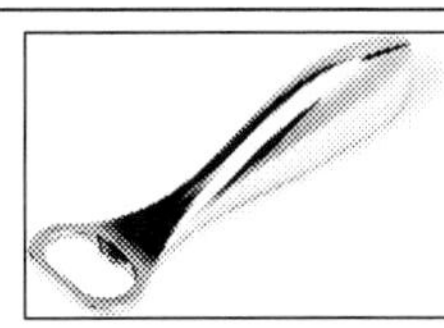
Bottle Sealers: For keeping liquors and other bottle contents fresh.	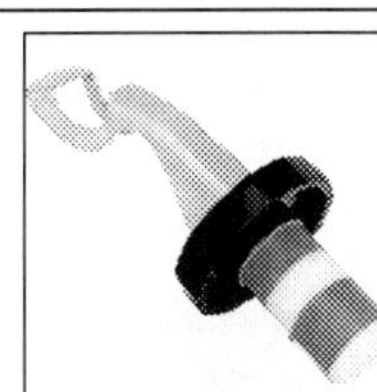

European Cocktail Shaker: Also known as a cobbler cocktail shaker. It has a cap and built-in strainer which makes it convenient to use. The cap can often be used as a measure for spirits or other liquids. Most common type of cocktail shaker is usually made of aluminium. **Note:** Always pour the least expensive ingredient into the cocktail shaker first.	
Boston Shaker: The Boston cocktail shaker does the same thing as the cobbler shaker, but looks and works slightly different. It consists of two cone-shaped parts, metal and a glass with the glass part fitting into the shaker. Shaking with this type of shaker is similar to shaking with a cobbler. Instead of using a cap to close the shaker, you tightly fit the two cones onto one another before shaking. One does need to be more careful than with a cobbler shaker. Put the ingredients in the glass cone, put the metal cone over it and give it a slight nudge to seal the two cones.	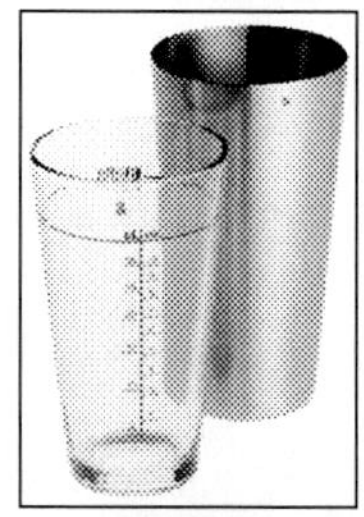
Electric Blender: Many cocktails require a blender to blend the ingredients smoothly together. Useful for drinks with fruit pieces or ice cream, etc.	
Grater: To grate spices like nutmeg and others.	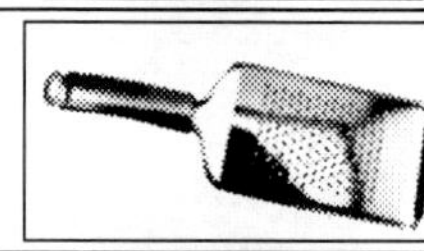
Ice Bucket: A metal or insulated bucket keeps your ice cold and clean.	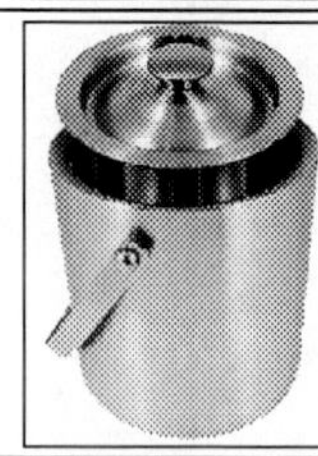
Ice Scoops and Tongs: Use these to add ice to drinks. Never handle ice with your hands, it's not only unhygienic, but the heat from your hand will begin to melt the ice. Don't use glassware as a scoop.	
Jigger: A measurement tool.	

Juice Squeezer/Extractor: Needed for getting the most juice out of your fruits. It helps to soak citrus fruit in hot water before squeezing.	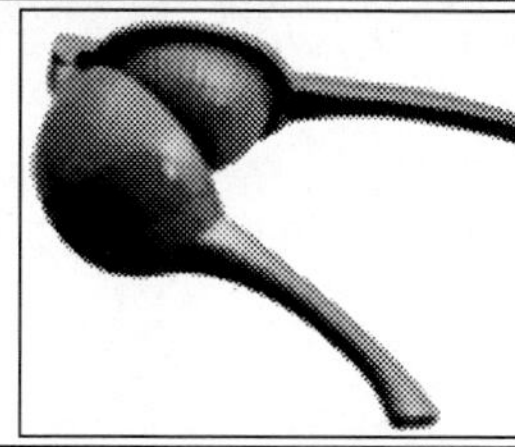
Bar Spoon: A bar spoon with a long handle and a muddler end will allow you to mix and measure ingredients as well as crush garnishes.	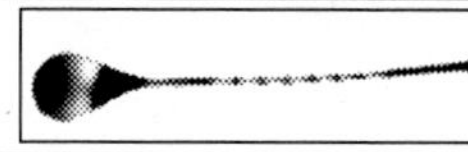
Mixing Glass: Useful for long drinks where it is required to mix the ingredients without shaking.	
Sharp Knife: For cutting fruit and garnishes.	
Strainer: Removes the ice and fruit pulp from juices. This may come with a cocktail shaker.	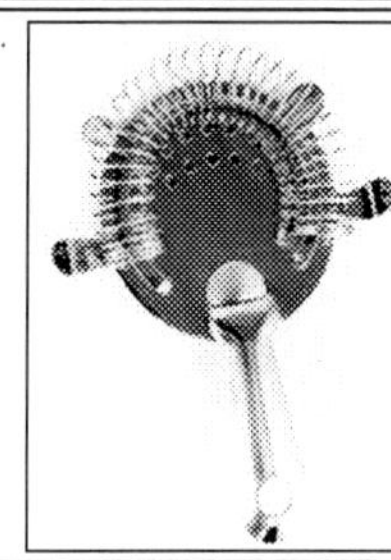
Straws and Stirrers: To stir the drink and to drink.	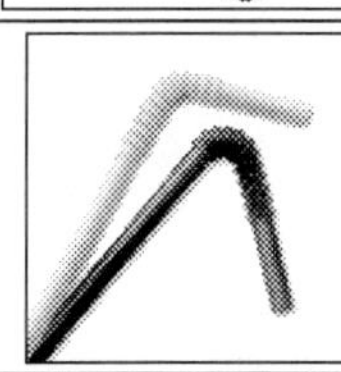
Muddler: To muddle the drink, generally made of wood.	

Garnish Tray/Condiment Tray: To place different garnishes into the tray.	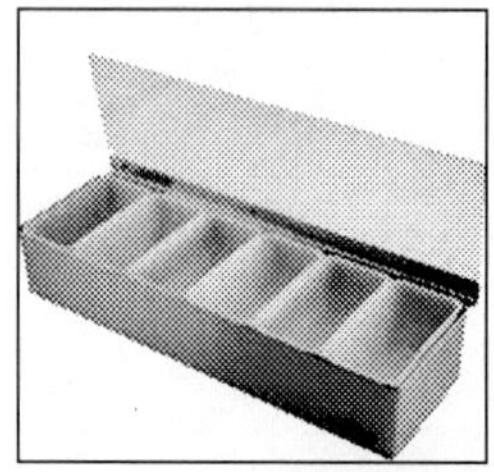
Salt Rimmer: Used to rim the glasses with salt.	
Speed Pourer: Helps in pouring drinks.	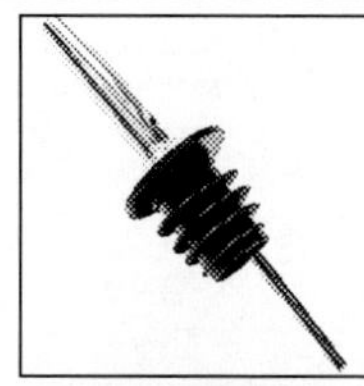
Beverage Round/Salver: Used to serve drinks on the table and to carrying glasses.	
Coaster: Glasses are placed on the coaster where there is no table-cloth.	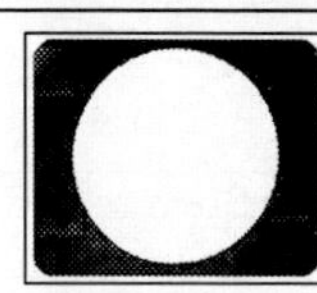
Cocktail Umbrella: Used to garnish drinks.	
Bar Caddy: To put straws, stirrers and paper napkins.	

Ice Machine: To make ice cubes.	
Bar Gun: A soda gun or bar gun is a device used in bars to serve various types of carbonated and non-carbonated drinks.	
Zester: To remove the zest of citrus fruits.	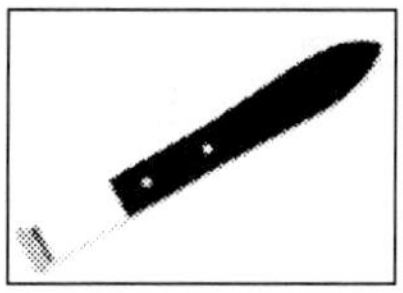

REVISION QUESTIONS?

1. Differentiate between stem glassware and flat bottom glassware.
2. Name any five stem glassware and any five flat bottom glassware used in bars.
3. Write a note on handling and storage of glassware.
4. List any ten pieces of equipment used in bars.

ACTIVITIES

- Visit any bar or pub nearby your place and list the various equipment and glassware available there along with their purpose.
- Visit any fine dining restaurant or a five-star hotel in a group and find out that which brand of cutleries and glassware they are using.

30 BEVERAGE PRODUCT KNOWLEDGE

MEANING

Beverage means any liquid intended to be drunk or you can also say any potable drink. It is a term derived from the Latin word *"bever"* means *"to rest"*. Beverages can be alcoholic and non-alcoholic. Non-alcoholic beverages sdo not contain alcohol. They can be classified as refreshing (juices, soft drinks), stimulating (tea, coffee) and nourishing (milk based drinks, ovaltine). Whereas alcoholic beverages contain 0.5% to 75% alcohol by volume such as spirits, beer and wine.

TYPES OF NON-ALCOHOLIC BEVERAGES

- **Refreshment:** Non-alcoholic beverages such as plain or carbonated water, lime juice, ginger ale and other bottled beverages, fruit juices and iced tea or coffee are refreshing drinks and are used to quench thirst.
- **Nourishment:** Pasteurized milk, butter milk, chocolate and cocoa drinks, eggnog made with rum, fruit juices, glucose water, lemonade provide nutrients and help in nourishing the body.
- **Stimulant:** Tea, coffee, cocoa and chocolate beverages help in stimulating the system.
- **Soothing Agent:** Warm milk and hot tea have a soothing effect.
- **Appetizers:** Soups, fruit juice and alcoholic drinks in limited quantities increase appetite and thereby food consumption.

TEA

Tea is the most consumed beverage in the world. It contains caffeine. It is a stimulating non-alcoholic drink. All teas come from the dried leaves of shrub *Camellia sinensis* – an evergreen shrub that may grow up to 60 feet in the wild.

Varieties of Tea

- **Ceylon (Sri Lanka):** Ceylon teas are black teas. They have an aromatic amber liquor and a rich, full astringent flavour. These are wonderful with a little cold milk and go well with a sweet breakfast or afternoon pastry.

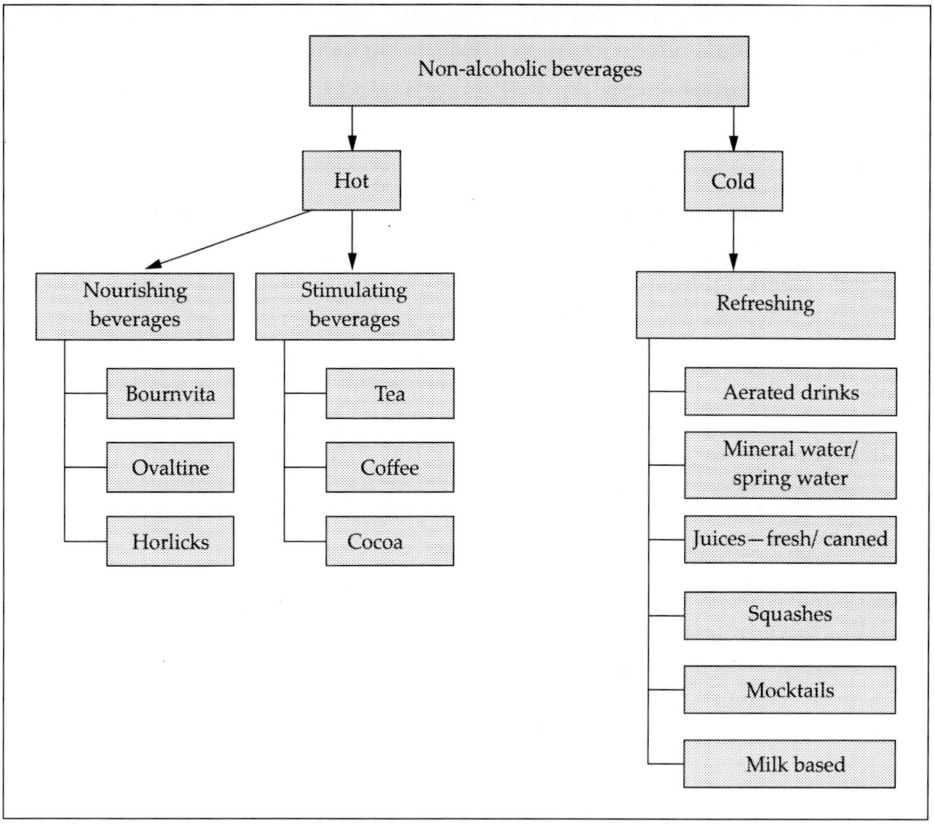

- **English Breakfast Tea:** It is a blend of fine black teas from India and Sri Lanka. A similar tea was made by a Scottish tea company and marketed as Breakfast Tea.
- **Keemun (China):** Keemun has a subtle orchid aroma and bright red liquor. The flavour is mild with a hint of sweetness, which makes it a good evening tea.
- **Lapsang Souchong (China):** This tea is produced by withering the tea leaves over open fires of pine. Lapsang Souchong is an assertive dark tea with a smoky fragrance and flavour. It yields a red brown liquor and is great accompaniment to salty and spicy dishes and with cheese.
- **Assam:** Assam teas are black bold tea with a strong malty taste and dark liquor, making them excellent morning teas. Assam teas are delicious with a drop of milk. This tea is generally served with milk in the morning.
- **Darjeeling (India):** It is the rarest and most prestigious black tea. Darjeeling teas have a distinctive taste depending on the season. Darjeeling tea is also known as "Champagne of tea" and can be served with milk or without milk along with lemon in the evening.
- **Tisanes:** These are fruit flavoured teas and herbal infusions which are often used for medicinal purpose and are gaining in popularity with trends towards

more healthy eating and drinking. Often these do not contain caffeine as they are natural botanicals which are not related to the actual tea plant.

- **Green Tea:** Full of antioxidants therefore good for health and is served without milk.

COFFEE

Coffee berries, which contain the coffee bean, are produced by several species of small evergreen bush of the genus *Coffea*. The two most commonly grown species are *Coffea canephora* (also known as *Coffea robusta*) and *Coffea arabica*. These are cultivated in Latin America, Southeast Asia, Africa and certain parts of India. Once ripe, coffee berries are picked, processed and dried. The seeds are then roasted, undergoing several physical and chemical changes. They are roasted to various degrees, depending on the desired flavour. They are then ground and brewed to produce liquid coffee which is also known as coffee decoction. Coffee can be prepared and presented by a variety of methods.

Types of Coffee Preparation

- **Espresso or Caffè Espresso:** Espresso is a concentrated black coffee brewed by forcing very hot, but not boiling water under high pressure through coffee that has been ground to a consistency between extremely fine and powder.
- **Espresso Macchiato:** A shot of espresso stained with a dollop of frothed milk. Also called 'Cortado' in Spain and Portugal, means quick and smooth sip of heaven.
- **Instant Coffee:** A thick coffee decoction is prepared first and then it is either spray dried to a fine powder or freeze dried to granules. When added to hot water it dissolves completely leaving no residue.
- **Caffè Americano:** Single or double shot of espresso combined with hot water, you'll get the rich and nutty flavour of espresso but with a lot less intensity and more to enjoy!.
- **Latte:** Single or double-shot of espresso combined with steamed milk and a little foam. A latte is usually a bit milder than its cousin Cappuccino.
- **Café Viennois:** Brewed coffee with a little whipped cream.
- **Mochaccino:** Single or double-shot of espresso, part hot chocolate and part frothed milk.
- **Cappuccino:** Single or double-shot of espresso, part steamed milk, part frothed milk and cinnamon or cocoa to top it – slightly stronger than latte.
- **Café Au Lait:** Half brewed coffee and half warm milk typically served in a bowl, à la Française.
- **Espresso Romano:** A shot of espresso with a little curl of lemon peel in Rome.
- **Iced coffee:** Fresh brewed coffee, cooled and served over ice.
- **Latte Macchiato:** Macchiato (means 'stained') is glass of steamed milk spotted with a shot of espresso.

CARBONATED BEVERAGES

Carbonated beverages are also known as soft drinks or mixers. They are popular items of bar stock as they are either sold on their own or as mixers with spirits such as:

- **Soda Water:** *Colourless and tasteless*
- **Tonic Water:** *Colourless and quinine flavoured*
- **Dry Ginger:** *Golden straw coloured with a ginger flavour*
- **Aerated Drinks:** *Coca cola, Pepsi, Thumps-up, Limca*
- **Lemonade:** *Lemon flavoured, sweet aerated water.*

> **Did You Know?**
>
> Sparkling waters are often consumed on their own and can be served either plain or with a twist of lemon or lime as garnish. They may also be used as the base for various cocktails and are sometimes recommended as a home remedy for an upset stomach.

BOTTLED WATER

It is of two types. **Mineral water (**which has a mineral content, which is strictly controlled) and **spring water** (which has fewer regulations apart from those concerning hygiene). Waters can be classified as:

- **Sparkling Water:** It is water that contains carbon dioxide or hydrogen sulfide gas, whether naturally occurring or introduced to create an effervescent drink. It goes by many names like fizzy water, seltzer and sometimes soda water.
- **Still Water:** Still water is plain water. It has no added carbon dioxide like the sparkling water. This can be tap water, spring water or plain bottled water.

Name	Type	Country
Appolinaris	Naturally sparkling	Germany
Contrex	Still	France
Perrier	Naturally sparkling (or in fruit flavours)	France
Royal Farris	Naturally sparkling	Norway
San Pellegrino	Carbonated	Italy
Spa	Still, naturally sparkling (or in fruit flavours)	Belgium
Spa Monopole	Still or sparkling	Belgium
Vichy Celestine	Naturally sparkling	France
Vittel	Naturally sparkling	France
Volvic	Still	France
Ashboure	Still or sparkling	England
Evian	Still	France
Highland Spring	Still or carbonated	Scotland

Mineral Water		Spring Water	
Vittel	France	Ashbourne	England
Contrex	France	Buxton	England
Perrier	France	Badoit	France
Spa	Belgium	Evian	France
San Pellegrino	Italy	High Land Spring	Scotland

Squashes

A squash is a sweetened fruit pulp. Squashes may be served on their own, mixed with spirits or cocktails, or used as the base for such drinks as fruit cups. They are indispensable in bars and an adequate stock should always be maintained, such as:

- Orange
- Lemon
- Grapefruit
- Lime juice

Syrups

The main use of these concentrated, sweet, fruit flavourings is used as a base for cocktails, fruit cups or mixed with soda water as a long drink.

S. No.	Items	Flavour
1.	Grenadine	Pomegranate
2.	Cassis	Blackcurrant
3.	Citronelle	Lemon
4.	Orgeat	Almond
5.	Cerise	Cherry
6.	Fromboise	Raspberry
7.	Gomme	White sugar syrup

Juices

Fresh fruit juices are prepared on order and a little extra is prepared for contingencies. These juices should not be stored for more than an hour. They have a low shelf life due to absence of preservatives. Fresh juices are generally served in hi ball glasses. These are also available in tetra packs or in cans. Some major brand names are:

- Morton (Indian)
- Tropicana (Indian)
- Ocean Spray (USA)

ALCOHOL AND ALCOHOLIC BEVERAGES

The term alcohol derives from the Arabic word *al-kohl. Kohl* is a black very fine staining powder used for cosmetic purposes by the Arab ladies for staining their eyelids. Afterwards the name was applied to highly refined chemical powders and essences and then to spirits produced by distillation. Alcohol in a better way can be regarded as a volatile liquid containing sugar, the strength of which can be further increased by distillation process. Beverages that contain 0.5% to 76% of alcohol by volume are considered to be alcoholic beverages. The only consumable alcohol is ethyl alcohol rest all other alcohols like methyl alcohol are poisonous. Alcoholic beverages can be made by fermentation, distillation and brewed and fermenting methods.

CLASSIFICATION OF ALCOHOLIC BEVERAGES

Alcoholic beverages have been classified into three categories:

(a) **Fermented beverages:** All alcoholic beverages begin with the fermentation of a liquid food containing sugar. Fermentation is the action of yeast upon sugar in solution, which breaks down the sugar into carbon dioxide and alcohol. The carbon dioxide escapes into the air, and alcohol, a liquid, remains behind the original liquid, which thus becomes a fermented beverages. Cider, perry and all types of wines like table wine, sparkling wines, fortified wines, aromatized wines are fermented beverages.

> **Compound Beverages**
>
> Apart from distilled, fermented brewed and fermented beverages there are compound beverages as well. These are the beverages which are made by combining either a fermented beverage or spirit with flavouring substances. Various types of liqueurs such as Benedictine, Tia Maria and various types of bitters such as Campari are examples of compound beverages.

(b) **Distillation/distilled spirits:** Spirits are potable alcoholic beverages obtained from distillation of an alcoholic liquid. The process of separation is called distillation. The liquid is heated in an enclosed container called a still. Brandy, whisky, rum gin, vodka, tequila are examples of distilled spirits.

(c) **Brewed and fermented:** Certain fermented alcoholic beverages like beer, sake, etc., are brewed before they are fermented, i.e., the mixture of grist (mashed cereals) and hot water is brewed to extract flavour, taste and aroma before being fermented.

DISTILLATION

Distillation is a process whereby two liquids are separated based on differences in their volatilities. It is a process where liquid is boiled to such an extent that it leaves vapour

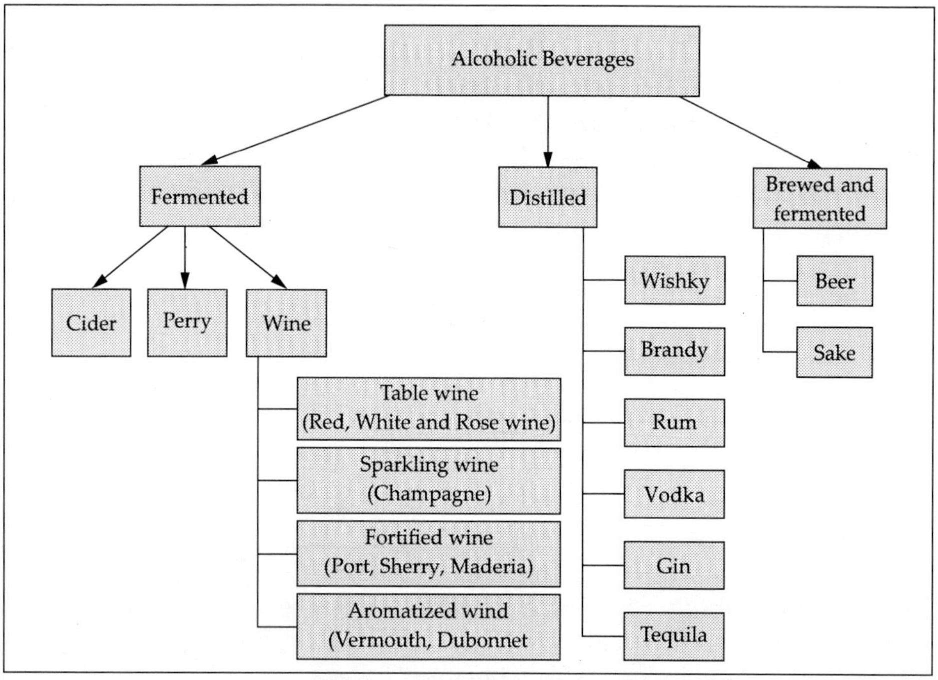

Classification of alcoholic beverages

behind and then condensing it back to liquid form. The liquid obtained is colourless. Equipment used to distill the spirit is called a still. It has three main parts:

1. Original container
2. Condenser
3. Receiver

Types of still used for distillation are:

1. Pot still
2. Patent still/continuous still/coffee still.

Proof - Measuring Alcoholic Strength

Alcohol proof is a measure of how much alcohol (ethanol) is contained in an alcoholic beverage. Earlier the strength of a spirit was tested or proofed by mixing equal amount of the spirit and gunpowder together, then the mixture was ignited. If the gunpowder didn't ignite it meant the alcohol was too weak and if it burned rapidly—the alcohol was too strong. If alcohol burned with a steady blue flame then the alcohol was considered to be of appropriate strength.

Strength of Different Beverages

- Low alcohol beer : 0.9% ABV
- Light beer : 3% ABV
- Beer : 5% ABV
- Table wine : 9-14% ABV
- Fortified wine : 17-22% ABV
- Spirits : 40 % ABV
- Over proof rum : 58% ABV

Note: ABV stands for "Alcohol by Volume"

Three types of system for measuring alcoholic proof are as follows:

- Sikes system/the British system
- Gay Lussac system
- American system

Sikes System/The British System

Bartholomew Sikes introduced a famous hydrometer in 1816. He determined that the steady blue flame is produced when the percentage of alcohol by volume in the spirit is 57.1% which is regarded as 100° proof. To convert the British proof into percentage by alcohol by volume, simply multiply the proof by four and divide by seven. Example: If according to the British system spirit containing 70°, will contain the percentage of alcohol by volume as:

$$\frac{70 \times 4}{7} = 40\%$$

Used mainly in Canada and Great Britain, now a new system called OIML (Organisation Internationale de Metrologie Legale), which is similar to what Gay Lussac used.

Gay Lussac or the GL System

Much easier to understand and adopted throughout Europe. Gives the exact amount of alcohol by volume. This system uses a scale of 0-100 means a spirit containing 60 contains 60% alcohol.

In this system degree is equal to the percentage.

American System

Here the proof of the spirit is precisely twice the alcohol content in the bottle by volume. Therefore, a spirit marked 90° proof would contain 45% of alcohol by volume. Remember that in America alcoholic beverages are measured differently. Spirits are measured by proof, beer by weight, and wine by volume.

BEER

Beer is a general term for all fermented liquors brewed from malted and unmalted cereals. Beer is an alcoholic beverage made from cereal grains, usually barley, but corn, rice, wheat, and oats are also used. Hops (a female cone-shaped flower from nettle family) is added while making beer to give it a spicy bitter flavour. It also increases the shelf life of beer. The fermented and brewed process typically produces beer with an alcohol content of 2 to 6 per cent.

BRAND NAMES

International Beer Brands	
Beer Name	**Country**
Foster	Australia
Corona	Mexico
Tiger	Singapore
Carlsberg	Denmark
Castle Lager	South Africa
Stroh	U.S.A.
Heineken	Netherlands
Amstel Light	Netherlands
Kalyani Black Label	India
Kingfisher	India
Budweiser	U.S.A.
Brahma	Brazil
Murphy	Ireland
Stella Artois	Belgium
Guiness	Ireland

WHISKEY/WHISKY

Whisky (or **whiskey**) is the name for a broad category of alcoholic beverages distilled from grains that are subsequently aged in oak casks. Whisky can also be defined as an alcoholic beverage distilled from cereal grains and matured in wood casks. The word whisky derived from ***'acqua vitae'***—the Latin equivalent of the Gaelic ***'usige beathe'***, or

Major types of whisky

'water of life'. The grains used to make various types of whisky include barley, malted barley, rye, malted rye, wheat, and maize/corn.

Scotch Whisky

Scotch whisky is a whisky made in Scotland. In the English-speaking parts of the world, the term is often abbreviated to "Scotch". In Scotland itself, however, the term *whisky* almost always refers to Scotch whisky, and the term "Scotch" is rarely used. Scotch whisky is divided into four distinct categories: single malt, vatted malt (also called "pure malt") blended and single grain. Scotch can only be Scotch if it has been both, distilled and matured in Scotland. It should be distilled at less than 98.4% in such a way that the distillate has an aroma and flavour derived from the materials used. Single malt whiskies are most prized by the whisky drinkers. For a whisky to be called a single malt, it must have been made using malted barley and come from one distillery alone, although single malts will most likely have come from more than one cask within the distillery.

Scotch Whisky Brand Names

Super Premium	**Regular**
Johny Walker Blue Label	Black & White
Royal Salute	Johny Walker Red Label
Premium	Cutty Sark
Johny Walker Black Label	Dewar's White Label
Chivas Regal	Grant's
Something Special	J & B Rare
Teacher's 50	Ballantine's
Single Malt	Bell's
Cardhu	John Haig
Glenlivet	Passport
Glemorangie	Teacher's
Glenfiddich	Vat 69
Oban	100 Pipers
Taliskar	
Laphroaig	

Irish Whisky

It is a grain whisky made in Ireland and triple distilled except connemara peated Irish Malt. There are several types of whisky common to Ireland. Irish whisky comes in several forms.

Irish Whisky Brands

- Tullamore Dew
- Bushmills
- Jameson

Canadian Whisky

This is a whisky made in Canada, by law it must be aged there for at least three years in a barrel. Most Canadian whiskies are blended multi-grain whiskies. These are often casually called "rye whisky" because they contain at least 51% rye. However, they contain proprietary blends of corn and barley in addition to rye.

Canadian Whisky Brands

- Canadian Club
- Black Velvet
- Windsor Supreme
- Firty Creek
- Crown Royal
- Wiser's Whisky

American Whiskies

American whiskies have two Regions—Bourbon/Kentucky and Tennessee

- Made from corn, rye.
- Should have 51% to 79% of a single grain (corn or rye).
- Aged in new American white oak casks.

Bourbon Whiskys

It takes its name from the Bourbon County in Kentucky and was first distilled by Elijah Craig in 1789 therefore it is also known as Kentucky whiskies. The mash should have at least 51% corn, the whisky should be distilled at 160 US proof and it should be aged in charred oak casks for a minimum of two years.

Bourbon Whisky Brands

- Jim Beam
- Wild Turkey
- Early Times
- Old Grand Dad
- Maker's Mark

Tennessee Whiskys

Should have 51% to 79% of a single grain means very similar to Bourbon except that it has an extra step of **filtration** through a bed of **maple charcoal**, which is also called mellowing.

Tennessee Whisky Brands

- Gentle Jack
- Jack Daniels
- George A Dickel
- Ezra Books
- RUM

Also called *Regular Used Medicine* by some drinkers is a distilled beverage made from sugarcane byproducts such as molasses and sugarcane juice by a process of fermentation and distillation. The distillate, a clear liquid, is then usually aged in oak and other casks.

RUM BRANDS

Light Rums

- Bacardi
- Ron Rico
- Dry Cane
- Rhum St. James
- Mount Gay
- El Dorado
- Malibu
- Carriba
- El Dorado

Dark Rum

- Captain Morgan
- Lambs Navy
- Appleton
- Myers
- Woods
- Hansen
- Coruba
- Barbancourt
- Old Monk

TEQUILA

It is not produced from the typical grains or fruits that most alcoholic beverages are made from. It is made from the distillation of an alcoholic wash obtained from the roasted centre (piña) of the blue agave plant and is obtained from the delimited Tequila region at the Jalisco district in Mexico.

Tequila Brands

- Sauza
- Two Fingers
- Camino Real
- Jose Cuervo

GIN

Gin is a spirit made from the distillation of white grain spirit and juniper berries which provide its distinctive flavour. Gin originally called Genever (French word for Juniper berries) was originated in Holland by a Dutch Doctor, Franciscus Sylvius. The juniper berries, which have medicinal value, were infused in the neutral spirit and the resultant product was Genever.

Gin Brands Names

- Aristocrat gin
- Beefeater
- Bols
- Bombay Sapphire
- Boodles
- Booth's
- Broker's Premium London Dry Gin
- Burnett's Gin
- Calvert Gin
- Cork Dry Gin Geek Gin
- Gilbey's Gin
- Gordon's
- Seagram's Gin
- Silver Wolf Gin
- Taaka (a London Dry Gin with a secret formula)
- Tanqueray

VODKA

Vodka known as Wódka in Poland and Voda in Russia means *'water'*. Vodka however, means *'little water'*, which signifies the love of the Russians towards it. Vodka may be defined as a neutral spirit distilled from any fermented material and treated in a way so as to be without any distinctive colour, aroma, or taste. It is a clear, colourless, tasteless and a neutral spirit originated in a laboratory at St. Petersburg in 1810. Vodka is generally made from agricultural products such as rice, wheat, corn, rye, molasses and sometimes with potato. Vodka exported from Russia, Poland, England, Finland, Sweden and United States are made up of grains.

Vodka Brand Names

- **Limmonaya:** Stolichnaya flavoured with lemon.
- **Okhotnichya:** Popular vodka flavoured with various herbs and heather honey, also known as 'Hunter's Vodka'.
- **Finlandia:** A classic from Finland
- **Pertsovka:** Russian pepper vodka. Made with black and red pepper pods and cubeb berries, it's a traditional Russian antidote to the cold.
- **Wisniówka Cherry Vodka:** A deep cherry-red, dessert vodka from Poland.

- **Zubrówka:** The famous bison grass flavoured vodka from Poland (a blade of the grass is included in the bottle). The vodka is slightly yellow and aromatic.
- **Starka:** This in Russian means 'old'. After production it is matured in wine soaked oak casks for 10 years, which imparts to it amber colour and a wine flavour. It is also known as the 'Brandy Lover's Vodka'.
- **Yubileyneya Osobaya:** Flavoured with brandy, honey, etc., it is also known as 'Jubilee Vodka'.
- **Grey Goose:** Neutral and citrus flavoured.
- **Absolut:** Swedish vodka made in the Åhus distillery in southern Sweden. Absolut vodka apart from neutral, comes in the following flavours.
  - **Peach:** Peach flavour launched in 2005.
  - **Citron:** Lemon flavour launched in 1988. Displays curious sweet/tart interplay of lively citrus. Develops an interesting salty tang in the finish.
  - **Kurrant:** Blackcurrant flavour launched in 1992.
  - **Mandarin:** Orange and mandarin flavour mix launched in 1999.
  - **Pears:** Pear flavour launched in 2007.
  - **Pepper:** The first flavoured Absolut Vodka launched in 1986, chili pepper flavour.
  - **Raspberri:** Raspberry flavour launched in 2004.
  - **Ruby red:** Grapefruit flavour launched in 2006.
  - **Vanilia:** Vanilla flavour launched in 2003.

BRANDY

Brandy known as "*Burnt Wine*" is an expression derived from Dutch word "Brandewijn" meaning burnt. Brandy, in its broadest definition, is a spirit made from fruit juice or fruit pulp and skin. Brandy usually contains 40–60% ethyl alcohol by volume. In addition to wine, this spirit can also be made from grape pomace or fermented fruit juice. Unless specified otherwise, brandy is made from grape wine. It is normally consumed as an after-dinner drink. Cognac and Armagnac are the famous French brandies.

Cognac Producers/Brands

- Braastad
- Courvoisier
- Rémy Martin
- Larsen
- Meukow
- Hennessey
- Martell
- Hine
- Camus

Armagnac Producers/Brand

- Delord
- Jean Sempe

- Janneau
- Chabot
- Alain Dauriac
- Sempe
- De Montal
- Darozze

WINE

Wine is pure, naturally fermented juice of ripe grapes or other fruits. In fermentation, yeast, which forms naturally on the grape and is most often added to the juice, converts the natural sugar of the juice into alcohol and carbon dioxide.

- **Table or Still Wine:** Wines which do not contain carbon dioxide.These are further classified into:
  - □ **Red:** Being fermented with the red grape skins from which the wine gets its colour.
  - □ **White:** Usually produced from white grapes and the grape juice is fermented away from the skins.
  - □ **Rosé:** The colour is controlled by regulating the duration the grape juice is kept in contact with the skin.
- **Sparkling wine:** The sparkling comes from the carbon dioxide in the wine, the most famous one being *Champagne,* but only sparkling wine made in the champagne region of France can be called *champagne,* others will be known as sparkling wines.
- **Fortified wines:** Are those wines which are strengthened by the addition of alcohol, usually a grape spirit. Their alcohol strength varies from 15%-22%, by volume. The famous ones being Port, Sherry, Madeira, Malaga and Marsala.
- **Aromatized wines:** As the term suggests it is flavoured wine. The flavourings range from herbs, fruit peels, fruit extracts, quinine. Examples: Vermouth (wormwood), Dubonnet (herbs and quinine), Lillet (herbs, fruit peel and fortified with brandy).

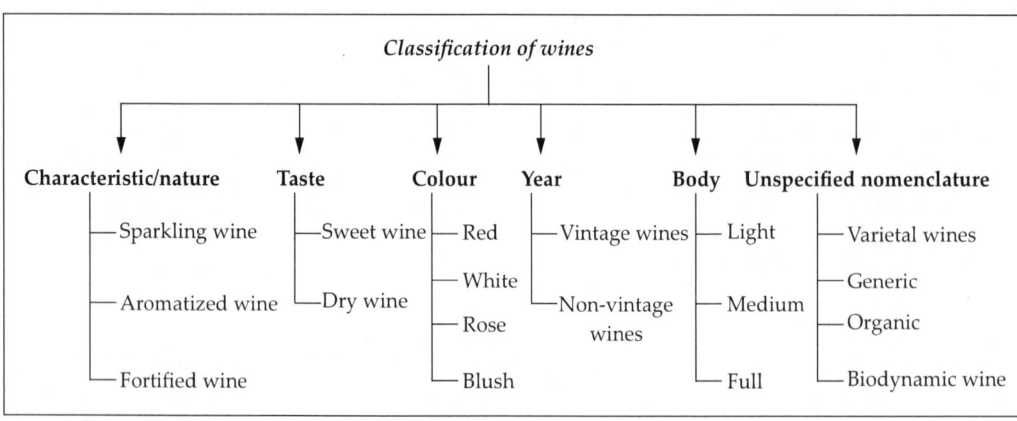

COMMON FLAVOURS FOUND IN WINE

When tasting wine, some find it useful to describe exactly what they are smelling and tasting. Common wine aromas are listed below. The aromas come from the grapes themselves as well as their cellar treatment (referred to as bouquet).

- **Herbs and Spices:** Dill, Tobacco, Bay Leaf, Mint, Green Grass, Straw, Basil, Vanilla, Black Pepper, Clove, Fennel, Nutmeg, Cinnamon, Lemon Grass, Thyme, Licorice/Anise.

- **Wood:** Smoky, Tree Bark, Sawdust, Tar, Raw/Green Wood, Eucalyptus, Cedar.

- **Fruit:** Plum, Cherry, Blueberry, Currant, Raspberry, Blackberry, Strawberry, Fig, Coconut, Grape, Watermelon, Cranberry, Mango, Orange, Lemon, Pomegranate, Grapefruit, Lime, Tangerine, Pineapple, Kiwi, Apple, Apricot, Peach.

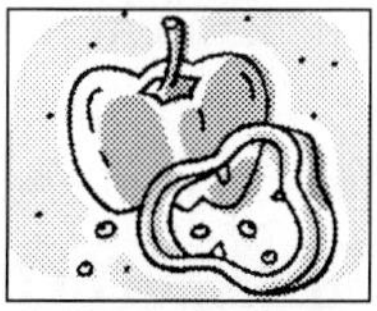

- **Vegetable:** Rhubarb, Bell Pepper, Black Olive, Green Olive, Tomato, Celery, Green Bean, Beet, Baked Potato.

- **Floral:** Violet, Rose, Lavender, Lilac, Honeysuckle, Orange Blossom.

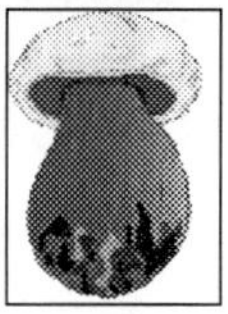

- **Earth:** Underbrush, Mushroom, Truffle, Humus.

- **Other stuff:** Chocolate, Grilled Meat, Baked Bread, Butterscotch, Caramel, Soy Sauce, Cherry Cola, Coffee, Walnut, Almond, Musk, Butter, Maple Syrup, Hazelnut, Honey, Baker's Yeast, Dusty, Chalky.

- **Off-Aromas:** Off-aromas indicate that the wine is flawed in some way. The most common off-aroma is wine spoiled by cork taint. The affected wine has a musty, unpleasant odour like garlic, onion, nail polish, burnt matches, vinegar and so on.

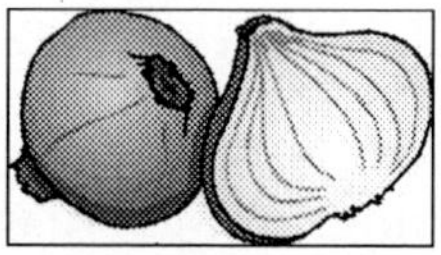

MAJOR CHAMPAGNE PRODUCERS

- Krug
- Lanson
- Bollingers
- Tattingers
- Charles hiedsieck
- Veuve clicquot pont sardin
- Mumms
- Laurent periere
- Piper hiedsieck
- Moet et chandon

Brand Names of Other Sparkling Wines

- **Carta Nevada:** *Spain*
- **Cordon Nigro:** *Spain*
- **Processo-Di-Valdob:** *Italy*
- **Henkel Trocken:** *Germany*
- **Marquise-De-Pompadour:** *Indian*
- **Sula Brut:** *Indian*
- **Henkel cardinal:** *Germany*
- **Lagenbach:** *Germany*
- **Dienhard Cabinet:** *Germany*
- **Asti Spumante:** *Italian*
- **Cobetchoe White:** *Russian*

Sparkling Wine Glossary

- **Vin Mousseux:** French term for sparkling wine.
- **Phil/ant:** French term for sparkling wine.
- **Perlant:** French term for light sparkling.
- **Spritzig:** German term for slightly sparkling.
- **Schaumwein:** German term for sparkling.
- **Perlwein:** German term for slightly sparkling.
- **Sekt:** German term for sparkling.
- **Spumante:** Italian term for sparkling.
- **Espumante:** Portuguese term for sparkling.
- **Espumosos:** Spanish term for sparkling.
- **Trocken:** German Dry sparkling wine.

Type of wine bottles

SERVICE TEMPERATURE OF WINES

Different types of wine are served at different temperatures:

Style of Wine	Example	Service Temperature
Medium-full-bodied white wine	Oaked Chardonnay	Slightly chilled: 12°C
Light-medium-bodied wine	Pinot Grigio	Chilled: 10°C
Light-bodied red wine	Beaujolais	Lightly chilled: 12-14°C
Medium-Full-bodied red wine	Shiraz, Cabernet Sauvignon	Room temperature: 16-18°C
Sweet wines	Sauterness	Well chilled: 6-8°C
Sparkling wine	Champagne, Cava	Well chilled: 6-8°C
Rose wine	Tavel Rose	Chilled: 6-10°C

Note: Always remember that over chilling can mask the flavours in white wine whereas the average room temperature varies due to the time of year, hating or due to other climatic factors, but be careful that red wines don't get too warm or too cold

WINE OPENERS

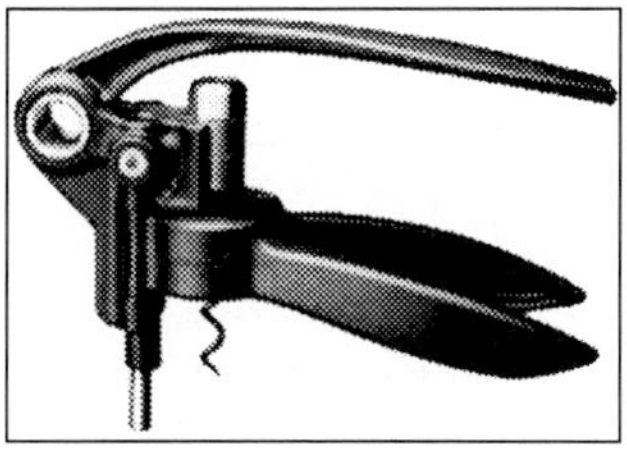

Lever style corkscrew/ the rabbit

Waiter's friend

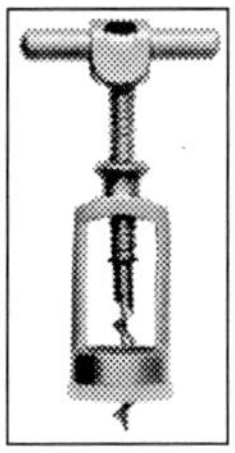

Twisting pull cork

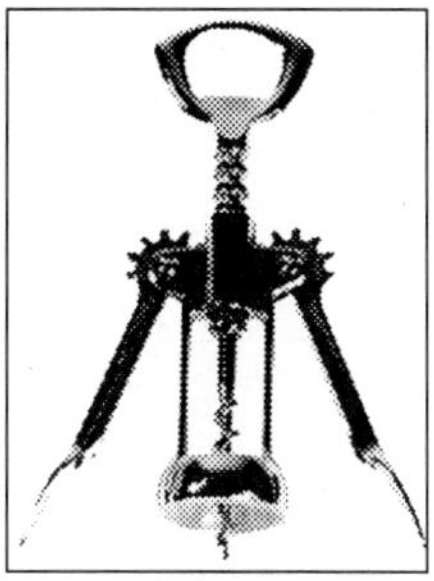

Winged corkscrew

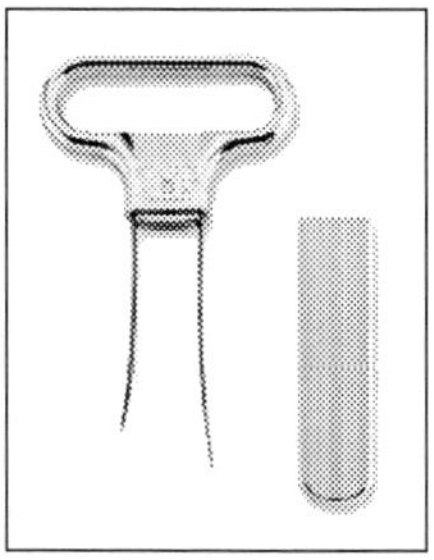

Two-pronged wine opener/ahso wine opener

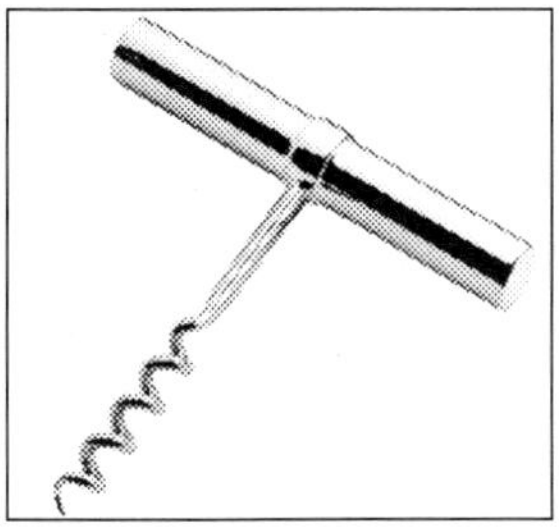

T-shaped wine opener

Types of wine opener

APERITIFS

Aperitif derives from the Latin word ***aperire,*** which means "to open," in the sense of opening up the appetite. It should be something to prepare the palate for the meal and should be offered within the first thirty seconds after the guests have been seated. An aperitif can be categorized as hors d'oeuvre (beverage appetizer) and treated as welcoming drink. It should be low in alcohol, so as not to numb the taste buds. It should be dry, so as to stimulate the appetite. As sweet drinks can cause the guest to feel full before the meal has even begun. All true aperitifs carry a bitter-sweet character that stimulates the production of gastric juices and promotes appetite. Aperitif can be said as before meal drink or pre-meal drink. Generally, aperitifs can be divided as wine based aperitifs and spirit based aperitifs. Wine based aperitifs include dry crisp white wines, sparkling wine or champagne, dry fortified wines like sherries (*Manjanilla and Fino*), Byrrh (*made of red wine, mistelle, and quinine*), slightly chilled light-bodied white wine like Chablis, Sauvignon Blanc and White Burgundies, Wine base cocktails like Kir and Kir Royale. Aromatized wines (*wines which are fortified and have been infused with botanicals that add flavour and colour)* such as Vermouth, Dubonnet and Lillet. Relatively low in alcohol from 16-24% and with distinctive bittersweet flavours as they promote conviviality without diluting the palate for the food to come. Some of the famous spirit based aperitifs include mixed drink like gin and tonic water, Cynar, Pastis, Ouzo, Campari, Amer Picon bitters and before dinner cocktails. Unlike aperitif digestifs are served after meal to aid in digestion. They are also known as after-meal drinks or post-meal drinks such as cognac.

BITTERS

Bitters refer to a spirit that is flavoured with roots, herbs and spices which are generally held to have medicinal properties. In other words bitters are an aromatic flavouring agent made from infusing roots, barks, fruit peels, seeds, spices, herbs, flower, and botanicals in a spirit. The origins of bitter lie in the flavouring elements that were commonly added to the very earliest spirits. Bitters were called 'elixir of life' means magical cure, taken as restoratives and remedies for any number of condition, ranging from headache, indigestion, stomachache to constipation. Three to five drops of bitters are used while making cocktails. Some of the renowned bitters are:

- Angostura bitters
- Aperol
- Campari
- Suze

LIQUEURS

A liqueur is a sweet alcoholic beverage, often flavoured with fruits, herbs, spices, nuts, flowers, leaves, citrus fruits, berries, seeds, roots, plants, barks, and sometimes cream. In short liqueurs are flavoured sweetened spirits, characterized by their flavourings and not base spirit. Liqueurs contain at least 2.5% sugar by volume. Liqueurs containing

2.5 to 10% sugar are in the dry range. Most liqueurs contain up to 35 or 45% sweetener. Whereas Cordials is derived from latin word *cordis*, meaning *heart*. This suggests the warming, heartening effect of liqueur on drinker.

Name	**Flavouring**	**Base**	**Colour**	**Alc%**	**Origin**
Amaretto	Almond, apricot	Brandy	Russet	28	Italy
Aurum	Orange	Brandy	Golden	40	Italy
Bailey's Irish Cream	Cream	Irish Whisky	Beige	17	Ireland
Benedictine	Herbs	Brandy	Dark amber	40	France
Chartreuse	Herbs	Brandy	Green, yellow	55, 40	France
Cointreau	Orange	Brandy	Clear	40	France
Crème de banane	Bananas	Brandy	Yellow	30	France
Crème de Cacao	Cocoa, vanilla	Brandy	Dark brown, clear	27	France
Crème De Cassis	Black currant	Brandy	Red-brown	30	France
Crème de Menthe	Mint	Brandy	Green, clear	30	France
Curacao	Orange	Rum	Clear, red, yellow, Green, blue	25-35	Dutch
Drambuie	Honey, herbs	Scotch	Amber	35	Scotland
Fraise de bois	Strawberry	Brandy	Red	30	France
Framboise	Raspberry	Brandy	Red	30	France
Galliano	Vanilla, liquorice, Anise	Neutral spirit	Yellow	35	Italy
Glayva	Heather honey, oranges	Scotch	Amber	35	Scotland
Gold-Wasser	Aniseed, caraway, gold	Neutral spirit	Clear with gold specks	40	Poland
Grand Mariner	Orange	Cognac	Amber	40	France
Irish Mist	Honey, herbs	Irish whisky	Amber	35	Ireland
Kahlua	Coffee	Neutral spirit	Dark brown	26.5	Mexico
Kummel	Caraway seeds	Neutral spirit	Clear	39	Germany
Malibu	Coconut	White rum	Clear	24	Barbados
Mandarine Napoléon	Tangerine	Cognac	Amber	38	France

Maraschino	Cherry	Neutral Spirit	Clear	30	Italy
Midori	Melon	Neutral Spirit	Green	23	Japan
Parfait Amour	Fruits, spices, violets	Brandy	Purple	30	Holland
Pastis, Ouzo, Ojen	Anise	Brandy	Golden	45	France
Peach Schnapps	Peaches	Spirit	Clear	23	Scandinavia
Pimm's	Fruit extracts	Gin	Deep red	25	England
Sambuca	Anise	Neutral Spirit	Clear	40	Italy
Southern Comfort	Peaches	Bourbon	Amber	40	U.S.A.
Tia Maria	Coffee	Jamaican rum	Dark Brown	26.5	Jamaica
Van der Hum	Orange, nutmeg	Brandy	Amber	25	South Africa
Wisniowka	Cherry	Vodka	Dark red	40	Poland

WINE TERMS

Acidity: Wines with high acidity are tart and zesty. Red wines generally have a lighter colour and more tart characteristics. White wines are often described with characteristics similar to lemon or lime juice.

Angular: An angular wine is like putting a triangle in your mouth – it hits at specific places with high impact and not elsewhere. It's like getting punched in the arm in the same place over and over again. An angular wine also has high acidity.

Austere: This is an unfriendly wine. It hits the mouth and then turns it inside out. It usually means the wine has very high acidity and very little fruit flavours. An austere wine is not fruit-forward nor opulent.

Big: Big describes a wine with massive flavour in your mouth that takes up all sections of your mouth and tongue. A big wine is not necessarily a fruit-forward wine, it can also mean that it has big tannins.

Bright: Bright wines are higher in acidity.

Buttery: A wine with buttery characteristics has been aged in oak and generally is rich and flat (less acidity). A buttery wine often has a cream-like texture that hits the middle of your tongue almost like oil (or butter) and has a smooth finish.

Cassis: The least fruit-like of all dark fruits. It means of the seedy and gritty character of actual black currants.

Charcoal: A wine that is described as tasting like charcoal tastes gritty, it's usually dry (with higher tannins) and has this rustic flavour. Charcoal is often associated with a similar characteristic: pencil lead (but less refined).

Cigar box: Cigar box flavours hint towards sweetness and cedar-wood with an abundance of smoke.

Complex: A complex wine simply means that while tasting, the flavour changes from the moment you taste it to the moment you swallow.

Creamy: Creamy is a popular description for white and sparkling wines fermented or aged in oak.

Crisp: The word crisp with wine is more often used to describe a white wine. A crisp wine is most likely simple but goes really well with a porch swing on a hot day.

Dense: Dense is flavoured for use in bold red wines such as Cabernet sauvignon and Côtes du Rhône but usually isn't a positive characteristic in other wines because it implies that wine is handicapped.

Elegant: It means that the wine is not fruity, not opulent and not bold. Off-vintages are often referred to as *elegant* vintages as they have higher acid. Elegant wines may taste like crap when they are first released but they also tend to age better.

Fat: Wide, big, massive, opulent, these are all similar synonyms of fat.

Flabby: Flabby means the wine has no acidity.

Flamboyant: Abundance of fruit.

Hint of: This wine definitely has this character like oak, herbs, fruits in the flavour when there is a *hint of* it in the description.

Jammy: In wine, jammy indicates a wine with a cooked berry sweetness that is syrupy and often is used to describe American wines like Zinfandel, Grenache, Cabernet Franc and Australian Shiraz.

Lees: Lees are an actual winemaking term describing the dead bits of yeast particles that generally sink to the bottom of a wine. Lees are stirred up once a day to make the wine have a thicker, more oily and creamy texture.

Oaked: The ultimate non-grape influence to the flavours in wine. In white wine it adds butter, vanilla and sometimes coconut. In red wine it adds flavours often referred to as baking spices, vanilla and sometimes dill.

Opulent: This word is a baseline word to a style of wine that is rich, smooth and bold.

Refined: Refined is a subset of elegant wines. This term is often used while describing tannins in a wine. These wines have the "less is more" ideology about them. GO TO ELEGANT.

Silky: Silky is the red wine equivalent word to creamy with white wines.

Steely: A steely wine has higher acid and more sharp edges.

Structured: A structured wine has high tannin and acid and is hard to drink.

Tight: This wine is not ready to drink. It usually has very high tannins, hard-to-identify fruit characteristics and is hard to drink. This wine could benefit from being decanted.

Toasty: Toasty is most commonly a reference to a wine that's oak-aged in *Medium Plus Toasted Oak*. It doesn't actually taste like toast, it's more like slightly burnt caramel on the finish.

Unctuous: When a wine is unctuous it is oily.

Unoaked: A wine that is unoaked doesn't have vanilla, cream, butter or baking spices in it. An unoaked white wine is more zesty with lemony flavours, while an unoaked red wine tends to be more tart.

Velvetly: Lush, smooth and silky are all synonyms of a velvety wine. To imagine velvety, visualize watching perfectly smooth chocolate pouring into a mold on a Dove chocolate commercial.

31 PRESENTING BEVERAGE MENU

Equipment Required

- Beverage menu
- KOT/BOT

Knowlege Required

- Knowledge of the food and beverages items
- Up-selling

Procedure

- The hostess/host after seating the guests comes back to the hostess desk and picks up the menus and approaches back to the table.
- Present the beverage menu to the guest, ladies first. Then present the beverage menu to the gentleman/host at the table. This menu should be presented irrespective if the guest chooses to have buffet or à la carte.
- The hostess/host should take the guest order if the guest is ready to order immediately.
- If the guest does not order at the same time the hostess/host should inform the guest that the steward would be at the table shortly to take the order.
- If the guest orders the beverages, the hostess/host/associate should collect back the beverage menus.

Standard

- Menu to be presented within 1 minute of seating the guest.
- The menus should be clean and stain free.
- The number of food menus should be the same as the number of adult guests.
- There should be at least 1 beverage menu for every 2-3 guests at the table.
- The hostess *should* hold the menu firm, from the right hand. The thumb should be on the upper side and forefingers should support the base.
- The menus should be offered from the right-hand side of the guests.
- The menu should not be presented to a group/guests with a pre-fixed menu.
- The menu should be handed over in the sequence:
  - □ Eldest lady
  - □ Other ladies

- Hostess
- Eldest gentleman
- Other gentleman
- Host

- In case the guest is occupied; the hostess should wait.
- Standard phrase for presenting the menu, "*The menu card for you Madam/Sir*".
- The hostess/host/steward should know the "not available" beverages and the other "off-menu" cocktails possible.

UP-SELLING

Equipment Required

- Beverage Menu
- KOT/BOT

Knowlege Required

- Knowledge of the food and beverages items
- Complete knowledge of the menu
- Pricing of various items
- Description and brief history of all items on the menu
- Up-selling techniques
- Knowledge of the hidden menu.

Procedure

- The steward suggests some alcoholic and non-alcoholic cocktails to the guest and other house specialties if the guest asks for simple aerated drinks or juices.

- The steward suggests wine to accompany the food and provokes impulse buying.
- The steward recommends the house specialities to the guest.

Standard

- *"Sir/Madam, I would recommend you to try our ____ (name of the drink and a brief description)".*
- *"Sir/Madam, I would recommend you to try _____ (name of the wine). It will complement with your meal really well."*
- *"Sir/Madam, I would recommend you try our specialty _________."* The steward should give a brief description about the dish and its spice level.
- *"May I recommend the Smirnoff vodka instead of the Magic Moments vodka in your Bloody Mary cocktail."*
- The guest should not feel like he is being forced.

32 SERVICE OF FRESH LIME WATER/ SODA/JUICE

Equipment Required

- Glassware
- Straw and stirrer
- Salver
- Cocktail napkin
- Coaster
- Creamer for sugar syrup and lime juice.

Knowledge Required

- Types of fresh lime soda available in the hotel.
- To prepare fresh lime soda sweet and salted.
- Other cold non-alcoholic beverages available in the hotel.

Service of Fresh Lime

- Whilst taking the order the order taker will check with the guest. How would you like your fresh lime Sir/Mr. Scott, sweet or salted? (get response), soda or water, Sir?
- While asking if another drink is required. May I repeat your drink/s Sir/Mr. Scott?

Standards

- Beverage orders will be taken within two minutes of seating.
- Fresh lime will be served within 5 minutes of taking order.
- Fresh lime will be served from a beverage round, unless served at the bar counter.
- Fresh lime will be served onto a coaster with a cocktail napkin. In case it is being served on to a tablecloth, the coaster and cocktail napkin may be omitted.
- An empty glass, swizzle stick holder or B&B plate will be placed for used stir sticks.
- The server shall ask for a repeat order when the glass is one-fourth full.
- All common courtesies such as "ladies first and host last" shall be followed.
- Glass will be cleared when the guest has finished the drink and declined a repeat order.
- All beverage orders shall be served from the guest's right (wherever possible).

Procedure

- Fill Collins glass with ice cubes, place a swizzle stick inside.
- Add lemon juice (30 ml)
- Put a lemon wheel on the rim of the glass.
- Add sugar syrup and/or salt.
- Add water and/or soda.
- Stir the drink.
- Place the following on salver.

Prepared Fresh Lime

- Sugar syrup in a decanter (in case fresh lime soda sweet).
- Straws in straw holder.

At the Table

- Place the straw holder in the centre of the table.
- Place the drink and the additional sugar syrup on right-hand side of the guest.

SERVICE OF ICED TEA

Equipment Required

- Glassware
- Straw and stirrer
- Salver
- Cocktail napkin
- Coaster
- Creamer for sugar syrup and lime juice

Knowledge Required

- Types of iced tea available in the hotel.
- To prepare iced tea.
- Other cold non-alcoholic beverages available in the hotel.

Procedure

- Fill Collins glass with ice cubes; place a swizzle stick inside, put mint leaves.
- Add lemon juice.
- Add sugar syrup.
- Fill with tea till top of the glass.
- Put a lemon wheel on the rim of the glass.
- Place mint leaves on top as garnish.

- Place the following on salver:
  - Prepared ice tea
  - Sugar syrup in a decanter
  - Straws in straw holder.

Standards

- Beverage orders will be taken within two minutes of seating.
- Iced tea will be served within 5 minutes of taking order.
- Iced tea will be served from a beverage round, unless served at the bar counter.
- Iced tea will be served onto a coaster with a cocktail napkin. In case it is being served on to a tablecloth, the coaster and cocktail napkin may be omitted.
- An empty glass, swizzle stick holder or B&B plate will be placed for used stir sticks.
- The server shall ask for a repeat order when the glass is 1/4th full.
- All common courtesies such as "ladies first and host last" shall be followed.
- Glass will be cleared when the guest has finished the drink and declined a repeat order.
- All beverage orders shall be served from the guests right (wherever possible).

At the Table

1. Place the straw holder in the centre of the table.
2. Place the drink and the additional sugar syrup on right-hand side of the guest.

Note: The tea leaves or tea bag should be brewed adequately before these can be poured over the ice. Most stewards do not allow the decoction to be brewed adequately, resulting in iced tea with very weak flavour of the tea itself. Also, brewing the mint leaf in the teapot with the tea helps enormously apart from the sprig of mint as garnish.

For Sugar Syrup

Boil up briskly, equal quantities of sugar and water, with lemon juice or egg white. When the scum rises take a skimming spoon and skim off the top. When the syrup is clear, it is done. Let it cool and bottle for future use.

SERVICE OF JUICE

Equipment Required

- Glassware
- Straw
- Salver

Standard

- Collect freshly squeezed juice or canned juice as ordered by the guest in a clean glassware as per the hotel policy on a salver.
- Juices should be well stirred and properly placed on a salver.
- Excuse me, Sir/Madam, (name of the juice) juice for you.
- Serve from the right-hand side of the guest.
- Always mention the name of the juice.
- Place on the right side of the water goblet.
- Place it carefully and slowly.
- Do not spill.

33 SERVICE OF TEA

Equipment Required

- Salver with cloth napkin
- Tea pot, creamer
- Tea cozy
- Tea cup and saucer
- Sugar caddy
- Tea spoon
- Tea strainer for masala tea

Tea tray set-up

Knowlege Required

- Service of tea.
- Varieties of tea available in the hotel.

Procedure

- F&B associate picks up the order.
- The teapot, sugar caddy, strainer with slop basin (in case of leaf tea), teacup, saucer and teaspoon are taken to the table on a salver.
- The F&B associate places the teacup, teaspoon and saucer in front of the guest.
- The F&B associate asks whether the guest would like the tea with or without milk.
- The F&B associate pours the tea from the teapot into the cup and takes the teapot back to the side station.
- The F&B associate asks for replenishment of the tea.

Standard

- The F&B associate should use tea leaves as per guests requirement of strength of tea and covers. Tea should be brewed for minimum of 3 minutes before being brought to the table.
- The milk should be processed from the coffee machine and filled in a creamer.
- In case of lemon tea, 3 deseeded lemon wedges should be carried in a bowl/ saucer (lemon wedges should be in a muslin cloth).
- In case of masala tea, the milk should be pre-mixed in the teapot and a dash of tea masala should be added.

- The teapot, teacup and saucer should be scrupulously clean and should be free from chips and stains.
- The teaspoon should be placed either parallel to the handle of the teacup or teaspoon should be placed at 4 o' clock position and teacup at 5 o' clock position on the saucer.
- The teaspoon should be sparkling clean and without water marks or stains on the surface.
- The teacup, teaspoon and saucer should be placed from the right-hand side of the guest using the right hand to grip the saucer.
- "Sir/Madam, would you like your tea with or without milk?"
- This step should be followed only if the specifications have not been reconfirmed at the time of order taking.
- The tea should be poured from the right-hand side of the guest.
- In case of tea with milk, the associate should pour the tea till three-fourths of the cup is full and then put 4-5 drops of milk at one go and allow the cloud of milk to come up. Ask the guest and pour milk again.
- In case of tea without milk, the associate should pour the tea till four-fifths level.
- The F&B associate should pour with a steady flow so as to avoid any spillage in the saucer or on the table.
- In the case of tea/coffee service 3 cookies are offered along with the coffee/tea. (1 person)
  For 2 people = 5 cookies
  For 3 people = 7 cookies
  For 4 people = 9 cookies
- The associate should ask for replenishment when the teacup is one-third full.
- "Would you like some more tea?"

TEA SERVING PROCEDURE

Step 1: Approach the table

Step 2: Place cookies on the table

Step 3: Place sugar basin, slop basin, tea cup and saucer

Step 4: Pour tea in the cup

Step 5: Pour milk in the tea

SERVICE OF COFFEE

Equipment Required

- Salver with cloth napkin
- Coffee pot, creamer
- Cozy
- Coffee cup and saucer
- Sugar caddy
- Teaspoon

Knowlege Required

- Coffee machine operations
- Classical service of coffee
- Types of coffee preparations available.

Procedure

Coffee tray setup

- The associate picks up the order.
- In case the guest orders coffee that is dispensed directly from the machine, pre-portioned in the cup.
- The sugar basin, cup, saucer, coffee pot and teaspoon are taken to the table on a salver.
- The station associate places the cup, teaspoon and saucer in front of the guest.
- The associate pours the coffee from the coffee pot/carafe into the cup and takes the pot/carafe back to the side station. (This step is not applicable in the case of coffee by the cup).
- The associate asks for replenishment of the coffee.

Standard

- The coffee should be processed from the coffee machine.
- The milk should be processed from the coffee machine and filled in a creamer.
- The outer surface of the cup should be clean and free from any coffee marks.
- Cup should be warm.
- Care should be taken that the coffee does not spill from the cup.
- The cup and saucer should be scrupulously clean and should be free from chips and stains.
- The teaspoon should be placed either parallel to the handle of the teacup or teaspoon should be placed at 4 o' clock position and tea cup at 5 o' clock position on the saucer.
- The teaspoon should be sparkling clean and without water marks.
- The cup, teaspoon and saucer should be placed from the right-hand side of the guest.
- The coffee should be poured from the right-hand side of the guest.
- In case of coffee with milk, the associate should pour the coffee till three-fourths level and fill the cup with milk.
- In case of coffee without milk, the associate should pour the coffee up to four-fifths level.
- The associate should ensure that there is no spillage on the saucer or anywhere on the table.
- In the case of tea/coffee service 3 cookies are offered along with the coffee/tea (1 person).

  For 2 people = 5 cookies

  For 3 people = 7 cookies

  For 4 people = 9 cookies

  The associate should ask for replenishment when the cup is one-third full. *"Would you like some more coffee?"*

COFFEE SERVING PROCEDURE

Step 1: Approach the table

Step 2: Place cookies the table

Step 3: Place sugar basin, coffee cup and saucer

Step 4: Pour coffee in the cup

Step 5: Pour milk in the coffee

34 BEER SERVICE PROCEDURE

Equipment Required

- Salver with cloth napkin
- Chilled beer goblet
- Bottle of beer
- Opener

Knowlege Required

- Product knowledge.
- Classification of beer.
- Brands available in the hotel..
- Basic knowledge of the beer of the world.

Procedure

- The F&B associate after taking the order from the guest gives the BOT to the bar, picks up the order and carries it to the station sideboard.
- The F&B associate to place the chilled beer glass on the table and then present the beer bottle to the host for approval.
- On getting the approval from the host, open the bottle and pour along the rim so as to avoid excessive head formation. Lift and tilt the glass to approximately 45 degree angle.
- Keep the bottle with remaining beer in the centre of the table on a coaster. Wish the guest while leaving the table.
- The F&B associate should ask for a repeat order when the glass is one-third empty.

Standard

- Beverage orders to be served within 5 minutes of the guest order.
- The beer glass should be placed at the 4 o'clock position to the water glass.
- The glass should be free from chips, stains and watermarks.
- Handle the glass from the base using the forefinger and thumb only, leaving no fingerprints on the glass.
- *"______ (brand name of the beer), Sir/Madam."*
- The bottle opener should be clean, free from dust and rust.

- Stop pouring 1 inch below the rim.
- The head should not exceed 1 cm.
- In case, the beer is not being shared place the bottle in front of the consumer's cover.
- *"Enjoy your drink, Sir/Madam."*
- *"Would you like to repeat your drink, Sir/Madam?"*.

BEER SERVICE PROCEDURE

Step 1: The station associate after taking the order from the guest gives the BOT to the bar, picks up the order and carries it to the station side-board.	
Step 2: The F&B associate to place the coaster on the table if tablecloth is not laid.	
Step 3: The F&B associate to place the chilled beer glass on the table.	

<table>
<tr><td>Step 4: The F&B associate to place the chilled beer on the table.</td><td></td></tr>
<tr><td>Step 5: The F&B associate to present the beer bottle to the host for approval. Host will check for the temperature of the beer.</td><td>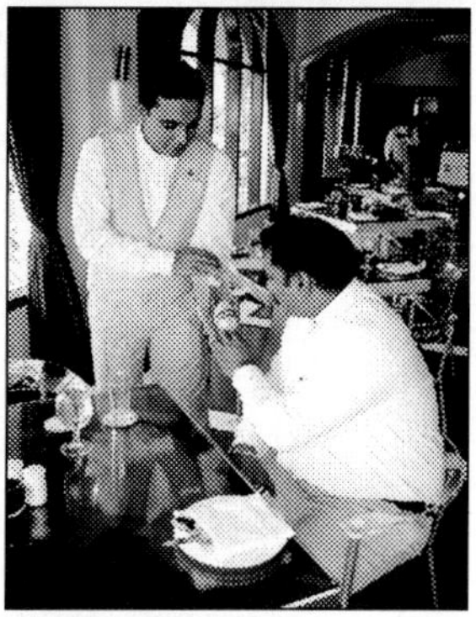</td></tr>
<tr><td>Step 6: Open the bottle and keep the crown cap in your pocket.</td><td></td></tr>
<tr><td>Step 7: Pour the beer along the rim so as to avoid excessive head formation. Lift and tilt the glass to approximately 45° angle.</td><td></td></tr>
</table>

Step 8: Serve the beer.	

35 SERVICE OF STRAIGHT DRINKS/SPIRITS

Equipment Required

- Whisky
- Salver with cloth napkin
- Appropriate glassware according to the drink
- Decanter
- Stirrer

Knowlege Required

- Product knowledge - whisky
- Principles of complementing mixers and spirits
- Types of glassware and hollowware.

Procedure

- The station associate should check with the guest which mixer she/he would like to have with her/his spirit.
- The associate after taking the order from the guest gives the KOT to the bar.
- The associate to pick up the drink order from the bar and approach the table.
- Place the pre-filled glass on the table on a coaster.
- Offer ice to the guest. After 2 ice cubes have already been placed, check with the guest if he would prefer to have some more ice.
- The associate should then top up the glass with the mixer or as the guest desires.
- The remaining mixer, if any, should be placed next to the glass.
- Wish the guest while leaving the table.

> Single malt whisky should always be served at cellar temperature. It is not intended to be a thirst quenching drink, so avoid ice, which will only numb the subtle flavour of single malt. A splash of water can be added but choose a spring water as it will not contaminate the flavour. Blended Canadian whiskey has a rounded, fruity taste and benefits from being served on the rocks whereas Bourbon whiskey is a highly versatile drink and mixes well with variety of mixers. Gin is mixed with tonic water and served with a slice of lemon.

Standard

- The F&B associate should always offer two relevant mixers. Example: *"Madam/ Sir would you like to have tonic water or orange juice with vodka?"*.

- Ice should be served with the help of tongs.
- The decanter should be neat and clean and never touch the rim of the glass.
- Stirrer should also be provided along with the drinks in the glass.
- If spirit is being served in the bar then cocktail napkin or paper napkin to be provided.

SPIRIT SERVING PROCEDURE

Step 1: Pick the drink order from the bar and approach the tables.

Step 2: Place the pre-filled glass on the table on a coaster.

Step 3: Offer ice to the guest. After 2 ice cubes have already been placed, check with the guest if he would prefer to have some more ice.

Step 4: The associate should then top up the glass with the mixer or as the guest desires.

Note: If tablecloth is laid on the table then coasters are not provided but if tablecloths are not laid then it is necessary to provide coasters along with the drink.

COGNAC SERVING PROCEDURE

Equipment Required

- Cognac
- Salver with cloth napkin
- Brandy snifter
- Decanter
- Lukewarm water
- Wine opener

Knowlege Required

- Product knowledge - cognac

Procedure

- The F&B associate takes the order and raises BOT.
- Give the BOT in the bar and collect the bottle of cognac with all the accessories.
- Carefully cut the capsule below the level of the cork in front of the guest.
- Remove the capsule and cork.
- With the help of neat napkin clean the neck of the bottle to remove any dust and debris from the bottle.
- Lay the brandy snifter on side of the bottle of cognac.
- Pour in the cognac until almost level with the lip of the glass. This will help to deliver the right amount of cognac in the glass and serve at the right-hand side of the guest.
- If brandy/cognac is desired only with lukewarm water then pour lukewarm water from the decanter in the guest's glass.
- Repeat the order after consumption of drinks in the glass.
- At last present the bill to the guest, take the money, deposit it to the cashier and pass a thanks note to the guest for his visit. If have any offers in future then discuss it with the guest for future business prospect.

TEQUILA SERVING PROCEDURE

Equipment Required

- Tequila
- Salver with cloth napkin
- Shot glass
- Lime wedge and salt

Knowlege Required

- Product knowledge - tequila

Procedure

- The F&B associate takes the order and raises BOT.
- Give the BOT in the bar and collect the drink with all the accessories.
- Bring the tequila in shot glass.
- Place the shot glass in front of the guest's right-hand side.
- Place salt and lime wedge on the table.
- Repeat the order after consumption of drinks in the glass.
- At last present the bill to the guest, take the money, deposit it to the cashier and pass a thanks note to the guest for his visit. If have any offers in future then discuss it with the guest for future business prospects.

GIN SERVING PROCEDURE

Equipment Required

- Gin
- Salver with cloth napkin
- High ball glass
- Decanter
- Tonic water
- Ice bucket with ice and ice tong
- Stirrer stick
- Lime slice (optional).

Knowlege Required

- Product knowledge - gin.

Procedure

- The F&B associate takes the order and raises BOT.
- Give the BOT in the bar and collect the drink with all the accessories.
- Bring the gin in high ball glass with a stirrer stick.
- Place the glass in front of the guest's right-hand side.
- Ask for the preference:
  - □ If gin is preferred on the rocks then ask for number of ice cubes to be placed.
  - □ If gin is desired only with tonic water then pour tonic water from the decanter.
  - □ If gin is desired with ice and tonic water then first place ice cubes then add tonic water to it.
- Repeat the order after consumption of drinks in the glass.

- At last present the bill to the guest, take the money, deposit it to the cashier and pass a thanks note to the guest for his visit. If have any offers in future then discuss it with the guest for future business prospects.

VODKA SERVING PROCEDURE

Equipment Required

- Vodka
- Salver with cloth napkin
- High ball glass
- Decanter
- Lemonade
- Ice bucket with ice and ice tong
- Stirrer stick
- Lime slice (optional).

Knowlege Required

- Product knowledge - vodka

Procedure

- The F&B associate takes the order and raises BOT.
- Give the BOT in the bar and collect the drink with all the accessories.
- Bring the glass with the vodka in it.
- Place the glass in front of the guest's right-hand side.
- Ask for the preferences:
    - □ If vodka is preferred on the rocks then ask for number of ice cubes to be placed in the glass.
    - □ If vodka is desired only with lemonade then pour lemonade from the decanter into the guest's glass.
    - □ If vodka is desired with ice and lemonade, then first place ice cubes then add lemonade to it.
- Repeat the order after consumption of drinks in the glass.
- At last present the bill to the guest, take the money, deposit it to the cashier and pass a thanks note to the guest for his visit. If have any offers in future then discuss it with the guest for future business prospects.

36 COCKTAILS

INTRODUCTION

A cocktail is a mixed drink containing two or more ingredients. Originally, a mixture of distilled spirits, sugar, water, and bitters. The word has gradually come to mean almost any mixed drink containing alcohol. Cocktail today is made by mixing spirits or wine with fruit juices, bitters, liqueurs or other ingredients either by stirring, shaking and blending all of them. The ideal cocktail combines two or more ingredients having a base of alcoholic beverages in a harmonious manner so that no element should dominate the other. The term cocktail was first introduced by American bartenders in the 1920.

INGREDIENTS OF COCKTAIL

Cocktails usually consist of three different 'classes' of ingredients.

- **Base:** It is most often some sort of spirit, like vodka, whisky, gin, tequila and sometimes wine.
- **Flavouring:** The main flavouring is added to bring out the aroma of the base and to modify its taste such as vermouth, fruit juices or even eggs or cream.
- **Special flavouring:** It is added to enhance the taste of the base, and often adds the colour to the cocktail. Common special flavourings include Grenadine, Blue Curacao and others.

EQUIPMENT

There are many types of equipment used for making a good cocktail. First out of the essentials is the cocktail shaker. There are two basic types of shakers available. A European cocktail shaker is usually made of metal, or glass with a metal top. It is basically a container which holds about half a litre, fitted with a top which closes tightly around the upper edges of the container. This top also has a smaller top, usually fitted with a built-in strainer, through which the shaken cocktail is poured. American shakers, however, consist of two cones about the same size. One is often made of glass, and the other is metallic. These cones are held together to form a closed container, and the shaken cocktail is poured from either one. Most American shakers do not have built-in strainers. Peg measures, also known as jiggers, are also essential. Jiggers are most often made of metal, but glass jiggers are common, as well. The standard measurements of a jigger can vary widely, depending on where you are. In India jiggers are available at 60 ml/30 ml and 50 ml/25 ml measuring. In addition to the equipment mentioned above, there are other equipment as well like ice bucket, water jugs, ice crusher machine, muddler, bar caddy, bar pad, salt and sugar rimmer, electric blender, ordinary kitchenware such as fruit knife, pairing knife, corkscrews, chopping board, lime squeezer, speed pourer, bar guns, lemon squeezer, store and pour, zester, scooper, straws, toothpicks stirrers (small stirrers known as swizzle sticks) and hand towel and cocktail napkin. To serve cocktail in an appropriate glass is also very important. Glassware like Cocktail glass, Martini glass, Margarita, Rolly Polly, Rock, High Ball, Tom Collins, Slim Gim, Hurricane are most common glassware used to serve cocktails.

MIXING A COCKTAIL

Not all cocktails are made in the same manner, only the ingredients vary. There are several ways in which to mix a cocktail. The most frequently used methods are:

- **Shaking:** The cocktail is mixed by hand in a cocktail shaker. The shaker is first filled three quarters with ice, preferably cubes, as crushed ice will tend to melt and dilute the cocktail. The ingredients are then poured on top of the ice, in order of alcohol content (highest first). When shaking a cocktail, hold the shaker in both hands, one hand on the top and the other supporting the base of the shaker, and shake vigorously. When water begins condensing on the outside of the shaker, the cocktail is sufficiently chilled, and the cocktail should immediately be strained into the glass. In general, shaking creates a colder cocktail than stirring does, but also a cloudier one.
- **Stirring:** The cocktail is stirred with a glass or metal rod in a mixing glass, before the cocktail is strained into a glass. As with shaking, crushed ice should not be used, and water condensing on the outside shows that the cocktail is finished.

Shaking Steps

- Add ice, spirits, liqueurs and mixers into a cocktail shaker.
- Place the lid and cap on the shaker facing over shoulder.
- Shake vigorously for ten seconds ensuring that ice hits the top and bittom of the shaker a number of times. Condensation on shaker base indicates that drink is ready.
- Remove the cap and pour drink gently in the glass.
- Remove cap and place Hawthorn strainer over shaker if using American shaker.

Stirring Steps

- Chill the glass.
- Add ice in mixing glass.
- Pour ingredients like spirits, liqueurs and mixers into mixing glass.
- Stir the ingredients in mixing glass by rotating bar spoon around edge of glass without melting the ice.
- Place strainer on top of mixing glass and pour gently into the chilled ice.
- Place garnish.

- **Blending:** An electric blender is used to mix fruit juices, alcohol, fruit, etc. Blending is an excellent way of mixing ingredients which do not blend easily in any other way. Blend the cocktail till it has reached a smooth consistency. If the recipe requires ice, add crushed ice last, but be careful not to add too much, as the cocktail gets watered down. Blending is a much disputed method of mixing a cocktail, and in general, blending should be avoided unless the recipe demands it.
- **Building:** When building a cocktail, the ingredients are poured into the glass in which the cocktail will be served. Usually, the ingredients are floated on top of each other, but occasionally, a swizzle stick is put in the glass, allowing the ingredients to be mix.
- **Muddling:** When one or more of the ingredients need to be crushed into the drink. It is commonly used to mix granulated brown sugar or white sugar with fruits and herbs like mint leaves which help to extract the flavours from them.
- **Layering:** In this mixing method a mixed drink is layered to create a contrasting colour effect. Usually, a 30 ml or 60 ml sort glass is used for this drink and alcohol chosen for making layered drinks should vary in its density so that layer can form.
- **Combination:** This mixing method applies combining any two mixing methods to create an interesting effect. Example:
  - Layer blended over shaken mixture.
  - Layer blended over built mixture.
  - Layer a shaken combination of ingredients over built mixture.

Building Steps

- Take glass and add ice.
- Pour spirits and liqueurs over ice.
- Add mixers and garnish.

Note: Glassware for built cocktails is usually larger.

Muddling Steps

- Add ingredients to an appropriate glass.
- Crush sugar and herbs/fruits by pressing muddler firmly downwards and twisting clockwise until ingredients are thoroughly mixed.
- Most of the bartender used to shake the cocktail after muddling to ensure consistent flavor throughout the cocktail.

Layering Steps

Take a shot glass and place mixing spoon upside down into glass and pour ingredients one by one over back of spoon, gently raising spoon as glass fills.

TYPES OF COCKTAILS

Following are the six major categories of cocktails.

- Pre-dinner cocktails
- Creamy cocktails

	Summary of Mixing Methods	
• Building	:	Ingredients poured over ice
• Shaking	:	Ingredients shaken with ice
• Blending	:	Ingredients blended with ice
• Stirring	:	Ingredients stirred over ice
• Muddling	:	Ingredients crushed using a muddler.
• Layering	:	Ingredients layered one over the other with no ice.
• Combination	:	Combination of two or more mixing methods to create an interesting effect.

- Long cocktails
- Sour cocktails
- Shot cocktails
- Mocktails

Pre-dinner Cocktail

These are usually intended for consumption before meals. The intention is to stimulate the appetite and increase the enjoyment of the meal. The base spirit for the pre-dinner cocktail is usually clear but rye whisky or brandy can be used.

Creamy Cocktail

These are usually served after a meal. They contain cream and heavy mixers.

Long Cocktails

These are served in long glasses and can be served any time during lunch or dinner. They consists mainly of fruit juices and soda and are generally lower in alcohol content by volume than the other categories. The base spirit for a long cocktail is nearly always a white spirit as they are more suitable to mix with soda and juices.

Sour Cocktails

These are balanced combination of spirits and liqueurs, lime/lemon juice and sugar syrup. Suitable for drinking in any occasion but are best consumed in the late afternoon or early evening.

Shot Cocktails

These are often served as accompaniments to other beverages. They are usually layered and served in 30 ml shot glasss and can be sipped or shot. Shot cocktails are often served to celebrate a special occasion and are mainly served later in the evening. In order to mix shot cocktails properly one must be acquainted with the density of a spirits and liqueurs. Density is determined by sugar content. Higher the sugar content the higher will be density. Example: Kahlua is heavier than a vodka as Kahlua has a higher sugar content. Spirits and liquers higher in density sink to the bottom.

Mocktails/Non-Alcoholic Cocktails

Also known as virgin cocktails and contain no alcohol. The base for these drinks is normally juice. As with cocktail, mocktails look and taste better than any of their individual component. Mocktail or non-alcoholic drink, you can say, is typically a blend of different fruits and juices with sugar syrup to provide sweetness.

RULES FOR MAKING COCKTAILS

- Use the appropriate glass.
- Make your tools ready, for example, cocktail shaker, peg measure, etc.
- Get equipped with cocktail recipes.
- Use only the finest ingredients.
- The chilling process: As soon as you are equipped and ready, start by chilling the cocktail glasses. It can be as simple as putting the glass in the freezer for some hours or pouring in water with ice. Take them out only when you are ready to pour the mixed drink, this way the drink is kept smooth and cool for a longer time after it has been served.
- Adding the ice. If ice is desired then it should be placed last into the cocktail shaker and in case of built cocktails it will be vice versa.
- Adding the ingredients in the order: **Base spirit>1st Mixer>2nd Mixer>Garnish.**
- If the cocktail needs shaking then shake it well near the shoulder hitting ice top and bottom inside the cocktail shaker, till the moisture can be seen outside the shaker.
- Dress up or garnishing the cocktail: Cocktail drinks will look empty without the proper garnishing. Garnishes generally used are sweet lime, lemon, orange, pineapple, strawberry, cherry, olives, etc. Right garnishes for right cocktail make it more appealing. A general rule for selecting garnish is:
  - » No garnish with dark spirits.
  - » White spirit should be garnished with that fruit which is used in the cocktail either as a juice or chunks, etc.

COCKTAIL GARNISHES

Almost all cocktails are garnished in one way or another, most often with some kind of fruit, but no matter the exact decoration. Garnishing is a part of the ritual of making cocktails. It adds to any drink a special feature than the others giving colour, flavour and style. Most of the classic drinks have their own garnish, but it is in your imagination and creativity where you can find lots of models. A garnish should be attractive for its main functions is to please the eye, which invariably pleases the palate. While garnishing any cocktail, it is always important to use fresh ingredients. The most common garnishes include fruits such as lemon, orange, apple, cherry, pineapple. Some drinks require more elaborated garnishes like olives, celery stick, berries, cherries, mint and cucumber.

Sometimes coffee beans, nutmeg, cinnamon stick can also be used depending on the creativity of bartender and nature of cocktail. Although garnishes for some classic cocktails never change but nowadays there is a trend towards less garnish and more cocktail hence giving better value for money to the customers. Following factors should be considered while preparing a garnish for any cocktail:

- **Colour:** Colour of the garnish should be compatible or a contrast to the colour of the drink. Example: a pink coloured drink benefits from a red cherry and a blue drink with a pineapple slice which is yellow in colour.
- **Taste:** If an edible garnish is used, it should be compatible with one or more of the ingredients in the cocktail. Edible garnishes also impart flavour to the drink. Example: A cocktail containing pineapple juice would be benefitted by a garnish of pineapple slice and a cocktail containing lime/lemon juice by a lime/lemon slice/wedge.
- **Shape and Size:** The shape of the glass helps in determining the garnish to use. Example: Lime/lemon wheels complement a Martini glass whereas adding pineapple slice in Martini glass will look odd with the shape of the glass. Size of the garnish should also be appropriate for the size of the glass. Example: a mixed drink in a small glass may benefit from a small cherry, but a large orange slice.

Garnish Can be Placed Like as Follows in a Glass		
Mounted	Place on the side of a glass.	Lime wheel in Margarita.
Floated	Floated in the mixture.	Lime/lemon slice in vodka and lemonade.
Sunk	Dropped into the bottom of the glass.	Cherry in Manhattan.

Garnishes are normally floated for normally mixed spirits and mounted or sunk for cocktails.

LIME GARNISH

Wedges	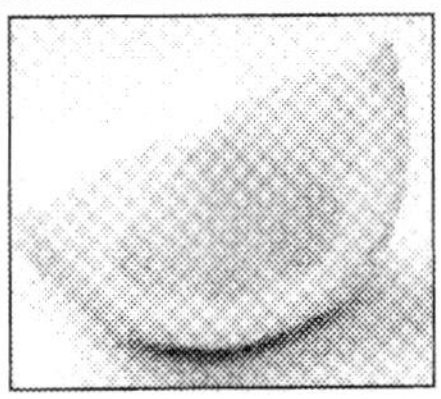
Slices	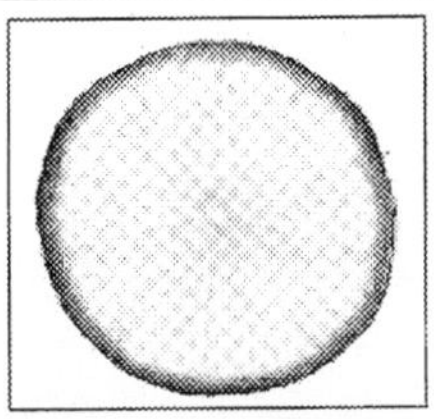

Half Moon	
Spiral/Twist	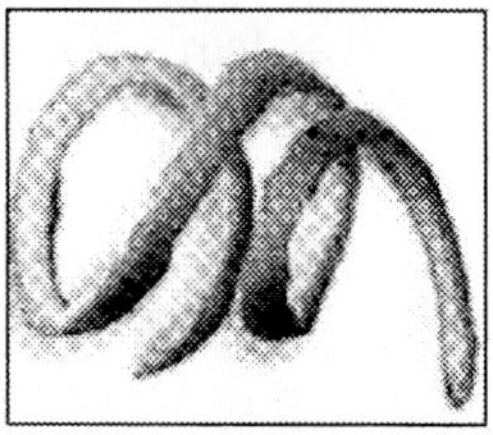
Zest	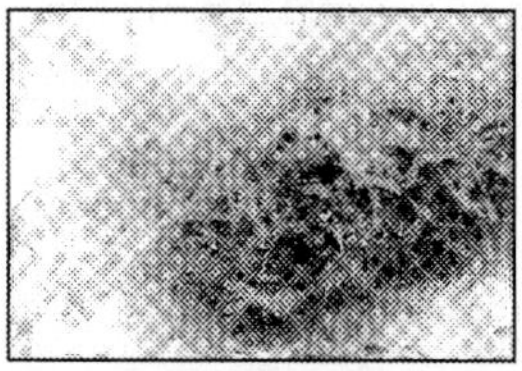

Orange Garnish

Orange zests are also flamed and garnished in some cocktails

Twist	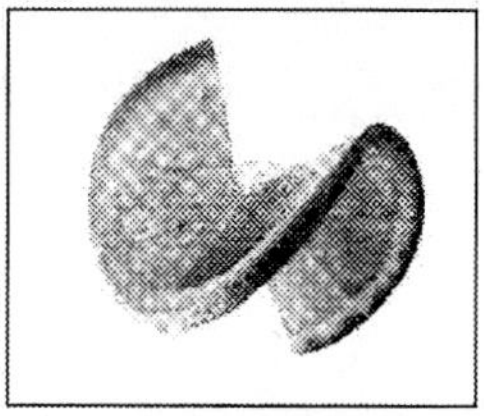
Spiral	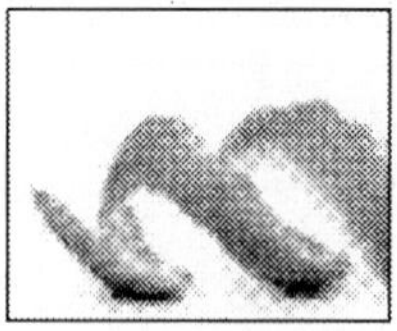
Slices	

Orange wheel	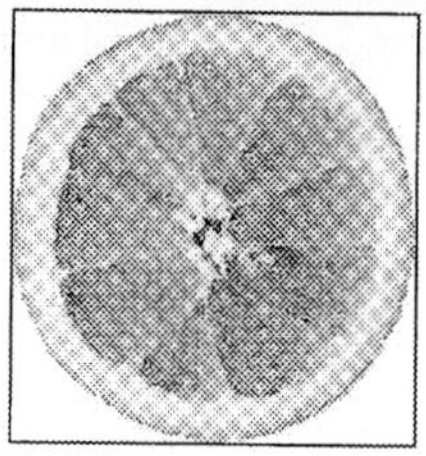
Wedges	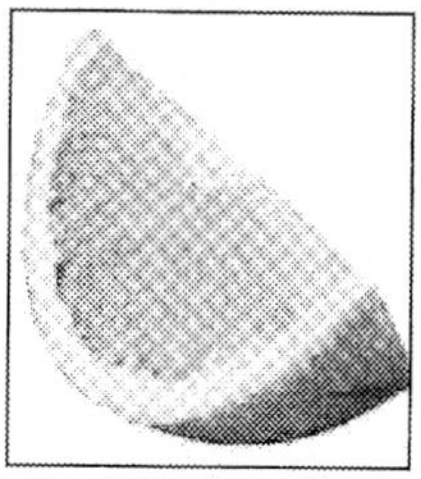

Pineapple

Wedges	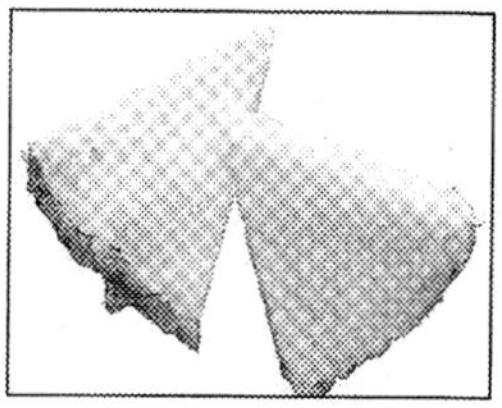
Slices	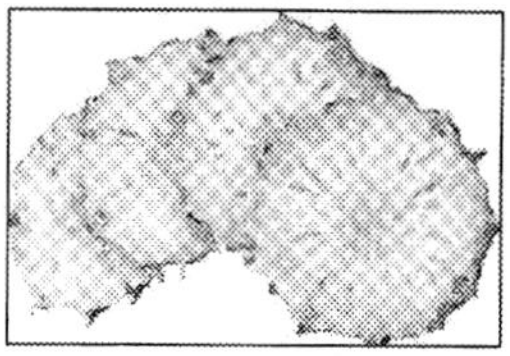

Olives

Famous for being the garnish of traditional Martinis.

Olive jewel	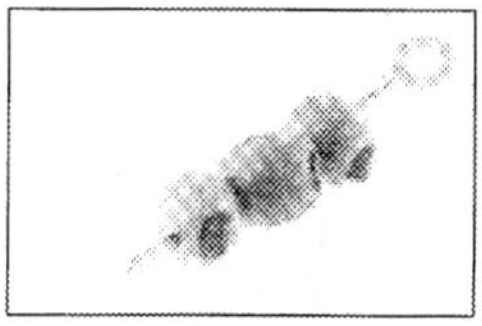

Apples

Apple slices	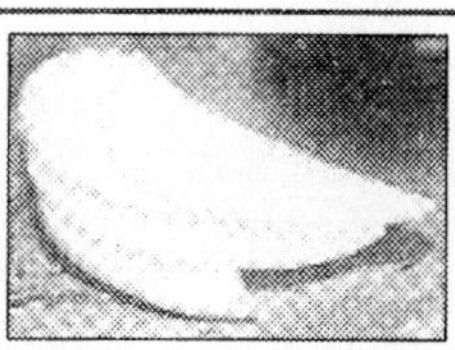

Cucumber

Cucumber Spear	

Cherries: Cherries are speared onto orange slices, pineapples, limes, and lemons. This type of decoration is called "flag" in the cocktails world. The most common are: Maraschino cherries, red cherries, yellow cherries, and green cherries.

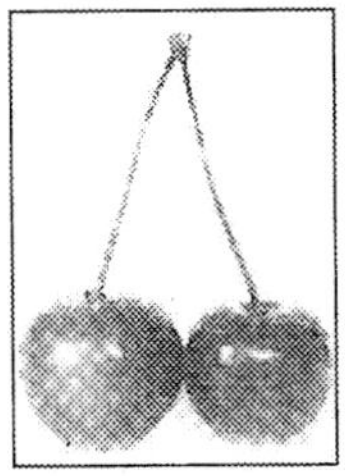

Flags: Fruit flags and boats are the flashiest of the standard cocktail garnishes. Flags are garnishes that skewer a maraschino cherry on top of another garnish, such as an orange slice or pineapple wedge whereas boats are the garnishes made from citrus fruit wheels that have been folded in half with a maraschino cherry pinned into the fold.

Pine apple flage

Orange boat

IMPORTANT COCKTAIL RECIPES

Screwdriver	Ingredients	Qty/ml	Method	
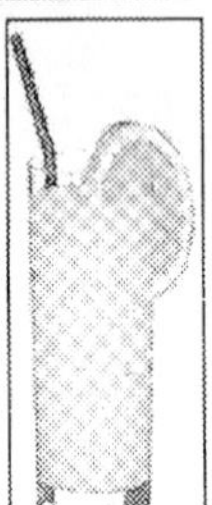	Vodka	60	Build the ingredients over ice into a Collin glass, stir and serve with an orange slice.	
	Orange Juice	150	Garnish	Orange slice
			Glass	Collin glass

Harvey Wallbanger

Ingredients	Qty/ml
Vodka	45
Galliano	15
Orange Juice	120

Method: Build the ingredients over ice into a hurricane glass, stir and serve with an orange slice. (You can float galliano on top as well.)

Garnish	Orange slice
Glass	Hurricane glass

Black Russian

Ingredients	Qty/ml
Vodka	30
Kahlua	30

Method: Shake the vodka and kahlua over ice and strain into an old fashioned glass filled with ice.

*For White Russian, float cream over the same cocktail.

Garnish	Cherry with stem
Glass	Old fashioned

Kamikaze

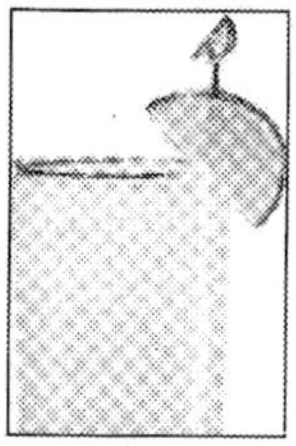

Ingredients	Qty/ml
Vodka	30
Triple sec	30
Lime juice	15

Method: Shake all the ingredients over ice and strain into the glass. Garnish and serve.

Garnish	Lemon wedge
Glass	Old fashioned

Caprioshka

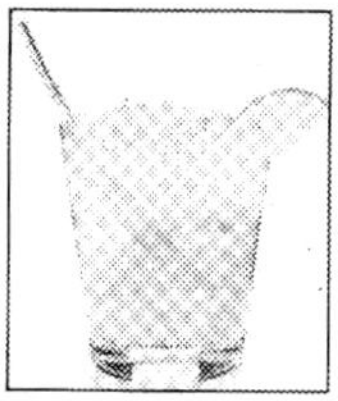

Ingredients	Qty/ml
Vodka	60
Lemon (chunks)	1
Brown sugar	10
White sugar	5

Method: Muddle lemon chunks with white and brown sugar in an old fashioned glass, add crushed ice and vodka, cover with mixing glass and shake well. Pour into another old fashioned glass.

Garnish	Lemon
Glass	Old fashioned

Bloody Mary

Ingredients	Qty/ml
Vodka	60
Tomato juice	120
Worcestershire	Dash
Tabasco	Dash
Lemon juice	15
Salt & pepper	

Method: Stir all ingredients in the mixing glass and strain into an old fashioned glass.

Garnish	Celery and lemon slice
Glass	Rolly polly/rock

Cosmopolitan	Ingredients	Qty/ml	Method	
	Vodka	45	Add all ingredients to a cocktail shaker with ice cubes. Shake and strain into a Martini glass.	
	Cointreau	15		
	Cranberry Juice	60		
	Lemon Juice	10		
			Garnish	Orange slice/zest
			Glass	Martini

Long Island Iced Tea	Ingredients	Qty/ml	Method	
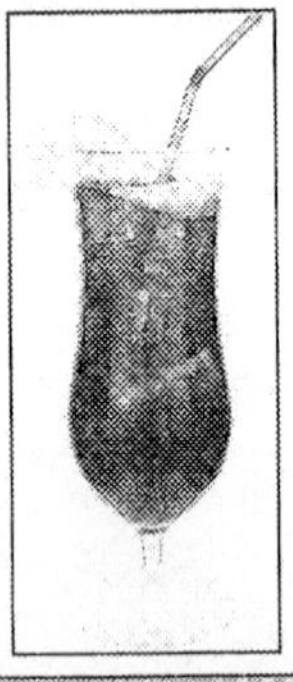	Vodka	15	Add all the ingredients in a hurricane glass put ice and top up with coke.	
	Gin	15		
	Rum	15		
	Tequila	15		
	Cointreau	15	Garnish	Lemon wedge,cherry
	Coke Lemon Juice	1 10	Glass	Hurricane

Perfect Manhattan	Ingredients	Qty/ml	Method	
	Rye whisky	45	Add the ingredients to a mixing glass filled with ice and stir the mixture until chilled. Strain into a cocktail glass, add the garnish and serve. (Can be made shaken as well.) *There can be variants like dry or sweet Manhattan, based on vermouth	
	Sweet vermouth	7.5		
	Dry vermouth	7.5		
	Angostura	Dash		
			Garnish	Cherry
			Glass	Cocktail/martini

Rob Roy	Ingredients	Qty/ml	Method	
	Whisky	45	Add the ingredients to a mixing glass filled with ice and stir the mixture until chilled. Strain into a cocktail glass, add the garnish and serve.	
	Sweet Vermouth	15		
	Angostura	Dash		
			Garnish	Cherry
			Glass	Cocktail/Martini

Rusty Nail	Ingredients	Qty/ml	Method	
	Scotch whisky	45	Add the ingredients to a mixing glass filled with ice and stir the mixture until chilled. Strain into an old fashioned glass, add the garnish and serve.	
	Drambuie	15		
			Garnish	Orange zest
			Glass	Old fashioned

Old Fashioned	Ingredients	Qty/ml	Method	
	Rye whisky	60	Place sugar in the glass and soak with the bitters. Muddle the mixture and pour whisky slowly on ice until all the whisky has been added and the sugar is dissolved. Run orange zest around the rim of the glass.	
	White sugar	15		
	Angostura	Dash		
			Garnish	Orange zest
			Glass	Old fashioned

Mint Julep	Ingredients	Qty/ml	Method	
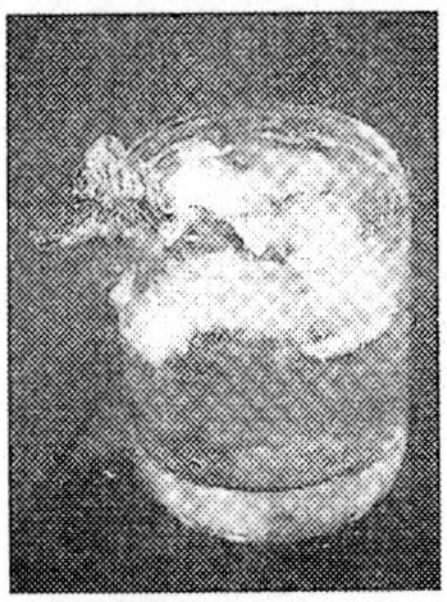	Rye whisky	60	Crush the mint and sugar in the glass. Fill the glass with crushed ice and add the whisky. Stir the mixture and serve.	
	White sugar	10		
	Lemon juice	10		
	Mint sprigs	5		
			Garnish	Mint leaves
			Glass	Old fashioned

Whisky Sour	Ingredients	Qty/ml	Method	
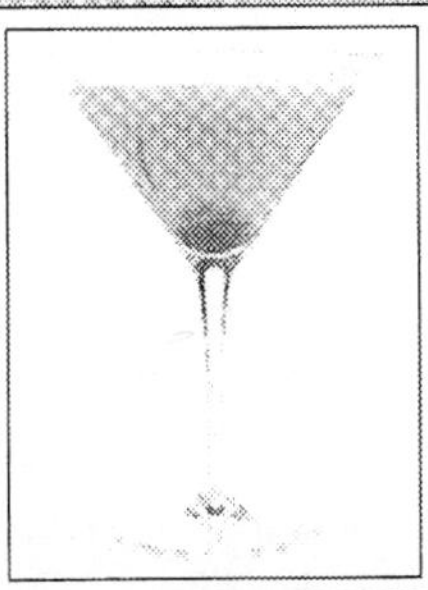	Whisky	60	Add all the ingredients to a shaker filled with ice and shake sharply. Strain the contents to a cocktail glass filled with ice, garnish and serve.	
	Lemon juice	15		
	Sugar syrup	10		
	Angostura	Dash		
			Garnish	Cherry
			Glass	Cocktail

Daiquiri	Ingredients	Qty/ml	Method	
	White rum	45	Pour all the ingredients into an ice filled shaker. Shake and strain into a cocktail glass. Garnish and serve.	
	Cointreau	15		
	Lemon juice	15		
	Sugar syrup	10		
			Garnish	Lemon slice
			Glass	Cocktail/Martini
Mojito	**Ingredients**	**Qty/ml**	**Method**	
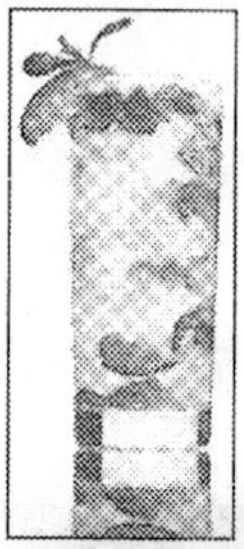	Bacardi	45	Crush the mint and sugar in the glass. Fill the glass with crushed ice and add the rum. Stir the mixture, top it with sprite and serve.	
	Dark rum	15		
	Sprite	120		
	Brown sugar	10		
	Mint sprigs	5	Garnish	Mint sprigs
	Lemon juice	10	Glass	Collins/old fashioned
Planter's Punch	**Ingredients**	**Qty/ml**	**Method**	
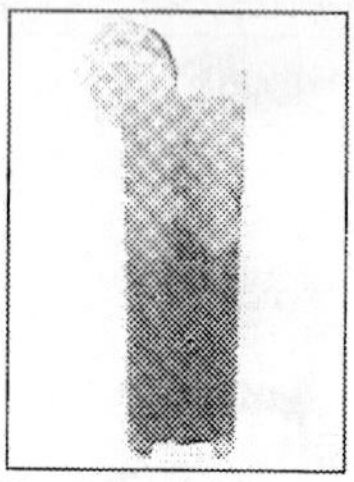	Dark rum	60	Build the ingredients into a Collins glass filled with ice. Gently pour the grenadine on the side of the glass, float the dark rum. Garnish and serve.	
	Orange juice	60		
	Pineapple juice	60		
	Lemon juice	10		
	Grenadine	5	Garnish	Orange slice
			Glass	Collins glass
Mai Tai	**Ingredients**	**Qty/ml**	**Method**	
	White rum	45	Add all the ingredients to a shaker filled with ice, shake and strain into an ice filled old fashioned glass. Garnish and serve.	
	Triple sec	10		
	Cherry brandy	10		
	Pineapple juice	60		
	Angostura	Dash	Garnish	Orange slice
	Sour mix	10	Glass	Old fashioned
Pinacolada	**Ingredients**	**Qty/ml**	**Method**	
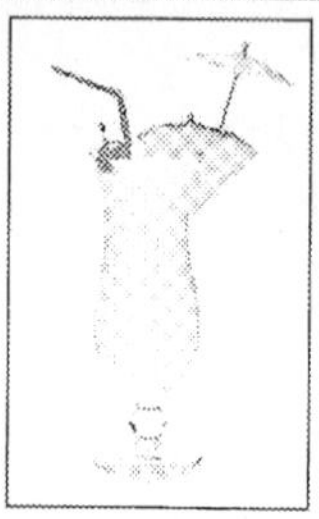	White rum	60	Put all the ingredients in a blender, add a scoop of crushed ice and blend. Pour into a hurricane glass, garnish and serve.	
	Pineapple juice	100		
	Coconut cream	25		
	Sugar syrup	10		
			Garnish	Pineapple slice
			Glass	Hurricane glass

Negroni	Ingredients	Qty/ml	Method	
	Gin	20	Shake all the ingredients together over ice and strain into a cocktail glass. Garnish and serve.	
	Sweet vermouth	20		
	Campari	20		
			Garnish	Orange twist
			Glass	Cocktail/Martini

Gimlet	Ingredients	Qty/ml	Method	
	Gin	60	Add the gin and cordial to a shaker filled with ice. Shake very sharply and strain into a cocktail glass.	
	Lime cordial	30		
			Garnish	Lemon slice
			Glass	Cocktail/Martini

Martini	Ingredients	Qty/ml	Method	
	Gin	60	Add both the ingredients to a mixing glass filled with ice and stir. Strain into a martini glass, garnish and serve.	
	Vermouth	Dash		
			Garnish	Olive
			Glass	Martini

Singapore Sling	Ingredients	Qty/ml	Method	
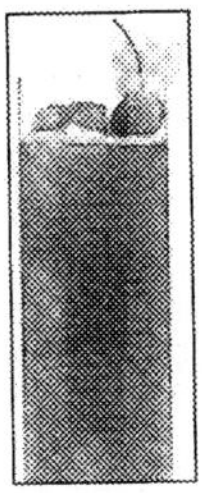	Gin	30	Add all the ingredients to the cocktail shaker, shake and pour into an old fashioned glass.	
	Cherry brandy	15		
	Triple sec	7.5		
	Benedictine	7.5		
	Pineapple juice	120		
	Grenadine	10		
	Angostura	Dash	Garnish	Pineapple & cherry
	Lemon juice	10	Glass	Old fashioned/Collins

Tom Collins	Ingredients	Qty/ml	Method	
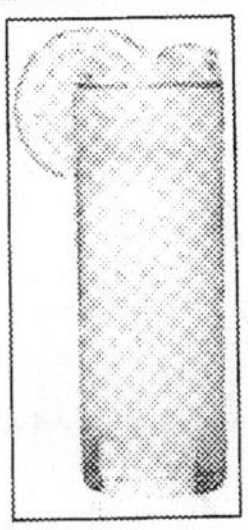	Gin	60	Build the ingredients into a Collins glass filled with ice. Stir gently, garnish and serve.	
	Soda	120		
	Angostura	Dash		
	Lemon juice	20		
	Sugar syrup	15	Garnish	Lemon slice
			Glass	Collins

Margarita	Ingredients	Qty/ml	Method	
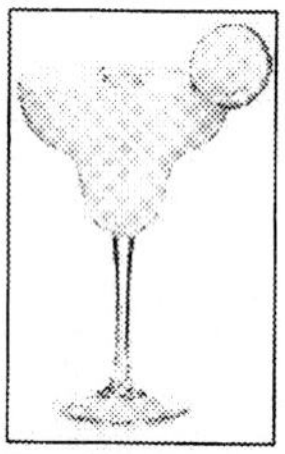	Tequila	45	Add all the ingredients into a blender. Add a scoop of crushed ice and blend. Pour into a margarita glass, garnish and serve.	
	Cointreau	15		
	Lemon juice	15		
	Sugar syrup	10		
			Garnish	Lemon slice
			Glass	Margarita/cocktail

Tequila Sunrise	Ingredients	Qty/ml	Method	
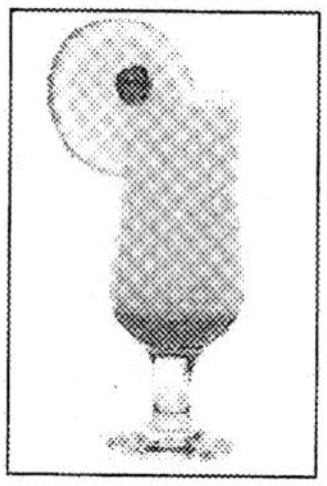	Tequila	60	Build the tequila and orange juice into the glass with ice. Gently pour the grenadine down the inside of the glass so the syrup fills the bottom. Garnish and serve.	
	Orange juice	120		
	Grenadine	15		
	Lemon juice	10		
			Garnish	Orange slice
			Glass	Hurricane/Highball

Kir Royale	Ingredients	Qty/ml	Method	
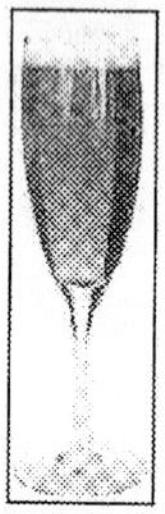	Sparkling wine	120	Add a small dash of crème de cassis to a champagne flute and gently top with sparkling wine. Stir gently and serve.	
	Crème De Cassis	5		
			Garnish	Not required
			Glass	Champagne flute

Bellini	Ingredients	Qty/ml	Method	
	Sparkling Wine	120	Add the peach schnapps and gently top with sparkling wine. Stir gently, garnish and serve.	
	Peach Schnapps	15		
			Garnish	Peach slice
			Glass	Champagne flute

Sidecar	Ingredients	Qty/ml	Method	
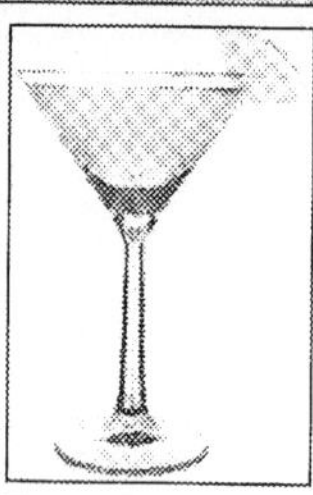	Brandy	45	Shake all the ingredients together over ice and strain into a martini glass. Garnish and serve.	
	Cointreau	15		
	Lemon juice	15		
			Garnish	Lemon slice
			Glass	Cocktail/Martini

Brandy Alexander	Ingredients	Qty/ml	Method	
	Brandy	45	Shake all the ingredients over ice and strain into the glass. Garnish and serve.	
	Crème De Cacao	15		
	Cream	15		
			Garnish	Grated nutmeg
			Glass	Brandy balloon/Martini

Grasshopper	Ingredients	Qty/ml	Method	
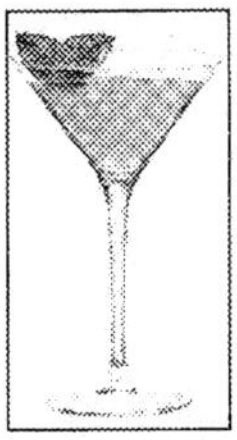	Crème De Menthe	30	Shake all the ingredients over ice, strain into a glass and serve.	
	Crème De Cacao	30		
			Garnish	Mint leaves and cherry
			Glass	Martini

B 52	Ingredients	Qty/ml	Method	
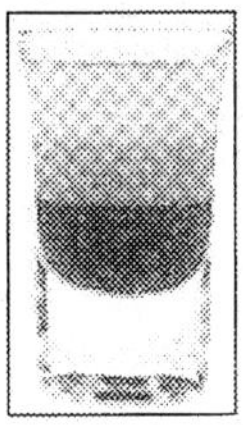	Kahlua	15	Make layers in the order of ingredients written	
	Bailey's Irish cream	15		
	Grand Marnier	15		
			Garnish	No garnish
			Glass	Shot

BAR TERMINOLOGY

For a good bartender it is important to have a good knowledge of beverages apart from food dishes and understand bar terminology as well.

After-dinner cocktail: Sweet cocktails, which are served after dinner.

Pre-dinner cocktail: Dry cocktails, which are served before dinner (sometimes standing cocktail) and should be stimulating.

Blend: To mix drinks, but as well to mix whiskys during production (blend of malt and grain whisky).

Blending: Mixture of 2-3 various components.

Build-in glass: The preparation of a cocktail or mixed drink is done in the glass served.

Chasers: Are long drinks which are filled up with tonic waters, bitter lemon, ginger ale, coke, fruit juice, beer, etc.

Chilled: Cooled down, chilled glass from the freezer.

Dash: Drop, "spritzer", is a pouring unit used with strong aromas like angostura, grenadine, syrups, etc.

Fill: "To fill-up", a drink up with fruit juice, lemonade, soda water or sparkling wine.

Filler: Other word for chaser.

Float: Kind of preparation technique, aromas which are put on top of the drink for garnish.

Frosted: Frozen, a glass or bottle is covered with a film of thin ice.

Gill: Original whisky pouring unit of 1½ oz, that is 42 g.

Gom, Ghomme: Another name for sugar syrup.

Grind: To grate or grind an ingredient finely to powder or fine substance.

Iced: Like frosted.

Jigger: Measuring unit of 20 or 40 g.

Sugar Syrup: 1 kg sugar and 1 litre water is boiled up and then cooled down, used for cocktails.

Long Drink: Name for every drink which has more than 8 cl content of beverage.

Marge: Spirits with high alcohol tend to lose slightly volume especially when heated.

Mixer: Other name for chaser or filler.

Muddler: It is like a pestle or the other end of the bar spoon, to grind or smoothen ingredients like rock sugar, herbs or fruits (Caipirinha).

Mug: Old description for big beer glass with handle out of clay or tin.

Nip: To drink a fairly small amount or taste.

Nutmeg: Freshly grated used in some cocktails.

On-the-rocks: Type of order for drinks served with ice (whisky on the rocks).

Peel: A piece of skin of citrus fruits, lemon, lime, orange to flavour drinks and for decoration.

Pitcher: Water pitcher, wine pitcher to be put on the table for self service.

Plain: Not diluted, not mixed, type of order for drinks (no ices!).

Poures: Pouring unit for bottles, with 20 or mostly 40 g. To be installed on the bottle neck.

Pouring drink: Is a basic drink like cognac, whisky, if the guest does not specify what kind without giving a brand or name.

Sediment: Also called depot, a deposit especially found with aged red wine, sherry or port.

Shake: A preparation technique using a cocktail shaker.

Short drink: Name for drink which contains less than 8 cl liquid.

Soothe: Conserved egg white in aerosol/spray bottles, used for creamy

Sparkling: Foam, sparkling wine.

Squeeze: To press, especially for citrus fruit

Stir: To mix or stir a drink as preparation technique whereby ingredients are carefully mixed in the glass served with a bar spoon.

Straight up: Other name for plain or up.

Strain: To strain or hold back ice or ice pieces in the shaker, when pouring the drink into the glass.

Straw: Formerly, the natural straw used for drinks, now of plastic in various colours and shapes.

Sugar edge: Sugar on the rim of the glass, dipped in lemon or lime juice and then into a sugar bed on a saucer.

Sugar lip: Like sugar edge, part of the garnish.

Sugar rim: Other word for sugar edge.

Swizzle stick: Used for mixing drinks, twirling stick (small).

Topped: Covering drinks with cream or whipped cream.

Twist: To twist citrus fruit on the rim of the glass to release the aroma.

Underliner: Underliner for the glass, usually out of small, round white linen, or paper with property logo.

37 SERVICE OF COCKTAILS AND MOCKTAILS

Equipment Required

- Salver with cloth napkin
- Appropriate glass as per standard of the drink
- Straw

Knowledge Required

- Beverage menu knowledge
- Standard phrases
- Types of glassware
- Point of sale

Procedure

- The F&B associate, after taking the order from the guest, gives the KOT to the bar, picks up the order and carries it to the station sideboard.
- The F&B associate to serve the beverage at the table. The F&B associate will announce the name of the beverage while doing so.

Standard

- The white copy of the KOT should be handed over to the bartender.
- Suitable glass should be used according to the standard recipe for the cocktail/ mocktail.
- The glass should be free from stains, chips and watermarks.
- The beverage should be picked up from the bar complete with garnish. The garnish should be fresh and according to the standard recipe of the cocktail/ mocktail.
- The juices to be picked up from the pantry kitchen.
- The associate to check with the KOT for the cover numbers – who is having what.
- Do not go to the table and ask who is having which drink.
- The glass is placed on the table to the right-hand side of the cover at 4 o'clock position from the water glass.

- The glass should be held at the stem or at the base using the forefinger and thumb only, leaving no fingerprints on the glass.

COCKTAIL/MOCKTAIL SERVING PROCEDURE

The F&B associate after taking the order from the guest the BOT to the bar and picks up the order from the bar.

Serve the drinks according to the cover number. Always serve from the right hand side of the guest starting with the ladies first.

Carrying Drink Tray Guidelines

- Salver/beverage round is carried on a slightly cupped hand on the pads of the fingers. This allows the waiter to adjust the balance of the tray as glasses are removed or added to the tray.
- When serving drinks to seated guests from a tray hold the tray behind the guest's head, and use your right hand to place the drink from the guest's right.

38 SERVICE OF WINE (RED AND WHITE)

Equipment Required

- Salver with cloth napkin
- Wine glass
- Wine
- Wine chiller with stand for white wine
- Waiter's friend

Knowledge Required

- Wine making and wine producing regions
- Wines available in the hotel
- Basic knowledge of the wines of the world
- Principles of wine and food pairing

Standard

- The wine glass should be placed at the 4 o'clock position to the water glass.
- The glass should be free from chips, stains and water marks.
- Handle the glass from the stem using the forefinger and thumb only, leaving no fingerprints on the glass.
- The F&B associate collects the wine bottle from bar. Check the temperature of the wine. In case of white wine the wine should be chilled.
- The F&B associate should present the wine with a napkin under the bottle from the right of the host.
- The bottle should be held in the left hand and the thumb and index finger of the right hand should support the neck of the bottle.
- Approach the host from the right-hand side.
- Label should face the host.
- The F&B associate should be carrying a waiter's-friend, which should be in immaculate condition, scrupulously clean, shining and free from rust.

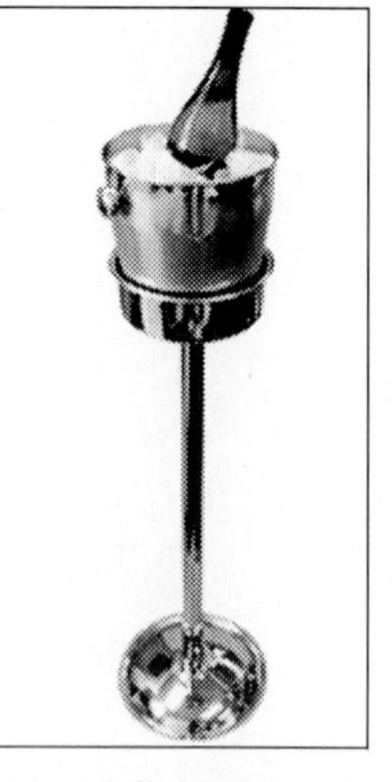

Wine chiller with stand

- Cut the seal with the knife of the waiter's-friend and discreetly place the seal in your pocket.
- Ensure there is little or no sound while removing the cork.
- The neck and mouth of the bottle should be free from fragments of the cork.
- The bottle should be wrapped with a clean napkin collar.
- The label should be facing the guest and not covered by the napkin.
- The service should be in the same sequence of etiquette.
- The wine should be poured gently without touching the rim of the glass.
- The glass should be twisted to one side with a jerk to avoid spillage.
- Place the bottle on the side station if table is too cluttered.

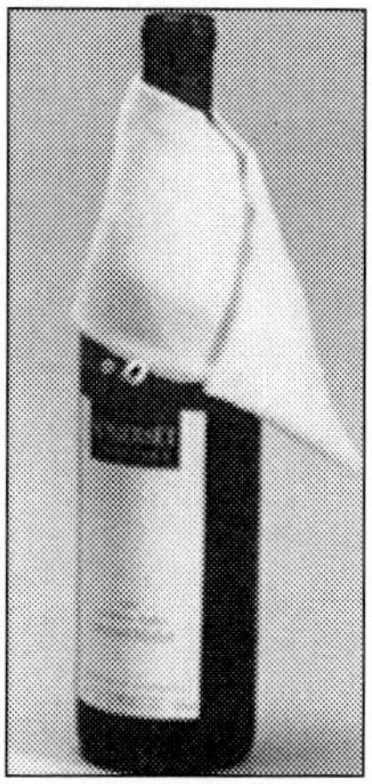

Wine collar

Standard for Service for Wine by Glass

- Hold the glass by the stem while placing it on the table.
- *"Madam/Sir, the wine by glass is Grover's Sauvignon Blanc 2002."*
- Place it at 4 o'clock position to the water goblet.

Procedure

- The F&B associate brings the wine glass on a salver and places at the table. (In case of white wine, chiller needs to brought along with the wine.)
- Present to the host the wine bottle placed on a white napkin.
- Announce the name of the wine with grape variety, and vintage year.
- Remove the seal after guest's approval.
- Unscrew the cork to open the wine bottle.
- Wipe the mouth and the inner neck with a clean cloth. Smell the wine. Do not serve if you have a doubt.
- Hold the bottle in the right hand so that the label faces the host, and pour about 30 ml into the glass for approval.

White wine in a wine chiller

- After the host has approved the wine, proceed to serve the guests.
- In case of white wines place the wine chillier on the right-hand side of the host or in a wine stand.
- In case of red wines the bottle of wine should be placed on the table having wine collar.

- The F&B associate should always replenish the wine when the glass is one-third empty. The bottle should be wiped dry when removed from the chiller for replenishment.

Service for Wine by Glass

1. The bus boy should get the glass of ordered wine from the bar. The F&B associate should announce the name of the wine to the guest while serving the wine.

SERVICE OF WINE

Step 1: The F&B associate brings the wine glass on a salver and places at the table.

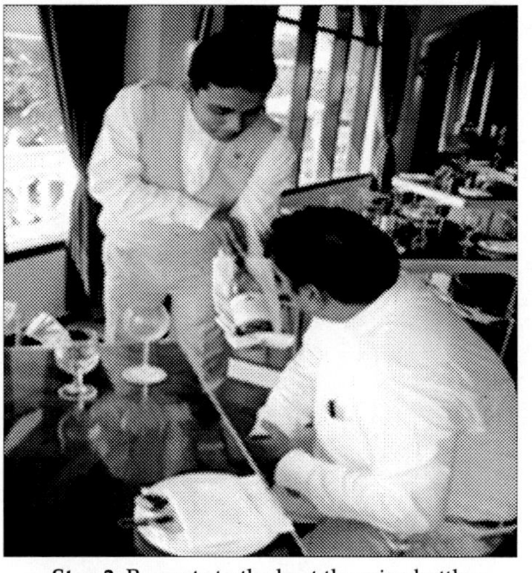

Step 2: Presents to the host the wine bottle placed on a white napkin.

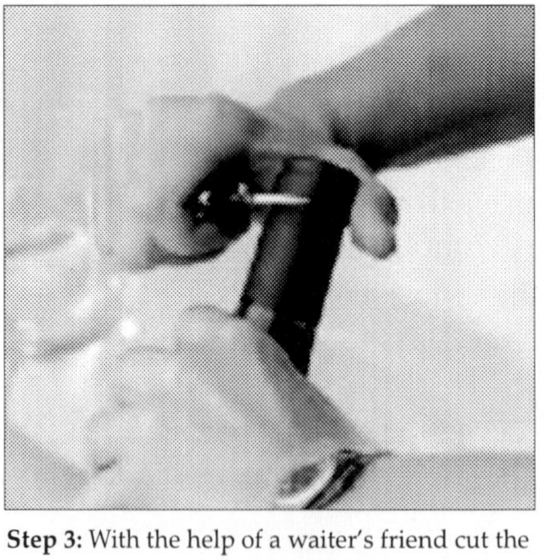

Step 3: With the help of a waiter's friend cut the capsule cleanly beneath the lip of the bottle. Rotate the bottle as you cut. Put the piece you have cut in your pocket.

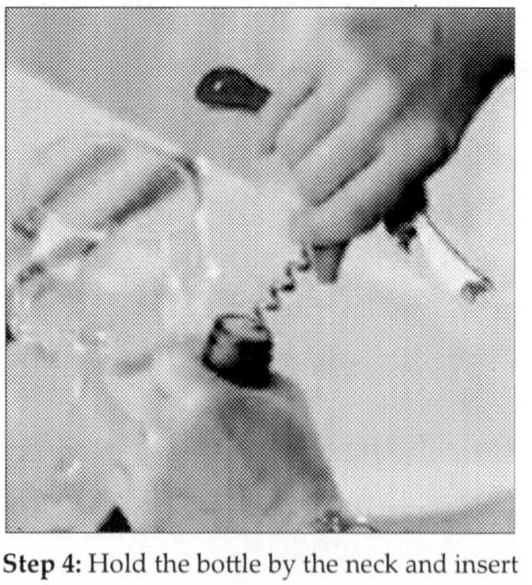

Step 4: Hold the bottle by the neck and insert the tip of the corkscrew at an angle and slightly off the center. This helps to prevent cork breakage. Turn the corkscrew until it is fully into the cork.

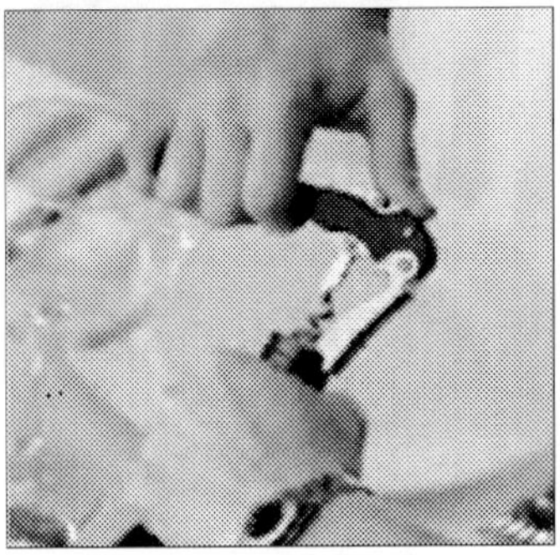

Step 5: After inserting the tip, turn the corkscrew just until the lever will sit on the rim of the bottle.

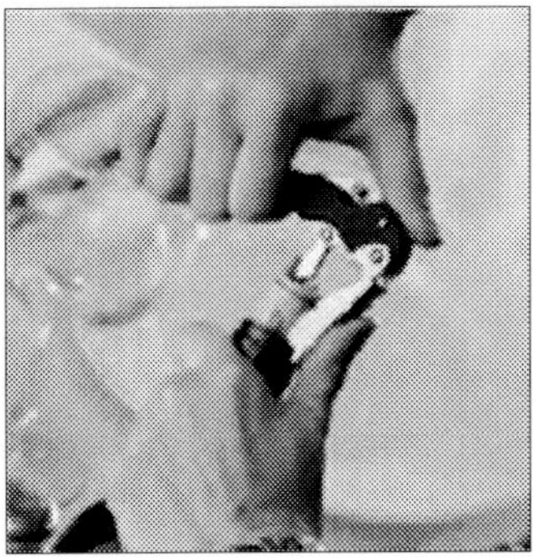

Step 6: Holding the lever in place, lift up the corkscrew until the cork is halfway or more out of the bottle. Turn the corkscrew the final turns it takes for it to be fully inserted, place the lever, and lift the cork out.

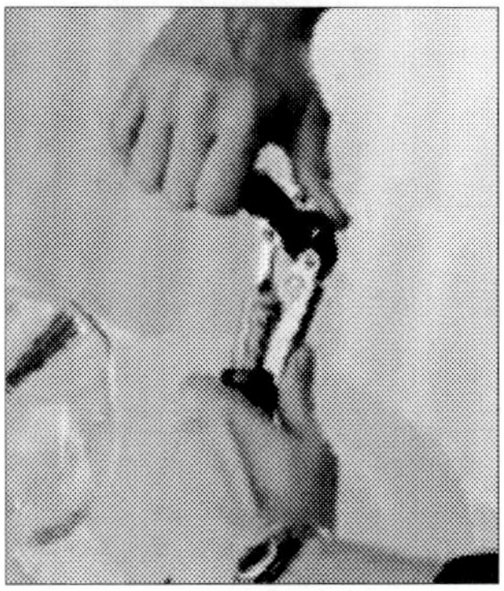

Step 7: Hook the lever of the corkscrew into the rim of the bottle. Hold the lever with the thumb of the hand that is holding the bottle. Lift up the corkscrew in one firm slow motion until the cork is fully extracted

Step 8: Wipe the mouth and inner neck with a clean napkin

Step 9: Hold the wine bottle with the right hand and pour 30 ml into the host glass for approval

Step 10: After the host approve the wine, start serving wine to the guest and serve host last.

WINE TASTING PROCEDURE

Wine tasting is not the same as drinking it. To experience the true flavour of a wine requires attention to the senses of sight, smell, touch, and taste.

See: Look at the wine colour against a white surface. Aside from the aesthetic value, colour tells a lot about the wine in the glass. As white wine ages, it becomes darker, more golden in colour while when red wine ages it loses its colour. Oak aging, grape varietal and climate also affect colour.	
Swirl: Swirling opens up the aromas and flavours and introduces oxygen which will help soften a young red wine's tannins.	
Sniff: Start smelling the wine a few inches above the rim of the glass. Do not plunge nose straight into the glass. Note the types of aromas, their intensity and harmony. If there are unpleasant smells, that may indicate that the wine is flawed.	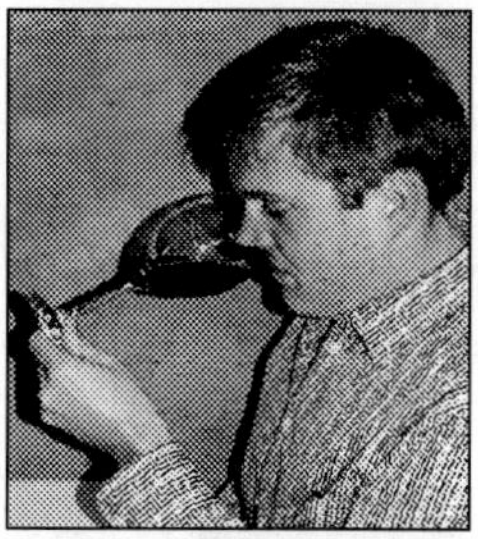
Sip: Take a sip and inhale the wine like a backwards whistle. Move the wine around mouth. There are only four things which are tasted, i.e., sweetness, saltiness, bitterness, and acidity.	
Savour: Think about the taste: is it seamless, angular, full, light, crisp, buttery, well-balanced, overly acidic? Does it have a long finish or an abrupt end? Do you like it or not?	

39 SERVICE OF CHAMPAGNE/ SPARKLING WINE

Equipment Required

- Salver with cloth napkin
- Champagne tulip
- Champagne/sparkling wine
- Wine chiller with stand
- Waiter's friend.

Knowledge Required

- Difference between champagne and sparkling wine and their making methods.
- All champagne/sparkling wines available in the hotel.
- Basic knowledge of the champagne/sparkling wines of the world and their characteristics.
- Principles of wine and food pairing.

Procedure

- Bring the champagne tulip on a salver and place it on the table.
- The F&B associate should carry the bottle in the chiller to the host at the table.
- The F&B collects the champagne/sparkling wine from the bar, checks the temperature as champagne/sparkling wine should be served chilled.
- The F&B associate should present the champagne from the right of the host.
- On getting the host's approval, hold the bottle with your left hand. Open the wire mesh using your right hand. Thumb to be placed on the bottle cork while unwinding the mesh. Index finger to be wrapped around the cork.
- Once the bottle has been opened, serve the host first and then the other guests.
- Place the bottle back into the chiller once every guest has been served.
- Top up the glasses regularly.
- When the champagne gets over, place it inverted in the chiller and ask the guest whether he would like to order for another bottle.

Standard

- Place the champagne tulip at the 4 o'clock position at the water glass.
- The tulip should be free from chips, stains and water marks.

- Handle the tulip from the stem using the forefinger and thumb only, leaving no fingerprints on the glass.
- The bottle should be twisted to one side with a jerk to avoid spillage.
- The champagne should not be popped.
- Should not be given for tasting
- The label should face the guest.
- The wine should be poured gently without touching the rim of the glass.
- The glass should be only three-fourths full (180 ml).
- The wine chiller should be placed next to the host.
- The bottle should be wiped dry when removed from the chiller for replenishment.

Champagne in wine chiller

OPENING CHAMPAGNE/SPARKLING WINE

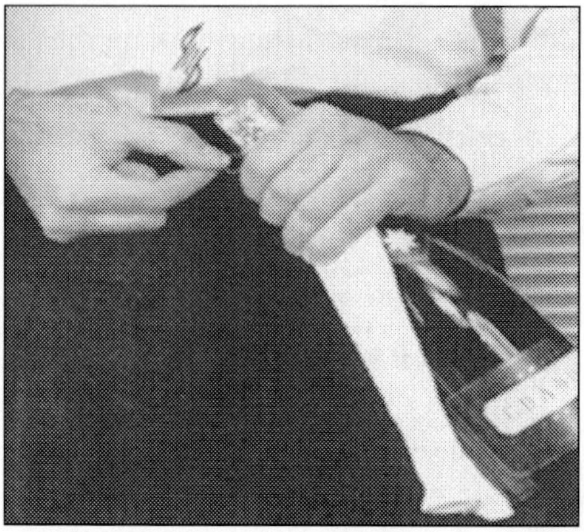

Step 1: Remove the foil wrap, untwist the wire mesh while keeping thumb over the top of the cork. Do not remove the wire cage.

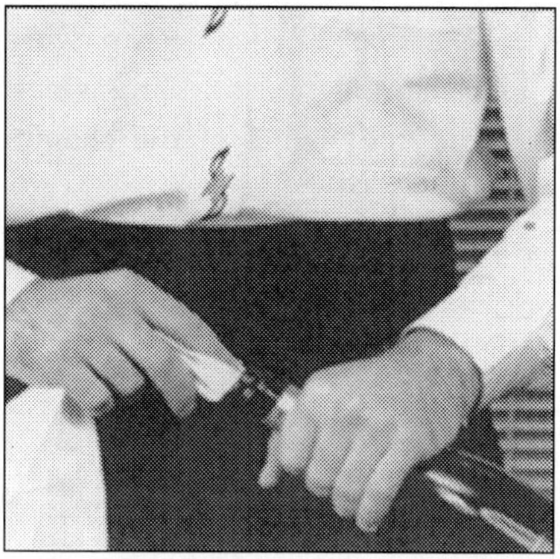

Step 2: Twist the cork off the bottle without shaking the champagne/sparkling wine

SAMPLE WINE MENU

Champagnes

Moët et Chandon, Brut Impérial, NV
Épernay, CHAMPAGNE

Moët et Chandon, Brut Impérial, NV
Épernay, CHAMPAGNE

Moët et Chandon, Cuvée Dom Pérignon, 1995
Épernay, CHAMPAGNE

Château Indage, Marquise de Pompadour, Brut, N/V
Narayangaon, Maharashtra, INDIA

White Wines

• Chardonnay

Chardonnays make consistently excellent, rich and complex white wines. Typically, these wines offer bold, ripe, rich and intense fruit flavours of fig, melon, pear, peach, pineapple, lemon and grapefruit along with spice, honey, butter, butterscotch and hazelnut flavours. This is a very versatile grape and grows well in a variety of locations throughout the world, particularly in Burgundy, Australia and California.

Albert Bichot, Puligny-Montrachet, 2000
Côte de Beaune, BURGUNDY

Louis Jadot, Pouilly-Fuissé, 2001
Mâconnais, BURGUNDY

Chinkara Wines, "Chinkara", 2003
Melbourne, Victoria, AUSTRALIA

Maison Louis Jadot, Bourgogne, 2000
Bourgogne AOC, BURGUNDY

Maison Louis Jadot, Meursault, 1998
Côte de Beaune, BURGUNDY

Château de Montpatey, Bourgogne, 2002
Bourgogne AOC, BURGUNDY

• Sauvignon Blanc

Another great white varietal, this one is with a notable grassy or musky aroma. The pure varietal is found mainly in Loire, at Sancerre and Pouilly-Fumé. New Zealand has had striking success with Sauvignon Blanc, producing its own perfumed, fruity style that spreads across North America and then back to France.

Henri Bourgeois, Pouilly-Fumé, 2002
St. Andelain, LOIRE VALLEY

Montana Wines, Marlborough Reserve, 2003
Blenheim, NEW ZEALAND

• Clairette

Originally from France, the Clairette grape is one of the Châteauneuf and Côtes-du-Rhône villages varieties. In its new "home" in Bangalore it produces an attractively fruity wine with low acid.

Grover Vineyards, Blanc de Blancs

Nandi Hills, Bangalore, INDIA

- **Pinot Gris**

Originating in Italy as Pinot Grigio, this varietal comes into its own in Alsace, also known as Tokay there. This varietal is soft, gently perfumed and gives out more colour than other white wines.

Domaines Schlumberger Grand Cru Kitterlé, 1998

Guebwiller, ALSACE

- **Gewürztraminer**

Best grown in Alsace the Gewürztraminer can yield magnificent wines. The grape thrives in cool climates that allow it to ripen fully. The Gewürztraminer produces a floral and refreshingly spicy wine with crisp acidity that pairs well with spicy food.

Domaines Schlumberger, Grand Cru Kessler, 2000

Guebwiller, ALSACE

- **Riesling**

The Riesling vine's hardy wood makes it extremely resistant to frost, therefore this variety excels in cooler climates. Although best known for the wines of Germany's Moser-Saar Ruwer, Pfalz, Rheinhassen and Rheingau, it also achieves brilliance in Alsace and Austria. Due to their higher acidity and distinctive floral, citrus, peach and mineral accents the Rieslings of Alsace have won many fans around the world.

Domaines Schlumberger, Grand Cru Kitterlé, 1999

Guebwiller, ALSACE

- **Muscadet**

A small district, Sevre-et-Maine, in Loire valley produces the best classic Muscadet in France. The wine is distinctive and musky in aroma and is very light, a bit tangy and a small bit sparkly. It goes very well with seafood and often has a light green apple flavour.

Gadais Père et Fils,

La Grande Réserve du Moulin, 2002

Muscadet de Sèvre-et-Main, Pays Nantais, THE LOIRE VALLEY

Rosé

E. Guigal, Tavel, 2002

Tavel AOC, SOUTHERN RHÔNE

Grenache, Cinsault, Clairette, Carignan, Mourvèdre, Syrah, Bourboulenc.

Red Wines

- **Cabernet Sauvignon**

This grape is a remarkably steady and consistent performer all over the world. In Bordeaux it is blended with Cabernet Franc, Merlot, and Petit Verdot to create some of the world's most famous great wines. In California, it produces wines of uncommon depth, richness and longevity. For our Cabernet Sauvignon collection we have selected a few outstanding styles of this great red grape.

Jordan Winery, "Jordan", 1998
Healdsburg, Sonoma County, CALIFORNIA

Dominus Estate, "Dominus", 1999
Yountville, Napa Valley, CALIFORNIA

Château Margaux, Premier Grand Cru Classé, 1997
Margaux, Médoc, BORDEAUX
70% Cabernet sauvignon, 20% Merlot, 5% Cabernet franc, 5% Petit verdot

Château Latour, Premier Grand Cru Classé, 1997
Pauillac, Médoc, BORDEAUX
80% Cabernet sauvignon, 4% Merlot, 15% Cabernet franc, 1% Petit Verdot

Château Cos d'Estournel, Grand Cru Classé, 1997
St. Estèphe, Médoc, BORDEAUX
60% Cabernet sauvignon, 38% Merlot, 2% Cabernet franc.

Stag's Leap Wine Cellars, "Napa valley", 2001
Napa Valley AVA, Napa County, CALIFORNIA

- **Shiraz**

Also known as Syrah in France, the Shiraz is a majestic red that can age for half a century. The grape itself seems to grow well in a number of areas and is capable of rendering rich, complex and distinctive wines, with pronounced pepper, spice, black cherry, tar, leather and roasted nut flavours, a smooth supple texture and smooth tannins.

Penfolds Wines, Grange, 1997
Barossa Valley, SOUTH AUSTRALIA

Mount Pleasant, Philip, 1998
Hunter Valley, AUSTRALIA

Cabernet - Shiraz

Grover Vineyards, Cabernet-Shiraz
Nandi Hills, Bangalore, INDIA

- **Zinfandel**

The most widely planted grape in California, it may have originally come from Southern Italy as a variant of the Primitivo grape. Although much of it is vinified into a blush wine, real Zinfandel, the red wine is a quintessential California wine. The grape has a zesty, spicy pepper, raspberry, cherry wild berry and plum flavours.

St. Francis Vineyard "Old Vines", 2000
Kenwood, Sonoma Valley AVA, Sonoma County, CALIFORNIA

Duckhorn Paraduxx, 2000
St. Helena, Napa County, CALIFORNIA

- **Pinot Noir**

Pinot Noir, the great grape of Burgundy offers the classic black cherry, spice, raspberry and currant flavours and an aroma that can resemble wilted roses, along with earth, tar, herb and cola notes. A fickle grape to grow as it reacts to environmental changes is therefore different in different parts of the world. Anderson Valley in California and Oregon produce interesting flavour variants to the classic Burgundy Pinot Noir.

Maison Louis Jadot, Bourgogne, 1999
Bourgogne AOC, BURGUNDY

Louis Jadot, "Damodes" Premier Cru, 1999
Nuits-St.-Georges AOC, Côte de Nuits, BURGUNDY
Pinot noir, Pinot gris, Pinot liébault

Louis Jadot, 'Gevrey Chambertin"Premier Cru, 1998
Nuits-St.-Georges AOC, Côte de Nuits, BURGUNDY

Château de Montpatey, Bourgogne, 2002
Bourgogne AOC, BURGUNDY

- **Merlot**

Merlot is the red wine success story of the 1990's: its popularity has soared along with its acreage. Although it dominates most of Bordeaux, it also produces great variants in Washington State and California. Unblended, the Merlots produce simple, light, balanced red wines highlighting their drinkability.

Duckhorn Vineyards, "Duckhorn", 2001
St. Helena, Napa County, CALIFORNIA

Stag's Leap Wine Cellars, "Napa Valley", 2000
Napa Valley AVA, Napa County, CALIFORNIA

Chinkara Wines, "Chinkara", 2003
Melbourne, Victoria, AUSTRALIA

- **Corvina Veronese**

Amarone della Valpolicella Allegrini, 1999
Valpolicella Classico, Veneto
75% Corvina Veronese, 20% Rodinella, 5% Molinara

- **Sangiovese**

Sangiovese is best known for providing the backbone for many superb Italian red wines from Chianti and Brunello di Montalcino, as well as the so-called super-Tuscan blends. It is distinctive for its supple texture and medium-to full-bodied spice, raspberry, cherry and anise flavours.

Marchesi de' Frescobaldi, Castel Giocondo, Brunello di Montalcino, 1999
Montalcino, Chianti, TUSCANY

Marchesi de' Frescobaldi, Nipozzano, 2000
Chianti Rufina, TUSCANY

- **Grenache**

The world's second most widely planted grape. Drought and heat-resistant, it yields a fruity, spicy, medium-bodied wine with supple tannins. Particularly widespread in the Southern Rhône, it is blended to produce the famous Châteauneuf-du-Pape.

E. Guigal, Châteauneuf-du-Pape, 2001
Châteauneuf-du-Pape AOC, Southern Rhône, THE RHÔNE VALLEY
Grenache, Syrah, Mourvèdre, Picpoul, Terret noir, Counoise, Muscardin

Wines By The Glass

- **White Wines**

Louis Jadot, Pouilly-Fuissé, Chardonnay

Chinkara Wines, "Chinkara", Chardonnay,

Maison Louis Jadot, Bourgogne, Chardonnay

Château de Montpatey, Chardonnay

Henri Bourgeois, Pouilly Fumé, Sauvignon Blanc

Montana Wines, Marlborough Reserve, Sauvignon Blanc

Grover Vineyards, Blanc de Blancs, Clairette

Domaines Schlumberger Grand Cru Kitterlé, Pinot Gris

- **Rosé Wine**

E. Guigal, Tavel

- **Red Wine**

Stag's Leap Wine Cellars, Cabernet Sauvignon

Grover Vineyards, Cabernet-Shiraz

Mount Pleasant, Philip, Shiraz

St. Francis Vineyard Old Vines, Zinfandel

Château de Montpatey, Pinot Noir

Duckhorn Vineyards, Duckhorn, Merlot

Chinkara Wines, "Chinkara", Cabernet - Merlot

Marchesi de' Frescobaldi, Nipozzano, Sangiovese.

40 SERVICE OF CIGARS/CIGARETTE

Equipment Required

- Cigars
- Humidor
- Ashtray
- Cigarette
- Matchbox
- Cigar cutter
- Side plate
- Beverage round

Knowledge Required

- Various types of cigars and cigarettes available in the bar/restaurant
- Handling cigars and cigarettes.

SERVICE OF CIGARETTES

Procedure

- A packet of cigarettes must never be carried by hand to a customer.
- Always place a packet of cigarettes over a side plate on a beverage round.
- Outside wrapper is opened, the inside wrap pulled out and one or two cigarettes are tapped out, and not pulled out.
- Serve it along with a matchbox.
- The waiter or server should then stand by with a matchbox ready to light a cigarette.
- The waiter should strike the matchbox away from the guest and hold the flame only.
- Before extinguishing the match, the waiter must be sure that the cigarette is well lit.

Presenting cigarette

- The used matchbox should not be disposed of in the guest ashtray.
- The waiter should clear the ashtray frequently.
- Cleaned ashtray should be placed on the table and it should be removed time to time.

12. Some famous well known imported cigarettes brands are :
    - □ Vogue
    - □ Benson and Hedges
    - □ Camel
    - □ Vin
    - □ Columbus
    - □ Gudangaram
    - □ Capri
    - □ Pine
    - □ Dunhill
    - □ Viceroy
    - □ Marlboro Lights

CHANGING ASHTRAY

Procedure

The following procedures are to be followed in the restaurant having smoking policy.

- Hold a clean ashtray in your right hand and place it over the dirty ashtray.
- The clean astray may be either way up.
- Remove the two trays together using the one hand.
- Transfer the dirty ashtray to your left hand .
- Use your right hand to place a clean ashtray the right way up where the dirty one was.
- Dirty ashtrays should be held in the left hand or on a service tray well away from the guests.

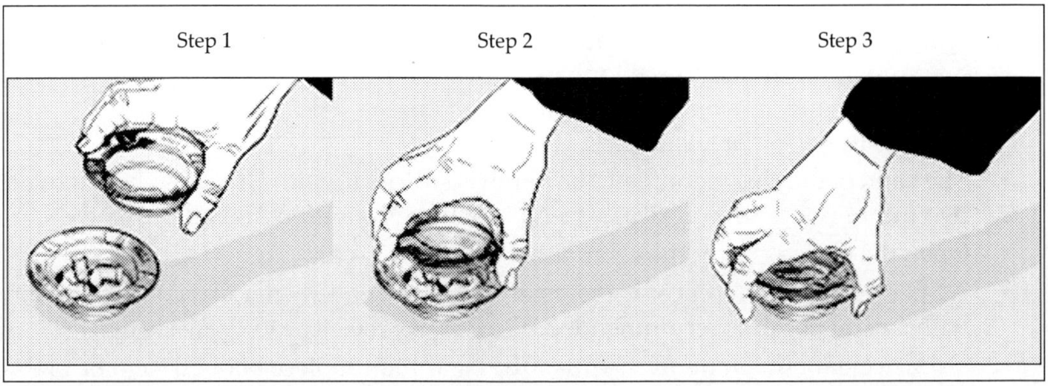

SERVICE OF CIGARS

Procedure

The best presentation and method of keeping cigars is in humidor. Humidor is a polished box with half a dozen sections each holding a different size and type of cigar. On the inside of the lid is a pad which is kept damp, but not wet, to maintain the humidity.

Presenting cigar in humidor

- Place a clean ashtray on the table.
- Present the glass case or humidor from the left-hand side of the guest to select the cigars.
- Present the cigars to the guest.
- Explain the different types, where they are from, sizes and how strong they are.
- Make recommendations as required.
- Carefully remove the selected cigar without any damage to the wrapper.
- A cigar should be smooth, firm and even to touch, it should be the same size and colour as its partners in the box.
- The wrapper should have a healthy glow to it and the open or cut end should be smooth and even.
- Collect the cigar from the guest for preparation. Ask the guest if the band of the cigar may be removed and what type of cut he/she prefers straight or V-cut before taking it to the sideboard.
- Within 5 minutes of order. Take the cigar to the sideboard to prepare according the request of guest.
- If cigar is wrapped in cellophane then carefully remove the cellophane by applying gentle pressure at the end of the cellophane tube. Put the cellophane in your pocket and later on throw it in the garbage box.

Cigar Brands

- Monte Cristo
- Romeo y Julieta
- Davidoff
- Cohiba
- H.Upmann
- Punch
- Partagas
- Hoyo De Monterrey
- Rafael Gonzalez
- Bolivar
- Cuaba
- Alcazar

- The band of the cigar should not be removed before lighting. It should be removed two minutes after the cigar has been lit with the consent of the guest.
- Open the closed end of the cigar either by flat or V-cut.
- As per guest's preference, if the cigar is not pre-cut, then a clear V-shaped cut with a cigar cutter is recommended. This allows the cigar to draw easily.
- Using a cigar cutter cut off the tip of the cigar mouth piece about 0.5 cm or to the guest's liking.

- Cigars should not be pierced as this allows inadequate draw and leaves a bitter taste in the mouth.
- Tap the cut cigar on the side plate to remove any tiny particles.
- Present the cut cigar on the side plate from the left-hand side.
- Strike a cigar match, hold the face of the cigar at 90° angle to the flames and rotate it between the thumb and the finger. From time to time remove it from the flame and wave it in the air. Within a minute the cigar will be lit and ready to offer.
- Once cigar is lit place gently in cigar ashtray on the right-hand side of the guest.
- Cigars must be lit with safety matches, cedar linings or a gas lighter and not a petrol lighter whose fumes would affect the taste of the cigar.

If the guest wishes to light his own cigar

- Place a box of cigar matches, which is especially made for lighting cigars on to a side plate with the cutter and the cigar.

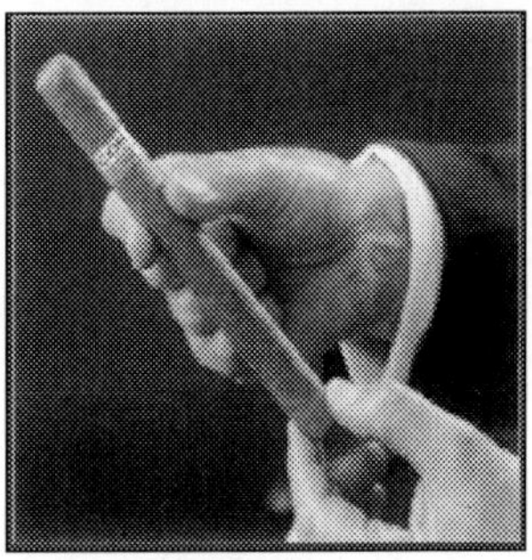

Judging a cigar

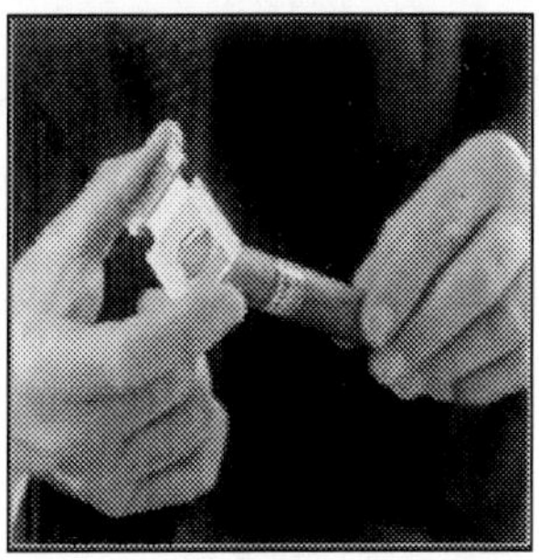

Cutting a cigar

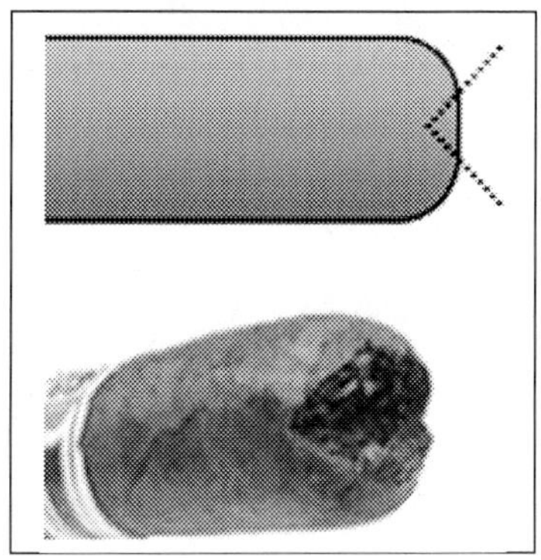

V-Cut for cigar

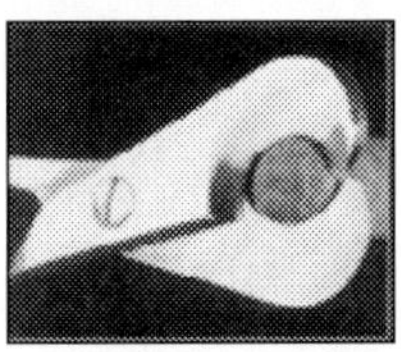

Cigar cutter

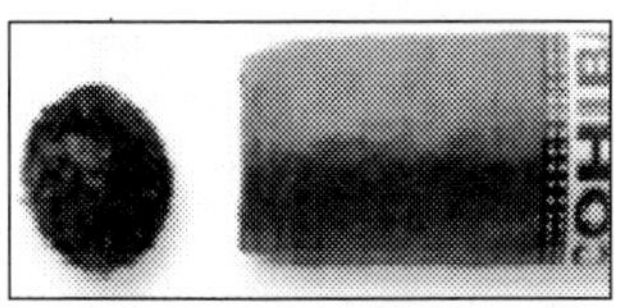

Cigar after cut

STORAGE OF CIGAR

- Cigars are kept in the humidor, which keeps it at a constant level of humidity and temperature.
- Humidor needs to be checked on a daily basis, by assistant operations manager and cigar hostess.
- Ideal temperature should be between 68 to 72% humidity.
- The colleague checking the humidor should take appropriate action which may include adding distilled water, requesting advice from operations manager and chief engineer.

- Action taken should be noted in the outlet logbook.
- Cigars are very delicate and are easily spoilt, if not looked after properly they will dry and lose their taste.

Lighting a cigar

Points to remember

- Offer cigar matches, ashtray, cutter and services detailed above to both customers who purchase cigars from the outlet and those who bring their own.

41 HANDLING MICROS

MICROS or better known as Machine Integrated Cash Register and Ordering System provides comprehensive restaurant point-of-service (PoS) solutions that can be scaled to meet the requirement of every type and size of restaurant, whether it is a mid scale, upscale, stand-alone or part of a hotel. This system can easily be expanded as required, and can fit the demands of every type of restaurant. Software and hardware of MICROS used in the restaurant industry primarily includes touch-screen computers for the serving staff to place orders, which are then sent to kitchen and bar printers for preparation. It can be regarded as a complete restaurant Point of Sale (PoS) system software provides solution with tools for the back-office, restaurant operations, and guest services. This fully-integrated restaurant point-of-sale system is both powerful and flexible and helps operations within the property flow more cohesively, efficiently, and profitably. It also offers restaurants multiple solutions that are designed specifically for table and quick service operations, as well as fast casual concepts. It helps restaurants manage complex employee environments, monitor inventory levels, streamline ordering and receiving processes, enhancing the profitability of restaurant operation with customizable reporting and analysis tools, compare operational conditions against established standards, create waitlists and reservations, and implement gift card and loyalty programmes for guests.

HARDWARE OF MICROS

- Integrated touch-screen personal computer system
- Slip printer
- KOT printer
- Cash drawer

MICROS: OPERATING PROCEDURE

1. **Sign in Procedure**
   - Observe the display on screen. It reads '*Sign In, Enter your ID number*'.
   - Swipe your appropriate shift card through the magnetic reader holding the card upside down and the magnetic reader facing to your right.

- The screen displays 'Ready for your next Entry'.
- The system is now ready for any transaction.

2. Beginning a New Check by Table Number

- Touch the Begin Check key. You are now prompted for Table Number.
- You are prompted to Enter Number of Guests.
- Select the number of Guests and press Enter.

3. Posting Menu Items

- Observe the display on the screen.
- Select the desired group (i.e., breakfast, liquor, lunch) by touching the respective key.
- You get a screen of menu items. Select the menu items by touching the keys.
- If the quantity of item required is more than one, e.g., 2 coffee, then select the quantity, i.e., 2, followed by the item desired, i.e., coffee.
- Press Save key to store the check in the system and allow you to do another transaction on the screen. Saving a check will also print the KOT and BOT on the printers in the respective preparation areas.

4. Pick up a Check (Pick up a Existing Check)

- Touch the Pickup Check key. All the checks open in the outlet and are displayed on the screen.
- Touch and select the Check to be picked up.
- Alternatively, you can also select the Table number and press Pick up table.

5. Printing a Check

- Pick up the check as above and touch Print Check Key.

6. Error Correction

Prior to saving the check, an item can be voided as follows:

- Touch and highlight the item to be voided followed by the Void Key.
- Pressing Void Key twice can void last item on the check.

7. Manager's Void

Manager's void are performed the same way as error correction with the following difference:

- As the items to be voided are of previous service round. System prompts you to 'Enter Authorization ID' that is generally assigned to supervisors/managers.
- The supervisor or manager swipe his ID card at this time.
- Corresponding "VOID" KOT or BOT is printed in the respective kitchen or service bar.

8. Transaction Cancel

This key cancels the current transaction.

- Press Transaction Cancel key. The system prompts "Cancel Transaction?".
- Confirm by pressing Enter. The current transaction gets cancelled, i.e., all items entered in the current round are cancelled.

9. Posting an Open Item

An open item is an item where the user can decide the name and selling price of the menu item to be served. This option is used only when a guest requests for a menu item, which is not listed in the menu.

- Select the Open Items from the main menu screen.
- Select the appropriate Open Item key as the case may be.
- Enter the selling price inclusive of taxes when the system prompts to do so, followed by the name of the item to be printed in the check and the KOT.

In order to post-multiple open items

- Press the quantity desired followed by the @/For key.
- Select the Open Item key as the case may be.
- Enter the selling price and the name of the item.

10. Settle a Check

Various modes of settlements are Cash, Credit Card, City Ledger and Room charge. You may settle a check to any of the above modes using the following procedure:

- Pick up the check to be settled.
- Select the charge/credit card through the settlement key.
- The system prompts you to enter Charge Tip Amount.
- Enter the charge tips amount.

11. Adjust Closed Checks

This procedure enables you to correct the mode of settlement or add/remove tips on a settled check.

- From the transaction screen touch Adjust Closed Check key.
- Type the check number and enter to continue.
- Touch the settlement posting followed by the Void Key.
- Re-enter the correct settlement.

12. Discount

- Pick up the check.
- Press the Discount Key.
- System will display the various discounts possible for food, beverage and liquor select the appropriate one and give the correct reference.

Note: When a 100% complimentary discounts are applied, the subtotal reduces to '0'. The zero balance check has to be settled to settlement code, namely, Complimentary Check.

13. Splitting a Check

- Save the check.
- Pick up the same check.
- Touch Misc Keys and select Touch Split key. You are presented with two checks on the screen. One is the Original check with all the menu items entered and the other is a Blank check created by the system.
- Touch New to create more blank checks on the screen.
- Items can be moved from one check to another by touching and placing on the destination check.
- In case of an item within multiple quantity, you are prompted to enter count to move.
- In case an item has to be shared by more than one check, touch the Share key. You are presented with all the checks, which can share an item. Select the checks which would share the menu item.

14. Transfer of Checks

- Open a new check and give the destination table #. If the check already exists then pick up the Check).
- Touch Misc keys.
- Touch Add/Tfr key.
- All open checks in the outlet are displayed. Touch and select the check to be transferred.
- The destination check remains on the screen. You may either post more items or settle check.

15. Correction of Covers

- Pick up the check.
- Press Misc keys.
- Press Change Covers keys.
- Enter the correct number of covers. In case you enter more than 9 (nine) covers the system will prompt you to confirm the entry. Do so by pressing Enter.

16. Reports

At the end of the shift following report has to be printed:

- Press Reports key. The system lists the different available reports.
- Select report number 3 Employee Financial Report and press 1 and Enter to print the report.

42 FRUITS, NUTS, HERBS AND SPICES

INTRODUCTION

Fruits are the edible seed bearing portion of some cultivated or wild shrubs, trees and plants. It can be eaten raw, cooked or in many other forms. A fruit is used widely in the preparation of various food dishes. Fruits are classified as follows:

- **Berries:** Blackberry, blueberry, raspberry, strawberry.
- **Citrus:** Blood orange, grapefruit, sweet lime.
- **Hard fruit:** Apple, pears.
- **Tropical fruits:** Dates, figs, melons, pine apples.
- **Stone Fruits:** Apricot, plums, peach, cherry.

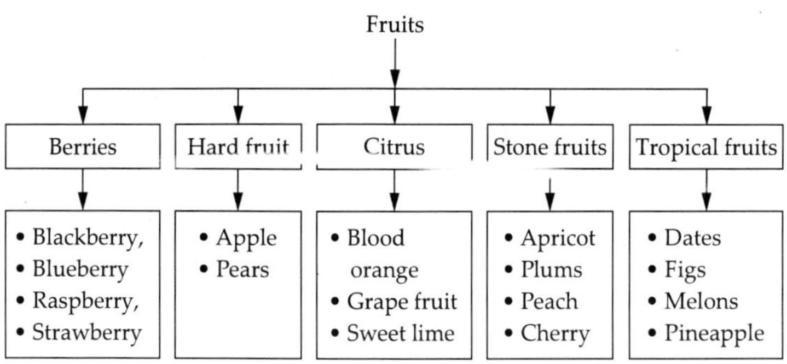

Food and beverages personnel must know the name of fruits as well as their uses.

Name	Picture	Uses
Apple *(pomme)*		• Eaten raw, stewed and poached • Generally, seen in fruit platter. • Used in salads, sauces (apple sauce). • Cooking apple is generally green, sweet and sour. • Cooking apples can be used as grilled and also goes with salads, and sauce.

Cooking apple		
Apricot (abricot)		• Eaten raw, stewed and in salads. • Used as garnishes, filling for pies, pastries and puddings. • Used in preparation of jam.
Avocado (avocat)		• Eaten raw. • Used in salads, soup and shakes.
Banana (banane)		• Eaten raw. • Used in shakes, desserts, ice creams. • Used in fruit platter. • Goes well with waffle, pancakes and deseert or as a banana fritter.
Blackberry (mure)		• Eten raw, steweds. • Used as a filling for tarts, pies, puddings, jam.
Cherry (cerise)		• Eaten raw. • Filling for tarts, flans, pastries and pies. • Used as a garnish in various foods.

Currant (groseille)		• Eaten raw. • Filling for tarts, flans, pastries and pies. • Used as a garnish in various foods.
Date (datte)		• Eaten raw. • Used as a flavouring for cakes, pastries and puddings.
Fig (figue)		• Eaten raw. • Used in salad and fruit salad. • Goes with yoghurt, dry fruit. • Used in marinating as it gives tenderness to the meat.
Gooseberry (groseille verte)		• Eaten raw. • Used as a filling for pies, puddings and tarts and as a stewed.
Grapes (raisin)		• Eaten raw. • Used as a garnish for pastries, custard, puddings fruit salad and in sorbet.
Grapefruit (pamplemousse)		• Eaten raw. • Used in breakfast. • Used in preparation of marmalade.

Kiwi		• Eaten raw. • Used in a fruit platter. • Served as a garnish in various pastries and dessert.
Lemon (citron)		• Used as a garnish. • Used as a flavouring agent. • Used in marination. • Used as an accompaniment such as with grilled fish. • Lemon rind is also used in bakery. • Used in various alcoholic and non-alcoholic beverages.
Mango (mangue)	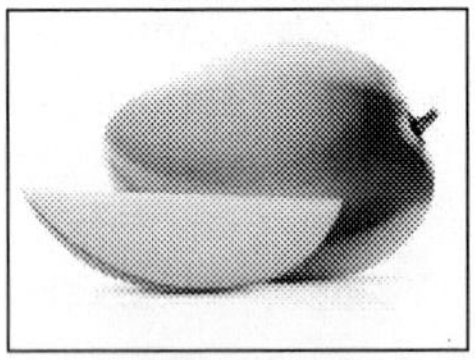	• Eaten raw. • Used in fruit platter. • In Ice cream, shakes.
Melon (melon) Types of Melon: • Casaba • Santa Claus • Charentais • Ogen • Cantaloupe • Honeydew • Crenshaw • Canary • Galia • Watermelon • Lavan • Honey ball		• Eaten raw in salads. • Used in cocktails, fruit salad and in sorbet and drinks.
Orange (orange)		• Eaten raw. • Used in fruit cocktails, salads, fruit salads. • Used as a juice, fresh and canned. • Used in various drinks, sorbets, mousse and souffle. • Widely used in the preparation of marmalades.

Papaya (papaye)	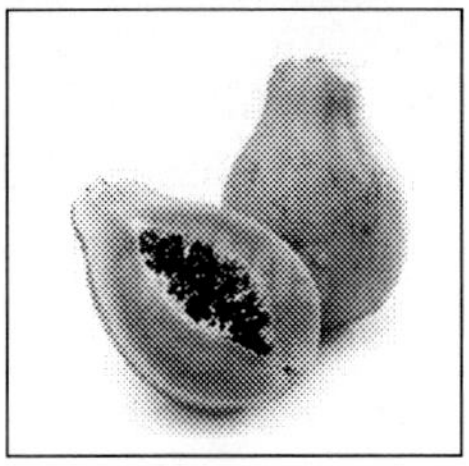	• Eaten raw. • Used in fruit salad. • Used in marination for tendering meat.
Peach (peche)		• Eaten raw. • Used in fruit salad. • Used as a filling for various pies and pastries. • Used in preparation of many dishes and garnishes.
Pear (poire)		• Eaten raw. • Used in fruit salad. • Used in tarts and also as a stewed fruits
Pineapple (ananas)		• Eaten raw. • Used in fruit salad. • Used as a juice and garnishes to many foods and drinks. • Used in many food preparations.
Plum (prune)		• Eaten raw. • Used in fruit salad. • Used in filling for tarts and pies as well as stewed.
Pomegranate (grenade)		• Eaten raw. • Used in fruit salad. • Used as a juice, syrup and in garnishes.

Raspberry (framboise)		• Eaten raw. • Used as a filling for pastrie, tarts and pies. • Used in souffles, mousse, ice creams and jam.
Strawberry		• Eaten raw. • Used in filling for tarts and pies. • Used in mousse and souffles. • Used as a garnishes in many foods and drinks.

Note: Fruits should not be stored in dry atmosphere. Hard, stone and citrus fruits are best stored in the boxes in which they are delivered. Berries are handled as little as possible and always stored in the refrigerator.

NUTS

Nuts are single seeded dry hard-shelled fruits that have to be cracked to open or nuts can be described as any seed or fruit with an edible kernel in a hard or brittle shell. The seed inside the shell is called kernel nuts are used in many food preparations.

Name	Picture	Uses
Almond (amande)		• Eaten raw. • Widely used in bakery and confectionery for preparation, decoration and garnishes. • Used in filling for various pies and tarts. • As an accompaniment for cheese.
Chestnut (marron)		• Braised, roasted and eaten hot. • Used as a garnish in many food products. • Used in bakery.

Coconut (noix de coco)		• Eaten raw. • Used in puddings, pastries cakes. • Used as a oil and in curries. • Used widely in South Indian food. • Coconut milk is also used in many food preparations.
Hazel nut (noisette)		• Eaten raw. • Used in filling of pie, tarts and in cakes. • Used as an oil.
Ground nuts (cacahouette)	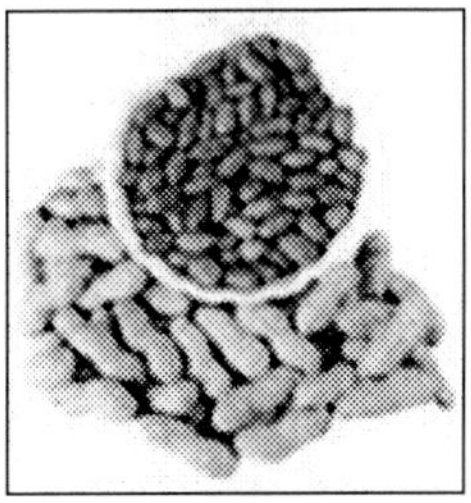	• Eaten raw. • Used as an oil. • Used in filling of pies and tarts.
Pistachio (pistache)		• Widely used in bakery and confectionery to decorate cakes and other desserts. • Used in salad and dressings.
Walnut (noix)		• Widely used in bakery and confectionery to decorate cakes and other desserts. • Used as a stuffing and in pate. • Used as a garnish, dressing and in many salads.

HERBS AND SPICES

The world **"herb"** comes from the Latin word *herba,* meaning *grass* or *herbage*. Herbs have been the main source of medicine throughout the human history. Culinary herbs are fresh or dried leaves used as food flavouring. There are literally hundreds of plants that can be grown for this purpose. Some more popular commercially grown herbs include basil, cilantro, chives, dill, mint, oregano, parsley, rosemary, sage and thyme. Both herbs and spices enhance the flavour of foods, and most of these have medicinal and nutritional properties. Herbs are the aromatic leaves of the fresh or dried plants whereas spices are aromatic parts of plants that thrive in the tropical region. They are usually in the form of dried buds, fruits, berries, roots or barks.

HERBS

In former times, the term 'herbs', when used in cookery, included all plants and vegetables that grow aboveground, or in simple terms various aromatic plants that are used in cookery. **Pot herbs** traditionally include six vegetables— chard, lettuce, orache, purslane, sorrel and spinach. They are used not only to flavour soup but also as vegetables, salad ingredient and as a garnish. **Herbes a soupe**, which was traditionally used to flavour soups and stews, consisted of various green vegetables (carrot and celery tops, radish leaves, parsley stalks. **Herbes de Provence** consists of a mixture of aromatic plants (thyme, rosemary, basil, bay leaf, savory). **Herbes Venitiennes** are a mixture of aromatic herbs (tarragon, parsley, sorrel and chervil), which are finely chopped and incorporated into beurre manie. The herbs have been highly prized for centuries for their endless uses in cookery as well as in the field of the medicinal and healing properties. In cooking, herbs can make a significant difference to a dish, making a simple meal great with full of aroma and flavour. Fresh herbs can be easily grown in home in the garden, or in a pot or window box, and are also widely available from supermarkets, as sprigs, leaves and growing in pots. They are available in dried and frozen as well as fresh form.

Though the range of herbs used in the cookery is endless, this study will take into account the main herbs that are usually seen and used on a day-to-day basis in the hotel kitchens. The most common herbs are as follows:

- **Basil:** It has two types, common and sweet; both originated in India. Its name is derived from Greek word *basilikos,* meaning royal. This delicate aromatic herb is widely used in Italian cooking. It is very important in Thai and Vietnamese cooking— also used in salads and curries. The herb has a slightly pungent perfume, which can be noticed just by brushing the leaves. Basil has a great affinity with tomatoes and other Mediterranean vegetables such as aubergines and fennel and is the herb that is most likely to associate with Provence in France and Italian cooking. There are numerous varieties of common basil. ***Purple basil*** has dark wine red leaves, while ***handkerchief basil*** has large leaves and ***Neapolitan basil*** has crinkly leaves. ***Sweet basil*** also known as Asian basil or Thai basil has a more aniseed flavour. There are a number of varieties and sweet basil comes closest to the basil with which we are familiar, with glossy pointed leaves. ***Krapow,*** commonly known as holy basil, is another sweet basil but narrower leaves that tend to be dull rather than shine. It has a lemony scent and a peppery flavour.

- **Coriander/cilantro:** Also known as ***Arab parsley*** or ***Chinese parsley*** in France and as cilantro in the United States can be used like parsley: the leaves feature especially in the cuisines of China, South-east Asia, South America and Mexico. It is an aromatic plant used both for its leaves and seeds. The origin goes back to the days of Romans who used this for preserving their meats. Its most classic use is for the preparation of ***vegetables a la grecque*** and of pickles in vinegar. Fresh coriander looks similar to flat leaf parsley, but the flavour is completely different with a piquant taste and intense aroma. Coriander is used extensively throughout the world, wherever a distinctive fresh pungency is required. In curries, dals and chutneys in India; in kebabs, meat balls and stir fries in the Middle East and Far East: and in salsas in South America. It is often sold with its roots intact. The roots have a more intense flavour than the leaves and can be used in curry paste. The leaves also make a good garnish.

- **Parsley:** A herb originated in southern Europe and cultivated mainly for its aromatic leaves, which are used to garnish or flavour many dishes. There are mainly two types; ***flat leaf parsley*** which has large, flat, relative smooth leaves, a strong flavour and ***curly leaf parsley,*** the most commonly available form which has bright green, crinky leaves and good flavour. There is another type, i.e., ***turnip rooted,*** which is cultivated for its swollen roots, which is cooked like celeriac and used in soups. It is one of the main ingredients of a bouquet garni. When mixed with garlic it is often served with sautéed or fried fish dishes. Parsley is frequently used chopped to garnish many dishes and to add a touch of freshness. It is also used in the preparation of the flavoured butters. It has a very good freezing quality also.

- **Thyme:** It is one of the basic herbs used in cooking and is one of the main ingredients of the bouquet garni. It has a very good aroma and that is the reason it is used so extensively in various dishes. The other variety, i.e., wild thyme also called *serpolet* in France has clusters of pink flower and has less pronounced flavour then garden thyme. It is used fresh or dried. It is very good for flavouring eggs, salads, tomato dishes and lentils. In Provencal cookery it is used to flavour ragout, mutton and rabbit. Otherwise it is considered to be a very mild herb and used most of the time as a great flavouring for chicken.

- **Dill:** Also known as ***Russian*** or ***Swedish parsley,*** it is an aromatic plant originated in the east and introduced to Europe in ancient times. It is commonly called false anise or bastard fennel but it has a very peculiar delicate flavour of its own. It grows wild in Spain, Portugal and Italy. It thrives in the warmer regions of the Northern Hemisphere and is widely used in Scandinavian cooking with salmon for making ***Gravadlax.*** Dill goes well in potato salads and with cucumber. It makes a good addition to creamy sauces and can be added to a wide variety of egg dishes. It is also used as a flavouring for dressings and dips, used in marinades and is a good partner of mustard. It should be added at the last minutes before serving as the delicate flavour goes away while cooking.

- **Fennel:** A plant of the Mediterranean origin, which is now widely cultivated. The feathery leaves have a slightly aniseed flavour. The leaves are also used as garnish. The plant is a member of the same family as parsley and dill. It grows abundantly near the sea and in damp places, and has been used in cooking for thousand of years. The herb goes particularly well with fish and chicken. Chopped fresh fennel leaves may be added to mayonnaise and other yoghurt based dressings, creamy sauces, stuffing and soups. The fennel bulb can be used raw in salads or cooked in a wide variety of dishes.

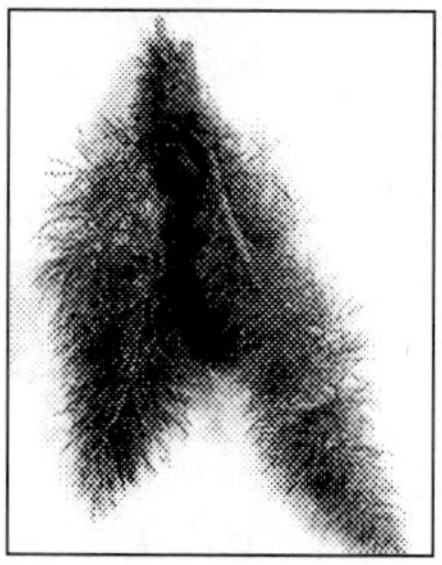

- **Tarragon:** This plant originated in Central Asia. Its name derives from the Arabic ***tarkhun***. The herb was formerly reputed to cure snakebites. Fresh tarragon is deservedly one of the most popular herbs. The slender leafed ***French variety*** has a unique intense sweet vanilla flavour and is considered superior to the coarser tasting ***Russian tarragon***. This herb has an affinity with egg and cheese dishes, tastes good with poultry and can be added to green salads. It is used to enliven dressings and mayonnaise, and is excellent finely chopped and stirred into cream and egg based sauces ***(Béarnaise)*** to serve with salmon and trout. Tarragon vinegar is a classic ingredient for many salad dressings and sauces. Tarragon leaves are used fresh or they may be preserved by drying or freezing.

- **Chervil:** It originated in Central Asia but now common throughout Europe. It has a delicate flavour that goes well with soups, omelettes, sauces (béarnaise, gribiche, vinaigrette) and fish. It also looks very close to the flat leaf parsley. In addition to the ***common chervil*** there is another variety which is ***curly*** and used for decorative. There is also ***bulbous chervil***; its tuberous roots, with high starch content, are eaten like Jerusalem artichokes. Chervil loses its flavour with prolonged cooking, so it is important to add it at the end of the cooking. It keeps very well when frozen.

- **Mint:** A very fragrant aromatic plant used in infusion, to flavour liqueurs, sweets and syrups, and as a culinary herb. There are many varieties of this very famous and versatile herb. Some common ones include; ***Spearmint***, the most popular mint. It has pointed serrated leaves with the fresh familiar flavour we mostly

associate with mint. This is the most preferred type for mint jelly or mint sauce to accompany roast lamb. It is also used in tea in North Africa and Middle East, and for Kentucky mint julep. ***Pepper mint*** with its darker, longer leaves have a stronger flavour. It produces very pungent oil used mainly in confectionery. ***Japanese mint*** is a species from which menthol is extracted. The soft green leaves of ***apple mint*** have a more subtle fruitier flavour. Mint is widely used as a flavouring in a wide variety of dishes. It is an essential ingredient to the Mediterranean salad ***Tabbouleh***. In India it is also mixed with yoghurt to make ***raita*** and ***mint chutney*** accompaniments to Biryani and kebabs. ***Asian mint*** is more strongly flavoured than most European types, with a sweet cool aftertaste.

- **Marjoram:** This herb, closely related to oregano, has three main known varieties; ***Sweet marjoram*** and more flaourful ***pot marjoram***. There is also another type known as ***wild marjoram*** which grows in abundance in Greece. Marjoram has a slightly sweeter flavour and a sweet, almost perfumed aroma. It goes particularly well in Mediterranean style vegetable dishes such as ***ratatouille*** or in casserole and tomato sauces. It should be added at the last minute as it has a mild flavour which diminishes as it is cooked for long. It is also used in marinades and sometimes also used in pizzas topping. In Greece it is frequently used with lamb.

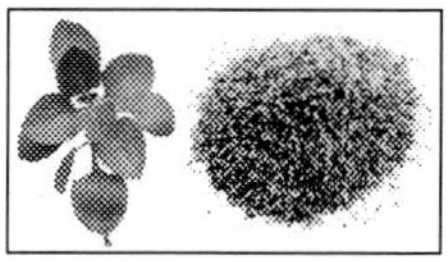

- **Oregano:** It is also known as ***wild marjoram*** and undoubtedly one of the most important herbs for pizza topping. This herb is most commonly related to Italy where it grows in abundance. It has a warm aroma and a pleasant slightly musty flavour that brings out the flavour of tomatoes and aubergines.

- **Rosemary:** This herb is a native of the Mediterranean countries. The name comes from the Latin word ***Rosmarinus*** which means rose of the sea. The sprigs or spiky leaves are used either fresh or dried. They have a strong flavour and only a few are needed to flavour a marinade, a ragout or a grill. It goes particularly well with lamb, chicken and game. Its flavour can also enliven bean and vegetable dishes.

- **Sage:** A herb that is widely cultivated in temperate climate for its leaves. The name comes from the Latin word ***salvus*** which means safe, in good health as traditionally it was considered to have curative properties. It also aids in digestion. It has a potent aroma and slightly peppery flavour and a little is required to flavour a dish. It is excellent with pork dishes, especially grilled pork. It is used most frequently in Italian cuisine: ***Saltimbocca, osso bucco, paupiettes and rice minestrone*** are flavoured with it. In France it is mainly used in Provence for flavouring white meats and certain vegetable soups. In the Middle East it is eaten with roast mutton and in China, the tea is flavoured with sage.

- **Bay leaves:** This herb is from the Mediterranean region, which is obtained from an evergreen tree—*Bay laurel* or *true lorel.*.It is widely cultivated in temperate regions for its glossy aromatic leaves known as bay leaf. It is one of the most commonly used culinary herbs. Its leaf is always incorporated into a bouquet garni to flavour any stock and soups, ragouts and various casseroles. This herb is hardly available fresh as most of the time it is sold dried. It can also be used fresh which gives a different flavour of its own.

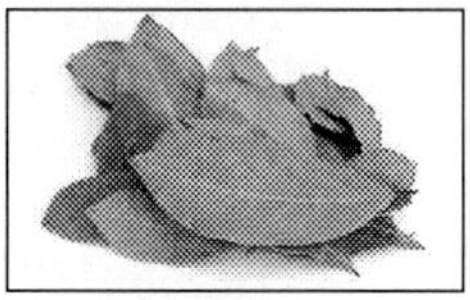

- **Curry leaves:** This strong flavour herb comes from a tropical tree of the citrus-rue family, which is a native to Southern India and Sri Lanka. The long leaves are shiny, dark green on top with paler undersides. It has a warm and spicy aroma when they are bruised or rubbed. It imparts a curry flavour that is unique to this particular herb. A classic way of using curry leaves is by adding them to the hot fat for few seconds. This way the flavour is best extracted from the leaves. They can also be used chopped or whole in the curries, but in the latter case they should be carefully removed from the dishes as some people do not enjoy the leaves coming into their mouth while enjoying the meal.

- **Chives:** These are members of the onion family and have a very mild onion flavour. On the other hand there is one more variety which is known as **Chinese chives** also called **garlic chives** have a delicate garlic aroma. They can be snipped with scissors and added to the egg dishes as garnish and for salads and soups also. They are an essential flavouring in **potato salad**. They are also a component of **fine herbs**. They make a good combination with soft cheese. When they are mixed into soft butter they make a good alternative to garlic butter. Caution has to be taken if they are to be cooked along with some hot dish. They should be cooked briefly as they lose this flavour on prolonged cooking.

SPICES

Spices are aromatic substances derived from plants, which have a fragrant or sharp taste and flavour and are used to season food. Most spices come from the east and the first spice to be introduced to Europe was the pepper from India. The use of spices in cooking was originally introduced by the Byzantines. Foodstuffs were preserved in spice sauces and sometimes to replace the flavour lost after lengthy cooking. Now the spices used in various cuisines are endless, everyone having his own style and way of using. The main purpose though remains the same that of providing flavour to the dish. Some of the main spices used in the kitchens are as follows:

- **Cardamom (*ilaichi*):** It is an aromatic plant from the Malabar region of south western India. It has pods whose capsules contain seeds which are dried and used as a spice. It is an essential spice which is also the main ingredient of the whole as well dried ground garam masala. The pungent and the warm bouquet of the cardamom seeds are unforgettable. It has a pleasing slightly warm lemon like flavour. India is responsible for **80%** of the total cardamom growth world over. There are two types; the **green cardamom** and **the black cardamom**. Green cardamoms are the most common and useful. They are used extensively in curries, sweets and most commonly in flavouring tea. White cardamoms are the same pods which have been bleached. The black ones are used in long cooked highly flavoured spicy Indian curries and chutneys. The spice is also used in German cooking in pickles, herrings and cakes. It is also widely used as a mouth freshener.
- **Coriander seeds (*dhania*):** It is used in Indian cuisine as one of the main ingredients, finding its place in almost any curry prepared in India. The seeds look like tiny, pale, creamy-brown peppercorns. When they are dry fried they have heady, slightly burnt orange aroma, which is very appealing. They are also used in the cuisines of Middle Eastern countries. In Germany they are used in game marinades and also for flavouring and seasoning cabbage. Whole or coarsely ground coriander must be used in dishes cooked a **la grecque**.
- **Cinnamon (*dal chini*):** It is a bark which is obtained from several tropical plants. The bark is removed, dried and rolled up to make a tube, light fawn or dark grey in colour depending on the species. The most popular variety is from **Sri Lanka**. It imparts a sweet penetrating aroma and has a mild warm and spicy flavour. It is also commonly found in the form of a powder used as a topping and flavouring for coffee. In India it is again used in garam masala and in France it is used in compotes and desserts. Apple and cinnamon are an all time combination (Apple pie and cinnamon Danish).
- **Nutmeg (*jaiphal*):** It is the seed of the nutmeg tree widely cultivated in **tropical Asia and America**. It is a native to the **Banda Island** in the **Moluccas**. The best known variety is the nutmeg tree of the Sunda Island. The nutmeg is oval and rounded in shape, greyish brown in colour and wrinkled. It has a spicy flavour and aroma and is always used freshly grated in little amount as too much of it can cause the dish to taste bitter. It should always be stored in airtight container as it tends to lose its flavour if left open. It goes excellent with béchamel base sauces, sautéed spinach, potato dishes, savory soufflés and cream based preparations. It is also used to spice cocktails and punches and is used in the manufacture of some fortified wines and spirits.
- **Mace (*javitri*):** It is also obtained from the same tree. It is nothing but the outer web-like covering of the nutmeg spice. It is pressed, dried and used as it is or

in powder form. It has a slightly **stronger flavour** than nutmeg. It is used in garam masala in Indian cuisines. In Europe it is a popular seasoning for sausage meats and force meats, and it has an affinity with pork dishes. It can also replace nutmeg in potato puree and soufflés but the precaution has to be taken to add a little lesser.

- **Cloves (*long*):** The name comes from the Latin word ***clavus*** which means a *nail*. It is a native to the **Moluccas** in the South East Asia, but they are now widely grown in Caribbean, Indonesia, Malaysia, Madagascar and Sri Lanka. They are picked when the buds are small and as they are dried in the sun the colour changes to a darker brown. They are of great culinary significance. They are included in Indian garam masala and **Chinese five spice powder**. They are also used in the onion cloute for flavouring the béchamel sauce. They are arranged in a diamond pattern for flavouring and appearance on the **baked ham**.
- **Cumin (*jeera*):** These are seeds having a spindle shape that are used either whole or ground. They have a piquant and slightly bitter taste combined with warmth that is evident in their aroma. It is of great use in the Indian cuisines used for tempering curries and dals and for making rice preparations as Pulau. It is also used in the middle Eastern dishes in dolmas and rice preparations. It is a classic flavouring for breads in Europe and also used in the preparation of cold meets and cheeses, such as **munster cheese**. It has two varieties; **the brown and black**. Black is also called **shahi jeera** in India and is more intense than brown cumin.
- **Turmeric:** This spice is hugely popular in India, and not only as a cheap alternative to saffron, it has a peppery aroma and adds a warm, musky flavour to food. It is used in dried form and commonly available in the form of powder. It resembles a great deal to ginger but it is rare to see it fresh as most of the turmeric produced in India is sold dried. It has an amazing shelf life provided it is stored in an airtight container to save its flavour. It is largely used in curries to provide colour and to lend a flavour which is unique to it. It is also used in various pickles and said to have great medicinal uses also.
- **Saffron:** One of the most expensive spices available on the earth, it is the **stigma** of a flower name **crocus sativus**. It has a distinctive and lasting aroma, and a pleasant pungency if used sparingly. Because of its striking colour it is used in celebration dishes, e.g., **pulau in India, Paella from Spain and Risotto Milanese from Italy**. **Bouillabaisse**, the classic French seafood soup is also flavoured with saffron. It is also commonly used in various sweets in India.
- **Mustard (*rai* or *sarson*):** The word mustard comes from the Latin word **mustum**, which is the name for the grape juice used to mix the ground seeds to a paste, known, in turn, as mustum ardens, the burning paste. There are three different types of mustard seeds; **white (alba), brown (juncea) and black (nigra).** The seeds has a very mild smell or almost no smell. The real taste comes when they are crushed and mixed with a liquid mixing powder mustard with a liquid activates an enzyme present in the seeds and it reacts with other constituents to develop the essential oil, which gives mustard its characteristic taste. Black seeds have the

sharpest taste followed by white and than the brown. It has several culinary uses, main being used as a condiment. It is also one of the main ingredients in salad dressings. In India its oil is used for cooking and in marinades. It is also used in lot of south Indian dishes as a tempering. It goes excellent with steaks giving them that extra tang as some people find the taste to be a little bland.

- **Carom (*ajwoin*):** This is a famous Indian spice particularly famous in *parathas*, an Indian bread done on a griddle. It is also used in savoury pastries, snacks (*samosas*), and breads. It goes very well with beans and pulses all of which illustrate the affinity carom has with starchy food. It has a powerful thyme like aroma, which can be simply found by crushing the seeds in the hands.
- **Nigella (*kalonji*):** These are the seeds of the onion, having little aroma. When they are rubbed they give off a peppery smell. They are sometimes used as a substitute for pepper also. It is widely used in Indian cuisines where it is known as *kalonji*. Kalonji is often sprinkled over naan, breads, etc. Nigella is one of the ingredient in **Bengali five spice mix**.
- **Chillies (*mirch*):** They are available in several different forms all around the world. The birthplace is **Mexico** where one can find the maximum varieties of chillies. They are available in all the supermarkets around the world in dried form as whole or powdered. They are largely used to provide pungency to the dishes. Chillies contain a pigment called **capsaicin** which is responsible for their flavour. It varies from species to species. The higher the capsaicin content in chillies the higher the pungency. There are sweet chillies to fiery hot chillies (habanero). They are used in Indian cuisine in powdered as well as fresh form to provide colour and pungence. They are also used whole for tempering several south Indian dishes. Some other varieties of chillies are ancho, nyora, serrano, cascabel, bird's eye and pasado, all having a fiery hot taste. **Serrano** chillies are used to make the classic **guacamole** in Mexico.
- **Fenugreek (*methi*):** It is a highly aromatic spice smelling of curry. The seeds are used in a wide range of curry powder. They are also used dried and whole as a tempering. They have a very good digestion property, which is the reason it is used in Indian cuisine to add it to the curries and dals to aid digestion. The seeds can also be used to make sprouts and can be used in sandwich fillings. The leaves after growing can be dried and used in gravies.

SOME COMBINATION SPICES

These are some of the combination spices that have been accepted worldwide in a standard combination of different spices and each of these has a specific use in their respective cuisines. Following are some of the examples of the combination spices.

- **Jamaican Jerk Spice:** It is a combination of nutmeg, cinnamon, cloves, thyme (dried), black peppercorn, paprika in the ratio of 1:1:1:2:2:2. All spices are briefly broiled and ground to a fine powder.

- **All Spice:** A spice also known as Jamaican pepper and in France as **poivre giroflee**, that is ground from the unripe berries of **Pimenta Officinalis**, a tree which grows in the Caribbean, Honduras and Mexico. It has strong odours of nutmeg, cinnamon and cloves, which is why it is sometimes mistaken as a mixture of spices. It is used to season sausages, salt beef and pork, pickles, sauces, herrings, stuffing and even Christmas cakes.
- **Seven Spice:** It is a combination of star anise, nutmeg, fennel, cinnamon, cloves, schezuan peppers and ginger. It is a spice associated to the oriental cookery.
- **Cajun Spice:** Spice mix made with 1 tsp black peppercorn, 1 tsp cumin seeds, 1 tsp white mustard seeds, 2 tsps paprika, 1 tsp chilly powder, 1 tsp dried oregano, 2 tsps dried thyme, 1 tsp salt, 1 tsp garlic powder, 4 tsps onion powder.

TYPES OF LETTUCES

- **Aragula:** With its peppery and slightly bitter flavour, arugula is a terrific green to be used in salads. It can be gently braised too.
- **Belgian endive:** These crunchy, slightly bitter leaves are often used to make hors d'oeuvres, but they can also be chopped and added to salads, or braised to make an exquisite salad.
- **Cress:** This is a peppery green that's great in salads, sandwiches, and soups. It's attractive enough to make a good garnish as well. There are several varieties, including **watercress**, **upland cress**, **curly cress**, and **land cress**. Cress is highly perishable, so try to use it as soon as possible after you buy it.
- **Curly endive:** This crisp, bitter green leave can be used in salads or cooked as a side dish. The outer leaves are green and somewhat bitter; the pale inner leaves are more tender and mild.
- **Iceberg:** This is prized for its crispness and longevity in the refrigerator, but it's a bit short on flavour and nutrients. It's one of the most readily available lettuces in India and is mostly used by a number of hotels to prepare salads.
- **Lollo Rosso:** This mild, tender lettuce has ruffled red edges.
- **Radicchio:** With its beautiful colouring and slightly bitter flavour, radicchio is wonderful when combined with other salad greens.
- **Romaine:** Romaine combines good flavour and crunch, plus it has a decent shelf life in the refrigerator. It's the preferred green for Caesar salad. Green romaine is the most common variety, but you can sometimes find red romaine, which is tender.
- **Red Sangria:** Thick rose blushed leaves over a blanched pale yellow heart make for an attractive lettuce.
- **Bibb:** This butter head lettuce has delicate, lose leaves and lots of flavour. The only downside is that it's usually expensive.
- **Mizuna or Spider Mustard:** Mizuna has tender leaves and a pleasant, peppery flavour.

- **Red mustard:** This has a pungent, peppery flavour that adds zip to salads.
- **Dandelions:** Dandelions have a somewhat bitter flavour, which Europeans appreciate more than Americans. Older dandelion greens should be cooked; younger ones can be cooked or served raw.

Types of Lettuces

ACTIVITIES

- Visit nearby vegetable market and make a list of the following along with their price:
  - □ Five continental fruits.
  - □ Five continental vegetables.
  - □ Five continental herbs used for cooking.
  - □ Five lettuces.
  - □ Ten Indian herbs and spices.

43 NEW TRENDS IN BAR

MIXOLOGY

It is another term for mixing drinks or bartending and a mixologist is another term for a bartender or bar chef. Mixology is generally accepted as a slang for a refined and in-depth study of the art and craft of mixing. In a line mixology can be defined as *"the art or skill of preparing mixed drinks"*. Mixology has become a more commonly used term in recent years and is generally accepted to be a refined, higher study of mixing cocktails and drinks.

MOLECULAR MIXOLOGY

> **Mixologist**
>
> He is the bar equivalent of a culinary chef. A mixologist not just pours the drink, he creates new ideas and signature cocktails by utilizing new culinary and savoury concepts and knowing how to use ingredients. A mixologist's objective is to showcase the versatility of beverage alcohol and enhance the guest experience by creating sophistication.

It is a special practice of mixing drinks using the analysis and techniques found in science to understand and experiment with cocktail ingredients on the molecular level. Inspired by the practice of molecular gastronomy (which works in similar ways with food dishes) this practice has become a popular study of many mixologists. The purpose is to manipulate states of matter to create new flavours, feels, textures and visuals that enhance the drink and make the drinker's experience more interesting. Popular techniques of molecular mixology include the use of foams, liquid nitrogen, gels, mists, heat, solidifying liquids, etc. There are many bartenders and establishments throughout the world that feature or specialize in molecular mixology, just as there are restaurants that specialize in molecular gastronomy. However, the practice is sometimes touted as novel, gimmicky and, with the absence of discretion, can be overwhelming for some drinkers. Bartenders and chefs leading the molecular mixology have created incredible cocktails and drinking experiences. Cocktail spheres that explode in the mouth, cocktail caviar, edible cocktails, multi-colour layered cocktails, cocktails that resemble lava lamps, cocktails with foams and bubbles, cocktails infused with surprising leather and cigar are all new trends given by molecular mixology. Molecular mixology equipment ranges from simple blowtorches to vacuum chambers, cotton candy makers, liquid nitrogen, rotary evaporators and dehydrators.

INFUSION: AN ART & SCIENCE IN A JAR

Herb-infused spirits whether they be whiskies, vodkas or gins are gaining in popularity. Infusing alcohol is an ancient practice. It is the process of adding flavours of herbs, spices, fruits and vegetables to alcohol to create a unique flavour combination. Infusing is a pretty simple process and has been used by distillers for centuries. Spirit infusions require inventiveness, a sense of adventure, product knowledge and the ability to control the process. It a simple practice of steeping or macerating a flavour into a spirit and letting it sit for a period of time. The time it takes for the spirit to absorb the flavours is all determined on the product and the environmental factors. The basic concept is to marry a variety of choice flavours into a base liquor to create a custom-flavoured spirit. Choosing an infused bottle of spirits can make drink a sweeter and smoother experience. It should also be noted that there is a difference between infused spirit and flavoured spirit. Makers of spirits have started adding flavours during production and now vanilla-flavoured rums and raspberry-flavoured vodkas sit side-by-side with perennial standards on the shelves of a bar. Infusing spirits is a lengthy process, taking about two weeks but it's certainly not difficult if working as a bartender. Take hard alcohol and add in a source of flavour such as a fruit peel, herb or spice. Store the two ingredients together in a tightly-sealed mason jar and shake it vigorously three to five times a day. A good rule to go by when infusing is to start with oil based flavours such as citrus, chilies and similar fruits and vegetables. Using more succulent fruits such as strawberries could result in a mushy mess without careful supervision. The combinations of flavours are only limited by imagination but requires a great deal of patience. Vodka is the easiest spirit for infusing, as it is neutral as well as it pairs well with any flavour. But light spirits like gin, sake, light rum can also be used for almost any flavour. The flavoured vodka market appears to have exploded in the past few years. Brands like Absolut and Smirnoff populating liquor store shelves with their fruity twists on classic vodka. From the flavours such as raspberry, citrus and vanilla to the unexpected treats like blueberry, mandarin and wild grape, there are options for every palate. Add just carbonated water and enjoy the enhanced taste of the guests. Tequila has also recently expanded into the infused drink market. Silver tequila from Sauza in both mango and açai flavours is one of the examples. In many countries tequilas and mezcal are also infused with rattle snakes and other insects. Though an infusion need not be alcoholic – water and sugar syrups can be infused, too. The higher the alcoholic proof, the faster and more pronounced the extraction of flavours. When very high-proof alcohol is used, bartenders refer to the infusion as a tincture, which typically highlights a single flavour. Below are some tips for preparing infusion.

Equipment Required

- Clean glass containers or mason jars.
- Empty wine bottles.

Just make sure they are very clean and free from any residue or odour of what was in them previously.

GATHER ALL FLAVOURING AGENTS

Add fruit, spices, herbs or other flavouring ingredients of your choice. Use your judgment as to how strong the flavour of the ingredient is for how much you add. A good rule for fresh fruit is to fill the container half way up with the produce and then add liquor to fill the bottle. With herbs, a good handful or two should be plenty. With something strong, like ginger, a three inch piece should be enough for a 750 ml bottle. More ingredients can be added after a few days if more pronounced flavour is desired. Remember to cut the pieces small if using a small necked bottle. Use creativity to personalize the creations. For best results, use fresh ingredients only. Wash the ingredients place them inside the mason jar or any other container.

ADD ALCOHOL

Fill the rest of the container with a decent spirit that is smooth and clean which will help in allowing the added flavours to shine. Remember to leave the little space in the container so that the spirit can be shaked. Cover and cork, close the container tightly.

INFUSION TIME

Store your infusion in a cool, dark place out of direct sunlight and shake it 3-5 times a day for the duration of the infusion. This can be done in the refrigerator. On average the ingredients should stay in the liquor for 3-5 days. Some of your more intense flavours will only need 3 days, less intense flavours should stay in the jar for a full week or more. Taste the infused mixture after every few days to see if the flavours are sufficient. The longer you leave it, the more prominent the flavour becomes, but it will level off eventually. Occasionally, tip the bottle gently to redistribute the alcohol.

STRAIN, STORE AND SERVE

When the infusion has reached its peak in flavour take the flavouring ingredients out of the jar. Use a fine strainer or paper coffee filter to strain the vodka into another clean jar or bowl and store in a cool place. Also note that containers and ingredients are thoroughly cleaned while infusing spirit. The high alcohol content should inhibit harmful bacteria from growing, but if at any point the concoction has an "off" smell, or starts to rapidly discolour or get cloudy, discard it. Remove rind and pith from citrus fruits as they will make the infused liquor bitter. Common flavouring agents which can be used in a bar for infusing spirit are as follows:

- **Citrus:** Lemons, limes, grapefruit, oranges, blood oranges and tangerines.
- **Herbs:** Thai basil, lemongrass, mint, rosemary, dill, cilantro.
- **Fruit:** Mango, melon, berries, cranberries (fresh or dried), peaches, pineapple, apricot (fresh or dried), pomegranate, pear.
- **Spices:** Use whole spices like cinnamon sticks, dried chili peppers, peppercorns, star anise, cardamom and bay leaf.

- **Vegetables:** Fresh ginger, hot peppers, fennel, olives, horseradish, cucumber.
- Exotic flavour combinations can also be experimented like lemon with honey, lemon grass and ginger, fig and cardamom, apple and cinnamon stick and many more with fresh and interesting botanicals.

OTHER TRENDS IN BEVERAGES

- **Flavoured tonics:** Tonic water is a simplest mixer, and an obvious staple to anyone serving drinks. A variety of new tonics are hitting the market.
- **Cask-aged cocktails:** Drink mixes aged in wooden barrels for added nuance continue to gain popularity in major urban centres around the world.
- **Cocktails on tap:** For speed and consistency, many bars are serving a selection of well-crafted cocktails.
- **Super-premium beverages:** Spirit enthusiasts and wine aficionados seem prepared to pay huge amount for a small taste of luxury potables. While they may not be willing to spend Rs. 2000–Rs. 30,000 for a bottle of top-top-shelf cognac or champagne more and more enthusiasts are showing a willingness to pay a premium amount for an ounce or two.
- **Smoked spirits:** Flash smoking is making a move from the chef's kitchen to the bar top. Still a relatively new phenomenon, bar-top smokers used to infuse spirits with a mild smokiness are beginning to be found in a number of popular bars in most major cities.
- **Combination drinks:** More and more bar owners are discovering the benefits of marrying two drinks and selling them together in order to boost sales. Whether it's the classic shot with a beer chaser, or a more inspired combination of two cocktails with complementing flavours, double-hitters promise to become a hit among bar patrons.
- **Return to the classics:** Cocktail menus have become chockfull of creative concoctions and signature drinks. More and more drinkers, however, are starting to embrace some of the classics.
- **Skinny drinks:** Expect cocktail menus to offer more and more low calorie beverages whether lighter versions of standard fare or entirely new concoctions. Popular among the ladies and health-conscious patrons wanting to limit the number of "empty calories" they consume, skinny cocktails are a good way for drinking establishments to cater to this growing segment of their clientele.
- **Vintage beers and lower-alcohol beers:** While higher-alcohol beers continue to be popular, rise in demand for flavourful, lower alcohol beers has also been increased.
- **Organic Beverages:** Bar situated in the hotels around the world have already gone beyond organic food to start serving organic alcohol as well. In a short time organic liquor has expanded beyond beer, wine and vodka to tequila, gin,

brandy, whiskey and rum. Wine made from grapes that are grown, harvested, and processed according to the principles of organic agriculture is gaining traction with wine connoisseurs, and as a result many of the Asian hotel chains such as Ritz-Carlton, Marriott and Hyatt Hotels now carry organic beverages in their bars.

COCKTAIL AND FOOD PAIRING

It is the new concept in bars to pair cocktail with food. Cocktails and food pair beautifully and already many trend setting restaurants and bars see cocktails as an inspired way to pair alcohol with foods and not just an aperitif. Following tips can be useful while pairing cocktail with food.

- Consider cocktail pairing with food as same like wine pairing. Detect the flavour profiles and create a complementary drink accordingly.
- Avoid cocktails that are overly sweet, especially when paired with a sweet dish.
- Bring an ingredient forward in a dish by using it in a cocktail pairing.
- Use fresh, quality ingredients in cocktails.
- If compiling an entire cocktail pairing menu, keep the cocktail portions small.
- Control the alcohol content as the high alcohol content tends to numb the taste buds.

DESIGNER ICE

One of the latest trends in the world of craft cocktails is using the designer ice. Different varieties, compositions, and shapes of ice are an essential ingredient in the new cocktail trend and with the help of such new innovations service of spirit has become more eye appealing. Serving whiskey on the rocks with the help of a ice ball is the latest trend in most of the high class establishments nowadays. Add just one big piece of ice that lasts longer in the drink, instead of a bunch of pieces of tiny ice that melt quickly.

Ice ball

INFORMATION TECHNOLOGY

Uses of online reservations is a rapidly growing trend, the use of the Internet to find where to go to eat and drink is common nowadays. Smart phones, majorly tablets, are being adopted more broadly in the hospitality industry not only as a PoS-integrated system but also as a replacement for the wait staff's order pads and as enhanced menus with photos, ingredients, the calorie count of foods, suggested wine pairings and much more. Many wine bars and restaurants are using tablets as a replacement to traditional wine menus. Tablets also provide an opportunity to provide cheap entertainment, in the form of interactive game play, to bar patrons. Using of social media has become a major marketing tool for the commercial bars as it combines the credibility of the word of mouth publicity with the reach of mass media. Many bar professionals are hiring social media managers to promote their bars. LEDs and new, cheaper and simpler-to-use DMX lighting software allows bars and nightclubs to modify the ambience with greater ease, without having to overhaul the entire architecture. Whether as means of creating an entirely fresh look or as a way of changing mood lighting to match an event, a season, or a time of day DMX lighting is being used more widely to create a fresh look and feel.

GLOSSARY

ABC: ABC stands for ashtray, budvase and cruet. ABC is kept at the centre of the table while laying the cover.

Aboyeur: Aboyeur aids communication between the kitchen and restaurant. He receives the food order from the service staff and announces the order to the kitchen. Baeyer is responsible for hot plate section of the pantry.

À la carte Menu: À la carte menu is a type of menu, where the food items are priced individually. Literary meaning of à la carte is "from the card".

American service: It is a type of table service. In American menu the food is pre-plated and portioned in the kitchen. This type of service is relatively less formal and seen in coffee shops.

Ancillary Areas and Services: Ancillary areas are the supporting areas of F&B service department. Without the help of the ancillary departments F&B service department cannot work smoothly. In this regard the ancillary departments are very important for F&B service department. Major ancillary departments in a five-star hotel are the following.

- Pantry
- Still room
- Silver room
- Linen Room
- Hot plate
- Wash-up area
- Kitchen stewarding

Back of the House: Back of the house is the ancillary area of the restaurant, where all the supporting service is carried out. Some of the back of the house sections are pantry, dishwashing, hot plate, still room, etc.

Bain Marie: Bain Marie is the equipment that holds the food hot. The equipment contains cylindrical drum, which is heated with water. Bain Marie is usually used in hot plate section of the pantry.

Banquet Service: Banquet functions are the services provided at a fixed time and at a fixed venue. The banquet service is inevitable in a hotel due to its revenue earning potential. The reason is that banquet can offer service to a large number of guests at a time. Banquet service can be formal or informal.

Barker: Barker is another term for baeyer. Barker is the person who communicates between service and kitchen and helps to pick up the food in time. Usually, the order taken by the waiter is handed over to the barker.

Bar Service: There are normally two kinds of bars in Indian hotels. One is the **public bar**, and the other is the **service** or **dispense bar**. The public bar is located in the public areas, and is used for the service of paying customers, be it in-house guest or non-residents. The dispense bar is used for dispensing drinks to other outlets of the hotel such as coffee shop, room service outlet, banquets and the specialty restaurant. It is generally located in the back area of the hotel and is open round-the-clock. It should be adequately equipped to meet the demands of all the outlets.

Bone China: It is a white translucent ceramic material made from kaolin, china clay and bone ash. It is used to serve various dishes.

Briefing: Briefing is done prior to the opening of the restaurant. In the briefing the senior-most staff gives instructions to the junior staff with regard to availability of dishes, special items of the day, and also some training.

Buffets: Buffet is a type of assisted service, where food and beverages is displayed at counters. Waiter assists at the counters to take the food from the counters or the guest help themselves.

Burnishing Machine: This is a revolving drum-like container used for cleaning silver-ware, with safety shield attached to it. The burnishing machines are attached with ball-bearing to run. Soap power is used to clean the silverware.

Bus Boy: Bus boy is a person who helps the waiter. The main responsibility of a bus boy is to bring the food from the kitchen and also do the clearance of plates from the table.

Cafeteria Service: This service exists normally in industrial canteens, colleges, hospitals and hotel cafeterias. To facilitate quick service, the menu is fixed and is displayed on large boards. The guest may have to buy coupons in advance, present them to the counter waiter who then services the desired item. Sometimes food is displayed behind the counter and the guest may indicate his choice to the counter attendant. The food is served pre-plated and the cutlery is handed directly to the guest. Guests may then sit at the tables and chairs provided by the establishment.

Carousel: Carousel is a circular counter that revolves to display the food items. The carousel is fitted in such a way that the one side is always inside the kitchen and other side is in the service area. As the carousel revolves the counter is filled up from the kitchen and guests select the food as it revolves.

Carte du Jour: Carte du jour me- "card of the day". It is used to highlight the special dishes of the day. carte du jour is actually an supporting menu to the main menu.

Carvery: Carvery is a type of assisted service. This service method includes both table service and self service. Some parts of the service is done by the waiter at the table and some parts of the service is done guests themselves.

Chafing Dish: It is a hollowware used to keep the food warm usually in buffet service. Chafing dish has a water container, which is the base, food container and place for fuel. Using the fuel the water is heated up and, in turn, the food is heated up with the hot water.

Coffee Shop: Coffee shop is a 24-hour, a multi-cuisine F&B outlet. Usually, coffee shops are situated near the lobby of a hotel. Style of service is American that is pre-plated. The menu of coffee shop is varied. Menu comprises full-day menu or according to meal session.

Counter Service: Counter service sometimes is called cafeteria service. The guests come in line, collect their food from the counter and seat at the table to have the food. Food may be grouped together such as cold and hot, or main course and desserts, etc. In some places the guests also have to clear the empty plates and cutlery after having the food.

Cover: Cover is the space on the table allotted for tableware to the guest to consume his/ her meal. The size of the cover is 24 inch × 18 inch.

Cutlery: Cutlery is all the cutting implements such as knives. Cutlery can be made of EPNS or stainless steel.

Demi-tasse: Demi-tasse means half cup. It is used to serve espresso coffee.

Dessert: This is the fruit course in the French classical menu and usually presented in a basket (Corbielle de Fruits) and placed on the table, as part of the table décor, and served at the end of the meal. All forms of fresh fruit and nuts may be served in this course.

Disposables: Disposables are use-and-throw products used in the service of food and beverages products. This is largely due to the increasing demand for fast food items. There are different types of disposables used in the catering business and mostly they are used in outdoor catering, vending machines, fast food outlets and hotels.

Drive Thru: The customer drives the vehicle to the counter and orders and collects the food and leaves the counter.

Dummy Waiter/Demi Waiter: Dummy waiter is another term for sideboard. It is a restaurant furniture and is used to keep all the serving equipment for a meal session.

Echelon: In echelon service the counters are arranged in such a way that it provides better view of the foods and is arranged in angular way.

Elevenses: Elevenses is a meal served at 11 o' clock. It includes the food items as biscuits, cakes and so on. It is usually offered to children.

English Service: English service is often referred to as "host service" The food is brought on platters by the waiter and is shown to the host for approval. The host then either carves/portions the food and serves to the guest or ask the waiter to carve/portion the food and serve to its guest.

Entrée: Entrée is the first meat in a French classical menu. It usually comprises a dish made up of steak, cutlets, casseroles or stews. Some examples are steak au poirre, veal cutlets, and Irish stew.

EPNS (Electroplated Nickel Silver): EPNS is silverware made of silver plating. Silver plating is a thin layer of silver on top of another metal. It is made by an electrical process, hence the name **Electroplated Nickel Silver**. Cutlery and crockery of high class establishments are made out of EPNS which includes different types of forks, knifes, pots, plates, salvers, etc.

Fast Food Service: There is a predominant American influence in fast food style of catering. The service of food and beverages in a fast food restaurant is at a faster pace, than at an à la carte restaurant as the menu is compiled with a special emphasis on the speed of preparation and service. To make this type of service financially viable, a large turnover of customers is necessary. The investment is rather large, due to the specialized and expensive equipment needed and high labour costs involved.

Food Courts: Food courts include series of individual counters where customer may either order and eat, or buy from a number of counters and eat in a separate eating area.

French Service: It is a very personalized service. Individual portioned food is brought from the kitchen in dishes and salvers which are placed directly on the table. The plates are kept near the dish and the guests help themselves.

Gueridon Service: This is a service done from the gueridon trolley. Cooking is done at the gueridon trolley place near the guest table and service is done at the guest table. The waiter plays an important role as he is required to fillet, carve, flambé and prepare the food with showmanship.

Gueridon Trolley: It is a mobile trolley from which the gueridon service is done.

Guest Service Cycle: Guest service cycle refers to the activities provided to the guests while in the restaurant. Guest service cycle is the process, which repeats to every guest. Learning guest service cycle is very important, because a good waiter should know what are the activities done in the restaurant during the service.

Hors d'oeuvre: Hors d'oeuvre course aimed to stimulating the palate, and consists of small tasty dishes, using a large array of different items such as anchovies, olives, cheese and smoked fish. They are often referred to a starters or appetizers. This course could also include salads.

Hot Plate: Hot plate is the food pick-up area of the pantry. The service personnel is not allowed to enter the kitchen nor wait till food is being prepared. The waiter hands over the KOT (Kitchen Order Ticket) to the aboyer, who is in-charge of hot plate and in turn, aboyer announces the order to the kitchen. Once the order is being prepared kitchen staff keeps the cooked food in the hot plate.

Hostess: Hostess is a member of restaurant brigade. Duties of hostess include taking restaurant reservation and receiving them at the door.

Indian Breakfast: It is a type of breakfast, which includes Indian dishes such as dosa, idly, chapatti, etc., served with chutney and vegetable curries. There are two types of Indian breakfasts, viz., north Indian and south Indian.

Kiosks: Kiosks are outdoor arrangements that provide food and beverages to people in a specific location.

Kitchen Stewarding: This department primarily controls the storage and issue of cutlery, crockery, hollowware, chinaware, glassware to the different food and beverages outlets and kitchens. Kitchen stewarding department supplies all cleaned service equipment to waiter. This department is also responsible for washing solid serviceware and subsequently furnishing clean items.

KOT/BOT Control System: A variety of control systems are used in the hotel industry. One such important control system is the KOT control. When an order is taken from a guest, it is ordered in triplicate on a KOT. One copy goes to the kitchen, against which the chef prepares the dishes ordered for. The second copy goes to the cashier to make the bill. The third copy is the waiter's copy, against which the food or beverage to be served to the guest is picked up.

Linen Room: The linen room is important back of the house service area in a hotel. The linen room should stock minimum linen and uniform required to meet the daily demands so as to ensure smooth operations. Linen is changed daily in the restaurant and it is exchanged on one-on-one basis from the linen room.

Lounge Service: It is a type of specialized service. Lounge service is done at the lounge of a hotel. Items such as morning tea, afternoon tea, and alcoholic beverages are served in the lounge.

Maitre d'hotel: Maitre d'hotel is the supervisor of the a F&B outlet. He looks after the day-to-day operations of a food service outlet.

Mechanical Shock: Mechanical shock in glassware is the direct result of contact with another object, such as a spoon, a beer tap, another glass, or a piece of china. This kind of contact can cause a minute abrasion, invisible to the eye, but a source of weakness in the glass, making it more susceptible to breakage from impact or thermal shock.

Menu: Menu is a list of food and/or beverages that can be served to a guest at a price. It helps guests to select what they would like to eat and/or drink. It is a document that controls and directs an outlet's operation and is considered the prime selling instrument.

Mise en scene: Mise en scene includes preparing the restaurant welcoming, create ambience with regard to cleanliness, furniture setting and temperature.

Mise en place: Mise en place is preparing the workplace for ultimate smooth service. To ensure that the restaurant is ready for service the waiter makes sure that this station has been efficiently prepared for service.

Napkin: Napkin is restaurant linen. Napkin is used to decorate the table using various folds and also used to keep on the lap of the guest to protect their clothes during service.

Pantry: Pantry is the area situated between the kitchen and restaurant. Pantry consists of the following sections. Hot plate or food pick-up area, Place to keep dirty plates and glasses, place or box to keep soiled linens, place to keep clean plates and cups, a sink to wash small equipment such as glasses and cups and dispense bar.

Polivit: Polivit is the one of the fastest methods of cleaning silverware. For this one needs aluminium foil, baking soda, shallow pan and a clean cloth. The baking soda will "polish" the silverware, removing dirt, stains, and grease. Rinse the silverware thoroughly under warm, running water. Air-dry the silverware on a clean towel. Buff the silverware with a soft, clean cloth.

Room Service: Room service also known as IRD or eat-in. It is offered to the resident guests. Guests order food and/or beverages to the kitchen and order is taken by the room service order taker. Once the order is taken then it is passed to the kitchen. Once the order is ready the room service waiter serves the food and/or beverage at the room. Along with the food, the bill is also presented to the guest to be signed or payment.

Russian Service: Table is laid with food for guests and presentation is done elaborately. Guests help themselves. This is an elaborate silver service much on the line of French service. Display and presentation are the major parts of this service. Some parts of the service such as carving and portioning, etc., are done by the waiter.

Salesmanship: The food and beverages service personnel are technical salespersons, hence they have a thorough knowledge of proper presentation and service of all the food and beverages served in the establishment.

Self-Service: In the self-service the service is done by customer themselves. The guests collect the food from the counters and then he/she may sit at the table or stand at high table to have the food.

Silver Dip: Instantly removes tarnish from silverware, silver plate, cutlery and small silver items. Quickly cleans even difficult to reach places such as between fork tines. Gives silver a brilliant shine. Just dip, rinse and dry.

Silver Room: Silver room is the place where all the silverware are stored and cleaned. Still room holds the complete stock of all the silverware such as flatware, cutlery, hollowware, etc. Separate storage areas are allotted to store different types of equipment. Silver room should contain space for silver cleaning.

Sommelier: Sommelier is the French term for wine waiter. He is responsible for the service of all alcoholic drinks during the service of meals, and is also a salesperson. He requires to have a thorough knowledge of beverages and wines and food accompaniments.

Special Equipment: Special equipment are for specialized services. They are not used in regular services. Specialized equipment are divided into trolleys and miscellaneous equipment. Some of the trolleys used in a restaurant are gueridon trolley, bain marie, vending machine, hot plate, etc.

Specialty Restaurant: Specialty restaurant is a restaurant serving specialized cuisines. Service in a specialty restaurant is both formal and stylish. The prices tend to be high because of higher overheads. The menu may be à la carte, buffet, or a table d'hote. Waiters should be highly skilled, as specialized services such as preparation of food at tables and flambés, may have to be done.

Specialized Service/In Situ: In situ service is the service provided at the place, which is primarily not meant for service. Examples of in situ services are room service, gueridon service.

Still Room: It is one of the most important supporting areas in the food and beverages department of the hotel. It provides the food and beverages for the service of meals which are not provided by the kitchen. The still room makes all the hot and cold non-alcoholic beverages needed for the restaurant.

Table d'hôte or a Fixed Menu: Table d'hôte refers to a menu of limited choice. It usually includes three to five courses available at a fixed price. It is also referred to as a **fixed menu.** This term is known to caterers by its abbreviation TDH menu. A table d'hôte menu is a complete meal at a predetermined price.

Tableware: Tableware is a type of restaurant equipment used to keep on the table. Tableware includes flatware, cutlery and hollowware. Tableware is made of either EPNS or stainless steel.

Thermal Shock: Thermal shock is the result of glass experiencing a sudden temperature change. Glass holds temperature, and a rapid change in temperature can cause enough stress to result in breakage.

Trancheur: Trancheur is the French term for carver. His responsibility is to carve the meat joints in front of the guests and serve them.

Tray Service: In the tray service the food and beverages are brought in a tray and given to guests. Such service is offered in hospitals, guest rooms, etc.

Table Service: It is a type of service. Table service is the service done at the table, where the guests are seated. In this service either service personnel or waiter serves the food to the guests or the guests help themselves.

Take-Away: The food order is placed at a counter and the food is collected from the same counter and take the food away from the premises for consumption.

Vending Machine: The customer inserts the value of the food item displayed in the vending machine and selects the food by pressing a knob. The vending machine dispenses the selected food. The vending machine can dispense hot or cold food.

Wash-up Area: The wash-up area comprises wash sinks, dishwashing machines, rack to keep cleaned dishes, and tables. All the utensils are washed, cleaned, dried and kept here for further use.

INDEX